ARCHITECTURE IN CINCINNATI

ARCHITECTURE IN CINCINNATI

AN ILLUSTRATED HISTORY OF DESIGNING AND BUILDING AN AMERICAN CITY

Sue Ann Painter

Photographs by Alice Weston

with additional text by Beth Sullebarger and Jayne Merkel

John G. Hancock, Editorial Advisor

OHIO UNIVERSITY PRESS

in association with the Architectural Foundation of Cincinnati

Front cover: Interior staircase of the Vontz Center for Molecular Studies, University of Cincinnati (architect Frank Gehry, with BHDP). Photograph by Alice Weston. *Back cover:* View of Cincinnati at night. Photograph by Alice Weston. *Page i:* Tyler Davidson Fountain in Probasco Place *(detail).* Ergott & Forbiger, color lithograph, 1872. *Frontispiece:* Tyler Davidson Fountain in Probasco Place *(detail).*

Photographs are by Alice Weston except as credited below.
i, vi, xi, xvi, 11, 12, 14 *(top and bottom),* 15, 16 *(bottom),* 17, 20 *(top and bottom),* 24 *(top and bottom),* 26 *(top and bottom),* 32, 33 *(top and bottom),* 34, 37, 39 *(bottom),* 54 *(bottom),* 55 *(bottom),* 56, 61 *(top and bottom),* 62, 64, 65 *(top and bottom),* 66, 67, 68, 69, 79 *(bottom),* 84, 86, 87, 90, 91, 96, 102 *(bottom),* 104 *(top and bottom),* 112, 120 *(bottom),* 122 *(bottom),* 130, 135 *(bottom),* 138, 152, 167, 168 *(bottom),* 169, 172, 173, 184 *(bottom),* 187 *(top),* 206 *(top and bottom),* 222, 229, 246, 252, 297, 332, 334: courtesy of Cincinnati Historical Society Library/Cincinnati Museum Center; 21: courtesy of Grouseland Foundation, Inc.; 98: courtesy of Gartner Burdick Bauer-Nilsen Architects; 110: courtesy of Procter & Gamble Archives; 148 *(bottom)*: courtesy of McGill Smith Punshon; 220: photo by Forster Studio, courtesy of Albert Kahn Associates, Inc.; 221: photo by Hedrich Blessing, courtesy of Albert Kahn Associates, Inc.; 226: courtesy of PFB Architects; 228: courtesy of Ohio National Financial Services; 232: photo by Longley Photo, courtesy of Skidmore, Owings & Merrill LLP; 300: photograph by J. Miles Wolf © 2006, www.jmileswolf.com; 324: courtesy of Glaserworks.

Ohio University Press, Athens, Ohio 45701
www.ohio.edu/oupress
© 2006 by Architectural Foundation of Cincinnati

Printed in China
All rights reserved

Ohio University Press books are printed on acid-free paper ⊗ ™

13 12 11 10 09 08 07 06 5 4 3 2 1

Library of Congress Cataloging-in-Publication Data

Painter, Sue Ann.
Architecture in Cincinnati : an illustrated history of designing and building an American city / Sue Ann Painter ; photographs by Alice Weston ; with additional text by Beth Sullebarger and Jayne Merkel.
p. cm.
Includes bibliographical references and index.
ISBN-13: 978-0-8214-1700-3 (cloth: alk. paper)
ISBN-10: 0-8214-1700-2 (cloth: alk. paper)
ISBN-13: 978-0-8214-1701-0 (pbk.: alk. paper)
ISBN-10: 0-8214-1701-0 (pbk.: alk. paper)
1. Architecture—Ohio—Cincinnati Region—19th century. 2. Architecture—Ohio—Cincinnati Region—20th century. 3. City planning—Ohio—Cincinnati Region—History—19th century. 4. City planning—Ohio—Cincinnati Region—History—20th century. I. Weston, Alice. II. Sullebarger, Beth. III. Merkel, Jayne. IV. Title.
NA735.C5P35 2006
720.9771'79—dc22

2006016684

Contents

Metalwork from Netherland Plaza Hotel, ca. 1930

Preface

THIS IS A book about the ongoing task of building a community. The City of Cincinnati is at the heart of that community, but its embrace extends beyond the political boundaries of the city, into the county and across the Ohio River into Northern Kentucky. Our focus is upon the built environment as it stands today, with reference to the architectural prototypes and planning efforts that have stimulated community building in Greater Cincinnati.

In *Architecture in Cincinnati,* we look at some significant and some typical structures that have enabled the economic, cultural, religious, charitable, and political life of the city and the region. This built environment has steadily evolved for more than two thousand years. Bridges, buildings, canals, roadways, and earthworks have come and gone. The landmarks that remain carry the cultural values of the Native Americans who roamed here before white settlement and the aspirations of the Anglo-Americans who established a city in the wilderness more than two hundred years ago.

In shaping Cincinnati's landscapes and cityscapes and designing its varied structures, these people were responding to a need, problem, or opportunity that was peculiar to their time and place. We believe that an understanding of the historical context in which planning and building took place will enhance appreciation of Cincinnati's significant buildings and public spaces.

One challenging task in this study has been to identify the patrons, planners, architects, engineers, and artists who designed and executed representative structures. Another has been to determine the artistic, political, and economic forces that most likely influenced their decisions about style and structure. The notion of a conscious selection of an architectural "style" first appeared in mid-eighteenth-century England, as evidenced by Horace Walpole's revival of a Gothic vocabulary for his country house, Strawberry Hill. Before that time, architects, builders, and craftsmen used the vocabulary common to their geographic location or appropriate to the client's station in life. For important urban buildings, designers usually relied on the books of the mid-sixteenth-century Italian architect Andrea Palladio or his intellectual ancestor, the Roman architect Vitruvius, as the preferred sources for "correct" classical forms and features, adapting them in ways that seemed right for their times.

By the time the Cincinnati area was settled in 1788, architects and patrons had a few more historical styles to choose from, such as the Common (vernacular), Doric or Corinthian (Greco-Roman Revival), and Gothic styles. By the mid-nineteenth century, the choices had expanded. Cincinnati's connoisseurs mentioned such exotic styles as "Norman," "Saracenic," and "Byzantine" to describe what we might call Romanesque, Ruskinian, or High Victorian Gothic. In the 1920s, architects and journalists used terms such as "Traditional," "Modernist," and "Traditional-Modernist" to describe an architect's stylistic emphasis. Today, though terms such as "Modern," "Postmodern," and "Deconstructionist" are often used, contemporary American architects are reluctant to discuss their work or that of their colleagues in those terms. In this book, we have tried to respect their wishes not to be categorized. Like their predecessors, present-day architects do emphasize that they aspire to design structures and places that are of their time.

Perhaps the standard of architectural excellence is still best summed up by Vitruvius, whose words are engraved on the Pritzker Architecture Prize medal. The prize is given annually to a laureate who has heeded Vitruvius's wise counsel "to build well" by endowing one's creations with "firmness, commodity, and delight"—or, to use the vernacular of our time, to build with regard to function, structural integrity, and aesthetic value.

In this book, we have tried to understand and describe the buildings and places represented here on their own terms, as their architects, engineers, designers, and builders—*and* the clients—intended them to be. We have used stylistic terms sparingly and refrained from clumping individual works into artificial categories. We do point out historical sources and precedents where they are known or obvious, but with the understanding that some ideas and design concepts are simply "in the air" at a particular time.

Our methodology fuses techniques employed by architectural historians, urban historians, and intellectual historians. And yet this work is not, strictly speaking, a history of ideas, nor a history of urbanization, nor a history of local architecture. Rather, it is about the process of creating a built environment as *part* of the process of building a new community in post-Revolutionary America. It is about building a place with the unlikely name of Cincinnati.

Cincinnati's buildings and urban places have been documented in several fine guide and interpretive books.[1] But no chronological survey of the important commercial, civic, and sacred architecture has been done. This volume came about in response to that perceived need.

Much of the information about nineteenth-century buildings and architects is based upon research conducted over several decades by Walter E. Langsam, an authority on local architecture and architects. The authors—Sue Ann Painter (chapters 1 through 6), Beth Sullebarger (chapters 7, 8, and 10), and Jayne Merkel (chapter 9)—and editorial consultant John Hancock have provided the contextual history and its interpretation, along with extensive research about individual projects. The many scholarly articles that have appeared over the years in the publications of the Cincinnati Historical Society, as well as news stories and critical articles in the local press, facilitated their work. The manuscript, photograph, and architectural drawing collections of the Cincinnati Historical Society Library–Cincinnati Museum Center have been an invaluable resource.

Alice Weston, a Cincinnati environmental artist, contributed the luminous color photographs. She has driven many miles and worked tirelessly over several years to document the architectural achievements of southwestern Ohio, from prehistory to the present. Her work captures the spirit of each building, and her cityscapes provide viewers with context and a sense of place.

The period photographs, paintings, and architectural drawings are from the collections of the Cincinnati Historical Society Library at the Cincinnati Museum Center. We are grateful for the expert assistance provided by Scott Gampfer, director of history collections, and Linda Bailey, photograph curator, and the library staff, especially Tina Bamert, who processed our many requests for historical images. One of the city's premier local historians, Dan Hurley, vice president for education at the Cincinnati Museum Center, and Walter E. Langsam critiqued the manuscript. The authors are grateful to OAAP Professor John Hancock for his expert guidance and scholarly editorial assistance. They thank all those who supplied information and assistance, including Dr. Compton Allyn, Neil Bortz, Stephen C. Gordon, Donald Junker, Stewart Shillito Maxwell, Mark McKillip, Michael Moose, Ed Rider, David Scott Ross, Timothy Rub, Peter Strange, and Alan Warner.

Sue Ann Painter wishes to thank her husband, Judge Mark Painter, who read each chapter as it evolved, critiqued her theories, and—as always—encouraged her efforts and turned a blind eye to the stacks of books and research papers that appeared in most every room of the house.

Alice Weston wishes to thank Sue Ann Painter for her excellent organization of the book material into a coherent whole as well as, along with Beth Sullebarger and Jayne Merkel, her insightful authorship. She acknowledges her husband, Harris, for his constant, steady, and emotional support. And she gives thanks to the City of Cincinnati, whose winding river and verdant hills provide a beautiful natural setting, and whose citizenry—with both individual initiative and public spirit—combined to inspire these photographs of its significant architecture.

This book is sponsored by the Architectural Foundation of Cincinnati, which was founded in 1981 to increase awareness and appreciation for the built environment of Greater Cincinnati. Publication of the book fulfills that mission in a most uplifting way. We would like to acknowledge the cooperation of the Ohio University Press, particularly David Sanders, the helpful and encouraging director, and John Morris, the ever-patient project editor. It is the hope of the foundation and the book project team that *Architecture in Cincinnati* will inspire renewed pride of place in residents and that nonresidents will enjoy this visual introduction to the Queen City of the West.

Sue Ann Painter *Managing Editor*
Alice Weston *Book Publication Chair*

Cincinnati from Price Hill

Bouquets to Patrons

The Architectural Foundation of Cincinnati and the publication team express deep appreciation to these generous and visionary supporters of *Architecture in Cincinnati.* They have helped to create this book as a gift to the people of Greater Cincinnati.

Platinum

Duke Energy Foundation
Hargreaves Associates
Kaplan Family Foundation
Patti and Buck Niehoff
Melody Sawyer Richardson
Alice and Harris Weston

Gold

BHDP Architecture
Otto M. Budig Family Foundation
Burgess & Niple
Cole + Russell Architects Inc.
GBBN Architects
Glaserworks Inc.
Harley Ellis Devereaux
Kolar Design
KZF Design
Messer Construction Co.
Miller-Valentine Group
Neyer Holdings Corporation
Christine Schoonover and George Verkamp
Ladislas and Vilma Segoe Family Foundation
Towne Properties
Waltek & Co. LTD

James W. McLaughlin, design for flower stand on Esplanade (Fountain Square), ca. 1871.

Mound at Fort Ancient,
500 B.C.–A.D.500
Warren County

Native American earthworks like this attracted the interest and respect of early Euro-American settlers in the Ohio country.

Introduction

Cincinnati is a city with a distinctive environment and a rich architectural heritage. It was the second permanent settlement in Ohio (after Marietta), and the third (after Vincennes, Indiana) in the Northwest Territory. Prior to Euro-American settlement, the Ohio country was hunting ground for and home to Native Americans, who left their own distinctive buildings. At the close of the American War of Independence, Congress offered Ohio lands for purchase. Thus, Cincinnati's city plan and its early architecture were the first expression of the building spirit of the new nation. A look at the early pioneer city tells us something of the builders' democratic aspirations, their desire for security and order, and their faith in progress.

John Cleves Symmes, a Revolutionary War officer from New Jersey, was the proprietor of the Symmes Purchase, which included all of what was to become Cincinnati and Hamilton County. Symmes and his fellow officers led the first settlers west. Many of these pioneers came as "boomers" intent on building a city in the wilderness. Blessed with an ideal location, imaginative leaders, and an inspired public-relations program, they succeeded beyond their wildest dreams. The city reaped the agricultural abundance of its hinterlands and grew rich on river commerce and the manufacturing that followed. By 1840, Cincinnati was the fastest-growing city in the United States, sixth in population, and third in manufacturing.

At midcentury, this "Queen City of the West" was a community with wealth, style, and an ambition to be bigger and better than its eastern or midwestern counterparts. Its leaders understood that competing successfully in the urban sweepstakes required urban amenities as well as basic services, so they built beautiful bridges, parks, churches, hotels, theaters, government offices, and emporiums. Famed architects such as Isaiah Rogers arrived, won lucrative commissions, and stayed to train a new generation of architects. Stylish buildings went up in Greek Revival, Gothic Revival, and Eclectic modes. Skilled craftsmen came—carpenters, woodworkers, and machinists for steamboat building—and they stayed to lend expertise to the construction industries. The noted landscape gardener Adolph Strauch took up residence here, and his "landscape lawn plan" for Spring Grove Cemetery became a national model. Famed engineer John A. Roebling made regular trips to Covington and Cincinnati to oversee the frequently interrupted construction of his Suspension Bridge, which opened in 1866, triumphantly uniting Northern Kentucky and Ohio.

Although growth slowed after the Civil War, Cincinnati continued to prosper. Its loyal boosters tried various growth strategies, and in the late nineteenth century they turned to cultural boosterism to shore up the sagging economy. Philanthropists created Fountain Square, the Art Museum, and Music Hall. In the early twentieth century, private investors and corporations put up handsome commercial buildings by well-known architects such as Daniel H. Burnham and Cass Gilbert.

In the Progressive era and up to World War II, Cincinnatians took a lively interest in municipal reform. The city's leaders were early advocates of the American planning movement. Cincinnati was a pioneer in adopting the city-manager form of government, and in 1925 it became the first major city in the nation to adopt a municipal master plan.

Modernism in design accompanied modern trends in governance, and landmark complexes such as Carew Tower and Union Terminal arose. They turned heads away from the equally beautiful but slightly old-fashioned Beaux-Arts masterpieces of the early 1920s—the Cincinnati Gas & Electric Co. Building and the Dixie Terminal. Cincinnati attracted national attention for its landmark buildings and for the suburban planned communities of Mariemont, Greenhills, and Forest Park.

In the second half of the twentieth century, urban development slowed. Like most mature midwestern cities, Cincinnati suffered from declining population, decentralization of the city, and the migration of jobs and young professionals to the Sun Belt. While politicians mouthed platitudes about the merits of being a city of "manageable" size, skeptics concluded gloomily that the city's best days lay behind it. Adding to the atmosphere of self-doubt, this most southern of northern cities has had its share of racial tensions and unrest, from its beginning to the present day.

Despite periods of anxiety and economic stagnation, a few influential boosters always emerged, keeping alive the ideal of the city as a civilized and civilizing place. In the late twentieth century, business, government, and institutional leaders came together with capital and commitment to reenergize the urban core. Beginning in the 1980s with the appearance of new public places and buildings—Bicentennial Commons on the riverfront, the Procter & Gamble and Federated Department Stores world headquarters, the adaptive reuse of historic buildings—the city and its environs moved ambitiously forward. The creative master planning and signature architects program at the University of Cincinnati produced remarkable buildings designed by Leers Weinzapfel, Bernard Tschumi, Frank Gehry, Michael Graves, and Thom Mayne on the Clifton campus, in conjunction with such local architectural firms as BHDP Architecture, GBBN Architects, Glaserworks, and KZF Design.

Cincinnati's historic core was enlivened with a theater complex, the Aronoff Center for the Arts by Caesar Pelli, the Rosenthal Contemporary Arts Center by Zaha Hadid, and a HOK football stadium that suggested movement and vitality. While downtown and uptown Cincinnati emerged as twin focal points for athletic, residential, and institutional developments, the neighboring Kentucky cities of

Covington and Newport developed their riverfronts with hotels, office buildings, and entertainment venues. Historic restoration projects in Over-the-Rhine and in Cincinnati and Northern Kentucky neighborhoods ensured an appealing mix of old and new architecture. With these buildings in place and new ones on the drawing boards, residents and visitors saw that significant architecture could set the tone for a dynamic new era.

This volume is a chronological survey of the community's rich architectural and cultural heritage. It begins with the mysterious Native American earthworks that welcomed the first settlers and concludes with the fascinating new earthworks that enliven the University of Cincinnati campus. George Hargreaves, the university's innovative landscape architect and master planner, inspired by the wonders of southern Ohio's oldest culture, made the earthwork concept an integral part of what may be Cincinnati's most aesthetically pleasing and stimulating built environment.

Designing and building Cincinnati is an incremental, ongoing process. This book attempts to illustrate some of the best examples of the city's ever-changing built environment. Our intent is to increase public understanding of and appreciation for Cincinnati's architectural heritage. We hope also that *Architecture in Cincinnati* will encourage excellence in new and imaginative designs that will elevate the spirits of the community and its people.

Hargreaves Associates
Mound, ca. 1990
University of Cincinnati

When landscape designer George Hargreaves came to Cincinnati to begin work on a master plan for the University of Cincinnati, he expressed a desire to visit Native American earthworks in the area. Environmental artist Alice Weston, who had photographed the works in Ohio, took Hargreaves to Fort Ancient. His subsequent designs for UC reflect that encounter with ancient art forms.

Map of Cincinnati in 1901.

ARCHITECTURE IN CINCINNATI

Monuments created by ancient Native American cultures were the earliest buildings in the Ohio River Valley. Euro-Americans settled between the Great Miami and Little Miami rivers in the 1780s, where they built fortified stations, towns, and one great city in the wilderness. Cincinnati's strategic location on the Ohio River—almost midway between Pittsburgh and New Orleans—made it the Queen City of the West by 1830.

1

Frontier City to Regional Capital

1788–1829

Attractions of the Ohio Country

NATIVE AMERICANS called the Ohio River "O-Y-O" (Grand River).[1] French explorers named it La Belle Rivière (the Beautiful River). In pre-Revolutionary America, the Ohio River was a beautiful temptress—the northwestern border that colonists were forbidden to cross. King George III's governors and generals wanted no battles with the natives. And since, by European standards, the eastern and middle Atlantic colonies were not overly crowded, the British maintained that their colonists had no need of lands north of the Ohio. All that changed when the British relinquished the Northwest Territory at the close of the Revolution. The Ohio Country became fair game for speculators and settlers.

Even before the 1783 Treaty of Paris was executed, American frontiersmen were floating down the Ohio River from Pennsylvania and crashing through the brush from Kentucky. They were scouting for prime locations for settlements—places where others would want to follow, where the land was fertile, timber abundant, and water routes to older settlements would facilitate trade.

Natural landings on the Ohio River at the mouths of the Little Miami and Great Miami rivers and another across from the mouth of Kentucky's Licking River caught the eye of Major Benjamin Stites, a German American from New Jersey.

Moon over Ohio forests

Before the arrival of Euro-Americans, this region was completely forested with oak, hickory, and other hardwood species. Deep and dark and laced with many rivers and streams, this woodland environment provided a rich abundance, and Native American cultures flourished here. The native people who lived in the Central Ohio River Valley from about two thousand to one thousand years ago not only exploited the full ecological diversity of the region, but also developed successful agricultural practices.

Ancient oak trees

Forest in fall

Clifty Falls

He must have envisioned rows of orderly houses rising here, with fenced outer lots for cattle and vegetable gardens. At the future site of Cincinnati, the land rose gently out of the river, becoming a forested plateau, which was framed by steep hillsides that formed a natural amphitheater. The basin was broad, flat, and deep, providing ample room for straight streets and regular blocks. The Ohio River was deep enough to be navigable year-round, but here it was narrow enough to ferry and bridge.

The location seemed ideal to speculators staking out a city site on which to build the London or the Paris of America.

Fall landscape

The Miami Purchase

Returning east, Stites touted the land between the Miami rivers to an influential friend, Congressman John Cleves Symmes, also of New Jersey. Symmes traveled to the Ohio Country himself, and he readily agreed that the area contained three or four Ohio River landings where a great metropolis could be built. The lush forests showed them that the surrounding land was fertile—an important factor for development of an agriculture-based commercial center.

Shortly after Congress adopted the Northwest Ordinance of 1787, Symmes arranged to purchase one million acres (later reduced to one-third of a million) between the Great and Little Miami rivers. It was called the Miami Purchase. Congress moved quickly to establish a civil government. General Arthur St. Clair was appointed governor of the Northwest Territory, and Symmes was named one of three territorial judges.

Symmes sold the lands at the mouth of the Little Miami for the Columbia settlement to Stites. The sections that became Cincinnati were sold to another New Jersey native, Matthias Denman. Denman formed a partnership with Colonel Robert Patterson, a Pennsylvania native and the founder of Lexington, Kentucky, and John Filson, a surveyor and Kentucky schoolteacher. Filson named their settlement Losantiville, a Latin-Greek-French combination meaning "village across from the mouth of the Licking." Symmes reserved for himself extensive acreage at North Bend, surrounding the mouth of the Great Miami River, as well as a large tract on the eastern perimeter of Losantiville.

Building Cities in the Wilderness

Each of the proprietary companies that owned the three land tracts hoped to establish the great regional capital city in the Ohio wilderness. The first group of permanent settlers arrived in November 1788 at Columbia, near present-day Lunken Airport. The Columbia settlers were exceptionally efficient. They stopped in Limestone (later Maysville), Kentucky, to purchase milled timbers for stockade and house construction.

The second party came in December to Losantiville. It was composed mostly of single men, adventurers who braved danger and hardship for the promise of free lots. They built houses from dismantled flatboats, cleared the land of trees, and erected fences, which first puzzled and then angered the Indians. Misunderstandings quickly turned into warfare, with atrocities on both sides. The Miami Purchase became known as the "Miami Slaughterhouse."

Judge Symmes brought a group to North Bend in February 1789. He tried to establish a high tone for his settlement by building a rare sixteen-cornered blockhouse. Its construction, begun on Christmas Day 1790, frustrated the amateur

View of Cincinnati in 1802

The settlement was incorporated in 1802. Ohio became a state in 1803.

builders, who protested that although the old judge claimed the design's purpose was to provide a better view of attacking Indians, the real reason was that he wished to boast of this near-circular architectural curiosity to his friends back in New Jersey.[2]

The three settlements competed with one another to become the dominant city of the Ohio River Valley, each trying to grow faster than the others. The matter was settled when a substantial U.S. military garrison, Fort Washington, was erected in 1789 in Losantiville. When the army arrived in Fort Washington, it brought federal funds with it. The military presence attracted additional settlers, who welcomed the extra security.

Cincinnati Name Honors Revolutionary War Officers

Most of the political and military leaders of the new nation were Revolutionary War officers and gentlemen schooled in the classics. They frequently made classical allusions in their writings and looked to Greek and Roman history for guidance in planning battles, towns, and buildings.

When Governor Arthur St. Clair visited the Miami Purchase in 1790, he approved of naming the county for Alexander Hamilton. But he found the name "Losantiville" peculiar and changed it to Cincinnati, in honor of the Society of the Cincinnati, an honorary organization of Revolutionary War officers. The society was named for Cincinnatus, a Roman farmer and military leader who returned to the plow after heroic service in battle. Cincinnatus was an idol to those Americans who glorified the citizen-soldier because they opposed keeping a standing army.[3]

Miamisburg Mound

Cincinnati once had large earthworks like this one at Miamisburg, Ohio. The tallest, at Fifth and Mound streets, was a favorite destination for evening strollers. By 1850, the earthworks downtown had been excavated and demolished.

Native American Earthworks

Settlers in the Miami Purchase found that talented builders had come before them. Native American earthworks, in various sizes and configurations, were everywhere. These remnants of ancient civilizations were a source of delight and awe for the more inquisitive explorers. William Henry Harrison (1773–1841), a nineteen-year-old ensign at Fort Washington, studied and documented the mounds. A Virginia patrician with a classical and medical-scientific education, he typified his generation's interest in cataloging America's natural and historical resources.

When Major General "Mad" Anthony Wayne arrived at Fort Washington in 1793 to command the Legion of the United States, Harrison took him on a tour of the earthworks. The ever-practical Wayne was impressed with the highest conical mound, but not for its archeological interest. He had the top cut off so it could function as a lookout platform for sentries.

The Ohio River Valley had been home to an advanced culture approximately two thousand years before settlement by Americans. The natives left a variety of earthworks: some conical, like Miamisburg Mound; others geometric, like those remaining at Fort Ancient near Lebanon, Ohio. The conical mound that Harrison took Wayne to visit was the highest in Cincinnati, at varying estimates of thirty to fifty feet high. It was on the western boundary of the town at Fifth and Mound streets (west of the present Convention Center).

Serpent Mound

As if to mark their relationships with the landscape, some Indian cultures created spectacular earthworks—not only burial mounds, but vast geometrical and hilltop enclosures and animal-shaped effigies. The most distinguished of these ancient earthworks is the Great Serpent Mound. Curling across a hilltop in northern Adams County, about ninety minutes east of Cincinnati, this is the most famous effigy mound in the world. Theories abound about its possible meanings, though obviously it was quite crucial to the culture of Native Americans who flourished here around AD 1000. Serpentine in form and echoing the twists and turns of the creek below, it may have been a symbol of the watery underworld, still part of Woodland Indian lore today.

Like many educated people of his generation, Harrison was deeply interested in the impact of the natural environment on plants, animals, and humans. Harrison and Dr. Daniel Drake had studied medicine with Benjamin Rush and Benjamin Barton at the University of Pennsylvania. Rush and Barton lectured students on their duty as educated citizens of the new nation to observe their natural environments and report their findings to the scientific community.[4]

In an 1837 address to the state historical society, Harrison said: "When I first saw the upper plain on which the city stands, it was literally covered with low lines of embankments. . . . The number and variety of figures in which these lines were drawn was almost endless . . . many so faint, indeed, as scarcely to be followed, and often for considerable distance to be obliterated; but, by careful examination and following direction, they could be found again." He had found traces of these low geometrical configurations across a broad plain from Third Street to Brighton, the northern boundary of the basin.[5]

Dr. Daniel Drake argued that the earthworks should be documented and, where possible, preserved. "These monuments are our only antiquities," he wrote, "memorials of a people who were lately the . . . sovereigns of the country which we inhabit."[6] Judge Jacob Burnet, who owned a city block in the heart of downtown, was also a devoted student of Native American culture. In describing a geometric mound he had carefully preserved on his property, Burnet noted that it was part of "an exact circle, about six hundred feet in diameter." [7]

Cincinnati boosters pointed to the earthworks when defending the natural environment of America against skeptics in the East and in Europe.[8] The mounds were powerful proof of a sophisticated indigenous culture. Cincinnati's Western Museum, which opened in 1820 with Joseph Dorfeuille and John J. Audubon on staff, had a collection of 215 American antiquities displayed alongside 150 Egyptian antiquities.[9]

Mounds and artifacts were found along the Ohio River from Anderson Township to Cleves, near the Indiana border. Remnants of Native American settlements or campgrounds were found along the Great Miami and Little Miami rivers, and many of the pioneer "stations," as the fortified settlements on the outskirts of the city were called, were located in places where earthworks testify that Indians had lived long ago, most likely for the same reasons the settlers chose them: water, fertile soil, and defensibility.[10]

Drake urged young people to complete their education by traveling to observe scientific wonders like these in their own country, rather than travel to Europe. "Such as rely on foreign journeys only, resemble scholars who spend their lives in the study of Greek and Roman literature, and die quite ignorant of their own," he told an audience observing the anniversary of the Western Museum Society in 1820.[11]

Straight Lines Map a City

When John Filson disappeared into the woods, Colonel Israel Ludlow became the surveyor of Cincinnati. Taking the city of Philadelphia, then the nation's capital and largest city, as a model, Ludlow established a grid of straight streets with the river as the main axis. He even named many of the streets in the Philadelphia manner, using numbers and native tree names.

The busiest streets in the first decade were Front and Water streets, which ran east-west along the river, and Broadway and Main streets, which ran north-south at right angles. The main streets were sixty to sixty-six feet wide, except for Broadway, which was one hundred feet wide. Originally, each square was divided into eight lots of 99 by 198 feet.

The proprietors were stingy with public land. The original commons consisted of a fractional square (Front Street to the river, between Broadway and Main) on the riverbank for the Public Landing, and a full square bordered by Fourth, Fifth, Main, and Walnut streets. Half of the latter was soon conveyed to the First Presbyterian Church, the first congregation established here; the other half was sold to the Hamilton County commissioners, who operated it as the Fifth Street Market.

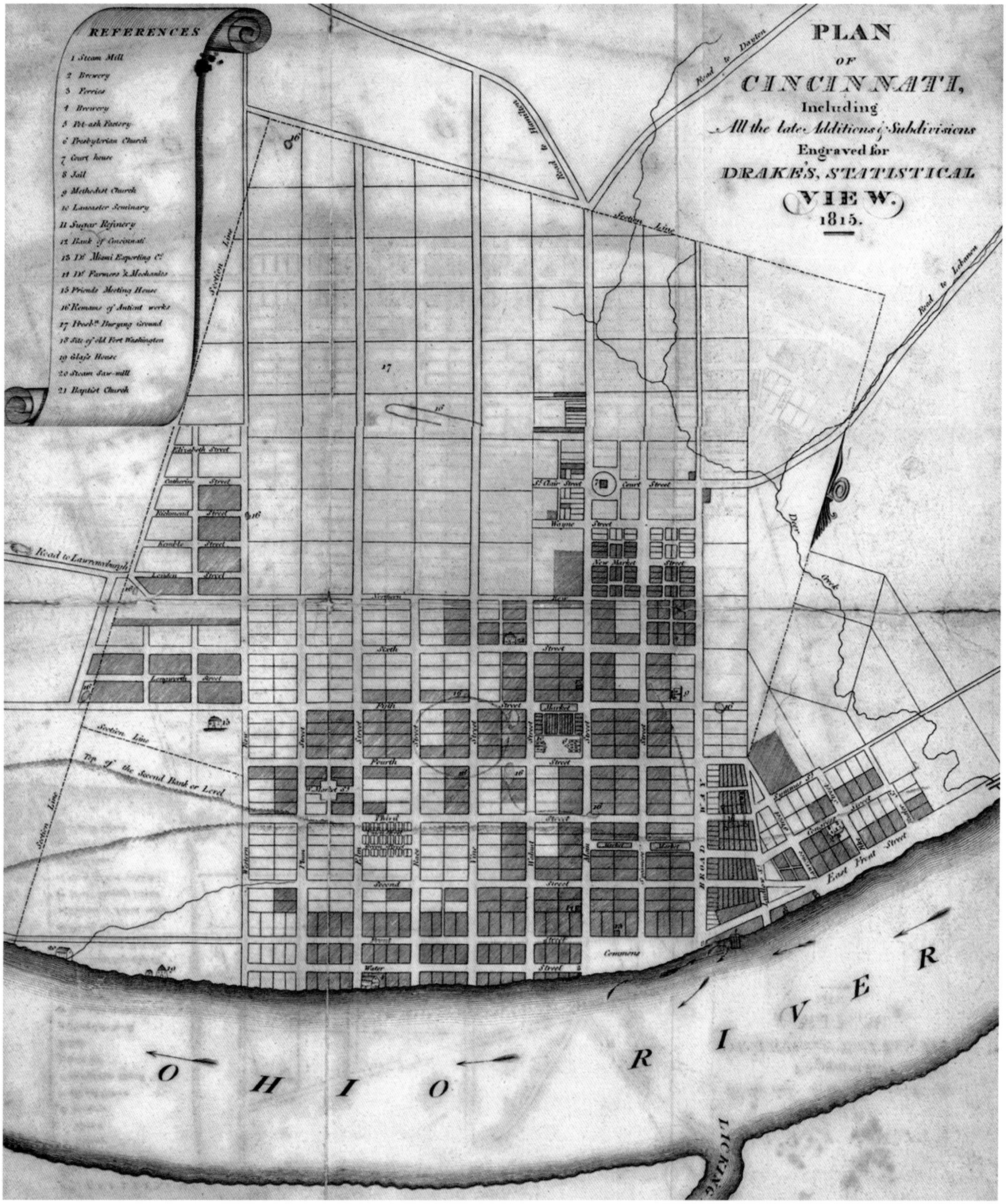

This map, published by Daniel Drake in 1815, shows Israel Ludlow's plan. Native American earthworks were marked with the number 16. The large circle, centered almost on Vine Street between Fourth and Fifth streets, is a geometric earthwork.

Daniel Drake (1785–1852)

Dr. Daniel Drake became the city's first statistician and chief promoter with several publications describing Cincinnati, beginning with a slender volume describing Cincinnati in 1810. He was a thoughtful critic as well as apologist. Entrepreneurs and professionals like Drake directed the city's institutions in its second decade, when local government activities were limited to the regulation of commerce. For the most part, Drake and his counterparts were native-born Americans and educated people of means, with a keen eye for the main chance. They became the community's volunteer boosters, promoting its virtues and opportunities to prospective settlers and investors. Drake founded the Ohio Medical College (now part of the University of Cincinnati) and numerous organizations.

Health and aesthetics were not considered—there was no recreational commons or leafy village square.

Early on, Cincinnati attracted an elite class of "boomers," or promoters, of which Dr. Daniel Drake, a physician, educator, and author, was one. He approved of Ludlow's gridiron because he believed straight lines signified the city. But he faulted the orientation of the plan, which he thought stifled the southwestern winds. He also lamented the lack of trees, open space, and porches. Drake worried that the city had too few alleys and commons to stimulate healthful breezes.

Drake believed that if Cincinnati were to become the dominant city in the West, it must offer a healthful natural environment and an attractive built environment. To attract desirable settlers, Drake wanted to expand economic, educational, and social opportunities and prohibit slavery. In his mechanistic view of civilization, if Cincinnati displayed all these attributes, the city was destined for limitless progress. It would become the first city of the West, and perhaps the London of America. His fellow civic leaders shared his ambitious goal.[12]

The City and the State

Building the city, its suburbs, and the state began in earnest after Major General Anthony Wayne vanquished the Native Americans in the Battle of Fallen Timbers in 1794 and the Indians relinquished all claims to southern Ohio. Strong community leaders emerged from the military officers who remained to become residents. Captain William Henry Harrison was elected the first territorial delegate to Congress in 1799, and Major David Ziegler became the first mayor when Cincinnati received its village charter in 1802.

Cincinnati residents and newcomers now moved confidently to the perimeters of Hamilton County. Some even went beyond into what became Butler and

Warren counties to the north and Clermont and Brown counties to the east. Settlers also flocked to Marietta and Chillicothe. Soon Ohio had sufficient population—5,000 electors—for self-government. In 1803, Ohio became the first state carved from the Northwest Territory.

Although Chillicothe, and later Columbus, became the political capitals of the state, Cincinnati was the undisputed economic and cultural center. Ideally located on the Ohio River, Cincinnati built up a rich trade with the East, North, South, and West. The introduction of the steamboat in 1811 greatly facilitated transportation of goods and passengers up and down river. When the state-sponsored Miami and Erie Canal was constructed in the mid- to late 1820s, it enriched local farmers and commercial traders. The town was incorporated as a city in 1819, although its powers were limited mostly to regulating commerce and responding to emergencies such as fires, floods, and epidemics.

Building Materials Were Plentiful

The first buildings in Cincinnati were crude structures made from native trees and planks salvaged from flatboats. Fort Washington was constructed of logs from trees felled on the site. Daniel Drake's pamphlets were intended to encourage settlement in the Cincinnati region, so he stressed that building materials for permanent structures were inexpensive and easy to obtain. Writing in 1815, he boasted that clay from the lower part of town made "excellent brick, about five million of which are used annually in this place"; the beds of the Licking and Ohio rivers furnished "excellent limestone," which was quarried when the water was low; and "marble of a fine quality" could be brought by water from Kentucky. White pine was floated downriver in large quantities from Pennsylvania, and native hardwoods—walnut, cherry, and oak—were abundant in the Cincinnati region.

As in Philadelphia, brick was preferred over wood, especially for permanent or public buildings. But growth was so rapid in the first two decades that frame houses were needed for speedy construction. Most were painted red to simulate brick. Cincinnati in 1815 had 1,050 houses, 250 of brick and about 800 of wood.[13]

Gentlemen Architects Determined Style

Professional architects were in short supply in the new nation. In 1815, Daniel Drake apologized that so few buildings had architectural refinements. But he praised the new Presbyterian Church (a predecessor of the one pictured in Wild's 1835 view) as a "spacious brick edifice" and the Baptist Church as a handsome brick building "finished inside with taste."

John Caspar Wild, *Fourth Street Looking West from Vine*

John Caspar Wild (d. 1846), an itinerant Swiss artist, did a series of gouache paintings of Cincinnati in 1835. This view of Fourth Street shows the Presbyterian Church with the cupola. The building with the crenellated tower farther west is the Unitarian Church.

Drake attributed several Greco-Roman designs for institutions to men who were either local or itinerant architectural designers. The Cincinnati Lancasterian Seminary, of which Drake was one of the founders, was an imposing two-story brick edifice with the style and flair of a Palladian villa. Its plan, which Drake tells us was furnished by one Isaac Stagg[e], boasted such fashionable features as a "colonnade," a "dome capped peristyle," and a "pediment with a Corinthian cornice," which Drake thought ill-proportioned. Later the building became the home of the Cincinnati College.[14]

Drake and his contemporaries were fascinated with taxonomies, whether for the categorizing of plants or animals or stylish buildings. They regularly associated a style name with any description of a building. It might be in the "common" (vernacular) style or a higher style—Gothic (sometimes ranked into subcategories of French, English, and Modern Gothic), Grecian, or Roman. Classical styles were sometimes described by the order of the most prominent columns or the cornice, so a building design might be classified as Doric, Ionic, or Corinthian. Not all of these taxonomies correspond to twenty-first-century definitions of styles.

First Cincinnati College

Amateur (or "paper") architects prepared many of the first building plans. In the late eighteenth and early nineteenth centuries, gentlemen of property made a point of becoming knowledgeable about architecture, much as young ladies were expected to be skilled in drawing and music.

Architectural principles for design and construction were transmitted readily by books. As many as eighty-seven titles about architecture were known in America before the

Revolution; the London works of Sir Christopher Wren (St. Paul's Cathedral) and James Gibbs (St. Martin-in-the-Fields) were especially popular. The United States contributed its share of printed guides to building. Asher Benjamin, a disciple of Charles Bulfinch (the famed Boston Statehouse architect), published seven editions of his book *The Country Builder's Assistant* (first edition 1796). It contained new designs for carpentry and architecture, as well as practical suggestions for economical use of native materials. After independence, a number of design-build contractors operated in the West, using books like Benjamin's as guides. Designers were aware of Thomas Jefferson's preference for Greek and Roman forms, and many Cincinnatians were caught up in the "Greek mania" that swept through the nation during the Greek War of Independence, which began in 1821.[15]

Building owners, women as well as men, often drew their own designs for master builders to execute. Susan Livingston Symmes, the fashionable wife of John Cleves Symmes, drew the plan in 1795 for their large and costly stone house in North Bend.[16] And Frances Trollope, the English author and businesswoman, surely had a say in the eclectic design of her ca. 1830 bazaar, which drew mixed reviews from residents and visitors.

The British tended to be more progressive than the Americans in design matters. William Bullock, a wealthy London collector and friend of Trollope, became infatuated with the Cincinnati area while touring here with his wife. He purchased extensive riverside acreage in what is now Ludlow, Kentucky, where he proposed to develop the town of Hygeia. In 1827, John Buonarotti Papworth (1775–1847), a well-known English architect and planner, drew up the planned community in the picturesque manner, with undulating roadways and provisions for cultural amenities. Hygeia failed to attract investors, and the discouraged Bullock sold the property by 1830.[17]

John Caspar Wild, *Public Landing in 1835*

The foundation of George Evans's nine-story steam mill was in the Ohio River bed. The structure was the first thing visitors saw as they approached the city by river.

War of 1812 Spurs Manufactures and Commercial Building

Cincinnati was at the center of the western theater during the War of 1812. Jefferson's embargo and then the war with England cut off trade with Europe. Cincinnati manufactories prospered and merchants profited from outfitting the troops in the Army of the Northwest. When the war ended, a flood of westward migration followed. New and improved roads that had been built to move the army facilitated peacetime development in the West.

Toward the end of the war, Cincinnati began to build steamboats, and the city quickly became the second-largest shipbuilding center in the nation. The industry brought to the city skilled carpenters, woodworkers, metal workers, and machine-tool specialists. Cincinnati's growth coincided with the beginning of steam power and the industrial revolution. The first commercial buildings and millworks were usually built according to the economical and functional plans of their owners. An amazing industrial complex, the nine-story Steam Mill, dominated the riverbank in the 1820s and 1830s. According to Daniel Drake, proprietor George Evans designed it in the "common style." The construction manager, an "ingenous [*sic*] mason and stone cutter" named William Green, put up the nine-story building, which "swallowed up 90,000 bricks, 14,800 bushels of lime, and 81,200 cubic feet of timber."[18]

By 1826, Cincinnati had 2,495 commercial, institutional, civic, and domestic buildings of substance—most three or four stories high. Only 18 buildings were built of stone; 1,541 were frame, and 936 were brick. But brick was clearly in the ascendancy. In the boom year of 1826, when 180 new structures were built, 128 were brick.

Foote's Row
Third and Vine streets

Below the Greek Revival house were offices for artists, physicians, and the waterworks company.

The Aesthetic of Good Taste

Cincinnati's avid promoters, along with other urban boomers in America, shared an evolutionary notion of city building. They believed that growth alone was not sufficient; it was necessary to grow at a faster rate than the competition. Some of the more sophisticated boomers argued that it took more than economic opportunity to attract capitalists to the community—aesthetics and amenities were also important. Therefore, the city should be neat and graced with plantings, and important buildings should have elegance and style. They seldom mentioned "beauty." More often, the criterion was "good taste," which to them meant appropriate, chaste (restrained), and well proportioned, often in the Palladian manner. The words "chaste" and "neat" appear frequently, always as terms of high praise.

In their *Cincinnati in 1826,* two young lawyers, Benjamin Drake and Edward Mansfield, praised the neoclassical U.S. Banking House as "one of the chastest specimens of architecture within the city." They were especially enthusiastic about the first Catholic cathedral, built according to a plan by Michael Scott, describing it as a "neat specimen of the Gothic architecture." Scott, an Irish carpenter-designer, worked in Cincinnati from ca. 1818–24. He was the city's first self-styled architect.

The Hamilton County Courthouse at Court and Main streets came in for harsh criticism from Drake and Mansfield. The second courthouse designed by Judge George Turner, a scholarly jurist who designed with the aid of pattern books, it exemplifies the typical Ohio courthouse model: a cube with a small attic story and cupola gave the building the appearance of an antique coffee-grinder. Drake and Mansfield, whose law office was blocks away near lower Market Street, found the courthouse too distant from the center, and they sniffed that the interior plan of the courthouse was "not in good taste."[19] Other ambitious city boosters wrote of the need for one or two trained architects.

George Turner
Hamilton County
Courthouse

This engraving of the Turner courthouse was published as part of an illustrated map of Cincinnati in 1845.

Architects Arrive with Regional Prosperity

Some of the city's wealthiest families suffered financial reversals during the Panic of 1819–20. But the opening of a portion of the Miami and Erie Canal in 1826 ushered in a period of unparalleled prosperity. The population swelled, building boomed, and high wages encouraged skilled tradesmen—carpenters, metal workers, and masons—to migrate here. Men who had trained as architects in England or the eastern United States set up practice in Cincinnati, realizing that the building boom would provide lucrative commissions. Seneca Palmer (ca. 1793–after 1855) of New York state and his associate John Jolasse, a native of the Swiss-German states, were among the first architects to locate here. Peleg Kidd was an early practitioner in Northern Kentucky.

The city attracted not only architects, but also professionals educated in the law, the ministry, medicine, music, and letters. They brought with them a cultivated taste for the arts and architectural refinements, which was soon manifested in the physical fabric of the fastest-growing city in the nation. Cincinnati in 1829 was a diverse but solidly middle-class collection of individuals, well prepared to create wealth and build a great city. The population stood at 24,148, including nearly 60 lawyers, 80 physicians, and 40 clergymen. There were around 2,900 mechanics (skilled workers) compared to only 1,000 laborers.

Cincinnati became known as the "great emporium of the West," and its success story attracted national and international attention. By the 1820s, foreign visitors publishing complimentary accounts in French, German, and English were referring to the bustling city as the "Queen of the West."[20]

The boom kindled a wave of optimism and belief in the inevitability of continued progress. It appeared to many people, especially those who had witnessed the transformation of the wilderness into a thriving metropolis, that the new American West, with Cincinnati as its center, was destined to become a national and world leader.

Distant view of Fort Ancient

Winter solstice
at dawn

Native American Earthwork
Fort Ancient

Warren County, Ohio

Just northeast of Cincinnati, overlooking a narrow gorge of the Little Miami River, stands one of ancient North America's greatest monuments. About two thousand years ago, a Native American culture we call "Hopewell" built the largest of their many hilltop earthen enclosures—Fort Ancient. The earthwork forms a rim for the irregular hilltop, enclosing about a hundred acres.

The term "fort" is something of a misnomer. Recent scholars have come to realize that these walls could not provide good military protection, since the ditches are on the inside, there are many open gateways, and the perimeter is far bigger than could have been defended by the small populations who lived here. More likely they were after a different kind of protection, involving spiritual powers. The ditches that followed inside the walls were designed to fill with water and reflect the sky; they helped to establish a sacred boundary. In antiquity, all visitors had to pass not only through the wall, but also across this water boundary.

(*top*) The pond
(*above*) Western embankment

More than twenty-five million cubic feet of earth was moved to level the hilltops, fill ravines, and construct this set of walls and ponds. That is enough to fill a bumper-to-bumper line of dump trucks from Cincinnati to Cleveland and back again. The outside surfaces and gateway openings were lined with hundreds of tons of limestone, carried up from the riverbanks below.

This was clearly a sacred place, where the society's largest conceptions of order and meaning were made visible. Inside the North Enclosure, for example, four limestone-covered mounds form a perfect square, 512 feet on each side, that was kept clean and clear of other buildings. The original stone surface on these four mounds was oxidized, red, and crumbly, suggesting that huge ritual fires had been set atop them. These ceremonies may have been connected with the sun and moon: From the southwesternmost of these four mounds, alignments through three of the gaps in the wall mark three major astronomical events: the summer solstice sunrise and the minimum and maximum northern moonrises.

Outside the northeast gateway, the locations of a number of specialized craft workshops have been discovered. Like other Hopewell sites, Fort Ancient may have been surrounded by thriving industries, with artisans making things for use in the ceremonies, or for pilgrims to take home as souvenirs. Many of the raw materials, like mica, obsidian, flint, and copper, were brought here from very far away.

From the early nineteenth century, Fort Ancient has been a favorite tourist attraction for Cincinnati-area residents and visitors. It featured

Twin processional mounds

prominently in America's early fascination with its ancient monuments and the advent of the modern science of archaeology, and it remains one of the best-preserved earthworks in the region. The Ohio Historical Society has made it a "Gateway" to other state-owned pre-Anglo sites and built an interpretive center for understanding Native American earthworks and culture in Ohio.

Fort Washington

The painting was made from a drawing that depicted William Henry Harrison drilling troops on the parade grounds. Harrison arrived at Fort Washington in 1791 and lived there—even after marriage to Anna Symmes and the birth of two children—until 1798.

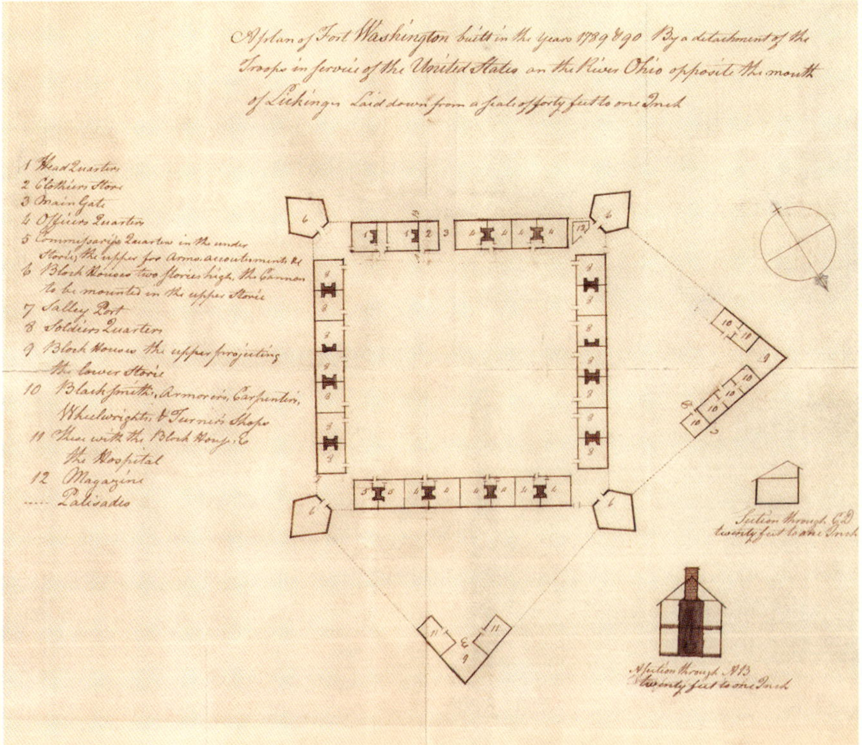

Plan of Fort Washington

The complex was nearly 200 feet square, with an interior courtyard.

Fort Washington

Engineer: John Doughty
Fort Washington, 1789; demolished 1809
Third and Broadway streets

The fort was the most important structure in the frontier city. Travelers arriving by boat received their first impression of Cincinnati from this handsome fortification on the plateau. Constructed on a fifteen-acre reservation east of Broadway, it consisted of a blockhouse sited on the rise above Third Street and outbuildings that rambled downhill to the river.

Fort Washington was constructed of logs from trees felled on the site. The two-story blockhouses and single-story barracks formed the outside walls. A slanted clapboard roof in the "shade" fashion was designed to overhang the walls, making it difficult for attackers to climb inside. At some point the rustic exterior was whitewashed and the roof painted red. Major John Doughty, the military engineer who designed the complex, followed a popular model that had been used for forts in Kentucky, Pennsylvania, and Marietta, Ohio.[21]

During the Indian wars, the facility was overcrowded, dirty, and noisy with visiting regiments and militia. Townspeople disliked the ruffian soldiers, but the fort guaranteed the safety of the settlement from Indians.

In times of peace, officers maintained pleasant apartments where they lived with their wives. Distinguished visitors were entertained—the celebrated Miami chief Little Turtle stopped here on his return from the White House to visit with newlyweds Anna Symmes and William Henry Harrison, who had risen through the ranks to become commander of the fort.[22] General and Mrs. James Wilkerson held balls within the fort and elegant dinner parties on their elaborately decorated riverboat. Several officers and government officials had private houses and attractive gardens adjacent to the fort. The army physician maintained a peach orchard, which was widely admired.

In 1809, the fort was dismantled, the timbers salvaged, and the ground sold by the secretary of the treasury. The closing of the fort marked the end of the frontier period.[23]

William Henry Harrison (1773–1841)

A Virginia native, Harrison came to Fort Washington in 1791 as an ensign and left in 1841 as the ninth president of the United States. His career is symptomatic of the rise of the West. He was elected the first delegate to Congress from the Northwest Territory (1799), named governor of the Indiana Territory (1800), and appointed major general in the War of 1812. He married Anna Symmes, daughter of Judge John Cleves Symmes. As a political leader, Harrison was a Whig and proponent of the American System, which would have tied the nation together with a public network of canals, roads, and railroads. The first Ohioan and westerner to be elected president, he died one month after his inaugural. An obelisk (ca. 1922) and entry designed by Cincinnati architects Frederick Garber and Harry Hake mark Harrison's tomb at North Bend, Ohio.

Whitewater Shaker Village, begun 1825
Exterior of South Family Group

The Shaker Millennial Laws determined the community's principles for architectural design and group planning. The South Family House is simple, symmetrical, and devoid of ornament.

Whitewater Shaker Village
Interior of Meeting Room, Center Family Meeting House

The Shakers created an aesthetic with their beautifully proportioned spaces and exploitation of the visual potential of common materials, especially wood.

Whitewater Shaker Village

Some of the suburban settlements were made by faith communities such as the Shakers, a sect founded in the late eighteenth century in England. They were in the Cincinnati area by 1805, taking advantage of a schism in the Presbyterian Church to convert New Light splinter groups. The Shaker way of life was based upon poverty, chastity, and industry. Union Village at Turtle Creek Township in Warren County became the center of western Shaker missionaries. From here, a colony moved southwest in 1825 to form a new community near the Whitewater River in northwestern Hamilton County. Beginning as a small settlement of eighteen people, who reaped a living from a mere forty acres, the community supported itself with seed, broom, and mat production.

The Shakers led a simple, spiritual life. They sought individual purity through life in a united socialist community. Their Millennial Laws established guidelines for proper conduct and architectural design. Each community was to include a site of great natural beauty for worship. Buildings were to be simple, symmetrical, and arranged along a linear axis in an orderly landscape. Odd or fanciful styles were forbidden. At Whitewater, the results were like many of the rural, vernacular buildings in southwestern Ohio. But the Whitewater Shaker community differed from its secular farm neighbors in the precise, harmonious layout of the structures and the well-ordered landscape.

The large brick South Family House, now painted white, is the most impressive, despite an ill-suited porch addition. Several adjacent outbuildings frame it. The former broom-making shop has decorative trim, an unusual feature in Shaker construction.

Around a bend of the road, beyond the county line, is the Center Family Group, which features a pair of fine brick buildings flanked by exquisite farm structures, each adapted to a specific agricultural or domestic/industrial use.

The red-brick two-story Center Family Meeting House is virtually unaltered. The first-floor Meeting Room is shown in the photograph. Originally completely open as a single rectangular space (made possible by a ceiling suspended through the second story from the impressive timber trusses of the roof), this served as a setting for the Shakers' ritual yet free-form dances, which gave them their name. Although their rituals sometimes became noisy and agitated, the symmetrical space is sublimely ordered and innately tranquil. As is typical, there are separate entrance doors—north for men and south for women. These are flanked by unusual fireplaces centered on the side walls and flights of stairs that lead to the second-story elders' quarters. The minimal woodwork includes Shaker pegboards that divide the surfaces horizontally.

The Whitewater Shaker structures consist of a Meeting House (1827), Dwelling House (1832), Office (1855), Broom Shop (1876), and other outbuildings. The property is owned by the Hamilton County Park Board, but the buildings are not open to the public. It is one of the least-known treasures of history and architecture in Hamilton County.

Miami and Erie Canal, 1825–45

Foot and cart bridges crossed the canal in downtown Cincinnati. In this photograph from the 1890s, the turrets of the city hospital at Twelfth and Plum streets are visible to the southeast.

Miami and Erie Canal

Engineer: Samuel Forrer

Inspired by the success of New York State's Erie Canal, Ohioans undertook a program of statewide canal projects. Cincinnatian Micajah Williams is regarded as the father of the Canal Bill, which passed with the enthusiastic support of Governor Ethan Allen Brown (who served two terms, 1818–22), also a Cincinnatian. Construction began on the Miami Canal from Cincinnati to Middletown in July 1825 and was completed in 1826. The next phase took it to Dayton and then to the Maumee River rapids below Toledo, a distance of more than 250 miles. Construction costs, which were covered by the state, were approximately $12,000 per mile. At one time more than 4,000 laborers were paid 30 cents a day to work on the two great Ohio canals: the Miami and Erie and the Ohio and Erie, which connected Portsmouth and Cleveland.

The supervising engineer for the project was Samuel Forrer (1793–1874), a Pennsylvania native who moved to Dayton in 1818 and practiced in many parts of Ohio and Indiana, including Cincinnati. He was held in high esteem, and the first boat to enter the Dayton-Cincinnati segment was christened the *Samuel Forrer.*[24]

The southern stretch included multiple locks and aqueducts. An aqueduct in Cincinnati crossed the Mill Creek near the "pleasure ground" amusement park of Chester Park on Spring Grove Avenue. Rock-faced spillways formed scenic waterfalls at Spring Grove, attracting sightseers and waders. Along the southern part of the route, where rock was readily available, the trenches and locks were made of sandstone. Some portions of the canal had locks made of wood, which deteriorated faster.

The products of the rich farmlands—corn, wheat, whiskey, fruit, vegetables, hogs, and cattle—came to Cincinnati wholesalers and meatpackers and direct to consumers at public markets. Shipping charges on canals were one-fifth of those for overland hauls, providing a boon to farmers and to commercial development of cities along the towpaths.

The canal followed the path of the Great Miami River in its southern stretch. North of Cincinnati, the canal turned eastward into the path of what became Central Parkway (the towpath was Canal Street) and Eggleston Avenue to the river. The canal stimulated trade and building along the towpath. The Cincinnati segment was drained in the 1920s, when the canal bed became a subway channel topped by Central Parkway. Portions of the canal and locks have been restored and are visible at Hamilton, Middletown, and Dayton. The best sites are in Piqua and five miles to its north at Lockington.

Seneca Palmer
Trollopean Bazaar, 1829;
demolished 1881

This lithograph of the bazaar appeared in the Cincinnati city directory of 1828–29.

Frances Trollope (1780–1863)

In 1827, Trollope left London with three of her children for a visit to America. She came at the invitation of the Scottish-born feminist reformer Frances Wright, who very likely recommended Cincinnati as a boomtown to the ambitious Trollope. Arriving here in 1828, Trollope took a cottage in the Mohawk section of Over-the-Rhine. She commissioned the Bazaar as a business venture for her son. When it failed, she went on to the East Coast, where she greatly admired New York City. Back in London, Trollope wrote *Domestic Manners of the Americans* (1832), giving permanent offense to Cincinnati society by portraying the city as a dull, dirty, pig-ridden place where the principal amusement was churchgoing, which was the pastime chiefly of women. Although she found the houses and public buildings "neat," in her eyes the lack of domes, towers, and steeples limited the city's architectural appeal. She extolled the beauties of the Kentucky landscape and praised the farmers' markets of Cincinnati.

Trollopean Bazaar

The Trollopean Bazaar, as it came to be called, was a shopping center, tearoom, and banquet hall. The building sparked a storm of amateur architectural criticism, much of it unflattering.

The building was a fantastic three-story edifice sited on a large, open property carved from the Fort Washington parade grounds. The architect was Seneca Palmer, but Trollope and her traveling companion, French painter and illustrator Auguste Hervieu (1794–1853), very likely helped to conceptualize the design. Trollope disliked the sameness of the American architectural scene—she described Benjamin Latrobe's Cathedral in Baltimore as one of the few significant edifices in the new nation. She obviously wanted her entertainment and shopping center to have a distinctive and light-hearted look, and coming recently from London, she would have been familiar with the latest fashions of Regency architects, such as the Peter Robinson design for her friend William Bullock's Egyptian Museum and John Nash's Brighton Pavilion for the Prince Regent, the soon-to-be King George IV. With an eye for the picturesque, she selected a site that allowed for gardens and river views.

The Bazaar was an amusing concoction of Moorish, Egyptian, and Gothic elements. It was one of the first examples of the spirit of Eclecticism—drawing upon historic styles from various and exotic cultures—which came to dominate American building for the remainder of the century. Here, the designers drew on several sources for a creative rather than authentic, single-style version of a historical design convention. Staid Cincinnatians and visitors, who were accustomed in public buildings to the simplicity of the vernacular, the chasteness of neoclassicism, and the spirituality of Gothic Revival, delighted in attacking what they regarded as the tastelessness of the "bizarre bazaar." Hervieu painted a panoramic mural in the building. He also painted a panorama of Lafayette's 1825 visit to Cincinnati, which became a traveling exhibit.

The city had always attracted far more merchants than it could support, and the shopping boutiques were never successful. But the banquet hall quickly became the favored site for important celebrations. The rooms were large, airy, elegant, and functional. Verandas opened on the sides, offering views of the hills and the river. The monumental and elaborate structure made a statement in the bland Cincinnati cityscape. Its orientation toward the scenic vistas offered by the river and the hills testifies to the growing spirit of Romanticism, which had appeared earlier in England and continental Europe. The Romantic movement stimulated an interest in primitive, exotic art and architecture and a taste for the picturesque in nature.

Although Trollope was forced to forfeit her interest in the Bazaar before it was completed, it continued to be known as the Trollopean. It became headquarters for the Ohio Mechanics Institute (OMI),[25] which purchased it for $10,000. The building served efficiently as a teaching facility; the earliest architectural education courses offered in Cincinnati were held here. Within a few years, however, OMI failed to make payments and lost the Trollopean, which then went through multiple uses, including a nursing facility for wounded soldiers in the Civil War. In 1881, Thomas Emery & Sons razed the building to erect the Lorraine apartment house.

Seneca Palmer was born around 1793 and came to Cincinnati from Albany, New York, after 1825. He worked here at least through the early 1850s. A complimentary essay about Trollope's new Bazaar in the 1829 city directory describes him as the architect, but in the street address and occupation section of the directory he is listed simply as "carpenter." This reminds us that in the original Greek, "architect" means literally "chief carpenter."

Palmer was the designer of some important projects in Cincinnati—in part because he had little competition. His longest-standing works were the Lane Presbyterian Theological Seminary in Walnut Hills (ca. 1830–32), where his residence for the Beecher family has survived, and the Western Baptist Theological Institute in Covington, Kentucky (ca. 1840). The president's and residence houses of the latter remain in Covington, at Twelfth and Russell streets. In both these academic complexes, Palmer made use of the Greek Revival conventions that were then in vogue for theological and educational buildings.

View of Ohio River and Northern Kentucky

Southwestern Ohio and Northern Kentucky grew rapidly between 1830 and 1860, and a poem by Henry Wadsworth Longfellow saluted Cincinnati, the "Queen of the West." The era was characterized by the influx of people from the German states and the establishment of churches, businesses, and self-improvement societies, all of which needed permanent buildings. Wealthy individuals and corporations recruited architects, engineers, and landscape architects to design important projects, but many of these works were demolished long ago. Foremost among the survivors are a handful of fine churches and landscape architectural places such as Glendale and Spring Grove Cemetery.

2

Queen of the West

1830–60

America's Original Boomtown

AMERICANS CONTINUED to move westward in the 1830s. Before good highways and railroads, the river route through Cincinnati was the standard choice. Settlers heading for St. Louis and the far West took a steamboat down the Ohio River to Cincinnati, where they stopped for provisions before beginning the overland journey.

Serving as the "Emporium of the West" made Cincinnati the "Queen City of the West" by 1830. In fact, the commercial focus became so strong that some residents and visitors complained of too many merchants. As investment capital became available, manufactories flourished, and food processing, shoe-making, brewing, distilling, and furniture-making became dominant industries.

Cincinnati suffered a cholera epidemic in 1831 and another in 1832, along with a devastating flood and a great fire. Citizens were concerned for their health and safety, so the municipal government, which served primarily to regulate commerce, was forced to assume responsibility for some public services. Shortly after Cincinnati became a city in 1819, elected officials found themselves in the business of hiring employees and erecting public works and public buildings. In 1839, the city reluctantly took over the troubled private water system, which it purchased from developers for $300,000. Theodore R. Scowden (b. 1815), a highly regarded hydraulic engineer from Pennsylvania, was appointed in 1845 to reconstruct and supervise the waterworks. Scowden replaced the original log pipes with about fifty miles of iron pipes and built a new reservoir and pump house, which was operated by an innovative low-pressure engine.[1]

Despite the disasters of the 1830s, settlers and transients continued to arrive. Between 1830 and 1840, the population grew by 85 percent, reaching 46,338 residents. By 1840, Cincinnati was the fastest-growing city in the United States, sixth in population, and third in manufacturing. It was hailed as a truly American boomtown—the first post-Independence settlement to demonstrate the urban potential of the new nation.[2]

The basin filled with buildings and people. At a time when walking was the chief means of urban transportation, the wealthy lived in the city center, which radiated outward from Federal architect Ammi B. Young's Greco-Roman post office at Fourth and Vine streets.[3] The poor lived on the periphery: free blacks and poor whites occupied shacks and tenements along the Ohio River and the Mill Creek in the west. They lived amid the more undesirable institutions and noxious industries such as slaughterhouses, brickyards, and tanneries.

The most desirable commercial-residential district occupied the plateau above the flood plain. Main Street was the original shopping street, while banks and financial services clustered on Third Street. On Fourth Street, fashionable residences were located at either end, with churches, Cincinnati College, fine shops, and hotels between. Visiting travel writers often commented on the neat red-and-white houses, the pretty, flower-filled yards, and the tree-lined streets. The houses and most commercial buildings were detached two- to three-story structures.

Cincinnatians took pride in what they had accomplished and in their city's reign as "Queen of the West." There was now a gentry elite, who wanted to advance the city's reputation in the nation and abroad. They turned to the arts, education, and urban amenities to project a positive image for the city. An itinerant artist, John Caspar Wild, painted a series of cityscapes that illustrate the young city's economic status and its early claims to architectural distinction.

Buildings to Improve Society

Between 1830 and 1850, Cincinnati participated in the national culture of societal and self-improvement through education. Institutions proliferated at a dizzying pace as local leaders dedicated themselves to creating a civilized and civilizing community. The development of voluntary institutions was tied to current political theory: If democracy was to work, if the precious and precarious Union was to survive, the people had to be educated, temperate, industrious, and devout. The young had to attend grammar school. Good mechanics and clerks required continuing education

Ammi B. Young
Column from old Post Office
Pioneer Cemetery, Wilmer Avenue, Columbia-Tusculum

Ammi B. Young (1800–74), a native of New Hampshire, was supervising architect of the Treasury when the Federal Building and post office were designed. Cincinnati architect James Keys Wilson may have collaborated in the design and construction of the Greek Revival–style edifice at Fourth and Vine streets. When the landmark government building was scheduled for demolition in 1885 to make way for the Chamber of Commerce Building, designed by H. H. Richardson, citizens tried to move and preserve fragments of the handsome structure. This ornate Corinthian column came from the portico.

Fourth Street with Pike's Opera House, built and rebuilt, 1857–66

The opera house, designed and constructed by New York City architect John M. Trimble in 1857, was described by contemporary Cincinnatians as a grand and exceptionally beautiful theater, but an article in the Architect's and Mechanic's Journal *published 1859 in New York gave the architecture an unfavorable review.*

classes and access to libraries, and the Ohio Mechanics Institute was established in 1828 and the Young Men's Mercantile Library Association in 1831 to fill those needs. In addition, the general populace needed churches, museums, and self-improvement societies to keep abreast of all that was new and best in religious thought, politics, philosophy, and science.

Civic leaders sought skilled architects to design buildings for their important institutions. As neighborhoods developed around the first permanent schools and churches, these buildings became the focal points of community life. Architects tried to give each institutional headquarters a distinctive character that underlined its intellectual or spiritual meaning and function. The varied churches, schools, and education buildings of the period gave the rapidly growing city a sense of place.

Some institutions and buildings arose in response to perceived urban problems of public safety. At midcentury, civic leaders in Cincinnati and other American cities came to the realization that some newcomers, such as immigrants and some rural native-born Americans, were not adapting well to urban life. "Strangers" (strangers being all those who behaved unacceptably) seemed to threaten the health and morals of their more successful neighbors. In the 1840s and 1850s, cities created social welfare organizations to deal with this perceived problem. Citizen demand for more vigorous government action led Cincinnati to create a professional police force, fire department, and a health department with enforcement powers. Municipal governments, both city and suburban, became important clients for architects, engineers, and building contractors. In the mid-1850s, Cincinnati built its first city hall in a park-like setting at Eighth and Plum streets. The simple structure with Renaissance Revival details housed all the public safety departments.[4]

Otto Onken (1815–60),
Third Street between Main and Vine in 1849

The phenomenal rise of this great city in the wilderness encouraged optimism among Cincinnati civic leaders. Some maintained that the city's location at the center of the U.S. population made it a logical choice to be the social and cultural center of the nation. The appearance of the city and the merits of its architecture were tools in the great American race for urban supremacy.

Building Projects Attract Famous Architects

Along with buildings for institutions, enterprising Cincinnatians were creating permanent buildings for businesses and industries. Moving beyond the functional and sometimes shoddy construction of the pioneer period, entrepreneurs of the 1850s demanded fine materials and "good taste" in architectural design, qualities that enhanced the status of their business and the city. In 1848, a stock company engaged famed Boston architect Isaiah Rogers (1800–69) to design a hotel on the prime city block that Judge Burnet had wanted the city to purchase for its municipal building. The financiers of the hotel, named the Burnet House, instructed Rogers to build not just the best hotel in Cincinnati, but the most modern and elegant

Isaiah Rogers
Burnet House Hotel, 1848–50; demolished 1926
Vine and Third streets

Rogers was the most prestigious hotel architect in the nation when he came to Cincinnati to design this grand hotel. Fine architecture demanded fine interiors. Francis Pedretti (1829–91), a fresco painter and decorator, arrived in the early 1850s to decorate the hotel and stayed to train his sons in the art.

Isaiah Rogers
Longview Asylum, 1860
Carthage

Hamilton County operated this facility where mentally ill patients resided, most at no charge. Using brick, iron, and cement, Rogers designed a fire-resistant building that was regarded as the "best finished and best appointed asylum in the United States" (Kenny, Illustrated Cincinnati, *50). The low-security design and restful landscaped grounds made it a model institution.*

hotel in the United States. They must have felt the expense of the imposing Greco-Roman Revival block was justified when the nineteen-year-old son of Queen Victoria and Prince Albert, the Prince of Wales and future Edward VII (1841–1910), registered at the hotel in 1860.

In a testimony to the thriving construction climate, Rogers remained in Cincinnati to practice. He trained other architects, and his skilled handling of Greco-Roman and Norman Romanesque forms influenced the architecture of his time. Rogers's plan for Longview Asylum in Carthage made it a model facility for the mentally ill, one that endured (well beyond its "modernity") into the twentieth century. Although he considered Cincinnati home, from 1861 until 1867, Rogers was in Washington, DC, where he served the U.S. Treasury Department (Cincinnatian Salmon P. Chase was President Abraham Lincoln's Secretary of the Treasury) as engineer-in-charge, Bureau of Construction, supervising architect of the Treasury, and as construction manager for the Treasury Building.

Other architects arrived and used the city as a base for commissions in the tri-state region. Henry Walter (1780s–1851), had a short but distinguished career in the city and the state—he won the competition for the Ohio Statehouse. English-born John R. Hamilton (died ca. 1905) and James Keys Wilson (1828–1894), Cincinnati's first professionally trained native architect, were distinguished architects who influenced later generations. James W. McLaughlin (1834–1923), the most important Cincinnati-born architect during the second half of the nineteenth century, trained under Wilson and worked with Hamilton. English-born Samuel Hannaford (1835–1911), whose architectural firm was the most prolific in Cincinnati history, trained with Hamilton.

By 1858, about the time McLaughlin and Hannaford began practicing, Charles Cist, the city's leading statistician and the historian who published the earliest list of Cincinnati architects and their buildings, noted a "marked improvement in pub-

John R. Hamilton and James W. McLaughlin
Masonic Temple, 1858–59

This building summed up the area's sophisticated antebellum architectural development. It was one of the first American designs to show the influence of the Venetian Gothic architecture promoted by the English critic John Ruskin (1819–1900). The polychrome mansard roof with corner tower-pavilions also acknowledged the emerging French Second Empire style. This fascinating hybrid survived into the twentieth century.

lic buildings."[5] By the 1860s, practicing architects were teaching courses at OMI and at the college that became Xavier University. Students often supplemented their apprenticeship in an architect's office with some classroom education in the evening.

Residential City Districts

In the 1830s and 1840s, Cincinnati's population was composed primarily of native-born Americans from the Eastern, Middle Atlantic, and Upper Southern states. Travel writers described it as a Yankee city with a pleasant blend of Southern ease and charm. But a new ethnic element appeared in the thirties, when people from the fragmented states of Germany discovered Cincinnati. Many of them clustered together north of the canal in an area that they called Over-the-Rhine, where they built churches, houses, tenements (street-level shops with residences above), and small commercial buildings.

James W. McLaughlin
St. Francis Seraph Church, 1858–59
Liberty and Vine streets

Built on the site of the first Catholic church in the area, St. Francis is a hall church, a type preferred by German congregations. The central and side aisles of hall churches are all one height, allowing for exceptionally high side windows. The interior was altered in the twentieth century. In 1925, S. Hannaford and Sons sheathed the exterior in glazed brick. Still, the German Romanesque qualities of the twin-towered composition come through.

Alfred West Gilbert
(1816–1900)
Findlay Market, 1852–55
Elm Street, Over-the-Rhine

Findlay Market is the oldest extant municipal market house in Ohio and an anchor in neighborhood revitalization. The original construction used an innovative cast-iron and wrought-iron frame. Glaserworks renovated the historic market house in 2002–4 and expanded the surrounding marketplace.

Cincinnati's early Anglo-Irish or native-born architects had no difficulty designing buildings that accommodated the taste of German American clients. James W. McLaughlin designed the church of St. Francis Seraph in Over-the-Rhine for the Franciscans who arrived in 1844 to minister to German-speaking Catholics. The German American architects and engineers who came to the area in the 1840s and 1850s were inclined to emphasize engineering.[6]

Whigs Engineer "Internal Improvements"

The new Whig party, intellectual successors to the Federalists, advocated government funding of "internal improvements," primarily canals, highways, and railroads that would bind the nation together. (Southern and eastern-based Jacksonians opposed federal funding for sectional projects that would chiefly benefit Kentucky, Ohio, and the "West.") The state-funded Ohio canal system and county and municipal roads radiating out from Cincinnati contributed to general prosperity by enabling the transfer of grain to mills and distilleries, produce to urban markets, and hogs to slaughterhouses. At midcentury, Cincinnati's pork-packing industry had grown to such proportions that the city bore the sobriquet "Porkopolis."

Myron S. Webb
Whitewater Canal, 1838–43
Canal section below Harrison house, North Bend

The Whitewater Canal was built in southern Ohio and Indiana between 1838 and 1843 to bring Indiana farm produce into Cincinnati's market. It terminated in Cincinnati's West End. Designed by Myron S. Webb with a 1,782-foot-long brick-lined tunnel engineered by Darius Lapham, the canal was a great engineering feat ("Canal Construction in Indiana," 6–7). The Ohio segment of the canal was constructed through William Henry Harrison's plantation. The exceptionally long tunnel, which is still visible in Cleves, Ohio (the canal entry is near Miami Avenue and Wamsley Street, Cleves), was a rarity in canal construction.

In the Cincinnati region, small gardeners and farmers prospered and city markets flourished. In 1855, one of the nation's first iron market houses opened one block east of the Miami and Erie Canal, at Findlay Market in Over-the-Rhine.

By midcentury, railroads were gradually replacing canals, as indicated by the closing of the Whitewater Canal in 1861 and sale of its right-of-way to the Cincinnati and Indiana Railroad Co. Railroads provided a faster, more flexible, and more efficient means of transporting goods and people. However, the Ohio legislature refused to finance railroad construction as it had the canal system. Extensive railroad operations were built in the state, but not in a systematic way. By the 1850s, entrepreneurial railroads radiated out from five depots in downtown Cincinnati like spokes on a half-broken wheel. As the century progressed, the lack of a coordinated rail network was perceived as Cincinnati's great failing, a major handicap in the race for urban supremacy. In truth, the relative slowdown in the city's growth resulted from the convergence of a number of internal and external factors.[7]

Northern Kentucky Branch, Northern Bank of Kentucky/Bank of Kentucky, ca. 1830
East Third and Scott Boulevard, Covington

In 1998–2000, this building by an unknown architect was returned to its original use as a banking office. It anchors an important corner at the center of Covington's thriving convention and tourism district. In the 1890s, a third floor was added and the roof and cornice altered. But the original structure, with its recessed Greek Revival entrance, is still identifiable.

The City and the Metropolis

Nineteenth-century urban boosters had a metropolitan, even a regional, vision. The Northern Kentucky cities of Newport (founded 1795) and Covington (laid out 1814/1815) prospered along with Cincinnati and were frequently included with it in statistical reports. Kentucky was originally part of Virginia, and its frontier towns attracted settlers from the South. Many of them came equipped with capital and cultivated tastes in architecture. Marriage and business alliances tied the Ohio River border cities to one another. Covington enjoyed an influx of settlers and economic prosperity in the 1840s and 1850s. Covington civic leader Amos Shinkle, who led a movement to bridge the Ohio River, was president of the Odd Fellows fraternal organization when it erected a grand hall in the downtown.

A number of fine nineteenth-century structures have survived in Northern Kentucky. The Northern Bank of Kentucky in Covington and Odd Fellows Hall display restrained Greek Revival forms and Doric features. These buildings express the character of local architecture in the decades before the Civil War, when Cincinnati was known as the Queen of the West and Covington was its thriving metropolitan neighbor.

Odd Fellows Hall, 1856
Fifth Street and
Madison Avenue,
Covington

This building has no interior supports—its weight rests on the two-foot-thick outside walls. The entire third floor and second-floor ceiling were suspended from rods running down from the attic, leading some historians to suspect that John A. Roebling (who was in the area) had a hand in the design. The hall was rebuilt after a fire in 2002 destroyed all but three outside walls.

After years of encouraging growth statistics, the 1855 local census, which counted 172,370 residents, confirmed what keen observers had suspected. The rate of population increase was falling year by year—clearly Cincinnati's boomtown days of effortless growth were waning. Clinging to the title Queen of the West, civic leaders of the 1860s and 1870s would formulate new strategies for focused economic growth. But from 1830 to 1860, individuals and institutional leaders concentrated on building an attractive and efficient city, one that would be a nice place in which to live, learn, and earn a living.

Anton and Louis Piket
St. Xavier Church and College, 1860
Sycamore Street

The church is on the site of the first Catholic Church, within the city boundaries, in a block that once included the Athenaeum of Ohio, St. Xavier College (now University), and a boys' school. The Pikets were teachers of architecture and mathematics at the college. They also designed the post–Civil War college building north of the church in the Second Empire style popular then. When the church burnt in 1882, the Pikets' design for the rebuilding of the tower was rejected in favor of one by Samuel Hannaford, who provided the existing combination of a Gothic tower with a somewhat classical dome. The firm of Samuel Hannaford & Sons then proceeded to rebuild the Pikets' college, school, and a chapel in a classical manner.

Over-the-Rhine

Over-the-Rhine streetscape
West side of Main Street looking north toward Liberty Street

Main Street above Central Parkway is lined with some of the best-preserved historic buildings in this impressive district.

From 1835, German-speaking people were coming to Cincinnati in large numbers. The first were predominantly Protestants and Freethinkers, but Roman Catholics soon outnumbered them. By 1840, one-third of Cincinnati's 75,000 citizens were German-speaking, of which an estimated two-thirds to three-fourths were Roman Catholic.[8]

The immigrants were attracted by the promise of economic opportunities and political freedom. Some, such as the "Forty-Eighters," were educated liberals disappointed in the failure of the German Revolution of 1848 and fleeing civil unrest in their native states.

Most immigrants sought low-cost housing on the periphery of downtown Cincinnati, but a number of the Germans settled on small farms in the townships and across the Ohio River in Covington and Newport, Kentucky. The Irish, who were also arriving in considerable numbers after 1840, were dispersed on the periphery of the river bottoms, the West End, and Over-the-Rhine.

North of Canal Street in Cincinnati became a predominantly German neighborhood. In jest or longing, the canal was often called the "Rhine," and in time the neighborhood became known as Over-the-Rhine. Although the Germans were remarkably diverse, vehicles such as German-language newspapers, building societies for home-construction finance, Turnverein clubs for gymnastics and socializing, and churches for religion and school education enabled them to establish a cluster of communities in Over-the-Rhine.

In architecture, many German-Americans favored brick and stone over frame. For churches, they liked the simple monumentality of the Greek Revival, the solid walls and sturdy towers of the German Romanesque and Gothic styles, and the exuberance of the Baroque. Italianate forms and trim were used for commercial and residential buildings. Many of these buildings have similar features: tall, narrow, round-headed windows, corner blocks or quoins at exterior wall edges, and bracketed cornices.

Because the area north of the canal (later Central Parkway) escaped the continuous piecemeal improvements of the nineteenth century and the sweeping urban renewal of the twentieth century, much of Over-the-Rhine's historic architecture remains. Constructed largely of brick in vernacular styles and closely corresponding cornice lines, the buildings make up the largest and most important Italianate urban architectural district in the United States. Main Street, at the heart of the Over-the-Rhine entertainment district, is home to nightclubs, art galleries, and residential and office condominiums. Old St. Mary's and St. Paul's churches are nearby. The historic district, which has its own chamber of commerce, is home to a diverse and energetic population.

Old St. Mary's Roman Catholic Church

(Old) St. Mary's Roman Catholic Church, 1841
Thirteenth Street, Over-the-Rhine

St. Mary's church and school, erected by a German American congregation, have served the social and educational as well as religious needs of the Over-the-Rhine neighborhood since the 1840s.

St. Mary's Church is the oldest functioning church in the city. The Reverend Johann Henni traveled throughout the Northwest Territory states in the early nineteenth century, organizing German Catholic parishes. Henni had a keen interest in architecture, and he was a prodigious builder. He eventually became archbishop of Minneapolis, where he initiated the building of a landmark cathedral. Cincinnati Bishop Edward Fenwick and his successor, Archbishop John Baptist Purcell, allowed the German Catholic churches under Father Henni a high degree of control over their own affairs. Archbishop Purcell, himself an Irish immigrant, praised the Germans for their thrift and industry.

The church's designer is unknown. It is possible that a sophisticated architect had a hand in the design of St. Mary's. Seneca Palmer and Henry Walter were working in Cincinnati at the time. Henry Walter's design for St. Peter in Chains Cathedral (then under construction) would certainly have been known to Henni and his design-build team. While Ignatz Erd is frequently proposed as the architect, designer, or builder, we suspect that he was a parish trustee who may have chaired the building committee. Erd is listed in city directories of the period as proprietor of a coffee house at 74 Canal Street.[9] In that capacity, he could easily have collected pledges and paid contractors. As keeper of the purse, he may also have advised on the scope and design of the project.

St. Mary's is a substantial but simple Greek Revival block with a Gothic tower and a few Renaissance details. There is a tradition that the brick—now painted in pale grays—was made by the parishioners. The shallow structural pilasters are molded of brick, and colossal Doric pilasters organize the pedimented façade and sides. The single barrel-vaulted interior is akin to the Protestant meetinghouse in shape, but the mellow trompe-l'oeil interior decoration, which dates from around 1890, draws upon Roman Catholic Bohemian art traditions. The school building beside the church is also painted brick.

The church was enlarged and remodeled in the 1860s, the 1890s, 1914, and 1937. In 1988, the year of the city's bicentennial, local German American organizations assisted with a major restoration project, which was carried out as a tribute to historic Cincinnati.

Henry and William Walter
St. Peter in Chains Cathedral, 1841–45
Remodeled:
Edward J. Schulte, 1952–55
Eighth and Plum streets

Archbishop Purcell's massive basilica shares an important urban intersection with the Plum Street Temple and City Hall (shown on the right). The 140-foot needle spire of the cathedral, which was modeled after that of Sir Christopher Wren's St. Bride Church in London, is profiled majestically in the city's western skyline.

St. Peter in Chains Cathedral

St. Peter in Chains Cathedral is the oldest monumental structure in the central business district. It is the seat of the Roman Catholic diocese, which was established in 1821, when there were few Catholics in the city. The first wooden church was built on an inexpensive lot outside the city limits at Liberty and Vine streets. The majority of the Catholics who came to the area in the next two decades were Irish and German immigrants. As their numbers grew, so did hostility from the native-born majority. The Nativist riots of the 1840s and the political activities of the Know-Nothing Party in the 1850s were indicative of the continuing bigotry toward Catholics and immigrants.

When Cincinnati became the seat of a new archdiocese in 1840, Irish-born John B. Purcell was made archbishop. Purcell was a learned, politically astute man who was determined to align the church in America with national values. He was befriended by the handful of wealthy Catholics in the city, including Reuben Springer, Sarah Worthington Peter, and the Piatt family. They assisted in funding a series of capital projects, including this monumental cathedral. Located on a conspicuous urban corner, the edifice made a powerful statement in a community where Catholicism was still regarded as foreign.

Archbishop Purcell came to Cincinnati from Maryland, where he would have been familiar with what was then the only Catholic cathedral in the United States, Benjamin Latrobe's Greco-Roman Cathedral for Baltimore. The archbishop's decision to build in the Greek Revival style manner was likely influenced by his exposure to Latrobe, but also by its political symbolism. Although a strong advocate of separation of church and state, Purcell believed that the American Catholic Church should participate fully in civic life. While a resident of Baltimore, he became close to the Jefferson family in nearby Virginia, and he was familiar with Thomas Jefferson's architectural scheme for Monticello. For the Cincinnati cathedral design, Purcell drew upon the architectural traditions of the ancient classical world—the Roman and Greek forms that Jefferson associated with Greek democracy and Roman republicanism.

Henry Walter had contributed the winning design for the Ohio State House in an 1838 competition. Walter, who had worked in Pennsylvania and Maryland, was probably the most important architect to work primarily in the Greek Revival manner in Cincinnati before the Civil War.

After his father's death, William Walter (1815–86) finished the handsome portico of the cathedral with twelve towering Corinthian columns: six fronting the porch and three on each side. The tower is expressed in a suave series of octagonal blocks that rise in diminutions upward. The base is punctuated by ventilating windows in unusual cross-shaped frames, and two of the octagons are adorned with miniature Corinthian columns. The exterior walls are of "Dayton marble," a high-quality limestone quarried near Dayton, Ohio. The walls are set upon a blue limestone foundation.

When it was dedicated on November 2, 1845, the cathedral was acclaimed one of the most beautiful ecclesiastical buildings in the country. St. Peter's lost its cathedral status when residents abandoned the basin in the twentieth century, and the area deteriorated along with the building. In 1938, the hilltop church of St. Monica became the cathedral. In the 1950s, Archbishop Karl Alter countermanded that decision. He led a fundraising campaign to expand the physical dimensions of St. Peter's church and restore its cathedral status, thereby reaffirming the urban mission of the Catholic Church in Cincinnati.

The building was enlarged and modified between 1952 and 1957 by Cincinnati architect Edward J. Schulte (1890–1975). The original main block was 80 by 200 feet, and 55 feet floor to the ceiling. The renovation extended the west end by nearly 200 feet and added transepts for a baptistery and chapel. The Renaissance and Baroque paintings and statuary were removed. The two angels (1848–49) ordered in 1845 by Reuben Springer and Archbishop Purcell from the studio of Hiram Powers in Florence are displayed in the Cincinnati Wing of the Cincin nati Art Museum. The angels were sculpted by Powers's assistant, Odoardo Fantacchiotte (1809–77).

The interior, where colossal Corinthian columns with gilded capitals repeat the columnar motif of the exterior, was dramatically revamped in a high style inspired by Greek vase paintings and Early Christian mosaics. Cincinnati artist Karl Zimmerman painted the Way of the Cross murals in the manner of ancient (600–400 BCE) Greek vase painting. Cincinnati artist Ernest B. Haswell executed many of the relief sculpture figures. Dayton artist Robert Koepnick sculpted the free-standing figures.

Seneca Palmer
St. Paul Roman Catholic Church/Verdin Co., 1848–50
Rebuilt:
Samuel Hannaford & Sons, ca. 1900
444 Reading Road, Pendleton

The former St. Paul Church building is now a museum and event center, an anchor for the thriving Pendleton arts district.

St. Paul Roman Catholic Church/Verdin Co.

Seneca Palmer, the architect of the Trollopean Bazaar and Lane Theological Seminary, was the architect for this Catholic church in Pendleton. Sited on a knoll in the midst of other red-brick buildings abutting narrow streets that form a historic district, the complex has a strong urban presence.

Like St. Mary's, which it resembled even more closely before the tower was lowered, this church for German Catholics was a community center as well as a house of worship. Both parishes had schools for boys and girls. St. Paul's first two pastors and many of the parishioners had immigrated from villages near Bremen, Germany. In the late nineteenth century, nearly one thousand families were members of St. Paul church. Those who were successful in business gave generously to the parish. At the 1893 Chicago World's Fair, a well-to-do couple from St. Paul's admired a stained-glass window made in Munich. They purchased the window, which represented the marriage of Cana, and presented it to the church to commemorate their wedding anniversary.

St. Paul's has been altered significantly over the years. Following a fire that took all but the walls and foundation, Samuel Hannaford & Sons rebuilt it around 1900. At that time, the interior was embellished with stained-glass windows made in Germany and the walls were wainscoted with marble.

The movement of German Catholics outward and upward from "the Rhine" began around 1900 and accelerated in the 1920s. St. Paul's and nearby St. Mary's were left with too few parishioners to support both parishes. In 1974, when St. Paul's religious mission ended, the city purchased the property, recognizing that the church and its ancillary buildings represented an urban asset. The city sold the property to the Verdin Co., a local company that has been a world-renowned bell-maker since 1842. Verdin converted the church into the Verdin Bell and Clock Museum, and the Bell Event Centre, a popular meeting center.

Church of the Immaculate Conception

Piket & Sons
Church of the Immaculate Conception/Holy Cross-Immaculata, 1859–60
30 Guido Street, Mount Adams

Evidence of Cincinnati's natural attributes and early progress comes together in this breathtaking location overlooking the meandering Ohio River, the crowded city basin, and the verdant Kentucky hills. The simple sculptural shape of Immaculata has made the church a favorite subject for artists.

Archbishop Purcell erected this landmark church to celebrate the papal doctrine that declared Mary, the mother of Christ, was born immaculate, her soul unblemished by original sin. Immaculata was commonly referred to as the "archbishop's church" because Purcell built it as a thanksgiving offering for his many safe voyages across the Atlantic Ocean in search of funds for his cathedral project. The site on Mount Adams's southern promontory, which provided river views in three directions, may have been selected for the symbolic allusion to Purcell's voyages by water.

In the early nineteenth century, most of the acreage that became Mount Adams was owned by millionaire Nicholas Longworth, who had acquired it with the Martin Baum house (now the Taft Museum). Longworth planted the hillsides with grapes used for production of his prized Catawba grape wines, which were immortalized by Henry Wadsworth Longfellow in an 1854 poem that popularized Cincinnati as "Queen of the West, in her garlands dressed, on the banks of the Beautiful River."

Longworth donated a site on what was then called Mount Ida for the first Cincinnati Observatory (the site was later the location of the Passionist Monastery). When former president John Quincy Adams traveled to Cincinnati to dedicate the observatory, America's first "lighthouse in the sky," the name was changed to Mount Adams in his honor. Access to the hilltop then was by a rough dirt road.

The church congregation was drawn from the working-class residents of this beautiful but once isolated suburb. Perched on a rock far above the basin, Immaculata became a pilgrimage site for the faithful, especially on Good Friday, when they climbed the hillside steps, pausing on each step to say a Hail Mary. The practice, which originally culminated in a visit to the Passionist Fathers Monastery of the Holy Cross, now continues only as far as Immaculata. When Holy Cross closed in 1970, the congregations merged.

Stone for the rustic exterior of Immaculata was quarried from the site,[10] and the structure looks as if it has been sculpted from the rocky terrain. The building's unadorned but majestic profile has simple pointed Gothic windows. The interior is a hall-church style with a choir loft above the entrance end. The altar murals are by Johann Schmitt.

Louis Piket (1839–1910), who designed St. Xavier Church on Sycamore Street with his father, Anton Piket, in 1859, is generally believed to be the architect of Immaculata (James W. McLaughlin may have contributed to the design, which is listed in his book of accounts). The former Holy Cross Roman Catholic monastery (1900) and church (1894–95), Monastery Street, Mount Adams, are also attributed to Louis Piket & Sons (two of Louis' sons joined his firm in 1888). The monastery was beautifully renovated by Towne Properties, which is headquartered there.

Spring Grove Cemetery, 1845
Spring Grove Avenue, Winton Place

The advanced landscape plan of Spring Grove Cemetery was emulated in the United States and Europe in the nineteenth century.

Spring Grove Cemetery and Arboretum

In 1844, several leading Cincinnati families, including the families of Robert Buchanan, Timothy Walker, Miles Greenwood, and Salmon P. Chase, formed a cemetery association.[11] The overcrowding of Cincinnati's basin had extended to the cemeteries. Burials were often delayed for want of space, raising concerns about public health risks and causing inconvenience to the bereaved. Many of the founders of Spring Grove were members of the Cincinnati Horticultural Society. They wanted a "rural" cemetery, patterned after the landscaped plan that was used in 1831 for the Mount Auburn Cemetery in Cambridge, a suburb of Boston.

Leaders purchased property at the foot of Clifton Hill and engaged John Notman (1810–65) of Philadelphia to design a plan. Notman's conventional design was rejected, and a local architect, Howard Daniels (1815–63), contributed a road plan that conformed to the topography. In 1855, the cemetery board turned to Adolph Strauch, who was in Clifton designing and tending park-like estates of wealthy residents. Strauch was given free rein to design his own plan. His lawn plan evolved from the natural contours of the land, complete with lakes supplied by natural springs. Spring Grove Cemetery was nationally recognized as a pioneer in the lawn plan cemetery.

Strauch became superintendent of the cemetery and remained its supreme authority until his death in 1883. Since the nineteenth century, the beautifully landscaped grounds and interesting monuments have made Spring Grove a favorite touring destination for city residents and visitors.

Adolph Strauch (1822–83), a German-born landscape architect, was educated in Birez and Vienna and trained in Germany with the noted author and garden patron Prince Puckler-Muskau, who was influenced by the English Romantic landscape designers. Strauch visited Cincinnati in 1852 and stayed to assist Robert Bowler as gardener for his Mount Storm estate in Clifton. Strauch's role in nineteenth-century American landscape planning and horticulture is perhaps second only to that of Frederick Law Olmsted, who admired Strauch's work.[12]

England native Joseph Earnshaw was in Cincinnati by 1856, practicing as a "landscape engineer." His firm, which later included T. B. Punshon, specialized in cemetery engineering. Earnshaw worked at Spring Grove with Strauch and at other cemeteries throughout the United States.

Alfred B. Mullett
Public Vault, 1859 (now White Pine Chapel)
Spring Grove Cemetery

The cemetery building's rough stone walls contrast with the boldly carved concentric Norman geometric arches at the heavy wooden doorway.

Public Vault (now White Pine Chapel)

Alfred Bult Mullett (1834–90), an English-born Glendale architect, designed the waiting vault, now called White Pine Chapel at Spring Grove. Mullett used some features of the massive round-arch Norman Romanesque that his mentor, Isaiah Rogers, had employed in his design for Cincinnati's most highly esteemed church, the Episcopal Cathedral of St. Paul (since demolished).

The waiting vault consists of a rectangular stone gable-ended block with a perpendicular wing sunk deep into the hillside. A cupola marks the crossing. Although it appears diminutive at a distance and even in illustrations, the vault is large scaled and boldly detailed inside and out. Inside, the wing is lined with drawer-like vaults that were used to store caskets temporarily during the winter, before graves could be conveniently dug in the frost-hard soil of the cemetery grounds.

Mullett mastered architecture through the apprenticeship system, working in 1857 for Rogers in Cincinnati. During the Civil War, Mullett began a career in government service. He moved ahead of (or ousted) his mentor, serving as the supervising architect of the U.S. Treasury from 1866 to 1874. Mullett's designs for Treasury buildings, post offices, courthouses, and customs houses included the Executive Office Building in Washington, DC, and the courthouses and post offices of Trenton, NJ (1873–78), Philadelphia (1874–84), and St. Louis. His magnificent Government Building for Cincinnati (designed before 1874), completed 1885) was demolished in 1913 to make way for the building now known as the Potter Stewart U.S. Courthouse.

Mullett was Cincinnati's most famous and most influential nineteenth-century architect. He continued to practice independently in the District of Columbia following his formal resignation from federal employ. When his petition for back pay was denied by the federal government, Mullett took his own life.

Suire Pharmacy Building (later Herschede Building)

This lyrical commercial structure with a painted stone façade began life as Suire's Pharmacy. It was designed by William Walter, son of Henry Walter, and Cincinnati's first native-born professional architect, James Keys Wilson. The building design is typical of the era's high-end retail stores. Architects drew upon Italian Renaissance palazzo (town house) design for the device of ornamented multiple stories of smooth walls organized by arcades of applied orders. In the 1850s, iron structural supports made five-story buildings such as this possible. (Cincinnatians marveled that the first five-story brick structure, erected at Pearl and Walnut streets in 1847, did not collapse.)[13]

When this building went up, Fourth Street was becoming the prime shopping district. Cincinnatians compared it to Fifth Avenue in New York. Its sidewalks served as the favorite promenade for elegantly attired shoppers. In this walking city, property costs decreased in relation to their distance from the center. Those who could afford the best locations lived close to the center, near the shops and their place of business.

William Walter and
James Keys Wilson
Suire Pharmacy Building, 1857 (later Herschede Building)
Fourth Street

Herschede's, a fine jewelry, silver, and china store that catered to the carriage trade, was headquartered in this building from 1939 until the mid-1990s.

Mitchell & Rammelsberg Furniture Co. (the McAlpin)

Cincinnati native James W. McLaughlin (1834–1923) was the most original local architect of his generation, and he won many of the best commissions. McLaughlin was trained about 1850 by James K. Wilson and was a partner in 1857 of John R. Hamilton, an English-born and trained architect. McLaughlin's father was a business partner of John Shillito, and this was the young architect's first major work.

As Fourth Street became the shopping center of downtown, buildings were constructed with party walls and with footprints stretched to property lines. The symmetrical building plan reflected John Shillito's highly organized approach to merchandising. The exterior skin of the façade, organized by Renaissance Revival motives, was the high-style design for the retail dry goods store (stocking clothing, yard goods, and "soft stuff"), which catered mostly to women.

When Shillito's outgrew the Fourth Street store and moved to Seventh Street, the original building was taken over by the McAlpin Co. McLaughlin enlarged it in 1892 to include the adjacent Mitchell & Rammelsberg Furniture Co. Store, which had been designed by Walter and Wilson in 1870. In 2006, Muller Architects reconfigured the interior of the complex for condominiums and restored the historic façades.

James W. McLaughlin
John Shillito Co. (the McAlpin), 1855–56
Fourth Street

James W. McLaughlin designed the eastern section of the Fourth Street Shillito's dry goods store. The building reflected architectural trends in New York City, Boston, and Philadelphia. McLaughlin enlarged the Shillito block in 1892 by incorporating the adjacent Mitchell & Rammelsberg Furniture Co. Store.

Robert C. Phillips
Village of Glendale, 1851

This detail from an early rendering of Glendale reveals the Romantic, naturalistic street pattern and landscaping features that made Glendale an exceptional example of mid-nineteenth-century American residential planning. The railroad encouraged development of distant suburbs.

Robert C. Phillips platted Glendale on farmland eleven miles north of Cincinnati. The village was founded by a group of developers, most of whom built their own homes there. They were speculating that the opening of the Cincinnati, Hamilton and Dayton Railroad, which ran through the village, would make this distant commuter suburb popular for family living.

Some historians regard Glendale as the first "romantic" landscaped suburb in the nation.[14] Phillips's plan was based upon principles similar to those found in Howard Daniels's plans for Spring Grove Cemetery.[15] Phillips laid out some of the streets in a meandering way, seeking to re-create the effects of rambling country lanes. He created a lake and landscaped islands, such as Floral Place, at the interstices of streets. Glendale residents commissioned picturesque public buildings and cottage residences. The architecture reflected the somewhat contrived informality of the village plan.

Two other railroad suburbs—Hartwell, which was laid out by a Glendale resident, and Wyoming—were designed with a number of curvilinear streets and central parks. But Glendale was more than a physical plan. Early residents shared an ideal that fostered a sense of community. The village became the most desirable of the residential railroad suburbs, attracting successful Cincinnati businessmen who sought an idyllic home in the country for their families. Artists and architects were drawn to Glendale as they were to the comparable romantic planned community of Llewellyn Park in New Jersey, where famed architect Alexander Jackson Davis made his home. James Keys Wilson, one of the city's foremost architects, was one of the incorporators and early residents of the village and designed some of the first houses.

The movement to railroad suburbs altered American family life. Men commuted to the city; women and children remained in the country. As the household became "women's sphere," the role of wives and mothers gained more authority, including making decisions about architecture and interior design. Gradually, women became the tastemakers for the family; the role was seen as a logical extension of a woman's position as the family leader in matters of religion and morality.

Church of the New Jerusalem

Mullett's earliest documented design is the Church of the New Jerusalem in Glendale. Based upon the writings of Emanuel Swedenborg (1688–1772), a Swedish scientist and theologian, Swedenborgism emphasizes freedom, diversity, and individualism, qualities that made it popular with early nineteenth-century intellectuals, including American Transcendentalists. In spite of the commission for the Glendale church, there is no indication that Mullett or his family was Swedenborgian; in fact, his family claimed that his first design was for an Episcopal church.[16]

Mullett's diminutive cruciform church is a simple hall with a gabled roof. The building's frame board-and-batten siding and Gothic detailing would have been considered appropriate for a church in a suburban setting. The architectural examples and books of Andrew Jackson Davis and Alexander Downing popularized the concept of architectural design that conformed buildings to their context. Davis and Downing extolled the merits of building designs that expressed "meaning" and "feelings." Sacred architecture of the period was intended to evoke an emotional or spiritual response in the user.

Alfred B. Mullett
Church of the New Jerusalem (Swedenborgian Church), 1861
Congress Avenue, Glendale

Mullett's design for this board-and-batten church is tailored to its leafy environment. The building's form is similar to that of the Spring Grove White Pine Chapel.

Between 1866 and 1875, some of the city's most beloved landmarks were completed: the Suspension Bridge, Plum Street Temple, Eden Park, and Tyler Davidson Fountain. These landmarks satisfied the American desire to combine beauty and utility.

3

Building Civic Pride through Engineering, Architecture, and Art

1861–75

Cincinnatians and the Civil War

CINCINNATI IN 1860 was torn by the talk of disunion. Families north and south of the Ohio River had been linked for generations by social and matrimonial bonds. As the most southern of northern cities, Cincinnati had strong economic as well as social ties with the South—approximately one-half of its trade went there. But when Confederates fired on Fort Sumter, South Carolina, in April 1861, residents of the Queen City rallied to the Union. A number of architects and engineers joined the Union forces.[1] Although Kentucky was a Southern slave state, it remained neutral, and many Northern Kentucky residents were pro-Union.[2]

At first, the war had a chilling effect on the local economy. But by 1863, Cincinnati manufacturers were among the chief suppliers to the military, filling large orders for iron and steel products, uniforms, and wagons. In a few years, the profits amassed into great fortunes.

At war's end, a building boom began that changed the face of the city and extended its physical limitations beyond the basin and the Ohio River. Between 1866 and 1875, some of the city's most beloved landmarks were completed: the Suspension Bridge, Plum Street Temple, Eden Park, and the Tyler Davidson Fountain. The proliferation of bridges, railroads, streetcars, inclined planes, gaslights, and the telegraph speaks for the technological advances of the period. These modern

James W. McLaughlin
Cincinnati Gas-Light & Coke Co. Building, 1872
305 West Fourth Street

McLaughlin's Italianate "commercial palace" reflects his rather hard-edged, bold approach to conventional styles. Founded in 1841 to sell flammable gas, the utility aided modernization of the city. By 1875, there were 5,290 public gaslights. In 1901, as a gas and electric utility, the company became known as CG&E, and in 1994, as Cinergy. It merged with Duke Energy in 2006. The company is now located on East Fourth Street, and this building has been adapted as apartments.

innovations united people and places, but they also encouraged the outward movement and segregation of people by class. In a decade, the cohesion of the old walking city disappeared.

Civil War Watershed for Technology

When the war ended, John Augustus and Washington Augustus Roebling returned to complete their great Covington-Cincinnati bridge. They were the most advanced engineers of the era, refining their techniques bridge by bridge. During the conflict, much of the science and technology of construction had changed. American scientists and industrialists, operating under wartime pressures, had made technological breakthroughs and streamlined construction practices. By the 1860s, the price of iron and steel had dropped, and metal was available to supplement masonry bearing walls. Iron became a popular material for the skin and trim of commercial buildings, and styles evolved to suit the new materials and technology.

Cast-iron storefronts were less common in Cincinnati than in eastern cities, but local manufacturers boasted that they supplied iron cornices for most of the Italianate buildings in the business district and for much of the Midwest. Warner Elevator, a Cincinnati firm, invented the hydraulic elevator in 1855, and by 1875 many local commercial buildings had a hydraulic or a steam elevator.[3] Taller buildings were possible when the elevator was coupled with iron- and, later, steel-reinforced construction. Rising land costs made tall, slender buildings ever more desirable.

Sophisticated clients demanded buildings with modern conveniences—central heat, gas lighting, ventilation systems, running water, and toilets. They wanted their offices, retail shops, manufactories, and institutions (except for the Workhouse, which was medieval in style and amenities) to reflect the prosperity of their business and their city. Architects and engineers who took on large projects soon found it difficult to work alone or with a single partner. The practitioners who adopted the organizational structure of the industrialists developed the more successful businesses.

Railroad Round House
Madison Avenue,
Covington

Railroad lines and service buildings proliferated in the 1850s and 1860s. Buildings, such as this rare survivor, were sturdy and functional. The unknown designer enlivened the wall surface with a round-arched motif.

Transportation Ties the Parts Together

Railroad travel was the wonder of the 1860s. Although some Cincinnatians had been hesitant to support rail transportation, once its merits became evident—especially as Chicago profited by it—the Ohio Valley became a maze of tracks. Every city built at least one station, as did many villages and hamlets.

Between 1853 and 1864, each of the major rail lines entering Cincinnati erected a depot along the city's southern or western border. The most convenient to downtown hotels was the Plum Street Depot, which was built in 1863 in the Second Empire style. It complemented the $1 million Grand Hotel—also a sumptuous Second Empire creation—at Fourth Street and Central Avenue. The CH&D depot, at Fifth and Hoadley streets, was an eclectic 1864 creation.

Although Cincinnati's population stood at 216,239 by 1870, St. Louis and Chicago had grown at a faster pace. Both cities were closer to the westward-moving frontier and tied by rail to the emerging urban-industrial heartland, which lay along an arch that stretched from New York City through the Great Lakes states to St. Louis. The Civil War had severely reduced the value of Cincinnati's southern markets, and residual hostility redirected what trade remained to Kentucky. Railroads from the South stopped in Northern Kentucky, short of Cincinnati.

Cincinnati, Hamilton and Dayton Railroad Depot, 1864
Fifth and Hoadley streets

Railroad depots were one of the few building types erected during the Civil War. This was a busy commuter depot for business people who arrived daily from the pleasant residential suburbs of Glendale and Hartwell. Contemporaries described the architectural style as "Byzantine."

Bellevue (Elm Street) Incline and Bellevue House, 1876–77
Elm Street

James W. McLaughlin designed the Bellevue House atop the incline to Clifton Heights. The Mount Auburn (Main Street) Incline had been built in 1872, earlier than the Bellevue Incline.

Rail and bridge enthusiasts looked to the genius of modern engineering to bind the region and nation together. The long-delayed bridge between Cincinnati and Covington was completed in 1866. Writing in 1867, Edmond Farrington, an architect-engineer who had worked on the Suspension Bridge, expressed a common sentiment about the perceived value of regional connections. He observed that the bridge would benefit not only Covington and Newport, but also Cincinnati by opening Northern Kentucky for "quiet suburban homes, while Cincinnati is given up to the dust, smoke and turmoil of business."[4]

From the Basin to the Hilltops

From its earliest days, Cincinnati had been acclaimed for the marvelous views afforded by the steep hillsides that overlooked the basin and the river: Mount Auburn, Mount Adams, Fairview, and Price Hill. But those who enjoyed the heights were chiefly adventurous day-trippers and the farmers or wealthy families who lived there. The commute to hilltop suburbs by carriage was too long and expensive for the wage earners who resided in the basin.

In the 1870s, engineers designed inclined plane railroads: steam-driven platform lifts that transported foot passengers, horse-drawn streetcars and then electric cars uphill. For the first time, working-class families could escape the heat, humidity, and disorder of the city. The German American tradition of bauvereins (building associations, known as the "people's banks") made home ownership possible

William Walter and William Stewart
First District Elementary School, 1867
412 Liberty Street, Prospect Hill

Cincinnatians of the postwar period took great pride in their public schools. The annual reports presented detailed descriptions of building projects. The First District Elementary was designed to accommodate more than 1,000 children from Over-the-Rhine and Mohawk. The builder installed the latest heating and ventilating equipment. School administrators emphasized convenience, comfort, and durability rather than style. The result was a simple, solid building that appeals to modern sensibilities. Although the heavy cornice is a late-Italianate device, the strong vertical accents suggest the designers were familiar with the Gothic aesthetic. The school has been renovated for residential condominiums.

for those of modest means. Developers platted subdivisions of small houses on narrow lots in Mount Adams, Corryville, Clifton Heights, Fairview, and Price Hill.

Cincinnati's neighborhoods began to develop their distinctive character in this period. Over the next two decades each of these working-class hilltop communities built at least one public and one parochial school as well as numerous churches. These buildings became centers for community and religious gatherings.

After the war, the populations in Northern Kentucky and Hamilton County towns and villages grew apace with the cities of Covington and Cincinnati. In each community, edifices for worship and education were among the first public buildings to appear. Because a church or school symbolized the status or aspirations of a community, civic leaders often called upon a prominent local architect to design an appropriate structure.

Providing for Public Health and Safety

Between 1860 and 1870, Cincinnati had grown by 50,000 to 216,239 people. It was the most densely populated city in the nation. Despite an obsessive fear of contagion that led to frenzied periods of street cleaning when cholera threatened, the basin was dirty, noisy, and smoky. As the condition of tenement houses and slum areas worsened, concerned officials attempted to ameliorate the conditions of the

Washington Park, 1855

Cincinnati developed this inner-city park with trees and water features as a "breathing spot" for residents of Over-the-Rhine.

poor by providing "breathing spots" and recreational parks. The city purchased Washington Park in Over-the-Rhine in 1855, and Lincoln Park in the West End was developed in 1858.

Rural cemeteries, such as Spring Grove, and then public parks, particularly Central Park in New York City, set the design standard for urban parks. In the 1860s and 1870s, city government and private entities acquired land for parks (large ones were sometimes known as "pleasure grounds"). Eden Park, Burnet Woods, Chester Park, and the Cincinnati Zoological Gardens in Cincinnati and the Lagoon in Kentucky offered outdoor recreation and entertainment.

The Cincinnati Zoological Gardens, among the earliest zoos in America, opened in 1875. Some of the surviving original structures predate those of the Philadelphia Zoo, which was founded shortly before Cincinnati's zoo.

The early leadership and staff of the Cincinnati Zoo were dominated by German Americans, who were inspired by the pioneering Berlin Zoological Garden (1844) and other European institutions. Although the landscape architect Adolph Strauch was consulted by the zoo's founders, it appears that the layout was designed in 1874 by Theodor Fundeisen, a landscape gardener-engineer.[5]

The growing complexity of urban life and technological advances in the delivery of water, fire protection, and sanitation systems put pressure on elected officials to adopt specialized departments and deliver enhanced services. In the 1870s, Cincinnati voters approved taxes for essential services and even educational amenities such as comfortable and attractive school buildings and libraries. The first public library in the city was a magnificent $400,000 building designed by James W. McLaughlin. The facility opened on Vine Street in 1874, and the main library re-

Cincinnati Zoological Gardens, 1875
South Avondale

The Zoological Society of Cincinnati began as a private corporation. The first structure visitors encountered contained the bear pits. James W. McLaughlin designed the monkey house, aviary (now the Passenger Pigeon Memorial), and restaurant, which stood on high ground and had multiple verandas from which guests could enjoy the fine views (Kenny, Illustrated Cincinnati, *306). McLaughlin produced the earliest completed specifically zoological structures in the United States. They display his sense of humor and flexibility in housing specimens in buildings inspired by their origins, a practice found in model German zoological parks.*

mained in the building for nearly seventy-five years. Its original collection had been assembled by the Ohio Mechanics Institute.

At mid-nineteenth century, the city had created public charities that assumed responsibility for care of the sick poor, homeless children, and convicted criminals. Construction of buildings to house these institutions was delayed until after the war. By then, the ornate Second Empire style of grand architectural design was in vogue, epitomized by Cincinnati's large, modern hospital erected at Twelfth and Plum streets. Architect Albert Nash organized the spaces in discrete but connected pavilions crowned by mansard roofs and turrets. One of young Samuel Hannaford's first major commissions was the Cincinnati Workhouse, a jail.

Albert C. Nash
City Hospital, 1867
Twelfth and Plum streets

Nash's distinctive design for Cincinnati's great public hospital reflected the architecture of the Second Empire in France. In the United States, it was sometimes referred to as the "General Grant" style.

Aesthetics Followed Affluence

Well-to-do post–Civil War Americans had money to spend on art and architecture, and they wanted style and beauty as well as utility. These affluent men and women read widely, attended lectures, and studied European examples of new and historic architectural styles. East Coast architects who had studied in Paris and clients who had traveled abroad brought back impressions of the latest architectural styles in France and England. The Second Empire Renaissance and Baroque (the American version was sometimes called the General Grant style) were popular in the 1860s. The symmetry and order of Second Empire made it especially suitable for institutional buildings because additions could easily be made. Alfred Mullett used the robust classical columns and mansard roofs of the Second Empire Baroque in his monumental federal buildings. Second Empire/General Grant

Samuel Hannaford and Edwin Anderson
Cincinnati Workhouse, 1869
Colerain Avenue

The crenellated workhouse was built in Camp Washington, which was then outside the city. Never a modern jail, the workhouse was kept open well beyond its useful life, even after courts ruled that incarceration there was cruel and unusual punishment. Although preservationists attempted to find an adaptive reuse of the outwardly picturesque structure, the building could not be safely or economically reclaimed. It was demolished shortly after serving as the film location for the 1989 movie An Innocent Man, *featuring Tom Selleck.*

Samuel Hannaford (1835–1911)

Born in Devonshire, England, on April 7, 1835, Hannaford came with his family to a farm in Cheviot in 1845. He attended the Farmers' College and was trained in architecture in the office of John R. Hamilton. In 1857, he opened his own firm, which was known as (Edwin) Anderson & Hannaford, then Hannaford & Procter, and from 1887, when his architect sons, Charles and Eldridge Hannaford, officially joined him, Samuel Hannaford & Sons. Hannaford was a charter member of the Cincinnati Chapter of the American Institute of Architects (1870) and later president (1889–90). He was a resident of Winton Place, where he was elected mayor when it was a village. A champion of manual training and technical education, Hannaford taught drafting and applied architecture at the Ohio Mechanics Institute and served on the OMI board. He had an extensive architectural library and for a time edited the journal *Western Architect and Builder,* which was published weekly in Cincinnati for almost fifty years. He retired around 1895, but the firm continued into the 1960s.

Alfred B. Mullett
Federal Building, 1874–85
Fifth and Walnut streets

Mullett designed this project while he was supervising architect of the Treasury (1866–74). Samuel Hannaford supervised the construction.

style fell from favor along with Emperor Napoleon III, whose reign ended in 1873, and President Grant, whose term ended in 1877.

The British taste for the Gothic Revival had many followers in the United States during this period.[6] Author John Ruskin praised the colorful natural stonework and thin, curvaceous profiles of Venetian Gothic. By 1875, eclectic designs that incorporated elements from several historical periods were also much in vogue.

Wealthy clients provided local architects with a number of interesting commissions, which they executed in a variety of styles. This was an exuberant, creative, and lavishly productive period for local architecture, engineering, and landscape design.

Cincinnati chapter of the American Institute of Architects, 1870

Standing: Samuel Hannaford, James W. McLaughlin, and Henry Bevis. Seated: Solomon W. Rogers, Albert C. Nash, James Keys Wilson (president), Edwin Anderson, and Arthur Bates. This photo, which documents the founding of the local chapter, was taken in McLaughlin's office. Other charter members were Charles Crapsey and George W. Rapp. The chapter periodically sponsored exhibitions of architectural drawings and models, and in 1887 Cincinnati hosted the simultaneous conventions of the Chicago-based Western Association of Architects and the New York–based AIA. At that meeting, the two associations merged.

Education and Professionalization of Architects

The 1860s and 1870s were good times for local architects, who united in 1870 to form the second American Institute of Architects (AIA) chapter in the nation.[7] The local members were an exceptionally talented group. James Keys Wilson, the first president, was as accomplished as any of his counterparts in the East. James McLaughlin, Samuel Hannaford, and Charles Crapsey had already demonstrated great promise. This was the last generation to be trained through the apprentice system. Formal schooling was the way of the future.

The introduction of professional schools and societies created a distinction between academically trained architects and designer-builders who called themselves architects. Since the 1830s, the Ohio Mechanics Institute (OMI) had conducted intermittent classes in architecture. By the 1860s, OMI had acquired a permanent home in Greenwood Hall, classes had become more regular, and the school's prestige had increased. Cincinnati College opened the School of Design in 1869, which in its early years offered an occasional course in architectural drawing.

In 1866, the Massachusetts Institute of Technology (MIT) became the first college to establish a school of architecture. By the 1880s, it was a favorite with young men from Cincinnati, most of whom had studied first at OMI.

John A. Roebling
John A. Roebling Suspension Bridge, 1866
Covington and Cincinnati Bridge over Ohio River
From Cincinnati, south on Race Street

When it opened on December 1, 1866, the so-called Covington-Cincinnati Bridge was the longest suspension span of any bridge in the world: its main span was 1,057 feet.

John A. Roebling Suspension Bridge

This first bridge to unite Northern Kentucky and Cincinnati was a long time coming. In 1846, engineer John Augustus Roebling (1806–69) made a proposal to the Covington and Cincinnati Bridge Co., which held a charter from the Kentucky General Assembly. Construction began in 1856, but the Civil War and economic recession delayed completion of the bridge until December 1866, when it was opened to pedestrians. Vehicular traffic began on New Year's Day 1867.

Public support for the beautiful structure was overwhelming. Contemporaries pronounced it the "most substantial, graceful and perfect" of all bridges and hailed its creator as a genius.[8]

Oddly enough, Cincinnati civic and industrial leaders had refused to support the venture. In fact, Ohioans, fearful of everything from business competition to encouraging runaway slaves, tried to stall the project. The Ohio General Assembly even forbade connecting the bridge to any existing Cincinnati street. Covington businessmen, led by coal baron Amos Shinkle, formed a private corporation for the project, and eventually Cincinnati iron manufacturer Miles Greenwood served on the board.

John Roebling had studied civil engineering in his native Germany. For his state engineering examination, Roebling wrote his thesis on the iron-chain, suspended-deck bridges of Germany and Switzerland. He came to the United States in 1831 and settled in Pennsylvania, where he worked on canal construction design. Roebling's first suspension structure, an aqueduct, used steel rope rather than the standard hemp rope.

Although he did not invent the modern suspension bridge (the first wire cable bridge was built in Geneva in 1823), Roebling was the first to exploit its potential by using steel cable, which he perfected and produced in his own factories in the United States.[9]

A suspension bridge has three major components: towers (at least two), bundled cables, and abutments. The cables are suspended between the towers and are anchored into massive abutments, which restrain the ends of the cables. (The cables are in tension and the towers are in compression.) The girders that support the roadway are suspended from the bundled cables. The result is a light and strong structure with intrinsic aesthetic appeal. Although such structures are expensive to build, because the main span can be long and high they can be used to span deep gorges or rivers that are used by tall ships.

Roebling's skill and daring increased with each project. He employed these techniques in his Brooklyn Bridge of 1884, which surpassed the Cincinnati prototype in every category (the major span was 1,595 feet). He anticipated the problems encountered in the operation of suspension bridges, including the tendency for the deck to act as a wing in high winds and the tendency of moving objects to set up harmonic vibrations. Roebling warned patrons to beware of allowing a herd of cattle to trot or a battalion of soldiers to march in unison across a bridge.

The massive, hollow piers for the Cincinnati towers are made of limestone quarried near Dayton in Montgomery County, while the rest of the towers are of rough-hewn sandstone cut near Portsmouth in Scioto County. The planking that formed the roadbed was originally resin-soaked oak. The cables were made from one million pounds of steel wire imported from Manchester, England. It was woven into steel rope at Roebling's Trenton, New Jersey, factory. The beams, girders, and posts for the truss railings were forged in works in Buffalo and Cincinnati. Local ironworks, among them Greenwood's, Niles, and Lane & Bodley, did some of the work.[10]

The delicate, undulating cables strung horizontally and diagonally across the water establish a visual energy that is controlled by the rugged, massive vertical piers. Envisioning a powerful structure in which the form would be largely determined by the function, Roebling predicted the bridge would be a thing of great beauty, and it was. It captured the adventurous, romantic spirit of post–Civil War America. Along with the Tyler Davidson Fountain, the great Suspension Bridge has won a

permanent place in the affections of Cincinnati-area residents.

An 1896 rebuilding by engineer William Hildebrandt altered the appearance and increased the load-bearing capacity of the bridge by installation of a second set of cables. The alterations were needed to handle the new high-speed electric streetcars. The first rates for automobiles were fixed in 1901.[11] Around this time, functional electric lights were installed and the brown structure was painted blue. (The palette used in each bridge repainting by the Kentucky Department of Transportation is the subject of public debate on both sides of the river.)

The bridge remained privately owned until the Commonwealth of Kentucky purchased it in 1955. Tolls were collected until 1963, when the open metal roadbed was installed. In 1983, the bridge was renamed in honor of John A. Roebling, and in 1984 decorative lights were installed on the bridge by a volunteer committee headed by Julia E. Langsam.

John Roebling died in 1869 of tetanus, the result of an injury he sustained while working on the Brooklyn Bridge. His son, Washington Roebling, the talented engineer who had assisted him in Cincinnati, finished the Brooklyn job, aided by his wife, Elizabeth. The younger Roebling had developed caisson disease while working underwater on construction of the Brooklyn piers.

Roebling's Cincinnati suspension bridge was a technological innovation —it was the first bridge in which both vertical suspenders and diagonal stays fanned from the towers.

Cincinnati Astronomical Observatory

For many years, John Quincy Adams had campaigned to have professional astronomical observatories—"light-houses of the sky," as he called them—built in the United States.[12] His anti-Federalist colleagues in Congress consistently refused federal funding for what most regarded as a frivolous pursuit. Pleased that one was to be erected in Cincinnati, the seventy-seven-year-old former U.S. president made the difficult trip west in 1843 to dedicate the nation's first professional observatory. Nicholas Longworth had given four acres for the building site at the summit of Mount Ida, which was subsequently renamed Mount Adams.

The observatory should have been built to the west, rather than to the east, of the city. In Price Hill, the prevailing winds would have blown the soot away. As manufactories proliferated in the 1860s, Cincinnati's atmosphere became increasingly befouled by smoke from soft-burning coal. Engravings from the period depict factories and steamboats proudly belching dark streams into the sky. The haze hung over the basin even at night, so that astronomers could no longer observe the heavens.

In a move that combined civic philanthropy with boosterism for his new eastern suburbs, transportation and telephone tycoon John Kilgour (1834–1914) offered to donate $10,000 and a hilltop site upriver from Mount Adams, where the air was clearer. The founding astronomer, Ormsby MacKnight Mitchel (1809–62), had raised $10,000 to build the original observatory. The second-largest refracting telescope in the world, which he had assembled with lenses purchased in Germany during a trip there in 1842, was relocated to the new building in 1873. The cornerstone of the original building was relaid at the site in Mornington (now called Hyde Park), and Kilgour's subdivision to the south was named Mount Lookout.

Samuel Hannaford, a Cincinnati architect with a growing practice in public projects, was selected to design the new observatory. Like the original Mount Adams observatory, it was a functional building, centered on the revolving telescope, which was anchored in bedrock to minimize vibrations. The telescope housing is a cylinder within the elongated cube of the building. The original roof of the Hannaford building had a flat, retractable lid, which was replaced with a retractable dome in 1904 when a new cylindrical drum with a larger American-made telescope was acquired.

The classical portico and chaste details mimic the original Mount Adams observatory building's Greek Revival design. The lofty interior is spare and elegant. A side staircase curves up to the circular viewing room, where, with the aid of a manual pulley system, astronomers open the domed roof to the sky. The geometry of the structure is simple, logical, and pleasing. The original woodwork and fresco details have been preserved.

In the first decade of the twentieth century, the Cincinnati architectural firm of Tietig & Lee designed a second observatory building on the property. This smaller structure houses the original telescope and education space.

Samuel Hannaford
Cincinnati Astronomical Observatory, 1873
Observatory Place, Mount Lookout

The observatory, which was restored and renovated in 2002, is owned by the University of Cincinnati and operated by volunteer staff. It is a National Historic Landmark.

City of Cincinnati
Eden Park and Waterworks Reservoir, 1869–78

Construction for the reservoir began soon after the Civil War. Although it was demolished in the 1960s, some of the massive limestone walls remain as picturesque ruins.

City Parks and Waterworks

Post–Civil War Cincinnati was home to a diverse mix of people. Establishment newspapers and Protestant clergymen regularly complained about the number of bars, especially on Vine Street and in Over-the-Rhine, and the inability or unwillingness of the police to enforce the Sunday closing law. The large German population responded that beer and wine were temperance drinks and that Sunday was the workingman's only day for recreation.

Cultural "reformers" adopted varied tactics: One approach, that of the Women's Christian Temperance Union, was to close bars and legislate prohibition; another solution, favored by social workers, was to provide healthful diversions that would lure working men (along with their families) from bars and alcohol. Parks and physical exercise offered a diversion that possessed widespread appeal. Public health workers regularly preached the importance of fresh air to good health, helping to justify public expenditures to further the park movement. In keeping with the new view of the city as a regulator of social welfare systems as well as commercial ones, Cincinnati City Council created a Board of Park Trustees (1860), and funds were allocated for property acquisition and park development.

In 1869, the public health need for purer water and the economic demand by manufacturers for more water forced the city to purchase a plot of high ground (where the elevation provided pressure) to erect a new reservoir. At the recommendation of the Water Works Department, the city decided to buy property in Mount Adams from the Longworth estate. Ironically, this was the "Garden of Eden" land that two decades earlier the first Nicholas Longworth had offered to sell to the city at a discounted price if it were made into a public park.

One hilltop saddle was set aside for the reservoir. The city waterworks department quickly called for engineers, whose profession had grown during the Civil War. With skilled direction and teams of laborers, a mammoth reservoir was built between 1866 and 1878. Its limestone walls were forty-eight feet thick at the base and eighteen feet wide at the top. The enclosure wall was 1,252 feet long. The reservoir was demolished in the 1960s, but near present Mirror Lake remnants of the old walls are still visible. The lake, which replaced the open reservoir, is a shallow pool atop a vast storage tank.

After land was allocated for the waterworks structures, the remaining acreage was developed as a naturalized park. Adolph Strauch (1822–83), the superintendent of Spring Grove Cemetery, was commissioned to organize Eden Park for passive recreational purposes. Longworth had denuded the hills for vineyards, so a reforestation program was the essential first move. Strauch believed that parkland should mimic nature. He disapproved of intrusive buildings or activities, and even disliked artificial walkways; he would direct strollers to walk on the grass. The park opened to the public in 1870. Citizens came to it to enjoy leisurely walks, picnics, and concerts. The Eden Park plan was a perfect merging of beauty and utility, the kind of marriage that won the hearts of American taxpayers, industrialists, and politicians.

Over the years, Strauch's vision has been compromised by paved roads, automobiles, and a number of structures and cultural institutions, including the Art Museum, Krohn Conservatory, and Playhouse in the Park. But the designers of these buildings have been sensitive to the setting, and the natural beauty of the terrain and the superb vistas continue to enchant visitors.

Strauch also created Burnet Woods during this period. Members of the pioneer Burnet-Groesbeck family had contemplated developing a subdivision on their Clifton property. Instead, inspired by the park movement and their desire to leave a family memorial, they decided to sell the land at a discounted price to the city. Elizabeth Burnet Groesbeck and William S. Groesbeck also provided a trust fund for concerts in the park, reflecting the contemporary belief that the arts and nature should be allied for maximum enjoyment and for the edification of the people. Strauch made only minimal improvements to the land, creating a lake and a few undulating roadways. Burnet Woods, which was named for Mrs. Groesbeck's father, Judge Jacob Burnet (1770–1853), was opened to the public in 1872. Strauch's plan was altered during the 1876–91 period, when the Board of Public Works managed the parks.[13] Burnet Wood's acreage was halved through appropriation for the University of Cincinnati campus, a park museum, and the erection of monuments—some adding aesthetic value, others inspiring only curiosity.

William Tinsley
Calvary Episcopal Church, 1867
3766 Clifton Avenue, Clifton

Clifton was an idyllic suburban village when an affluent congregation built this church in a leafy grove.

Calvary Episcopal Church

As the city grew increasingly disorderly, wealthy residents simply moved out from the center. Some established enclaves on Eighth Street, bordering Piatt Park; others built elegant town houses on Dayton Street in the West End. Even before public transportation, the wealthy desiring lawns and gardens escaped to the hilltop suburbs of Mount Auburn and Walnut Hills. Those in the market for larger estates went to northern Clifton.

From the 1860s, Clifton acquired a reputation as a prestigious, park-like suburb.[14] For a time, its residents were the tastemakers for the city, particularly in matters pertaining to horticulture and architecture. Although the economic and ethnic makeup of Clifton village was diverse, British models seem to have shaped the culture. When the community decided to build a church, the English country church was a logical prototype.

Henry Probasco, a Clifton community leader, sometime village mayor, and the second president of Spring Grove cemetery, had commissioned Anglo-Irish architect William Tinsley (1804–85) to design Oakwood, his Norman Revival mansion off Lafayette Avenue. Probasco had retired from business with a great fortune, which he applied to art, architecture, rare books, and travel. He did not make hasty aesthetic judgments. Probasco and his wife had interviewed several distinguished national architects before deciding upon Tinsley. As a lead donor and building committee member, Probasco doubtless helped select Tinsley to design Clifton's Calvary Church. Several years later, he asked his favorite architect to design the esplanade for Fountain Square.

The selection of the English Gothic style for Calvary Church was likely made with knowledge that British author John Ruskin and the French architect A.N.W. Pugin had decreed that Gothic was properly associated with religious buildings.

Calvary Church is of modest scale, suited to its site and to the taste of a congregation of suburban gentlefolk. At the time the church was built, Clifton was a park-like village of fewer than 1,000 people. A rural English church must have appealed to the building committee, several of whom had been involved in the development of Spring Grove as a rural cemetery.

Tinsley was a sophisticated designer who manipulated Gothic idioms in a fluid, seamless way. His church hugs the ground and conforms to the contours of the hilly site. The rock-faced walls have an aged, organic quality. The asymmetry of the single tower and the entry doors placed off center give the church a pleasing informality. (By comparison, the adjacent Victorian [1888 and later] parish house by the Hannaford firm is dry, crisp, and upright.) The church interior has a high open ceiling supported by wooden arched trusses. The rectory by Elzner & Anderson dates from 1913.

Tinsley was an architect of national stature who executed a number of prestigious commissions. He was born in Clonmel, County Tipperary, Ireland, where he worked as an architect for a number of years, primarily in the Gothic style. In 1851, Tinsley came to America and settled in Cincinnati. He designed buildings for Rockwell, Kenyon, and Wabash colleges, Ohio Wesleyan and Northwestern Christian (Butler) universities, and the University of Wisconsin.[15]

Mother of God Roman Catholic Church

Walter & Stewart designed large, stylish new churches for Protestant and Roman Catholic denominations on both sides of the Ohio River. The firm's work is characterized by a strong emphasis on the vertical and a bold, sculptural quality in their ornament. Mother of God (originally Mutter Gottes Kirche) is Walter & Stewart's most important church design in the Cincinnati area.

Built to serve a German American congregation, Mother of God recalls German-Austrian models, such as St. Charles Borromeo Church in Vienna. Two tall, narrow towers flank the wide-gabled entrance porch. The generously scaled crossing dome is a unique feature in the area. The domed cupolas of the towers and the crossing dome form a memorable image on the Northern Kentucky skyline.

The church has been modified inside and out. After an early-twentieth-century storm, the Hannaford firm classicized the façade by adding a severe pediment. After another destructive storm in the 1960s, the exterior and interior were returned as closely as possible to their early twentieth-century state.

Mother of God is a "hall church," derived from German medieval examples. The term is applied to aisled basilicas in which the side aisles are almost as tall as the nave, providing the sense of a large, unified space. The tall side aisles allow huge expanses of glass in the outside walls to flood the interiors with colored light—an advantage in the northern European climate. Hall churches seem to have appealed particularly to German Americans: St. George's Roman Catholic Church in Corryville, almost exactly contemporary with Mother of God Church, shares the form, if not the style, of the Covington church. Both have tall, thin cast-iron columns so as not to interfere with sight lines.

The interior of Mother of God is brilliantly lit. The transept crossing is broad and deep. The semi-octagonal chancel behind the altar was decorated in 1890 with large framed wall paintings by Johann Schmitt (1825–98), a mural painter trained in Munich. In Covington, Schmitt was a member of the Altar Building Stock Co., which produced ecclesiastical art works, primarily for German Catholic churches.[16] He became the mentor of Covington-born painter Frank Duveneck.

William Walter (1815–86), a son of Henry Walter, assisted in the design and construction of St. Peter in Chains Cathedral and helped supervise construction of the Ohio Statehouse and others of his father's designs. William Walter had a series of partners, including James K. Wilson from 1853 to 1863 and Stewart from 1864 to 1872.

William Stewart (1832–1907) was born in York, England, the son of a builder and architect. He served his apprenticeship in Toronto, Ontario. In 1862, he settled in Covington, Kentucky, and worked in the Cincinnati area with William Walter until at least 1872, when he went to Hamilton, Ontario. There he practiced with his son Walter Stewart until his death.

Walter & Stewart
Mother of God Roman Catholic Church (Mutter Gottes Kirche), 1871
119 West Sixth Street, Covington

Mother of God Church, which served a middle- and working-class urban congregation, has some German Romanesque features.

Covenant-First Presbyterian Church

William Walter
Covenant-First (originally Second) Presbyterian Church, 1875
717 Elm Street

The design of this church was influenced by the form of an English tithe barn.

This church serves as the visual western terminus of Garfield Park. Its original tower, before it was taken down, was one of a cluster of spires and finials (the Catholic Cathedral, Jewish Temple, City Hall, and former dome of the Unitarian Congregational Church) that have long attracted artists and photographers.

Covenant-First (originally Second) Presbyterian's merged congregation traces its ancestry back to the first group of worshipers in Losantiville, and two famed clerics—the Reverend James Kemper and the Reverend Lyman Beecher. The first Presbyterian church came close to being the established church of the settlement. Local government officials granted the church a prime lot on Fourth Street.

Just as his Mother of God Church in Covington acknowledged the Germanic roots of its congregation, Walters's design here paid tribute to the cultural heritage of the Presbyterians. The primarily Anglo-Saxon parishioners would have been pleased with this rusticated stone church based on British country models. The limestone was hand-cut from a quarry on Colonel Peter Neff's estate atop Mount Harrison (now called Price Hill). To this day, it sparkles in the morning sunlight.

The interior, which retains most of its original features, was patterned after a medieval English tithe barn. The symbolism of the tithe barn, where the best wheat was presented as a tithe to the church, likely appealed to the building committee. William Morris, the apostle of the British Arts and Crafts movement, regarded a tithe barn near his home in Great Coxwell, Oxfordshire, as one of England's architectural treasures.[17]

For Second Presbyterian, Walter adapted the open-ended form of the high barn, placing window walls at the east and west ends and centering the lectern on the long south side. The pews encircle the minister's stand, suggestive of Presbyterianism's emphasis on the centrality of the word. The abstract, geometrically patterned colored glass windows date from the original construction period; the figurative, Munich-style, stained-glass windows were made locally by the Third Street Studio in the 1920s. Behind the low pulpit are wood-carved chairs and a bench by Henry and William Fry, the English educators and craftsmen who introduced artistic wood carving to Cincinnati. The entire ensemble, from the handcrafted exterior to the rich, dark interior, has an Anglo-American Arts and Crafts flavor.

Henry (1807–95) and William Henry (1830–1929) Fry, English-trained wood-carvers, began their long careers in Cincinnati shortly after 1850 as professionals working with local architects. After the Civil War, they increasingly turned to artistic carving and teaching. Many of their students were women. One of the most talented professionals was Henry's daughter Laura (1857–1943), a ceramic artist and educator.

William Stewart, the recent partner of Walter and frequently the main designer, may have assisted with the design of the church prior to his return to his native Canada.

Edward Hurley, etching of Garfield Place

Edward Hurley's wintry etchings and Paul Briol's misty photographs, depicting Garfield Place enveloped in snow or fog, capture the charm of this pocket of green space surrounded by (mostly) distinguished buildings.

James K. Wilson
B'nai Yeshurun/Isaac Mayer Wise/Plum Street Temple, 1864–67
Plum and Eighth streets

The interior glows with light from original brass chandeliers. Light played a symbolic role at the dedication of the temple. Rabbi Wise ordered the light level kept low until the ceremonies and speeches were completed. Then candles were flamed, illuminating the dramatic interior.

B'nai Yeshurun/Isaac Mayer Wise/Plum Street Temple

Early Jewish immigrants to Cincinnati were primarily English, but by 1838 enough German Jews had arrived to form a new congregation, B'nai Yeshurun, and erect a modest temple on Lodge Street (the façade is still visible). Reform Rabbi Isaac Mayer Wise (1819–1900), who was born in Bohemia and educated in Vienna, arrived in 1854 to lead the congregation. Wise believed in molding Judaism to the times and to the American environment. In Cincinnati, he found a progressive religious atmosphere that suited his mission.

The congregation purchased a prime corner opposite St. Peter in Chains Catholic Cathedral and City Hall. The emerging religious and civic district was highly desirable except for the nearby livery stables.[18] James Keys Wilson (1828–94) was asked to design the synagogue. In the temple, Wilson, who was one of the first Cincinnati architects to study abroad, displayed his familiarity with the latest European fashions. He devised an eclectic model that combined the forms of a Gothic cathedral—a triple façade, rose window in a pointed arch, and basilican plan—with Moorish minarets and abstract patterns.

At first conservative Cincinnatians were puzzled by the design. Some "sidewalk superintendents" sneered that the bulky red-brick and stone-trimmed building, with its two tall stacks, bore a "resemblance to a river steamer."[19] But skepticism changed to admiration as the building reached completion. Conforming to the current fashion for pale, monochromatic surfaces, Wilson painted the red-brick exterior gray to resemble stone. (The paint over the brick has been removed.) The interior culminated in thirteen shallow "Byzantine" domes.

The exterior was enlivened only with shallowly carved detail in Moorish patterns (or "Moresque" or "Saracenic," as it was called then). Moorish decorative motifs had been combined with Gothic and Byzantine forms in earlier synagogues in Germany and Eastern Europe. The German architect Gottfried Semper was among the first to use Saracenic features, in a Dresden synagogue in 1838–40, and the concept was used at Leipzig in 1855 and Cologne in 1856.[20] These precedents may have influenced Wise and Wilson.

Wise selected the Hebrew inscriptions and the symbolic program in the frieze bands, which may have been painted in by 1867. The remainder of the interior decoration was not completed until 1874, when Charles and Raphael Pedretti stencil-painted the walls and domes.[21]

The artists used the saturated colors and exotic patterns popularized by British designer Owen Jones in his *Grammar of Ornament* (1856), a book that celebrated Moorish, Persian, and Egyptian patterns.[22] Jones's replica of the Alhambra Court for the 1856 exposition at Sydenham, England, was surely known in Cincinnati, a center of Anglomania. Whatever the sources, this creatively eclectic building was apparently the first of its stylistic type in America and was an indication of the sophisticated state of architecture in the city at the time.

Contemporary accounts reported that the temple was designed "after the fashion of the Alhambra at Granada."[23] The Temple's Moresque style very likely influenced Leopold Eidlitz's Temple Emmanuel (1868) on Fifth Avenue in New York City. But the style, as with most exotic and highly decorative fashions, did not have a long life.

In 1949, when the congregation was building a new temple in Avondale, the Plum Street Temple was threatened with demolition. Cincinnatians of all faiths spoke out for the building's preservation, and the Temple has been designated a National Historic Landmark.

*Speaking at the dedication on August 24, 1866, Rabbi Wise called the Plum Street Temple "a monument of modern architecture, of American art, and the progress of both civil and religious liberty" (*Cincinnati Daily Gazette, *August 25, 1866).*

Main Entrance Gate, Spring Grove Cemetery

James K. Wilson
Main Entrance Gate
Spring Grove Cemetery, 1863–67
Spring Grove Avenue, Winton Place

Wilson's designs for the entrance gate (1863) and carriage-waiting station at Spring Grove Cemetery were said to have been inspired by fourteenth-century Norman Gothic architecture, but they are a free interpretation of historicist forms.

By the 1860s, people had grown tired of the restrained rationalism of Neoclassical architecture. Especially in buildings with a spiritual purpose, patrons preferred structures that symbolized religion and inspired elevated emotions. The Gothic tradition filled that need. Gothic had developed during the great period of ecclesiastical building in medieval France and England and was thus associated with Christian religion and learning.

The nineteenth-century Gothic Revival was encouraged by numerous literary sources. *The Ecclesiologist* (1841–68) was an influential British journal that discussed appropriate Gothic design for churches. Books by English critic John Ruskin won converts to the Gothic style, including *Seven Lamps of Architecture* (1849), which was widely read in the United States. Ruskin advocated the Gothic tradition for religious buildings because he believed it was the architecture of the "Age of Faith." For him it followed that the Gothic expressed the beauty, clarity, and moral purpose that characterized the Christian faith.

The European Gothic Revival had reached the United States as early as the 1830s, but Cincinnati's surviving structures date from the 1860s. Wilson was skilled in creating churches and monuments that evoked the Gothic romanticism of monumental European originals while meeting the American demand for economy and a smaller scale.

Wilson's main entrance gate building is somber and imposing, as befits its spiritual, emotive role. At the same time, it was practical, housing the cemetery's administrative staff and functions. The gatehouse and matching women's carriage waiting room are instructive examples of a creative architect handling an eclectic blend of historic elements.

Edmund Dexter Family Mausoleum/Chapel

Advocates of the Gothic Revival became more archeologically minded over time, just as students of the Classical Revival had been in the eighteenth century. Wilson's Edmund Dexter Mausoleum/Chapel at Spring Grove forms one of the nation's most "authentic" tributes to the late Gothic Sainte Chapelle in Paris. Sited picturesquely above one of the lakes, the chapel immediately became a destination for tourists.[24]

The Gothic style was popular for rural and suburban settings such as Spring Grove Cemetery because its irregular massing, pointed arches, and spiky finials reflected the organic forms found in nature. Wilson's design for Scarlet Oaks, the George K. Shoenberger "castle" in Clifton that overlooks Spring Grove Cemetery, is also an "authentic" Gothic work.

James Keys Wilson was a native of Cincinnati who was brought up in Philadelphia, where he trained with Charles Mountain. Wilson apprenticed with two of the leading American practitioners in New York City, Martin E. Thompson (1789–1877) and James Renwick Jr. (1818–95). Renwick was designing the Smithsonian Institution (1846–55) around the time Wilson worked for him.

Shortly before 1850, Wilson returned to Cincinnati as a well-trained and creative architect. In his designs for the Plum Street Temple, Spring Grove Cemetery entrance gates, and the Dexter Mausoleum, Wilson introduced Cincinnati to innovative versions of the High Victorian Gothic style. Wilson was a founder and first president of AIA Cincinnati chapter. His leadership and distinguished work brought new prestige to the architectural profession.

James K. Wilson
Edmund Dexter Family
Mausoleum/Chapel, 1866–70

Dexter, who made his fortune in liquor, built this much-admired mausoleum-chapel. Wilson's design was one of the nation's most "authentic" tributes to the thirteenth-century chapel of Sainte Chapelle in Paris, which was restored around 1840 by Viollet-le-Duc and other admirers of Gothic forms.

Tyler Davidson Fountain and Esplanade, 1870–71
Henry Probasco, donor
Ferdinand von Miller and sons, Royal Bronze Foundry, concept, sculpture, casting
August Von Kreling, sculpture design, ca. 1840
William Tinsley, architect for esplanade
Christian Herter, Herter Brothers, designer, esplanade accessories

The Cincinnati fountain became the centerpiece of an urban place: an oval esplanade one hundred feet long, sixty feet wide, and two feet high. The sawn limestone esplanade was ringed with sixteen pyramidal granite posts that shielded pedestrians from runaway carriages.

The Tyler Davidson Fountain marked a new way of thinking about the role of art and architecture in enhancing the image of the city and promoting the common good. The fountain was the first public art work in the city, and one of the first public fountain sculpture pieces in the nation. The fountain idea was conceived by Davidson and his brother-in-law, Henry Probasco, who were successful dry goods merchants and business partners. They had discussed contributing a fountain to the basin area as early as 1860, but the Civil War interrupted their plans. When Davidson died in 1865, his devoted sister and brother-in-law decided to erect a memorial in a public place rather than in a cemetery, and they revived the fountain idea. Providing utility as well as beauty, it would be a fitting memorial to Davidson and a gift to the people of Cincinnati.

Probasco traveled to Europe in 1866–67, where he inspected fountains and visited foundries looking for the perfect model. In Munich, he visited the famed Royal Bronze Foundry, owned by the Ferdinand von Miller family, where he rejected scores of designs that featured water nymph and Neptune figures before being shown the model for the realistic work that he ordered.

The European market had rejected the design, which had existed only in sketches since 1840, because it portrayed real rather than mythological figures. But the earthy human quality of the figure studies was exactly what the American merchant was looking for. He wanted this "gift to the people" to feature attractive, healthy-looking, real people—not pagan gods. The top figure, the "Genius of Water" is idealized, but she is clearly a symbolic, Madonna-like figure, representing an idea: the blessings of water.

Writing to Cincinnati's mayor from Palermo in 1867, Probasco offered to purchase the fountain if City Council would provide a suitable site and agree to maintain the monument. Determined to bring the project to perfection and sparing no expense, Probasco established delivery and installation deadlines with the foundry and the city before he left Europe. From then until dedication day, the retired merchant devoted himself to providing a suitable setting for his prized fountain. To ensure the quality of the fountain project, Probasco insisted that his favorite architect, William Tinsley, and designer, Christian Herter (b. 1839), be entrusted with the city-paid part of the project—the esplanade space and furnishings.

Tinsley, who designed the site, had solid experience in city planning. His most ambitious project in his native Ireland had been remodeling the entire town of Cahir for the Earl of Glengall. Herter, principal of the prestigious New York City firm that had furnished the Probasco house, designed the street architecture to encircle the esplanade. Herter Brothers, established in New York City in 1864 by Stuttgart natives and half-brothers Gustave and Christian Herter, was the first interior design firm in the United States. The accessories reflected the flowing, curvilinear shape of the fountain and the esplanade. The ensemble had a proto-Art Nouveau quality that reinforced the sight and sound of the falling water. Herter designed elegant gaslights—sixteen iron lanterns mounted on bronze posts. Forty wrought-iron cages, holding young sycamore trees, completed the stone, metal, and bronze ensemble. Probasco had assured a skeptical City Council that trees protected by such metal enclosures flourished in London and Paris.

In rallying public opinion to his vision of Fountain Place as a new centerpiece for the city, Probasco displayed exceptional public relations skills. The first proposed site for the fountain was in the middle of Fifth Street, between Main and Walnut streets. But Tinsley told Probasco early on that the site was inadequate and that the only space wide enough for the esplanade was the site of the Fifth Street Market, between Vine and Walnut streets. The market was a deteriorating one-story building occupied mainly by butchers.

Probasco organized a fountain preview party for City Council members at his opulent Clifton mansion. The men bonded over a fine dinner and multiple toasts. Caught up in Probasco's grand vision of an artistic fountain such as no other American city possessed, the councilmen all pledged to throw over Cincinnati's market heritage for the sake of art and plentiful cool drinking water. The butchers filed suit (years before, some

The Lady figure atop the sculpture group symbolizes the Genius of Water. Probasco's gift altered popular perceptions of the propriety of government participation in aesthetic improvements.

of the land had been taken by eminent domain expressly for a marketplace), and the case went to the Ohio Supreme Court.

When the court ruled in favor of the city, a demolition crew was dispatched immediately. In four hours, the market house was down. (Architect James McLaughlin designed a flower sales cart, which the city installed in token tribute to the lost marketplace.) Cincinnati's first great wave of urban renewal was under way.[25]

More than twenty thousand people gathered for the dedication on October 6, 1871, exceeding all expectations. Because city workers had discovered that water pressure was insufficient to power the fountain, a new line had been run from the Mount Auburn reservoir. People were delighted that the drinking spigots dispensed ice water, an unusual feature that Probasco had requested. The free drinking water, which he regarded as a substitute for bar drinks and therefore a temperance incentive, fulfilled the donor's goal of providing utility as well as beauty in this "gift to the people of Cincinnati." The Genius, her hands outstretched bestowing the blessing of water, became an icon and symbol of the city.

Admiration for Fountain Place led civic leaders to question the quality of its surroundings. The Reverend Dr. Max Lilienthal, rabbi of the Mound Street synagogue, was one of many dedication speakers. Lilienthal proclaimed a "new era" for the city that was "losing her diadem as Queen City of the West." He urged his fellow citizens to do away with the "lethargy and want of enterprise" that had exposed the city to ridicule. "Down with these old buildings," he cried. "They are no longer suited to this place." Crediting the donor with providing the noble example that would inspire a "metropolitan resurrection," Lilienthal declared the fountain esplanade would henceforth be known as "Probasco Place." And so, it was, for at least a decade.[26]

The Cincinnati Commercial congratulated Probasco on being the first citizen to put more than "one hundred thousand gold dollars in a work of art." The newspaper editor predicted that the gift would become a "radiant educator in our midst," transforming the dingy blocks about it. Transformation came slowly, but the prolonged discussion about the proper site for the fountain, the proper role of municipal government in funding aesthetic improvements, and the court battle over public rights and private rights make the Fountain Square project an early exercise in modern city planning.

The young woman giving a drink of water to her aged father was part of the original design by August von Kreling (1819–76). When Probasco requested that more figures be added to the composition, the foundry owner's son Frederick von Miller sculpted the children in the niches of the base; the youths playing with animals on the rim of the basin are the work of his younger brother, Ferdinand.

View of Cincinnati looking west toward Music Hall

While energetic entrepreneurs built department stores, breweries, packinghouses, and soap factories, wealthy cultural boosters organized Music Hall and the Cincinnati Art Museum. A new American type, the suburbanite, commuted by railroad to villages outside the crowded city. Local architects designed creatively eclectic buildings to house new business, government, and cultural entities. Cincinnati's attempt to reposition itself as the "Paris of America" helped make this a golden age for architects.

4

The Paris of America

1876–95

Cultural Boosterism Spurs Golden Age for Architecture

"It all began with the fountain," proud Cincinnatians explained. Henry Probasco's "liberality and public spirit" led the way for an outburst of philanthropy that resulted in the city's most enduring arts institutions and landmark buildings.[1] It was a golden age for Cincinnati architecture, art, and engineering.

Citizens of the era realized that something special was happening. They marveled at the handsome new buildings that arose and at the signs of progress all around them. Although its boomtown days were over, by 1880, Cincinnati's physical territory had increased to 22.2 square miles and its population had grown to 255,138 people, up 18 percent in the decade. The city continued to attract immigrants from Germany, but the "new immigrants" from southern Europe went elsewhere, to places such as Detroit, Cleveland, and Chicago, where work for unskilled labor could be found in heavy industry. Cincinnati, Newport, and Covington turned to annexation as a strategy for growth. In the years between 1875 and 1895, these three central cities erected numerous government buildings, churches, and schools to serve their expanding populations.

Private corporations joined government in contributing to the boomer atmosphere. In the spirit of progress, the Cincinnati Chamber of Commerce engaged the

Henry Hobson Richardson
Chamber of Commerce
Fourth and Vine streets
Painting by Louis Vogt

One of America's great architects, Louisiana native Henry Hobson Richardson (1838–86) studied architecture at the École des Beaux-Arts in Paris. He is considered the spiritual father of Chicago architect Louis Sullivan and therefore the creative "grandfather" of Frank Lloyd Wright. Fellow architects and discriminating clients admired his powerful and highly personal style, which came to be called Richardsonian Romanesque. Inspired by Early-Medieval Romanesque architecture, which in turn had been inspired by the ruins of ancient Roman imperial structures, the style seemed to capture the raw power and unaffected manner of the nation. It was the first American architectural achievement to be widely imitated in Europe, rather than the other way around.

In 1885, the Cincinnati Chamber of Commerce selected Richardson to design its headquarters. Completed in 1888 after Richardson's death, it was the most visible and important commission of the decade. In 1911, fire destroyed much of the building.

most famous architect in the United States, H. H. Richardson, to design its headquarters.[2] A group of local attorneys organized the country's first all-professional "base ball" team, the Cincinnati Red Stockings. James W. McLaughlin designed their first ballpark in the West End around 1870, and Charles Crapsey laid out a new park and stands in the Mill Creek Valley in 1884.

Cincinnati residents considered themselves fortunate to live in what they increasingly referred to as a "great city."[3] Some of the improvements to the built environment were motivated by profit, others by the desire to provide education and healthful entertainment for the public. Whatever their inspiration, the quality and quantity of the projects built in the period attest to an awakened interest in high-

Richardson monument, 1972
Burnet Woods

University of Cincinnati students used eighty-four tons of the pink granite salvaged from Richardson's Chamber of Commerce building to construct a monument in his honor in Burnet Woods opposite the College of Design, Architecture, Art and Planning.

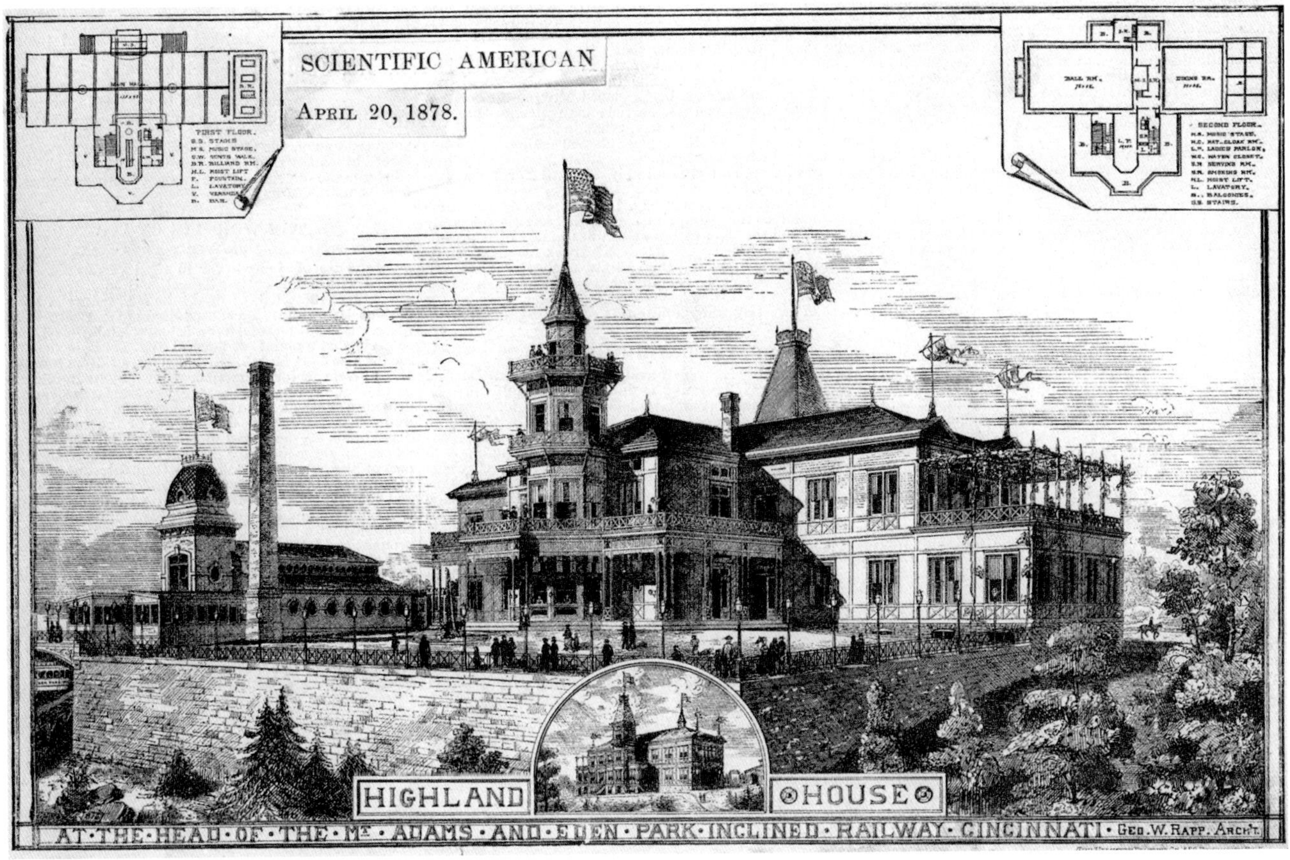

George W. Rapp
Highland House, 1875–76 (demolished 1895)
Mount Adams

Victorian confections atop Cincinnati's inclines featured pitched roofs and turrets with flags rippling in the hilltop breezes. This was festival architecture appropriate to the recreational purpose of the buildings. The architects of Lookout House, Bellevue House, Highland House, and Price Hill House looked to summer resorts and seaside hotels for inspiration. The buildings were designed for indoor-outdoor living, with large-glazed window walls, wide verandas, and beer gardens where orchestras performed nightly in summer. The Highland House, designed by Rapp (1852–1918), could accommodate 15,000 people.

style architecture among patrons, and something approaching a shared vision for a national architecture. Local architects were now self-confident and sophisticated professionals. They had worked with Cincinnati's natural and built environment. Within that context of hills, streams, and densely built city blocks, they proposed additions and alterations that would create a unified composition, one that reflected the diversity and picturesque character of the city. Visitors had always praised the beauty of the natural environment; now they complimented the built additions as well, especially those improvements that took advantage of the hills and views.

Samuel Hannaford and Joseph Steinkamp & Brother
Palace Hotel, 1882
Sixth and Vine streets

Luxurious "palace" hotels were a new type modeled after the town houses of European royalty and America's new class of multimillionaires. They allowed middle-class people to experience briefly the lifestyle of the rich. Dining, visiting, and even residing at palace hotels became a popular recreational activity in the so-called great cities. The Palace's best rooms were priced at $2.50 per day. The building exterior is distinguished by a steep slate mansard roof, which is pierced by two floors of dormers and the lightly incised limestone walls. Samuel Hannaford was the preferred architect for the Emerys until a construction problem on this job led them to change architects. The exterior base of the Palace and the interiors were dramatically altered in a Postmodernist fashion during a 1987 renovation by Trebilcock, Whitehead with KZF, Steven Schaefer Associates, and Frank Messer and Sons.

The Paris of America

For the first seven decades of the city's existence, Cincinnati boosters had tried to emulate English urban models. They aspired to make the city a great commercial and manufacturing center like London or Manchester. But in the late 1870s, some leaders suggested that Paris or Vienna might be more appropriate models. A number of Cincinnatians had acquired great fortunes (by midwestern standards), and many of them were looking for rewarding leisure pursuits. Following Henry Probasco's lead, wealthy families such as the Dexters, Ingalls, Longworths, Shillitos, Sintons, Springers, Tafts, and Wests turned to art, culture, and civic improvement. Civic leaders saw an opportunity to combine art with industry and cultural institutions with tourism to create a more livable, prosperous, and progressive city.

The city had become, almost accidentally, a tourist and meeting destination. Over-the-Rhine entertainment establishments, and then the hilltop incline resorts, which were large enough to accommodate conventions, contributed to the atmosphere of gaiety. Architects for incline owners expanded the hilltop cable houses with viewing platforms and elegant halls. This was festival architecture appropriate to the recreational purpose of the buildings. Most were constructed of wood and had a temporary character that suited their short-lived popularity. The celebrated orchestra leader Theodore Thomas conducted summer concerts to large audiences on the verandas of Mount Adams's Highland House, which opened in 1876.

Author George Stevens suggested as early as 1869 that by building additional entertainment and meeting facilities, Cincinnati might become a cultural capital, the "Paris of America." Cincinnatians found much to admire in Parisian architectural style. Many of the new downtown buildings, such as Mullet's government building, sported French Second Empire details. Shillito's new department store followed Parisian models. Thomas Emery & Sons built the first "French flats" (apartments with kitchens and bathrooms) and one of the most desirable "modern" hotels (it had incandescent light), the Palace. The hotel referenced the French Second Empire Neo-Grec style and the current taste for a lighter palette.

As real estate developers, the Emery family had a significant—and beneficial—impact on Cincinnati's built environment. Their developments are remarkable because they consistently demonstrate intelligent land use, modernity, and sophisticated styling. (This was the first Emery hotel. Nephew and business heir John J. Emery opened the Netherland Plaza Hotel in the 1930s and the Terrace Plaza in the 1940s.)

In the 1870s, Cincinnati's elite sought to emulate not only the high culture of Paris, but also the achievements of the various arts capitals of Europe and of Boston and New York City. The May Music Festival was the opening volley in the campaign for national recognition of the city as a cultural mecca.

Music and Manufactures

Serendipity played a role in transforming the city into a cultural center and a tourist destination. The music-loving German population had made Cincinnati and Over-the-Rhine the center for Saengerfests, as their choral festivals were called. In 1870, the Saengerfest society engaged architect Sigmund Kutznitski to design a quasi-temporary wood structure on city-owned property between the Miami Canal and Washington Park. The hall opened in June of that year with a Saengerfest. In September, the Ohio Mechanics Institute, the Chamber of Commerce, and the Board of Trade combined to host an industrial exposition in the hall, and new wings were built for that purpose. The railroads and Cincinnati hotels promoted the exposition throughout the region, and the influx of visitors, along with the favorable media attention, encouraged city boosters to plan annual expositions. The Queen City and volunteer organizer Alfred T. Goshorn won national recognition.

Search for a National Culture

Goshorn was named director general of the United States Centennial of its Independence, which was celebrated in 1876 with a world's fair in Philadelphia. The celebration encouraged Americans to reflect upon their past and examine their accomplishments. People associated with the arts attempted to identify what was peculiar to American literature, art, and architecture, and Cincinnatians, who were highly visible at the fair, joined in that quest. Many of the city's participants in the fair were women artists, china painters, and wood carvers. Their work, displayed in the "Cincinnati Room," won honors and praise.

Those who participated in the Centennial came back intent on applying to their own artworks what they had learned from the French, British, and Japanese pavilions. Many of the women had concluded that their nation and city fell below the standards of artistic excellence and good taste exhibited by their foreign counterparts. Determined to improve the city's art education and decorative arts manufacturers, in 1877 they formed the Women's Art Museum Association (WAMA) to encourage the "establishment of an Art Museum and Training Schools." The group was motivated by a desire for social reform as well as artistic advancement—one of their objectives was improving the status of women. They contended that a teaching museum and school could help their "poor sisters" acquire the skills needed for suitable employment.[4]

The new institutions for cultural boosterism required suitably impressive buildings. Music Hall, the Cincinnati Art Museum, and the Art Academy were perhaps the most celebrated buildings of the era. But even minor and utilitarian structures, such as those commissioned by the Cincinnati Water Works, were assigned to top architects to endow with style and character.

The Best of Times and the Worst of Times

In the 1870s and 1880s, Cincinnati was a prosperous city, and the philanthropic impulse was strong. But the disparity in wealth was growing. Native-born Americans often blamed poor pay and labor conditions on the surplus of recent immigrants and freedmen. In Cincinnati's overcrowded basin, the crime rate rose as the pay rate fell. Social and political tensions grew over issues of class, race, ethnicity, and

Charles E. Hannaford, Samuel Hannaford & Sons
"Elsinore Tower" or "Gate" Valve House, 1883
Gilbert Avenue and Elsinore Place, Eden Park

The Hannafords' three waterworks structures in Eden Park were designed in a historicist manner. Samuel's son Charles designed the valve house in this shape at the request of a waterworks director who had admired the stage prop of Elsinore Castle in a traveling Shakespearean production. Positioned at the foot of Mount Adams, the gate served as a symbolic entry to the Cincinnati Art Museum building at the top of the hill. The valve house has Richardsonian stone textures and rough-hewn "primitive" details.

criminal justice. The city had a record of street violence, but there was no precedent for the Cincinnati Courthouse Riot of 1884, one of the bloodiest riots in American history.

Several landmark buildings—Hannaford's new Music Hall and Isaiah Rogers's 1850s Hamilton County Courthouse—were the staging grounds for events that led to the riot. What began as a meeting in Music Hall called by a few staid civic leaders to discuss corruption in the justice system (a bribed jury had found a confessed murderer guilty of manslaughter only) ended with a lynch mob engaging law enforcement officials in a bloody three-day street battle. The riot ended with 54 dead, more than 200 injured, many of the county's records destroyed, and the courthouse and jail in a shambles. The prolonged battle terrorized downtown residents and attracted sensational coverage in the national media.

James W. McLaughlin
Hamilton County Courthouse
renovation, 1884–86

Architect James W. McLaughlin was assigned the task of rebuilding the 1853 courthouse, which had been damaged in the 1884 riot. He took a startling approach, attaching a Richardsonian Romanesque façade to the building's classical body. The strange marriage was clearly visible at the corners of the freestanding building. But courthouse patrons were pleased, and the Cincinnati bar held a dinner in McLaughlin's honor. (This clash of styles was rejoined in 1907 when Daniel H. Burnham added a wing to the Art Museum, concealing the north side of McLaughlin's Romanesque 1884 building.)

After the riot, Cincinnati turned to George "Boss" Cox to stabilize city government. Civic boosters joined arts advocates in setting out a building program aimed at restoring pride of place and repairing the city's tarnished image. In what seems like an oddly modern choice, they turned to art and architecture. New and splendid government buildings were required, and local architects were called upon to supply "palaces for the people."

Golden Age for Architects and Architecture

The postwar revolution in communications and travel allowed patrons to become increasingly knowledgeable and sophisticated about developments in architecture outside the region, but for the remainder of the nineteenth century, local patrons selected local architects for almost all of the best commissions. That practice would change in the next century, when Cincinnati patrons began to recruit Chicago and New York architects for the more important projects. (Roman Catholic institu-

Francis G. Himpler
St. Francis de Sales Church, 1877–79
Madison Road and Woodburn Avenue, East Walnut Hills

St. Francis de Sales is remarkable for its exquisite, well-preserved interior, with a Gothic vocabulary that is attuned to the soaring exterior. The parish was a focal point in the Village of Woodburn and of the present historic district. Himpler, who was educated in Munich and at the Royal Academy in Berlin, lived in the New York City area. He designed churches in many American cities.

tions, which had a national network of sorts, frequently engaged national architects.)

For the most part, architects in the late nineteenth century designed solid and functional structures, which they clad in creatively eclectic styles that satisfied their clients' taste for historicism by referring to precedents such as Gothic churches, Tudor castles, and Renaissance palaces. The archeological historicism of the 1850s and 1860s was dismissed, and a more creative eclecticism (albeit still using historical motifs) came into vogue.

Most architects and designers of the period expressed the desire to create work that was "modern," in the sense that it was of their time. Signs of cultural independence from European sources became more pronounced following the 1876 Philadelphia Centennial celebration, when many architects returned to Colonial American architecture for inspiration. And in technology, American and Cincinnati architects led in the development of tall "elevator" buildings based upon metal rather than masonry frames.

Because European cities had cultural or legal prohibitions against excessively tall and bulky structures, the elevator building, which became the twentieth-century skyscraper, evolved in the United States. Chicago gets most of the credit for developing the type. There, engineer and builder William LeBaron Jenney led a firm of talented young architects that included, at varying times, Louis Sullivan, Daniel H. Burnham, John Wellborn Root, and Frank Lloyd Wright. But Cincinnati played a critical role in the evolution of the tall building.

James McLaughlin, Cincinnati's most innovative architect, used wrapped steel supports for the lower floors and domed atrium of his new Shillito's building. This seminal building was described in a 1877 national publication and has been proposed as a prototype for Jenney's landmark First Leiter Building (1878–79) in Chicago.[5] Jenney, who had relatives in Cincinnati, visited here the year McLaughlin's building was under construction. McLaughlin went on to design a number of tall commercial buildings in the central business district, primarily on Fourth Street and on Fifth Street at Fountain Square. None of McLaughlin's survive, although

James W. McLaughlin
Shillito's Department Store Interior, 1878
Seventh and Race streets

Downtown commercial buildings became larger and more lavish in the 1870s. This trend climaxed in McLaughlin's new uptown Shillito's Department Store. "Elevator buildings," as the first tall commercial structures were called, permanently altered the skylines of urban America. These tall buildings were a new type made possible by the development of the steel frame and the electric elevator. The atrium design was inspired by Parisian models.

James W. McLaughlin (1834–1923)

James McLaughlin was born in Cincinnati in 1834 and died in his home in New York City on March 4, 1923. His parents had come to Cincinnati from Pittsburgh in 1818. The family was well connected and artistically inclined. James's sister, M. Louise McLaughlin, was a talented ceramic artist, wood carver, and art theorist. His father was a dry goods merchant and for a time a business associate of John Shillito. McLaughlin was trained in Cincinnati with English architect John R. Hamilton, and the two were practicing together by 1858. In the Civil War, he served as bodyguard to Major General John Fremont. Some of his military drawings were published in Frank Leslie's *Illustrated Newspaper*, 1861–62. He married in 1862, lived on McGregor Avenue in Mount Auburn, and had nine children.

McLaughlin was a founder and president (1878–81) of the AIA, Cincinnati chapter, which he helped to organize in 1870. In his more than fifty-year career, he was responsible for such monumental structures as the Masonic Temple, the Public Library, the new (after the riot) Hamilton County Courthouse, the YMCA (later the Shubert Theatre), and the Wiggins Block. He did pioneering designs for the great department stores: McAlpin's, Shillito's, and Mabley & Carew. Like most architects of the period, McLaughlin moved offices frequently, usually into buildings he had recently designed. In 1876, he had "elaborately furnished offices, equipped with every convenience," in the Johnston Building, which he had designed.[6]

Gustave Drach's Textile Building and Samuel Hannaford's Hooper Building are representative of this type.

By the 1890s, the Hannaford firm appeared to have the inside track with public jobs, winning the competition for University of Cincinnati's new campus in Burnet Woods, Cincinnati City Hall, and numerous courthouses in the region. The well-staffed Hannaford firm also supervised construction of works by out-of-city architects.

Architects in smaller partnerships found interesting commissions. Some developed highly individual styles based on Arts and Crafts and Richardsonian aesthetic ideals. Crapsey & Brown designed a series of distinctive urban and suburban Akron plan churches, in which they combined and contrasted forms and materials in original ways. Henry Siter, the Board of Education's official architect from about 1890 to 1899, designed weighty Romanesque schools and churches crowned by distinctive high-pitched roofs.

Many of the best works from this era have survived, and they contribute significantly to the distinctive quality of the city's built environment.

Samuel Hannaford
Church of the Resurrection/St. Luke Episcopal, 1877
7350 Kirkwood Lane, Sayler Park

Charles W. Short erected this tiny chapel in the manner of an English Gothic parish church as a memorial to his parents. The character of the building reflected the quiet country setting of the downriver community.

H. E. Siter
Fairview Heights (30th District) School, 1890
Warner and Stratford streets

The giant pyramidal Richardsonian roof proclaimed the school's role as a neighborhood landmark. It probably also provided a form of insulation, as did the thick masonry walls. The generously curved towers contribute to the grandiose scale of the building. Henry E. Siter (1851–1913) was born in Philadelphia and trained in Boston, where he was influenced by Richardson's work. He moved to Cincinnati in 1884 but returned to Boston in 1899.

H. E. Siter
Mt. Auburn
Presbyterian Church,
1889–90
103 W. H. Taft Road,
Mt. Auburn

This solid "masculine" structure has interesting variations in form and complex massing. The mysterious depths of the wood-paneled interior are illuminated by the large stained-glass windows.

Samuel Hannaford and Edwin R. Procter
Cincinnati Music Hall, 1877–78; Exposition Buildings; 1879
1241–43 Elm Street, Over-the-Rhine
Alterations:
Samuel Hannaford & Sons, 1895
Renovations:
George Schatz & Associates, 1969–76

Music Hall replaced Saenger Halle, which Sigmund Kutznitski designed in 1870 for the German-American Saengerfest Society.

A storm disturbed the otherwise perfect opening night of the first Cincinnati May Festival on May 17, 1873. The 1,000-voice chorus and maestro Theodore Thomas's magnificent orchestra competed with heavy rains that pounded the thin tin roof of Saenger Halle, causing a long unplanned intermission. According to contemporary reports, Ruben Springer then vowed to build a proper hall to house this glorious choral festival, which had brought thousands of visitors to the city. Springer challenged his peers to match his pledge of $125,000.

Cincinnati merchants and manufacturers were feeling affluent and civic-minded. Although newspaper articles in New York and Boston had praised Cincinnati for producing an outstanding musical festival, they also reminded readers that the city had until recently been known as Porkopolis. Springer presented Cincinnati's emerging philanthropists with the opportunity to make both an architectural and a cultural statement, and they took the bait. His challenge was met within five months. When exposition fans threatened to stop the Music Hall project because their demand for space for industrial fairs was ignored, Springer made a second challenge grant to build two adjoining exposition wings. The north wing was originally described as Machinery Hall, and the south was known as Horticulture Hall (and later, when it was home to art classes and collections, as Art Hall). Springer's gifts for construction of the complex and the organ totaled $185,000. He went on to donate $50,000 for the College of Music, which opened next door to Music Hall, and to establish a trust fund for a Music Hall endowment.

The Music Hall Association was chartered as a nonprofit corporation, with shares issued to contributors. Julius Dexter, chairman of the building committee, took his job seriously. He traveled to the East to look at model buildings. Two that must have caught his eye were the Harvard Memorial Building, then under construction in Cambridge, and the Jefferson Market House, built in New York City in 1876. The Harvard building served multiple purposes, as the Cincinnati music and exposition center would. Some of its American High Victorian Gothic stylistic qualities reappeared in Music Hall.

Because this was an important architectural commission, the Music Hall building committee held a national competition to select the architect. Local and out-of-town firms were invited to submit presentation drawings. The best-known competitors were William Ware and Henry Van Brunt of Boston, architects of the Harvard Memorial Building, and Alexander F. Oakey, an acoustics expert from New York. James McLaughlin and Samuel Hannaford represented the local firms, in what was likely their first public competition against one another.

Several of the entries, including the Hannaford firm's winning design, were published in the *American Architect and Building News.*[7] The proposal from Ware and Van Brunt may have been a surprise to Dexter. Unlike the firm's chromatic, lively Harvard Memorial Building, their submission for Music Hall was in the restrained, classical Neo-Grec style that was becoming fashionable in France. The committee selected the more flexible plan and exuberant exterior submitted by Samuel Hannaford and Edwin Procter, who were partners from 1874–76.[8] Ironically, the winning entry resembled Ware and Van Brunt's Memorial Hall at Harvard (1865–78), with its highly wrought and by then slightly dated mannerisms.

Music Hall's plan is liturgical in shape and attitude. The main entry on Elm Street faces east toward Washington Park. The east façade is organized around a huge (150-foot-high) central gable with a large rose window embedded in a giant recessed arch. It somewhat resembles the façade of James Keys Wilson's 1866 Plum Street Temple. Both of these monumental buildings use features common to French and German Gothic cathedrals. Hannaford and Procter conceived of Music Hall as a cathedral or temple of music.

The architects used texture and color to make the exterior surfaces sing. The high-pitched roof was originally covered with alternating bands of red and gray slate; the patterns are now replicated in cementitious tile. The towers and roof ridge were originally decorated with spiky finials that energized the roofline and led the eye skyward.

The Elm Street façade received the most lavish ornament and (perhaps because it would be in shadow much of the time) the highest

May Festival, the oldest choral festival in the Western Hemisphere, was the original tenant of Music Hall. Since the 1930s, Music Hall has been the home of the renowned Cincinnati Symphony Orchestra. More recently, it became the principal performance venue for the Cincinnati Pops and Cincinnati Opera.

Cincinnati's artistic wood carvers created the case for the pipe organ.

contrasts in color and texture.
In describing their intentions, one of the architects (presumed to be Hannaford) wrote in the *American Architect and Building News* article that the red-pressed bricks "were laid in black mortar with a sunken joint, 8/16 inches deep. The effect is to give a decided structural appearance to the surface, which in so large a building is an advantage."[9] The central Gothic arch is edged with brick corbeling and enlivened with diaper-patterned brickwork. The bricks have lost patina through sandblasting since then, and the joints have been filled with pale gray mortar.

On the Elm Street façade, sandstone carvings in roundels symbolize the function of the three main sections of the building. For the central section, musical instruments (a lyre and horn) are garlanded with laurel and oak leaves. The south wing, Horticultural Hall, was designed to house exhibitions from Hamilton County's important floral and horticultural industries. The carved roundels for this wing feature native birds and sunflowers. Gear wheels, ratchets, and architect's tools appear above the doors leading into Machinery Hall to the north of the concert hall entrance.

The Central Parkway façade, which faced west toward the canal, caught the afternoon sun. Here the architects selected the "best quality common red brick laid in yellow mortar with flush joints. The effect is to enhance greatly the body color of the building; so that in the glow of an afternoon sun it warms to the intensity of coral."[10] Anyone who has witnessed the effect of the setting sun on the west façade can testify to the magical moment when the walls begin to glow, just as the architects intended.

Music Hall's main lobby has a lofty and elegant character, which intimates that a superior musical experience lies ahead. Cylindrical iron columns support a high balcony that rings the lobby. Escalators have replaced the south stairs, but the lobby balcony and the north staircase retain the original square, vertical-incised balusters. The stair railing design is reminiscent of motifs (seed-germ), popularized earlier in the century by the French architect Viollet-le-Duc.

The main hall was not the auditorium of today. The original program had called for a multipurpose hall, and it must have suggested a gymnasium track or classical stadium (indeed, it was used briefly by an equestrian school in 1890). Narrow balconies ran all around the main seating area, except for the choir or stage area on the west end. Cast-iron columns rose within the sidewalls between the tall, narrow bays. They supported the coved ceiling vaults, which curved to meet the flat-coffered main ceiling (a few cast-iron columns remain at the back of the auditorium).

The interior walls of the concert hall were originally lined with oiled tulipwood, which was curved slightly in an effort to enhance the acoustics. Unfortunately, the wood darkened quickly and in the vast space became oppressive and gloomy. Hannaford was not satisfied with the effect of the original interior, which his firm was able to alter in 1896.

The Boston firm of Hood and Hastings won the contract to produce what was then the nation's largest pipe organ, which was placed in the apse-like space at the west end of the concert hall. The organ was housed in a spectacular carved wild-cherry case, the result of a collaboration between Cincinnati artistic wood carvers Henry and William Henry Fry and Benn Pitman (1822–1910). Much of the carving for Pitman's panels was done by his female students. The organ and its case have been replaced, but some of the carved panels survive on the stage front and in local collections. Pitman articulated the nationalist sentiment among artists when he described the design goals for the Music Hall organ case: "It was felt that our art work should be the expression of our needs and delight" and be "truly the product of American civilization."[11]

Samuel Hannaford & Sons directed major alterations to Music Hall in the mid-1890s. In the concert hall, which the board had decided should be reserved for musical presentations rather than available for general space rental, a more dignified, classical mood was evoked. The wood walls and ceilings were replaced with plaster and a coffered ceiling. A proscenium arch and a spacious stage were installed. The updated interior design complemented the classical foyer. The hall and the exposition wings were renovated again in 1927 and in 1969.

Since the 1930s, Music Hall has been home of the renowned Cincinnati Symphony Orchestra. More recently, it became the principal performance venue for the Cincinnati Pops and Cincinnati Opera. May Festival, the oldest choral festival in the western hemisphere, is held each May.

To a rare degree, Music Hall has benefited from the generosity of those who care about the building and the arts organizations that perform there. From Springer and Dexter in the 1870s to the Corbetts, Nipperts, and Herschedes in the 1970s and beyond, major benefactors have preserved and improved the hall. The Corbett Foundation was the lead donor in an extensive renovation and modernization, which began in 1969 and was notable for its careful attention to historic restoration as well as the installation of new systems and equipment. The wings, which are used primarily for administrative offices and social events associated with performances, have been renovated as recently as 2005, when Machinery Hall was adapted for Cincinnati Opera offices. The exterior, much of the main lobby, and the scale of the auditorium have remained faithful to the Hannaford and Procter design. The superb acoustics were retained through all the renovations.

Music Hall is one of the city's chief architectural and cultural landmarks. With Memorial Hall next door, the Crosley Telecommunications Center connection across the Parkway, the relocation in 2005 of the Art Academy several blocks southeast, and the proposed School for the Creative and Performing Arts nearby, Music Hall has gained support for its role as a downtown cultural anchor. Reuben Springer, who first proposed that Washington Park be home to the art museum so that the city's cultural resources could support one another, would have been pleased to see his envisioned arts district coming together.

Germania (later Columbia) Building

Cincinnati's strong German American population grew in power as it grew in economic strength. Successful brewers and manufacturers, such as the Hauck, Moerlein, Mullhauser, and Windisch families, held intellectual and cultural achievements in high regard. They made significant contributions to local music, architecture, education, and athletics.

Henry Ratterman (1832–1923), the multitalented founder of the German Mutual Insurance Co., was a prolific writer and gifted amateur musician as well as a successful entrepreneur. Ratterman was active in German singing societies, a leader of St. John's Evangelical Church on Elm Street, and a volunteer consultant for Maria Longworth and George Ward Nichols's first May Festival.

Ratterman hired Johann Bast to design his corporate office at Twelfth and Walnut streets. The distinctive insurance office building recalls German Baroque examples and anticipates the Beaux-Arts tradition, which embellished architecture with sculpture. Free-standing figures were seldom used on the exterior of secular buildings in Cincinnati. Cincinnatian Leopold Fettweis sculpted the Germania statue. In April 1918, because of anti-German sentiment arising from World War I, the insurance company changed its name to the Hamilton County Mutual Fire Insurance Co. and the identity of this statue was changed from Germania to Columbia.[12]

John (Johann) Bast
Germania (later Columbia) Building, 1877
Walnut and Twelfth streets, Over-the-Rhine

This delightful building with free-standing sculpture would not create much of a stir in European capitals, but it stands out in Cincinnati.

Sohn (Cliffside) Brewery

Sohn (Cliffside) Brewery, 1887
244 West McMicken Avenue,
Mohawk

Brewery engineering and construction were a specialized type that engaged many German American architects from Cincinnati and Chicago firms. Some architect-engineers went to Germany to study the technology.

The Sohn brewery was built for the John G. Sohn Co. in the Mohawk neighborhood, not far from where Frances Trollope and Charles McMicken lived many years before. It was a typical Cincinnati brewery —big, stolid, and functional, with Romanesque arched portals and windows.

The architecture of Sohn and some other Cincinnati breweries is in the Germanic tradition. It recalls the traditional Rundbogenstil or German Romanesque revival, which started in the Munich area around 1830 and was transported to England by Prince Albert when he left Germany to marry Queen Victoria in 1840. By the 1870s, the number of German American architects practicing in Cincinnati had increased. Brewery engineering and construction was a specialized type that engaged German American architects from Cincinnati and Chicago. Some of them went to Germany for training in brewery design.

Sohn was not as large as the largest breweries, Moerlein on McMicken Avenue and Lion (later Burger) on Central Parkway, but the surviving Sohn building is notable for its distinctive details. The panel above the main door is decorated in terra-cotta sculptural relief with three beer barrel heads, two grain shovels, and two frolicking cherubs.

The Sohn Brewery was near the southern terminus of the Elm Street incline. Some of the incline's stone foundation walls may be seen on McMicken and Mohawk streets, near the Cincinnati Metal Blast (built 1860 by the old Jackson Brewery), which awaits renovation as an integral part of Cincinnati's Brewery District. The Mockbee Co. (founded ca. 1850 as Bellevue Brewing Co.) buildings on West McMicken have survived.

Hannaford & Procter (Samuel H. and Edwin R.)
Alms & Doepke Department Store complex, 1878
222 East Central Parkway
Multiple additions by Samuel Hannaford & Sons
East addition:
D. H. Burnham & Co., 1912
Restoration and new interior:
GBBN Architects, 1995

The Hannaford firm designed the original building and the red-brick additions. Shallow wrought-iron balconies and decorative corbeling gave the store a stylish look that appealed to women shoppers. D. H. Burnham & Co. designed the restrained buff-brick addition to the rear.

Alms & Doepke Department Store complex

Almost since its founding, Cincinnati and its hinterlands had supported a number of fine specialty shops that attracted the carriage trade to Fourth Street. Duhme specialized in fine jewelry, silver flatware, fine china, and art pottery. Burkhardt's sold custom and ready-made fur garments, hats, and throws. Mitchell & Rammelsberg's manufactured furniture in its plant on Second Street and distributed a small portion from its retail store on Fourth Street. Dry goods stores like Shillito's sold clothing and other soft goods, such as bedding, curtains, and fabric. Many of these retailers designed and manufactured some of the goods they offered for sale. In the late nineteenth century, urban retailing changed. A trend toward department stores began in Paris, where Le Printemps built a giant retailing outlet with multiple departments and a great variety of merchandise, most of it produced by outside manufacturers.

Returning from duty in the Civil War, William H. (d. 1920) and Frederick H. (1839–98) Alms teamed with William F. Doepke (1838–1908) to form the Alms & Doepke Dry Goods Co. The store, which opened in 1865, enjoyed exceptional success by catering to the cost-conscious middle classes. In 1878, the partners engaged Samuel Hannaford to design a new store outside the central business district on the southern edge of Over-the-Rhine. The entrance façade on Central Parkway originally fronted on the canal, a short block from the Hamilton County Courthouse.

The area north of the canal lacked the prestige associated with Fourth Street. It was a low-rent district, home to manufactories, warehouses, and first- and second-generation German Americans. The selection of Over-the-Rhine for Music Hall upgraded the status of the neighborhood. Alms & Doepke emulated Music Hall benefactor and retired dry goods merchant Reuben Springer and his fellow philanthropists by selecting Hannaford & Procter as the architects for their store. Construction work for the Alms & Doepke store and Music Hall proceeded simultaneously.

The original building at the corner of Main and Central was a six-story eclectic composition, a striking tapestry of red-brick walls and pale stone trim. Checkerboard corbels between the third and fourth floors enlivened the exterior walls, much like the vitrified brick patterns on Music Hall dance across the Elm Street façade.

As with their design for Music Hall, the architects reduced the massiveness of the structure by breaking it into separate and projecting pavilions. A broken mansard roof, punctuated by dormers, crowned the pavilions. The 1886 Main Street addition on the northwest side was seven stories high. It has a simpler, cleaner surface, but the texture and rhythms of the windows and cornices complement the original. The roof is flat rather than mansard. Giant Corinthian pilasters mark the bays and unify the new and old sections.

Eventually, the Alms & Doepke complex covered two blocks and encompassed about fifteen acres of floor space. Additions were made to the original building by Samuel Hannaford (later Hannaford & Sons) in 1886, 1890, and 1897. In 1906, D. H. Burnham & Co. of Chicago designed an addition on the southeastern section of the block (Sycamore Street and Central Parkway to Hunt Street). With its pale buff brick and restrained classical trim, the Burnham section makes a different architectural statement, one that alludes to the Beaux-Arts preferences of the time.

Alms & Doepke targeted the middle market, but the firm's extensive inventory and sensible prices brought affluent customers as well. As the population in Over-the-Rhine dwindled and the middle class moved farther from the core after World War II, the store downgraded merchandise to appeal to cost-conscious shoppers. Alms & Doepke did not follow Shillito's, McAlpin's, and Pogue's example of opening satellite stores in suburban shopping centers. On August 18, 1955, "Alms & Doepke on the Parkway," as it was advertised, closed its doors for the last time.

Following the store's departure, the building was occupied for many years by Hamilton County Municipal Court and other county offices. The absentee landlord allowed the building to deteriorate, and demolition was pending when an appeal by historic preservationists persuaded county commissioners to save the exterior shell.

GBBN Architects directed the 300,000-square-foot restoration using LEED sustainable design principles for the all-new interior. The A&D, as county employees have long called it, reopened in 1995 as home to the Hamilton County Department of Job and Family Services. It was the first comprehensive sustainable design facility in Hamilton County, and it remains one of the largest.

Solon S. Beman
Ivorydale, Procter & Gamble Co. Plant, 1884–85
5209 Spring Grove Avenue

Ivorydale continues to look cool and pristine with its polychromatic, roughly textured wall surfaces and windows hooded in striped green-and-white awnings. The central clock tower building dates from 1913.

The original Ivorydale plants from the 1880s were designed to be functional and provide good working conditions. Devices such as shallow pitched roofs with tall clerestory windows admitted maximum light.

Ivorydale, Procter & Gamble Plant

Procter & Gamble is Cincinnati's largest multinational company, with operations in eighty-four countries. The company's corporate office—Cincinnati's most visible business complex—is at Fifth Street and Broadway.

P&G began in 1837 when William Procter, an English candle maker, and James Gamble, an Irish soap maker, married two sisters and formed a business partnership based upon byproducts of the pork-packing industry. Soap quickly became the sales leader. The firm supplied some of the Union troops in the Civil War, introducing thousands of soldiers to P&G products. James Norris Gamble, son of the founder and a trained chemist, developed the formula for Ivory soap in 1879. "The soap that floats" was an instant sensation.

Procter & Gamble's plain, functional buildings on Second Street burned in 1884. By then the plant was producing 200,000 bars of Ivory soap per day, and the firm had outgrown its site. The founding families had moved their residences to the suburbs—the Procters to Glendale and the Gambles to Westwood. They then became pioneers in the industrial suburban movement, selecting a plant site north of the city in the Mill Creek Valley because it was convenient for shipping by railroad.

The company had achieved national prominence, and it sought to make the new plant, Ivorydale, an architectural statement commensurate with its status. P&G hired Solon Spencer Beman (1853–1914), one of the most prominent industrial architects in the nation, to design its new facility. Beman, a native of Brooklyn, trained in New York City with the renowned Gothic-minded architect Richard Upjohn. He moved to Chicago in 1879 at the invitation of George Pullman to design the company town and manufactory of Pullman. In 1896, Beman won an award for his design of the "perfect town," even after an especially bloody labor riot at the Pullman plant in 1894.

Although there has been a good deal of alteration, demolition, and rebuilding at Ivorydale, enough remains to give a sense of Beman's program. The campus, which grew from 55 acres to more than 240 acres, originally had a suburban, park-like appearance. There were dual entries: the front entry faced Spring Grove Avenue, while the back entry welcomed workers and visitors who arrived by train.

Beman's use of brick trim around the rock-faced stone body of the buildings is one of the most decorative and individual features of the design. (It reverses the usual order of using stone to trim brick construction.) The device is especially effective around the windows and cornice line, where the dark brick borders the gray-white body, making the windows and doorways seem larger than they are. (Fellow Chicagoans Burnham and Root would use this device in their design for Maxwelton [1886–87], a house in East Walnut Hills.) The complex is varied with playful motifs such as the stepped gables. Early additions to the plant reflected the style and materials of Beman's original design. The clock tower entry by an unknown architect dates from the early twentieth century.

Supposedly, Harley Procter considered building homes for Ivorydale workers nearby and, at the suggestion of railroad executive Melville Ingalls, sought the advice of George Pullman. Although Pullman reportedly advised against pursuing anything beyond the industrial park, P&G did engage Pullman's architect.

To the Pullman labor force, which deeply resented hiking to the next town to buy a beer, nurturing (or supervising) the habits of adults was unwelcome paternalism. Procter & Gamble managers were much wiser: William Cooper Procter (1862–1934), a grandson of the founder, is credited with the "drastic industrial experiments and innovations that first startled the industrial world." Procter introduced the Saturday half-day in 1885 and an employee profit-sharing plan in 1887. Profit sharing inspired loyalty and put a steady stream of dividends back into the community. St. Bernard, the small city where Ivorydale is located, became something of a company town for factory workers, and it benefited significantly from the P&G presence.[13]

Although P&G sold the Ivorydale facility in 2003, the current plant operators continue to manufacture Ivory soap for Procter & Gamble.

James W. McLaughlin
Cincinnati Art Museum complex: museum, 1882–86; academy, 1887
Eden Park
Additions:

D. H. Burnham & Co.: Schmidlapp Memorial Library Wing, 1907; now entrance pavilion
Garber & Woodward: Ropes, 1910, and French, Emery, Hanna wings, 1930
Rendigs, Panzer & Martin: Alms Wing, 1937
Potter, Tyler, Martin & Roth: Adams-Emery wing, 1965

Interior renovations:

Garriott and Becker, Carl Strauss & Associates, Glaser & Associates, KZF

The first Art Museum was a romantic building that invited visitors to enjoy the beauty of the setting as well as the displays inside. In massing and materials, McLaughlin's design comes close to what Henry Hobson Richardson was doing in the 1880s.

Cincinnati Art Museum complex

The art museum idea originated with the Women's Art Museum Association. WAMA members believed that art education for craft and industrial workers would improve the city's manufactured products, improve their market appeal, and thereby give the city a badly needed edge in the urban sweepstakes.[14]

The museum itself was also presented as a vehicle for cultural boosterism—it would bring visitors to the city, much like the successful spring May festivals and fall expositions of the 1870s. The visitor-attraction concept appealed to Big Four railroad president Melville E. Ingalls, who was well aware that recreational opportunities inspired tourists to take the train to Cincinnati. Ingalls persuaded flour manufacturer Charles West to make a lead challenge gift of $150,000. In September 1880, West's gift was announced. One month later, the challenge had been met, and by December, there were 445 subscribers of gifts ranging from $25 to $10,000. The Art Museum Association was incorporated in 1881 with Joseph Longworth as president and Alfred Goshorn as director.

City officials agreed to provide a building site in Washington Park, Burnet Woods, or Eden Park. The choice of a basin or hilltop location was hotly debated in the popular press, much like the location of the Reds baseball park in the 1990s. Since WAMA had promoted the museum as a tool for the education of working people, critics questioned placing a museum and training school out of reach of the less fortunate who resided in the basin.

The debate polarized wealthy donors. One faction believed that the cultural center of the city should remain in the basin; the other believed that transportation improvements meant the future rested in the suburbs. Reuben Springer lobbied for Washington Park, arguing that Music Hall was already attracting visitors to it. Downtown advocate David Sinton, who had patented a smoke consumer and was lobbying City Council for mandatory pollution controls, admitted that the city was dirty, smoky, and disorderly. But he believed that scientific and moral advancements could clean the air and rid the city of vice.[15] Springer and Sinton were hoping to

The stairs in the Great Hall have moved around quite a bit. In McLaughlin's original building, the staircase was on the north wall, opposite the entry. The stair began in the center, rose to a landing, and then split into two runs: one to the east and one to the west. Burnham redesigned the stair so visitors could reach the Schmidlapp Pavilion. His stair began at the east and west, then rose in an arch to a landing at the center. In 1907, Burnham's Beaux-Arts classical wing (now the main entrance) was added to the north. During the unfortunate renovations from the 1950s, the stair was removed, a floor was added at the second level, and the four sets of columns were enclosed. In the Glaser Associates renovations in 1993, the floor was removed, the columns were uncovered, and a new stair was installed on the south wall.

cleanse the city, making it more like the suburbs. They saw the museum as an asset for civilizing the central city. But the supporters of the Eden Park location prevailed.

The public museum was then a new type, and James W. McLaughlin, who was selected to be the architect, traveled to other cities to look at art museums. For materials and a look suitable for the park site, McLaughlin used forms and decorative details that he described as Italian Romanesque. The result was a romantic building that invited visitors to enjoy the beauty of the setting as well as the displays inside. In massing and materials, McLaughlin's design for the museum comes close to what Henry Hobson Richardson was doing in the early 1880s with his designs for Austin Hall at Harvard Law School and smaller suburban library buildings.

The Romanesque character of the building was expressed by large granite arches and massive walls of blue limestone. Window openings and ornament were minimal. The roof of red Akron pantiles was a victory for the architect. McLaughlin had specified the tile roof because he considered it "appropriate" for the suburban park setting. But when the board learned that construction was over budget, slate roofing was proposed to cut costs. Throughout the summer, the board argued about sacrificing aesthetics to economy. At a special meeting four months later, an anonymous donor pledged the $710 needed for the upgrade to red tile. The roof cost-cutting measure was only one of many economies; when the museum was dedicated on May 17, 1886, McLaughlin's scheme was only partially realized.

The Art Academy began as the School of Design (established 1868). It was the first school in McMicken College (renamed University of Cincinnati in 1872) when the college opened in 1869. Art museum leaders, who thought the school should share a common campus and educational mission with the museum, persuaded the city to transfer the school to the museum. Generous gifts from Joseph Longworth and his heirs facilitated the transaction.

McLaughlin's design for the school was even more Richardsonian than the museum. The Academy's half-domed west end was intended to echo a semicylindrical east end proposed for the museum, but never built. The Academy building was altered years later. The top floor was removed, the entrance tower truncated, and the wonderful half-dome replaced by a conical version.

Over the decades, the museum building has been altered to the point that the original was almost completely concealed. The first addition changed the style of the structure from free-flowing Romanesque to a formal Beaux-Arts plan. In 1904, museum donor Jacob Schmidlapp specified that Daniel Burnham be the designer of a classical library addition, which is now the main entry. It must have been a cruel blow to McLaughlin, but changes in taste and use suggested a new style and building orientation that accommodated the automobile and the city's aspirations to emulate Chicago and Cleveland. The Schmidlapp wing was completed in 1907. Shortly thereafter, McLaughlin abandoned the city of his birth and greatest triumphs to practice in the East.

First ("Linton") Unitarian Church

Founded in 1830 by New England families who settled in Cincinnati, the Unitarian Church began in the basin as a Congregational Church. It was the parish church of William Howard Taft while he resided in Cincinnati.

The new church in the then-fashionable suburb of Avondale was one of McLaughlin's most accomplished works. The building is small in scale, as befits its suburban congregation, but it is bold in design. The church demonstrates the architect's personal interpretation of Richardsonian Romanesque principles, chief of which is the steep roof, which imparts great power to this design, as it did in his designs for the Art Museum and Art Academy. In an unsigned article, a *Cincinnati Times-Star* journalist who regularly traveled home via the Reading Road streetcar labeled Linton Unitarian the "Church of the Holy Roof." He proclaimed it "one of the very handsomest churches" in the city and described the architect as as a "man of originality who is an iconoclast and a master."[16]

George Thayer, pastor of the congregation from 1882 until 1916, worked with the architect on the building. McLaughlin acquiesced to the requests of frugal, sentimental Cincinnatians, who were still trying to salvage remnants of their beloved Greek Revival post office by incorporating stones reclaimed from the old building into the body of the church.

McLaughlin and Thayer took care in designing and furnishing the interior. Henry Fry did some of the original woodcarving. His work contributes to the Arts and Crafts ambience, as does the spectacular Tiffany rose window by Frederick Wilson. Installed in 1900, the stained-glass composition casts a glow over the sanctuary.

The church's excellent acoustics and intimate spaces (the nave seats 260 people) make it a favorite site for chamber music concerts. An addition dates from 1956. The original church building was renovated in 2005.

James W. McLaughlin
First ("Linton") Unitarian Church, 1887–88
536 Linton and Reading Road, Avondale

Several years before Richardson's Chamber of Commerce Building began in 1885, McLaughlin was developing a similar type that he termed "Italianate Romanesque." The rebuilt Hamilton County Courthouse and Shubert Theatre (originally a YMCA) represent an early phase of his Romanesque period, which extended through the Art Museum and culminated in Linton Church.

Albert C. Nash
Campbell County Courthouse, 1884
24 West Fourth Street, Newport

Nash's eclectic designs were distinguished by their varied and interesting rooflines.

Campbell County Courthouse

Newport was a thriving city of more than 20,000 people in 1883, when the courthouse construction began. In the years that followed, much of the population moved to the city's highlands. But beginning in the 1990s, the riverfront several blocks north of the courthouse square was revived with a popular aquarium and entertainment center, Newport on the Levee, which Messer Construction built for the Columbus, Ohio, developer.

The courthouse square has a welcoming small town look that belies its twenty-first-century setting in a major metropolitan area. Antique cannon and historical markers adorn the lawn, reminding visitors that the Kentucky militia assembled here for an ill-fated journey north during the War of 1812. The faceted-stone Gothic steeple and red wood door of St. Paul Episcopal Church (1871) by John R. Neff (d. 1895) grace the north side of the square; late-nineteenth-century houses and commercial buildings frame the other two sides. The Verdin Co.'s World Peace Bell is on display one block south.

Campbell and adjacent Kenton are among the few U.S. counties with two county seats apiece. This oddity came about because of the long, narrow shapes of the counties, with most of the population concentrated at the north ends, facing Cincinnati. The original and still functioning official seat of Campbell County is Alexandria.

Newport was settled in the 1790s. The first courthouse was the typical coffee-grinder type: a modest Federal-style cupola topped by a hipped roof, which rested on a cubic two-story block. The first floor was used for daily business and the second for the less-frequently occupied courtrooms. It was replaced by this building in 1883 at the behest of a committee representing both the city and the county.

The courthouse is a three-story rectangular brick block. The mansard-roofed mass is articulated, like A. C. Nash's now-demolished Cincinnati General Hospital, by corner towers and a dominant tower with convex roofs set to one side of the central one-story entrance porch.

The eclectic exterior is virtually intact, lacking only the original roof cresting and finials. The massing of Nash's building is robust, and the rosy red brick and pale, vaguely classical limestone trim contribute to its lively air. Gables and towers of varying shapes punctuate the steep-pitched roof. The interior retains little of its original appearance.

Additions to the north and south sides of the building are from 1911–12. A Richardsonian jail and police headquarters addition, designed by Crapsey and Brown in the 1890s, has been demolished.

A. C. Nash (1826–90) is listed locally as an architect as early as 1868, after practicing in Connecticut and Milwaukee, Wisconsin. For a time, he was in practice with Arthur Bates, a resident of Ludlow, Kentucky. Both Nash and Bates were charter members of the AIA, Cincinnati chapter (Nash was president from 1873–77). Their office was at 241 West Fourth Street in Cincinnati.[17]

In his early years of practice, Nash won some of the larger local commissions, including the Sister of Charity's first Motherhouse (1883) in Delhi Township and the mammoth Cincinnati Hospital near Music Hall. The hospital, completed in 1869, was an ambitious up-to-date pavilion-style building in the newly fashionable Second Empire style.

Nash probably designed the former newspaper office building opposite the Campbell County Courthouse square. His other Newport buildings include two ambitious factories for the Dueber Watch Case Co., one of which still stands on Washington Street. He designed the Baptist Church on Burns Avenue in Wyoming in 1882. Nash's swaggering design for the diminutive Fort Washington Hotel on Main Street in downtown Cincinnati contributes period charm and visual variety to the streetscape. (The hotel was converted to condominiums in 2005.)

Nash was obviously held in high esteem as late as 1885, when he was one of only three local architects invited to enter the competition—won by H. H. Richardson—for the Cincinnati Chamber of Commerce building.

Samuel Hannaford & Sons
Krippendorf-Dittmann Shoe Co. Building, 1888
Seventh and Sycamore streets

Samuel Hannaford's sons H. Eldridge (1857–1923) and Charles E. (1859–1936), who joined the firm officially in 1887, were probably responsible for the design of the Krippendorf Building.

Krippendorf-Dittmann Shoe Co. Building (Sycamore Place)

At the end of the nineteenth and into the early twentieth centuries, Cincinnati was a center of shoe manufacturing. The factories were concentrated along Sycamore Street north of Seventh Street, extending into Over-the-Rhine. The Krippendorf-Dittmann complex was perhaps the closest to the downtown core. Its main building remains one of the most conspicuous survivors of that lost wholesale industry.

The Krippendorf-Dittmann Shoe Co. was founded by Charles H. Krippendorf (b. 1836), a German immigrant shoemaker who arrived in Cincinnati in 1867. Krippendorf had a series of jobs and partners here before establishing his own women's shoemaking business with E. Timm in 1870. In 1885 Krippendorf became associated with George W. Dittmann. At its peak, the Krippendorf-Dittmann plant produced annually between 20,000 and 27,000 pairs of fine shoes for women, girls, and boys, making it the largest business of its kind in the United States. The plant employed as many as 1,300 workers.

Krippendorf and Dittmann had used Piket and Son as the architects of their previous plants on Sycamore Street, but in the late 1880s they switched to the Hannaford firm. The grand Richardsonian Romanesque block on Sycamore, which cost $90,000 in 1888, is the first and most impressive part of half a dozen structures built for the company at a total cost of well over $200,000 from the late 1880s until 1915. It is one of the most important surviving late-nineteenth-century commercial structures in Cincinnati.

The façade of the seven-story structure displays a strong rhythmical composition in the plainer commercial or "Chicago" variant of the Richardsonian Romanesque style.

Like several of Richardson's own commercial and industrial designs, the Krippendorf Building is a massive single block topped by a deep but nontraditional cornice supported by classical modillions, small blocks that create a rhythmic shadow pattern. Below this the brick surface is corbeled, that is, each course gradually projects above the one below; corbeling was a Germanic practice. Larger wedge-shaped corbels articulate the major bay system of the front, between the round arches of the top story. The ends of the façade are accented by narrow vertical stacks of smaller windows: on the right they are capped by stone keystones, and on the left they are longer, spaced between the stories, indicating that the stairs to the upper floors were located at that end, over the entrance to the factory.

In a rather daring and proto-Modern gesture, most of the ground floor is given over to storefronts that are almost entirely glass. The heavy walls above had to be supported by a long, exposed steel beam. From a distance, the façade is dominated by the four oversized round-arched window openings on the top story. In typical Richardsonian fashion, they emphasize the height of the structure while horizontal groupings and belt-courses counteract the upward movement.

Samuel Hannaford & Sons was so proud of the new shoe factory that the firm included a full-page photograph in a 1894 monograph that celebrated its major works in conjunction with the recent completion of the Cincinnati City Hall. This rare publication, called *Selections from Executed Work and Sketches,* features such prominent commissions as Music Hall, the former Workhouse in Camp Washington, the Phoenix Club Building, and the original University of Cincinnati buildings on Clifton Avenue.

Many of the Krippendorf shoe-factory structures have been incorporated into a loft rental apartments complex, which was developed by North American Properties and Al Neyer, Inc. in 2002. Cole + Russell Architects designed the renovation, which appropriately restored the original color relationships of the exterior and created deluxe loft-style apartment units. The Krippendorf Building, now known as Sycamore Place at St. Xavier, stands opposite St. Xavier Church, whose glowing golden sandstone façade boasts elegant Gothic Revival details. The developer and architects have succeeded in creating a lively urban place with meaningful historic references.

Samuel Hannaford & Sons
Cincinnati City Hall, 1887–94
801 Plum Street

The flared base and massive roof, forms popularized by H. H. Richardson, impart a sense of power and strength to City Hall.

The interior features an impressive marble staircase that winds up to Council Chambers.

Cincinnati City Hall

Cincinnati in the 1870s and 1880s was remarkably diverse, and citizens were easily moved to violence. The 1884 courthouse riot and a labor riot in 1886 suggested to many frightened downtown residents that the city was out of control.

The circumstances that surrounded the riots were similar to those found in other late-nineteenth-century American cities. Everywhere, cities were growing larger and more disorderly. A new authority figure emerged —the political boss. In Cincinnati, the boss was George B. Cox, a man of humble origin but considerable executive ability. Cox understood the importance of a functioning bureaucracy and the efficacy of political symbolism, such as the erecting of civic monuments. His job was to exercise control, and his methods were not unlike those of the so-called captains of industry who were combining businesses into trusts, or the labor leaders who were promoting the unionization of workers. To maintain his position as head of the organization, it was in the boss's interest to provide efficient city services. In an effort to enlarge the city in the early 1890s, the Cox administration annexed suburbs in exchange for essential services such as water. Cox defeated himself years later by trying to offer something to every interest group. Eventually, he offended all of them.

Samuel Hannaford, an able architect and businessman and one of the preferred architects of the Cox organization, won the 1887 competition for Cincinnati City Hall. Hannaford was active in local politics; as mayor of Winton Place, he worked for reforms in the delivery of government services. For more than a decade, he worked closely with Boss Cox and his lieutenants to build firehouses and park buildings. Hannaford's most monumental municipal project, the Richardsonian Romanesque City Hall, epitomized the late-nineteenth-century city. When it was completed in 1894, the Hannaford firm was building a Corryville mansion for Cox and his wife.

City Hall is a powerful, bulky building. The "masculine" style suggested the power of the political boss, even though Cox rarely stepped inside it. He had a suite of offices in the business district, as well as favorite saloons, such as Weilert's in Over-the-Rhine, where he conducted business after hours.

Although City Hall is on a lesser scale than Richardson's Allegheny County Courthouse in Pittsburgh, up close it has the same power to awe. The massive, rough-cut, red-sandstone boulders suggest a superhuman hand at work. The vertical profile resembles Richardson's 1886 Chamber of Commerce building in Cincinnati. Although the roof is not so steep, the corner towers and turrets have a similar effect: they seem to compress the massive wall toward the middle, as though forcibly containing the structure within a too-small city block.

Hannaford had demonstrated his love for chromatic effects in Music Hall, but there the smooth brick walls have a sedate, urban texture. At City Hall, the rich burgundy and pink-tinged stones strike a jarring note in the heart of the city. The rough-cut rocks sparkle in the sunlight; their bristly texture tempts one to touch, but cautiously.

Romanesque cushion capitals on short compressed columns are incised with typical Richardsonian foliate carvings. An occasional gargoyle appears; some are half-hidden in the foliage. On the north side, a carved-stone lintel indicates a small door leading to the former police court, long ago moved to the county courthouse. Windows are trimmed in dark stone. Their shapes vary to suggest the height and shape of the rooms they light. The polychrome mansard roof is punctured with dormers, and the roofline is spiked with crockets.

The interior was richly decorated. Pottier and Stymus's imagery-rich stained-glass windows are backlit by an interior court, which opens to the sky. Raphael M. (b. 1860) and Charles A. Pedretti (b. 1864) of Cincinnati, the sons of the fresco painter Francis Pedretti, designed and executed the murals, except for the one over the Plum Street entrance vestibule. The mosaic floors were designed by Herter Brothers. Although by the 1950s city officials were complaining that the building was overcrowded and hopelessly old-fashioned, City Hall survived proposals to demolish it and build new city offices on the site. The exterior and public areas have been beautifully restored.

H. Neill Wilson
Rookwood Pottery, 1891–92
1077 Celestial, Mount Adams

Within a decade of the opening of this picturesque factory and showroom, Rookwood Pottery became the most prestigious art pottery in the western world.

The founder of Rookwood Pottery, Maria Longworth Nichols, created a successful business by applying art to industry.

Rookwood Pottery

Founded in 1880 by Maria Longworth Nichols (ultimately Storer), Rookwood was named for her father's Hyde Park estate. The pottery combined American technology and Longworth capital with English, French, and Japanese techniques and aesthetics so successfully that its products were internationally acclaimed. Rookwood's art pottery won gold medals in international expositions in Paris (1900) and Turin (1902).

Mrs. Nichols wanted to create fine art pottery equal to that of Dalton Lambeth in London or Haviland in Limoges, France. But she was also determined to "make useful things beautiful" and to run a profitable business. She produced inexpensive stamp-decorated dinnerware in her first kiln. Over the years, Rookwood produced a variety of molded wares—vases, ashtrays, bookends, and figurines—that were artistically glazed but not artist-decorated. Architectural faience, introduced in 1902, was another useful and beautiful product. The common commercial wall tile was used in many Cincinnati schools, hotels, and institutions. Rookwood made fountains and fireplaces, some artist-designed and lavishly sculpted or painted under the glaze. Faience panels from the Sinton Hotel and a fireplace and fountain designed by sculptor Clement Barnhorn are on exhibit at the Cincinnati Art Museum.

The first pottery was located in Cincinnati's East End, in an old schoolhouse near the Ohio River. Record floods in 1883 and 1884 interrupted operations and damaged merchandise. A move to Mount Adams, where the Longworth family had extensive holdings, was planned. The selected site was directly north of the Mount Adams incline, in a conspicuous and dramatic location on the brow of the hill overlooking downtown Cincinnati.

When Maria Longworth Nichols retired to marry Bellamy Storer in 1890, William Watts Taylor (1847–1913) assumed management and ownership of the Rookwood enterprise. Taylor was active in civic affairs, served on the Municipal Art Society, and was regarded as an authority on design issues. He collaborated with the architect H. Neill Wilson in the design of the Mount Adams building. Taylor wanted an artistic structure that complemented the aesthetic principles of the art industry and took advantage of the magnificent site.

Wilson was the son of James K. Wilson, architect for the Plum Street Temple. The younger Wilson spent most of his career in Pittsfield, Massachusetts. He was influenced by English Arts and Crafts and Japanese architecture—idioms that are expressed in his design for Rookwood. The building has a rambling, suburban character. Lavish grounds laid out for the cultivation of cut flowers supplied artists with models for their slip-painted decorations on art pottery. (Hand-decorated and signed artist pieces brought higher prices than the plain molded and glazed wares.)

Although the base of the pottery has Richardsonian Romanesque stone arches, the stucco and half-timbered superstructure exhibits Tudor and Arts and Crafts elements, such as the tile roof and cylindrical brick flues that mark the location of the kilns. The mix of styles reflected the diverse functions of the building, which contained factory workrooms for molding and firing, tasteful studios for artist decorators, and a bright, spacious sales room.

In 1903–4, Elzner & Anderson designed compatible additions, which give the building its present form. Wilson had embellished the plaster sections between the timbering with hand-patterned ginkgo-leaf fans and sprays. This fascinating technique was incompletely recreated in the sensitive 1976 renovation by Carl Strauss & Associates and Hefley-Stevens Architects for offices and a restaurant. Some of the dining areas are set inside the original kiln rooms.

Village Halls

Samuel Hannaford
College Hill (former) Town Hall, 1886

The architect once studied at the Farmers' College in College Hill.

From around 1860 through the first decade of the twentieth century, Cincinnati was ringed by small, incorporated villages. Most of them, such as Westwood, Linwood, and College Hill, were absorbed by Cincinnati in a series of annexations. Others, such as Glendale and Terrace Park, far removed from the sprawling city, remain self-governing villages today. (Under Ohio law, a village becomes a city when the population reaches 5,000.)

By the 1880s, many villages in the sphere of Cincinnati were affluent enough, and their services complex enough, to warrant town halls, which often incorporated police and fire departments. Residents viewed village life as different from city life. They thought of themselves as being ideally situated. Suburban residents were close enough to be of, but not in, the city. Villagers wanted the architecture of their public buildings to reflect their suburban status. They preferred informal building and planning styles that reflected the sinuous qualities and irregularities of ever-changing organic forms in nature.

College Hill Town Hall

College Hill began as a pleasant upper- to middle-class commuter village. It was distinguished by the presence of several early and important schools: the Female Seminary and the Farmers' College (later Ohio Military Institute). Cincinnati statistician and author Charles Cist lived there, as did the Cary sisters, who achieved fame in the nineteenth century as poets.

The College Hill hall is an eclectic building by Samuel Hannaford. It has some Italian Villa features (an asymmetrical façade and four-story campanile) and an open aspect that suggests its suburban location. College Hill was annexed by Cincinnati in 1911, and the town hall was leased to local organizations.

Linwood Town Hall, 1875
Eastern Avenue, Linwood, East End

An unknown designer created this delightful "Stick style" hall, which later became a church.

Hannaford attended Farmers' College in College Hill in the mid-1850s but did not graduate. He probably went from there in 1854 to architect John R. Hamilton's office.

Linwood Town Hall

When it incorporated in 1874, Linwood was a prosperous Little Miami Railroad suburb, much like Glendale. Linwood lost its identity when the village annexed to Cincinnati. The former town hall is a frame structure; exaggerated edges and board surfaces express the timber fabric of the skeletal structure. The bargeboard gable decoration is reminiscent of the vernacular Gothic Revival domestic architecture that filled villages and hamlets in the early 1800s. Architectural historian Vincent Scully identified buildings with the characteristics of the Linwood Town Hall as a type peculiar to America, which he named the "Stick style."

Crapsey & Brown
Westwood Town Hall, 1888–89
Harrison Avenue, Westwood

Crapsey & Brown used a wide variety of materials, often in striking combinations. Westwood Hall displays their talent for interesting massing, polygonal forms, and varied roof shapes. The architects frequently juxtaposed plain stone masses with elaborate shingle surface treatments.

Westwood Town Hall

Westwood was incorporated as a village in 1868. Its most prominent residents were the Gamble and Werk soap-manufacturing families. Village residents decided to build a meeting hall in 1884, for which they obtained three acres in the center of Westwood. Crapsey & Brown were asked to develop presentation drawings to persuade residents to vote for bonds. The picturesque structure was approved, and construction began in 1888. The plan called for a typical village government center containing a variety of government and community activities: council meeting hall, mayor's office, jail, janitor's room, fire department, auditorium, dressing rooms, kitchen, and ticket office.

James N. Gamble and Mrs. Gamble were members of the dedication committee for ceremonies held July 28, 1888. Westwood was officially annexed by Cincinnati in 1898, and the village hall's value was set at $50,000. The city committed to preserving the building. At various times it served as a community center, YMCA, and performance venue for the Westwood Choral Society. In the mid-1960s, the city tried to demolish the hall for a parking lot, but community stalwart Bob Brodbeck (also known as "Mr. Westwood") led the movement to save it.[18] The building was rebuilt and restored in 2004–5 by Michael Schuster Associates, architect; Steven Schaeffer Associates, structural engineer; and HGC Construction, general contractor.

Charles Crapsey (1849–1909) was born in Fairmount, a West Side neighborhood of Cincinnati. He studied and worked with James Keys Wilson from 1865–75, then practiced on his own until 1888, when he formed a partnership with William R. Brown (dates unknown), a specialist in church design. They worked together until 1895. Some of Crapsey's best designs date from that period. Most of the work by Crapsey & Brown has a distinctive artistic character. Their work is often more fanciful than that of contemporaries such as Hannaford or McLaughlin.

Crapsey was a lifelong member and fellow of the AIA and served as secretary from at least 1874 until 1895. He was an active Methodist, and many of the firm's ecclesiastical commissions were for Methodist congregations. The Westwood Town Hall commission may have come about through the architect's acquaintance with the Gamble family, who were civic leaders and donors to Westwood projects, as well as prominent Methodists.

Adolph Druiding
Mount St. Joseph Motherhouse, 1884–86
5701 Delhi Pike, Delhi Township

Motherhouse chapel, 1884–ca. 1900

Cole + Russell Architects designed the renovation for the chapel in accordance with Vatican liturgical standards. Elements from the two historic side altars were incorporated in a new main altar, which was moved forward toward the congregation. A lighter color scheme and enhanced lighting revealed the beauty of the architecture and its Renaissance-inspired details. Druiding's original design for the chapel won an award in Paris; the renovation also won architectural and preservation awards.

Mount St. Joseph Motherhouse

The Sisters of Charity arrived in Cincinnati in 1829 at the invitation of Bishop Edward Fenwick. Almost immediately, they established an orphanage, parochial school, and academy opposite the old cathedral on Sycamore Street. In 1852, the sisters opened a Motherhouse and Good Samaritan Hospital in downtown Cincinnati. In 1854, they purchased the country residence of architect-engineer Major General William Rosecrans (1819–98) atop Mount Harrison (now called Price Hill). Here the sisters established Mount St. Vincent Academy, which offered "young ladies a thorough education in all branches of useful and polite learning."

In 1869, the Motherhouse was moved to a farm in Delhi Township upon the initiative of Sister Anthony O'Connell, the Civil War "Angel of the Battlefield," who had decided that the bluff overlooking the Ohio River was "a charming place for the Motherhouse, novitiate and academy." The property was christened Mount St. Joseph, and the farmhouse became the Motherhouse. The first new building, a limestone convent with a mansard roof designed by Cincinnati architect A. C. Nash and completed in 1883, was destroyed by fire two years later. One of the original structures remains. Mother Mary Blanche Davis thought the order needed a comprehensive plan that could be carried out over a period of several years. Adolph Druiding (1839–99), a German American architect, was engaged to design the complex. His building plan included a convent, infirmary, laundry, academy, library, and a magnificent chapel.

Druiding was born in Hanover, Germany, in 1830, and practiced over a wide area in the midwestern United States. He was a favorite architect for Roman Catholic institutions. Some of his churches remain in Chicago, Celina, and Cleveland. In Cincinnati, he designed St. Lawrence Roman Catholic Church (1886) in neighboring Price Hill.

Druiding's work at Mount St. Joseph, with its Queen Anne character, resembles his previous commissions for religious orders in St. Louis and Detroit. The substantial brick buildings are sited along a ridge on the north side of Delhi Pike. The burgundy-brick walls are articulated by light stone lintels and window hoods. The buildings face south, and the sun reveals the molded brick columnar details of the façade. The interior spaces of the Motherhouse are large and well-proportioned, with handsome natural wood doors and moldings. When Adolph Druiding died before the Motherhouse was completed, Samuel Hannaford & Sons took over supervision of its construction. Work on the chapel had been delayed until funds were in place.

The Motherhouse Chapel of the Immaculate Conception is the size of a church. The four-story interior is ordered by a transept and semicircular apse. In 1899, Mother Sebastian Shea traveled to New York to engage experienced mural painters. She selected Wilhelm Lamprecht, a native of Germany and graduate of the Munich Academy who had worked on churches in Cincinnati and northern Kentucky years before (1866–70), with young Frank Duveneck serving as his assistant. Lamprecht designed all the murals for the chapel and painted the apse mural of Mary Immaculate himself. A New York sculptor-decorator, Joseph Sibbel (ca. 1850–1907), who had done work there for St. Patrick's Cathedral, designed the main altar, the Lady altar to its left, and the Stations of the Cross. The right side altar, dedicated to St. Joseph, was a gift to Sister Anthony from Cincinnati philanthropist Reuben Springer.[19]

In 1920, the College of Mount St. Joseph was established adjacent to the Motherhouse in new red-brick buildings with streamlined Tudor details. In 1962, Western Hills architect Larry P. Cotter designed a seventy-five-acre campus of eleven buildings on the south side of Delhi Pike, on the bluff of the Ohio River.

Cincinnati Water Works intake pier building
Ohio River opposite California, Ohio

The aesthetic power of architecture and the logic of city planning made turn-of-the-century American cities desirable places in which to live, work, and play. The unparalleled success of corporations and the ingenuity of scientists and engineers stimulated an urban building boom that brought a new American type, the skyscraper, to Fourth Street. Seeking an orderly society, the growing urban middle class united in Progressive reform movements that expanded the powers of government. Hamilton County built Memorial Hall and the Courthouse. The City of Cincinnati built schools, parks, and waterworks.

5

The New Order of Things

1893–1919

Era of Big Business, Big Government, Big Buildings

At the turn of the century, Cincinnati's built environment expanded upward and outward. Cities grew by annexing adjacent villages; and office buildings towered ever higher into the sky, transforming the urban space. The hallmarks of the period were innovation, industrialization, and urbanization. In this age of big business and big government, everything seemed to grow larger and superficially better.

In the "Gay Nineties" and the early twentieth century, Americans first drifted, then rushed, to the cities. Young people were attracted by the promise of jobs, modern conveniences, and the experience of living in a community with stimulating leisure-time activities. The Jeffersonian suspicion of city living and industrialization was far from the minds of young people fleeing small town and farm life. Technological changes appeared first in the cities, adding to their appeal.

The reform impulse known as Progressivism was most evident in urban areas. There the latest inventions were found first: electric lights, telephones, and moving pictures. Cities had paved roads for bicycling, which became hugely popular in the 1890s, and for the motorcar, which appeared on Cincinnati streets in 1891. New building types followed advances in technology. The skyscraper, which James McLaughlin and others pioneered in the 1870s, came into its own as a distinctive urban and American type. Cincinnati's "skyscraper district" at Fourth and Walnut streets was created at the turn of the century. Throughout Hamilton County, big

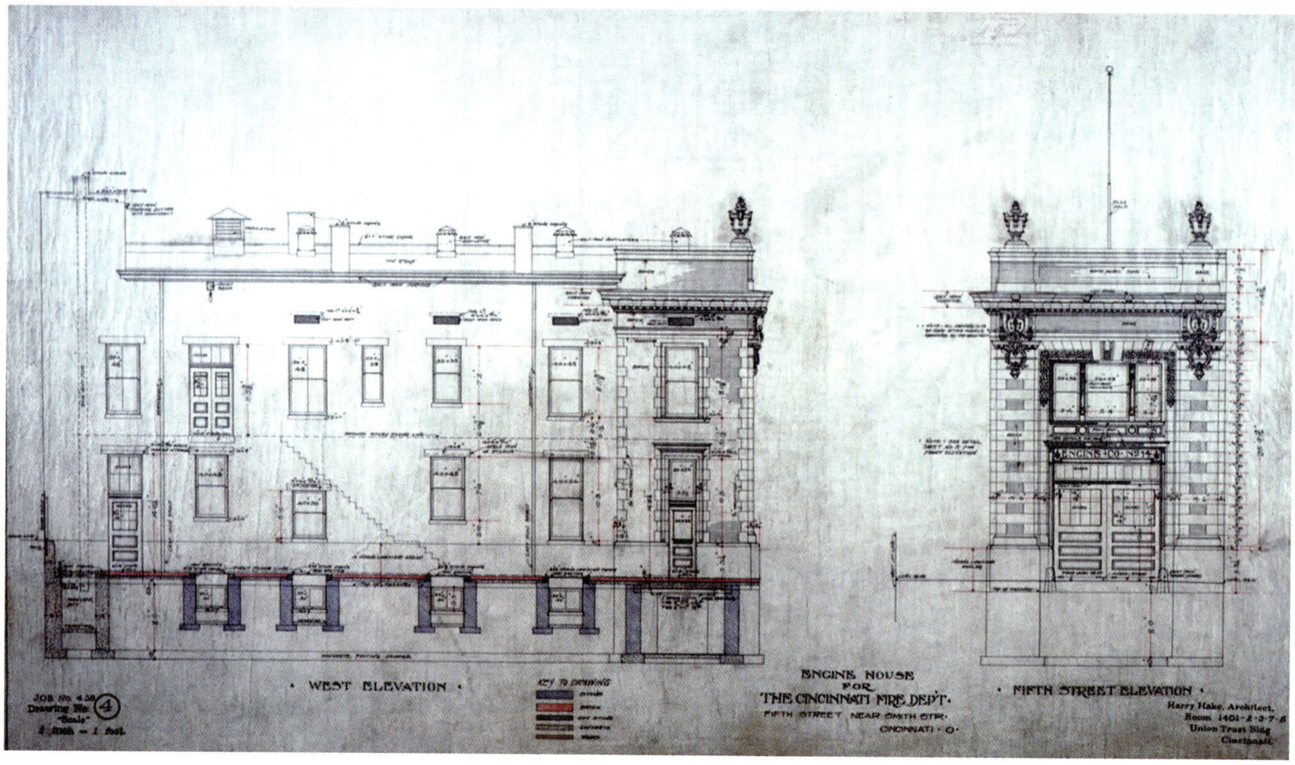

Harry Hake, architectural drawing, engine house for Cincinnati Fire Department

business invested in dignified corporate structures and big government commissioned a variety of public buildings in the central business district, hilltop neighborhoods, and outlying villages.

Cincinnati and the nation endured a major depression in 1893, the same year that the World Columbian Exposition opened in Chicago. When recovery came around 1898, a building boom ensued that lasted until 1917, the year in which the United States entered World War I.

Between 1896 and 1914, Cincinnati annexed the old hilltop suburbs in several waves, creating city "neighborhoods" from distinct villages.[1] About the same time, the repulsion hilltop dwellers of the 1880s had felt for the deteriorating basin area gave way to an enthusiastic embrace of the refurbished "downtown" and the better, more comfortable life that the "new" city began to offer. The City Beautiful movement, which emphasized fine architecture and planning, and the Park and Parkways movement, which attempted to make the city look more like a leafy suburb, contributed to this shift in taste.

Between 1906 and 1915, Cincinnati built thirty new public schools. And between 1912 and 1914, the taxpayers of Cincinnati and Hamilton County spent $11 million for other public improvements: the county erected a $3 million courthouse; and the city invested $1.75 million in parks, $550,000 for additions to the new University of Cincinnati campus in Corryville, and $600,000 for streets.[2] The city also built a number of modern firehouses for its new motorized fleet, and a new general teaching hospital, which opened in 1914 near the university.[3] The number and scope of capital projects—built largely with borrowed money—was so large that interest payments brought Cincinnati to the edge of bankruptcy by the 1920s.

Gustave W. Drach
Cincinnati California Water Works, ca. 1893–1907
5651 Kellogg Avenue, California, Ohio

The beautiful buildings of the modern waterworks and its sophisticated systems partially restored public confidence in city government and contributed to the optimistic attitude that Progressive reforms—even under boss regimes—were working.

Progressive Reformers Embrace Planning for Health and Beauty

The Columbian Exposition heralded a return to classical formality in architectural design. It also established the profession of city planning, an innovation that appealed to the government bureaucracies, which grew along with progressive political reforms. For the first time, shaping the natural and built environments was identified as one of the strategies for addressing urban problems. Progressive reformers in municipal governments (in Cincinnati this included the Republican machine) expanded government to cope with social and economic problems. Boss Cox and his followers on City Council had won the approval of citizens and the business community when they restored order after the 1884 riots and instituted a series of building programs. These reforms were designed to protect the health and safety of citizens and provide them with educational institutions, parks, playgrounds, and other amenities.[4]

Beginning in the 1890s, the city made major improvements to its water delivery and purification systems, which culminated in the construction of costly water treatment plants upriver at California. The plants were beautiful as well as functional. The pumps and engines installed in 1903 at the River Station in California and the intake pier near the Kentucky shore were in use until World War II. The engines, which pumped water into reservoirs on the California Golf Course, were the tallest steam engines ever built.[5] The architect-designed buildings served as advertisements for the pure, abundant water, which was an attractive benefit of living in the city.[6]

Garber & Woodward
Withrow High School, 1915–19
2488 Madison Road, Hyde Park

Withrow's thirty-acre campus included an agricultural section with conservatories and a poultry house, a manual-training shop, and a fine gymnasium. Garber & Woodward made the difficult challenge of a ravine across the front of the site into a dramatic asset by means of a Palladian bridge leading to the tall bell tower, which resembles the campanile in St. Mark's Piazza in Venice. The main building is a graceful, balanced composition with horizontal lines. Two matching wings are attached at a slight angle so that they spread across the wide entrance court to embrace the visitor.

Reforms in the education system were accompanied by a new school facilities program. In 1914, Cincinnati journalists published *Cincinnati: The Queen City*, a book in the tradition of the booster literature that Daniel Drake initiated in 1815. The book's first paragraph states that there is a "new" Cincinnati. As one of the first pieces of evidence, the authors present the "new" school system built in the last "five years," which took the city from an "undesirable position" to the "very first rank as an educational center."[7] At the end of the period, Cincinnati was the only U.S. city to have a public education system that extended from kindergarten through municipal university. The Cincinnati Public Schools' adoption of the "German idea of continuation schools," which encouraged factory apprentices to supplement their elementary-level education, was an innovation, as was the University of Cincinnati's cooperative engineering program.

Withrow High School illustrated the advanced thinking of Cincinnati public school educators. The facility offered manual, physical, and intellectual training on

Garber & Woodward Withrow High School library, 1915–19

The libraries in the new Cincinnati Public Schools were embellished with murals, panel paintings, and fine woodwork.

a collegiate-type campus that was superior to that of its college preparatory counterpart, the first Walnut Hills High School, then located on Ashland Avenue off Victory Parkway. Although segregation had been illegal in Ohio since 1887, Cincinnati had de facto segregation through the 1970s. As part of the facilities-improvement program, the all-black Harriet Beecher Stowe junior high school, designed by the prestigious firm of Tietig & Lee in 1916, was planned for the West End. Construction was delayed by World War I, and the school did not open until 1923. The architects created a handsome structure (since adapted for offices) from cream-colored brick crowned by a tile roof. The school closed in 1962.

Despite the many improvements Cincinnati had made to its infrastructure and community welfare, the city's momentum continued to slow. The U.S. Census of 1910 showed a growth rate of only 11.6 percent, below that of other major cities.[8] In an "interpretive history" of the city, the Reverend Charles Goss placed much of the blame on the city's reputation for "bossism" in government. But few politicians or businessmen were inclined to overthrow a political system that worked to their advantage. After being elected U.S. president in 1908 (with the help of the Republican machine), William Howard Taft denounced Cox. In 1911, Cox resigned in favor of a new boss, Rud Hynicka. Although the modified machine lumbered along for another decade, the reform impulse grew along with middle-class prosperity.[9]

Government and Private Sectors Fuel the Building Boom

Government and corporate building programs increased dramatically in the 1890s as new technologies, including steel framing, fireproofing, and electrification, made existing buildings seem unsafe and inefficient. At the same time, wealthy individuals selected capital projects for philanthropic support. Inspired by the reform rhetoric of social workers from the public and religious sectors, philanthropists seeded projects that would encourage factory and office workers to "better" themselves and the conditions in which they lived. Andrew Carnegie's foundation was a model; it provided financial assistance for construction of nine neighborhood libraries in Cincinnati, Covington, and Newport. Banker and philanthropist Jacob Schmidlapp added a library wing to the Art Museum, and Mary Emery's gift of $500,000 allowed the Ohio Mechanics Institute to construct a new facility where engineering and architecture were taught.

Civic pride was not limited to the wealthy. Cincinnati schoolchildren pooled their pennies to embellish schools with fine paintings by local artists. A Kentucky

Samuel Hannaford & Sons
Ohio Mechanics Institute/the Emery, 1909
100 East Central Parkway

The towers of the Emery echo the spiky, perpendicular Gothic profile of the previous OMI building on Sixth Street, but the Hannaford building displays more contemporary Tudor and Jacobethan revival influences. Mary Emery was devoted to the arts, and the Emery Auditorium at OMI was for many years the home of the Cincinnati Symphony Orchestra, which was established in 1894 by Nellie Taft, wife of William Howard Taft, with generous financial assistance from Mary Emery and Anna Sinton Taft. OMI became the Ohio College of Applied Science in 1958, and it merged with the University of Cincinnati in 1969. The building has been converted to upscale rental apartments, and named the Emery.

schoolgirl started the fund for Covington's Cathedral Basilica of the Assumption when she presented Bishop Camillus Maes with her savings—a single dollar.

Cincinnatians and the Columbian Exposition

Chicago's Columbian Exposition in 1893 reflected the state of American architecture and planning and had a tremendous effect on the designs that followed. Described in the literature of the time as the "Great White" or "Dream" city, the world's fair dazzled its millions of visitors. The master plan was the work of Frederick Law Olmsted (1822–1903), the dean of American landscape architects, and Daniel H. Burnham (1846–1912), an entrepreneurial Chicago architect who had contributed to the evolution of tall steel-skeleton commercial buildings. Seeking a harmonious,

Leon Coquard
Cathedral Basilica of the Assumption (window), 1895–1910
1130 Madison Avenue, Covington

Detroit architect Leon Coquard modeled the Catholic cathedral after the French Gothic Abbey Church of St. Denis. The façade (1908–10), by local architect David Davis (1865–1932), is an abbreviated version of Notre Dame in Paris. Bishop Maes contributed ideas for the iconography of the exceptional stained-glass windows. Most of the eighty-two windows were designed and produced in Munich by Mayer Studios. One measures twenty-four by sixty-seven feet, making it the largest in the United States. Frank Duveneck (1848–1919) painted the panels in the Blessed Sacrament Chapel. Clement Barnhorn sculpted the tympanum.

unified effect, they required all buildings in the centerpiece Court of Honor to be designed according to the classical principles taught by the École des Beaux-Arts of Paris, where some of America's leading architects and educators had been trained. Water features, electric lights, and rapid transportation contributed to the allure of the lakeside exposition, which seemed to prophesy the city of the future.

Cincinnati architects and artists were represented at the fair. James McLaughlin designed the Ohio State Building. Cincinnati women who were ceramic artists or wood carvers were given an entire exhibition floor in architect Sophia Hayden's Women's Building. Their male counterparts displayed paintings in the Charles Atwood–designed Palace of Fine Arts, adjacent to the Ohio Building. Sir Alfred Goshorn, who attended in his capacity as director of the Cincinnati Art Museum, purchased fine art for the museum collections.[10]

James W. McLaughlin
Ohio State Building, 1893
Columbian Exposition, Chicago

Only a portico of Ionic columns ornamented James McLaughlin's sleek, tasteful building. The "staff" façade of hemp and plaster was painted a dark cream color. A splendid bronze group stood to one side on the front lawn. Its circular composition incorporated life-sized statues of Ohio heroes. Intended to be viewed in the round, the sculpture echoed the semicircular rhythm of the porch. Many states erected picturesque late-Victorian buildings; Ohio's contribution met the fair committee's preference for classical symmetry. McLaughlin and his client state understood the new order of things.

The City Beautiful Movement

Americans went home from the Columbian Exposition with notions of how to transform narrow, brown streetscapes into vistas of white marble. Most of the accolades for the fair's success were heaped on Burnham, who succeeded Richardson, the celebrity architect of the 1880s, and Olmsted, the pioneering planner, as the nation's favorite consulting architect and planner. Burnham was comfortable wearing both hats. After the exposition, he focused almost exclusively on the planning aspect of his firm's practice.[11] In short order, he developed city plans for Cleveland, San Francisco, Manila, and Chicago. A memorable admonition attributed to Burnham —"Make no little plans, they have not the magic to stir men's blood"—reflected the mood of a nation caught up in expanding business at home and empire building in the Caribbean and South Pacific.[12]

From this point on, many of the best Cincinnati commissions went to firms from outside the city. Chicago, Philadelphia, and New York City had several large architectural firms capable of handling complicated projects. Many wealthy executives believed that a tall building designed by a famous architect would enhance the firm's corporate image. And frequently, it did!

Samuel Hannaford & Sons
Phoenix Club (detail of façade), 1893–94
Race Street near Piatt Park, Garfield Place

The adjacent Cincinnati Club absorbed the facilities of the Phoenix Club in 1911 and converted the elegant spaces for athletics. Beneficiaries of enlightened private investment and oversight, the Piatt and Lytle park historic districts have evolved as the most successful and attractive urban places in downtown Cincinnati. The Phoenix was restored in 1986.

Hake & Kuck
Western & Southern Life, 1916
Fourth Street and Broadway

The Taft and the Williams families guided the admirable twentieth-century redevelopment of Lytle Park and its environs, beginning with massive Beaux-Arts complexes for Western & Southern Life and the Masonic Temple/Taft Theater. Harry Hake Sr. (1871–1955) and Charles H. Kuck worked together from 1915 to 1947.

In the first decade of the twentieth century, Burnham designed six important Cincinnati buildings, all in the classical manner. Another celebrated designer, the Kansas City landscape architect and planner George E. Kessler, who had won fame with his plan for the 1904 St. Louis fair, was engaged to create a park plan for the city.

The interest in planning and ordering the built environment animated citizen groups as well as the growing ranks of planning professionals. These activities were often characterized, especially by nonprofessionals, as the City Beautiful movement. Interest in urban planning reached all the way to the White House. As secretary of war for President Theodore Roosevelt, William Howard Taft appointed Burnham to create the master plan for Manila, which was to be the capital of the Philippines. Intrigued by the prospect of imposing order and control on an unpredictable future, then-President Taft called the first national conference on city planning in 1909. Kessler and John Nolen, who designed Mariemont in the 1920s, were presenters.[13]

Classical Impulse Signaled a Search for Order

In the years before the Chicago fair, people had tired of the sometimes startling contrasts and excessive ornamentation of late-nineteenth-century architecture. The Beaux-Arts strategies of symmetry and axial planning imposed a sense of direction and logical order upon individual buildings and ensemble plans (Burnham called them "group" plans) that people found satisfying. Architectural historian Leland Roth saw the search for classical order and harmony in architecture and in city group planning as a parallel to the progressive political reform movements.[14] Burnham's

Elzner & Anderson
Cincinnati Country (and Golf) Club, 1901–2
2348 Grandin Road, Hyde Park

The clubhouse for the Cincinnati Country Club was built in 1900 and rebuilt in 1916 following a fire. The first course had been laid out in 1893 by Nicholas Longworth II, Edmund P. Harrison, and Charles Hinkle. When the club incorporated in 1895, William Howard Taft became its first president. Taft was also the first U.S. president to play golf and to own a presidential car.

William Howard Taft (1857–1930)

Cincinnati's most famous son, William Howard Taft was the only person to have been both U.S. president (1909–13) and chief justice of the Supreme Court (1921–30). His personal and professional history reflects main currents in American life in the 1895–1919 period.

Taft was the quintessential progressive reformer, seeking to bring order, discipline, and equity to an increasingly complicated and unpredictable world. In Cincinnati, Taft reassembled the law library after the courthouse riot and was the first dean of the University of Cincinnati law school. As governor of the Philippines and then secretary of war for President Theodore Roosevelt, Taft established self-government in the Philippines, commissioned Daniel H. Burnham to create a city plan for Manila, and supervised construction of the Panama Canal. An appreciation for architecture was part of his heritage. Taft accepted the nomination for the presidency of the United States from the portico of his brother's house (now the Taft Museum), and he laid the cornerstone for the new Woodward High School (his alma mater) the day after his 1908 election to the presidency. In the White House, he called the first national conference on city planning in 1909. As chief justice, he reorganized the judiciary and persuaded Congress to fund a separate building for the Supreme Court. Taft oversaw the design by Ohio native Cass Gilbert, but construction did not begin until 1932, after Taft's death.[15]

Although not a gifted politician, Taft was a superb executive with exceptional talents for planning and organization. In this respect, he resembled the era's business leaders, such as J. P. Morgan and John D. Rockefeller, whose conglomerates were targets for the trust-busting operations of the Roosevelt and Taft administrations.

Samuel Hannaford & Sons
The Citadel, 1905
114 East Eighth Street

The Hannaford firm, which kept a large architectural library, excelled at meeting requests for designs in any number of popular styles.

group plan created a controlling civic space in Cleveland, but a comparable group-planned civic center proposed for Cincinnati was never realized. In the absence of government action, business leaders and families who engaged in development came together informally to shape downtown districts. Mixed-use "club and office districts" emerged around Piatt Park (Garfield Place) and at Fourth Street and Broadway near Lytle Park.

Cincinnati architects responded to the revived interest in classical and Renaissance forms with a number of beautifully composed fraternal and institutional buildings. In support of the quest for harmony and repose, the use of color became more restrained, even monochromatic. The Phoenix Club, which Hannaford modeled after Chicago's Calumet Club, and the Cincinnati Country Club by Elzner & Anderson were in that mode.

In downtown Cincinnati, the classic principles of the so-called American Renaissance were adopted for grandiose government and corporate projects, such

Ernest Flagg
Gwynne Building (detail), 1914
Main and Sixth streets

William Procter and James Gamble began manufacturing soap and candles on this site in 1837. They rented a building from David Gwynne, a Virginia investor, whose granddaughter, Alice Gwynne Vanderbilt, commissioned New York architect Ernest Flagg in 1914 to design the present building. Flagg was an innovative and socially conscious practitioner who had trained at the École des Beaux-Arts. He designed skyscrapers with setbacks that allowed sunlight to reach the streets, model tenements, and attractive housing for wartime industrial workers. The Procter & Gamble headquarters was here from 1935 to 1956. The Gwynne Building is far more elegant than most Beaux-Arts commercial construction in Cincinnati.

as the Courthouse and Western & Southern Life Insurance Co. Classical elements produced the desired effects of dignity, solidity, and authority.

Most architects and civic leaders of the 1890s regarded the White City as an object lesson for a new urbanism, where beauty was employed to promote civic virtue and allegiance. But a few contemporary architects, later joined by historians, maintained that the effect of the Columbian Court of Honor was to stifle the emerging modern movement in U.S. architecture. That was the view of Louis Sullivan, whose Transportation Building was the most original structure at the fair. In Cincinnati, most mainstream architects tried to accommodate their work to the emerging demand for Beaux-Arts formality. (There were exceptions, such as the innovative Coppin Building, now Covington City Hall, by James Gilmore [1875–1962]). Some architects and clients favored late Gothic and Tudor styling, which could be balanced and symmetrical and also picturesque. One good example, Hannaford's Citadel for the Salvation Army is a small building embued with a quiet air of monumentality.

Architects, artists, and aesthetes might disagree on the proper use of ornament or what style one should build in, but most then believed that it was beauty—whether expressed in the classical orders, natural materials, or perfectly proportioned functional designs—that elevated architecture to an art above mere "building."

Architecture and the Cincinnati Aesthetic Movement

M. Louise McLaughlin, sister of the architect James W. McLaughlin and herself a talented artist, wrote several books about art and aesthetics. George McLaughlin, another brother, wrote the text to accompany a one-volume set of photographs titled *Art Work of Cincinnati.*[16] In a manuscript essay on architecture (probably from ca. 1895–1900), Louise McLaughlin argued for simplicity and emphasis on construction, maintaining that a building should be "complete in itself without ornament."[17]

"We cannot go back to the old times, we would not if we could," she wrote. "What we want, in the rush and whirl of modern life, is to produce something which shall breathe the spirit of our time but which nevertheless may be beautiful." As she observed, "modern life" was a rush and a whirl. People and places changed in response to new technologies that at times benefited them and other times overwhelmed them. The most enduring changes were in communications and transportation.

The telephone, telegraph, elevator, and, most of all, the automobile altered the shape of buildings and places: skyscraper buildings became ever more vertical in the city, factories spread horizontally in the suburbs, and Mayor Henry T. Hunt's administration initiated traffic rules and regulations for the operation of motor vehicles. There was even a proposal to "rip out Fountain Square and replace it with a parking lot."[18] The automobile sales and service building took on the functional shape and barn-door entry of the carriage house. These automobile buildings often were given a proto-Art Deco form and integral ornament, which "breathed the spirit" of the time. The Central Parkway Barlow Motors Building, designed by Harry Hake in 1915–17 and renovated by Bruce Robinson in 2002, is a good example of this trend.

Cincinnati Urban Parks

Fritz von Empergen
Melan Arch Bridge, 1894
Eden Park

The Melan Arch Bridge employed new reinforced-concrete technology, using steel I-beams. Stone eagles from the Richardson Chamber of Commerce were mounted on the bridgework after fire destroyed the chamber in 1911.

Cincinnati's first large public parks—Eden Park, Lincoln Park, and Burnet Woods—were laid out by Adolph Strauch (1822–83), the highly respected "landscape gardener" of Spring Grove Cemetery. Strauch, who was also park superintendent for Cincinnati, had been opposed to buildings—even walkways—in his parks. But after Strauch resigned, the city authorized a number of building projects on park grounds, usually with the admonition that the designs enhance rather than detract from the natural settings.

Eden Park was purchased with the intent that it be used primarily for waterworks, but the Hannaford firm respected its dual use as a park with romantic, Chateauesque forms in designs for a pumping station and "water stand pipe" tower. Erected in 1894, the tower quickly became a favorite local landmark.

A number of other structures were built in Eden Park in the 1890s. The first public greenhouse opened in 1894 on the site of the present Krohn Conservatory, and in the same year the structurally innovative Melan Arch Bridge was built over Eden Park Drive. In 1902, the fanciful gazebo was built over a springhouse at the edge of Mirror Lake.

At a time when Cincinnati lagged behind comparable cities in its ratio of parkland to population, all of these tasteful "improvements" subtracted

Samuel Hannaford & Sons
Eden Park Water Tower, 1894

Samuel Hannaford's 172-foot water tower in Eden Park created a picturesque landmark. Set at 576 feet above low-water level, it is visible from the Ohio River and Kentucky. The water standpipe, which cost $135,000, was useful as well as beautiful: water pumped into the tank flowed downward into the Walnut Hills supply mains.

from parkland. Mayor Edward J. Dempsey, in his one term (1905–7), and several park board members, who viewed social welfare as a responsibility of the modern city, proposed that the city acquire suburban parkland and build inner-city playgrounds. Some newspapers and taxpayers opposed more "park-making" as wasteful and unnecessary, but voters approved a bond issue of $15,000 for a professional study by George E. Kessler.[19]

A landscape architect, Kessler (1862–1923) was born in the United States and educated in Europe. Like Strauch, he was an admirer of the work of Prince Herman von Puckler-Muskau. Kessler first made a name for himself in Kansas City, Missouri. Cincinnati engaged him to conduct a needs assessment for parks and boulevards. In his report, which council accepted in 1907, Kessler urged Cincinnati to take advantage of its exceptional hilly topography. "Few cities in the world are provided with precipitous hills which thrust themselves directly into the hearts of the community," Kessler observed.[20]

Kessler's first priority was creating a series of river-view parks. He also recommended the purchase of additional parkland in neighborhoods throughout the city. The parks would be connected by a system of boulevards bordered by wide strips of greenery. The concept was something like Olmsted's 1887 "emerald necklace" for Boston. But unlike the necklace, the Cincinnati plan circled the hilltops along the Ohio River and looped east, north, and west, connecting neighborhoods as well as parks. Although council shelved the boulevard plan, some parkways were eventually built: Central Parkway, Columbia Parkway, Victory Parkway, Westwood-Northern Boulevard, and West Fork Road.

Kessler's park plan, which did not differ radically from an 1890s park board plan except in its romantic yet progressive concept of the whole city as a park, drew immediate action. New suburban parks were added beginning in 1908, starting with Mount Echo in Price Hill. In 1911, the city increased total park acreage from 569 to 1,289 acres by purchasing land for Mount Airy Forest and Mount Storm. The same year, Levi Addison Ault, president of the park board (1908–27), and his wife, Ida May Holtzinger Ault, donated 150 acres overlooking the Ohio River on Cincinnati's East Side; their gift was the beginning of the 223-acre Ault Park. In the summer of 1911, play directors were hired to organize youth activities. In 1917, Alms Park was created.

The Kessler plan was Cincinnati's first and last comprehensive park plan. After World War I, the notion took hold that piecemeal planning for parks (or anything else) was less effective than comprehensive planning for all functions of the city and the metropolis. Even so, the Kessler plan remained a reference tool for city projects in the 1920s and for federal projects of the Depression era, which are described in chapter 7 of this book.

Carnegie Libraries

James W. McLaughlin
Walnut Hills Branch Library, 1904
Kemper Lane and William Howard Taft Road

This library was one of McLaughlin's last commissions in the Cincinnati area. The materials in the Beaux-Arts classical design are striking: charcoal gray brick set in burnt sienna–colored grout forms the body, which is trimmed in buff stone. The pediment is richly embossed and sculpted in the classical manner.

Walnut Hills Branch Library

Andrew Carnegie, a poor Scottish immigrant, accumulated great wealth as owner of the company that became U.S. Steel. Carnegie attributed his success to self-education in the private library of a wealthy Pittsburgh gentleman. Carnegie, who viewed private wealth as a sacred trust, applied the fortune he obtained from the sale of his company to expanding opportunities for poor youths. Having selected the new type of public circulating library as the best vehicle for encouraging upward mobility, Carnegie made challenge grants to communities for the construction of new neighborhood libraries in the city.

To qualify for these library grants, the community provided the site and pledged an annual allocation of 10 percent of the library's construction cost to support operations. Carnegie gave at least $250,000 for Cincinnati. (The system is now known as the Public Library of Cincinnati and Hamilton County.) The outlying areas of Norwood, Covington, and Newport also received Carnegie libraries. Community participation in the selection of the buildings' style contributed to the sense of ownership. The buildings are essentially classical in their symmetrical, block forms. Decorative motifs were drawn from a number of historical sources, including Spanish Colonial. Many of the designs exploited inexpensive natural materials in a manner characteristic of the American Arts and Craft movement. The interior of McLaughlin's Walnut Hills Library is a handsome example of this aesthetic.

The Walnut Hills Library marks a prominent corner in this historic neighborhood. A partially below-grade "English" basement floor is bridged by a double flight of stairs leading up to an oversized entry portico. A skylight centered in the low-hipped roof illuminates the interior.

McLaughlin designed the library with his last (and only, except for John R. Hamilton some fifty years before) partner, James Gilmore. Their building was selected from nine sets of competition plans. In 1907, it was included as an example for a model Carnegie library in Theodore Wesley Koch's *Portfolio of Carnegie Libraries*.[21]

McLaughlin usually worked in a more picturesque style, but this pristine, small structure, which recalls the formal clarity of his Ohio Building for the Columbian Exposition, was a fitting finale to his career in Cincinnati. He left shortly thereafter to live and work in New York and New Jersey.

Corryville Branch Library

A perspective drawing and plans of the design appeared in the *Inland Architect* in 1907.[22] The symmetrical façade of the Corryville library has a distinctive portico capped by a pediment and supported by rectangular pilasters and round columns. The low hip roof is covered with decorative red tile. The exterior of this building has been sensitively restored, and the new interior has been modernized and enlarged. The blue-and-gold coffered dome was restored and is once again spectacular.

From its earliest years, Cincinnati had a strong literary, printing, and publishing tradition. In the early twentieth century, it was still a national center for book publishing and consumption. Many readers used libraries to access world news and keep current on the proliferation of knowledge. As the number of book titles and press runs grew, the price of books dropped and library collections grew apace.

The sometimes conflicting needs for book storage, retrieval, and customer service affected library design. McLaughlin and Tilton addressed these problems in their designs for circulating libraries. In traditional reference libraries, the staff controlled the collections, allocating books and reference materials to patrons upon request. Circulating libraries were tailored more to school-age children and novice adult readers.

The plans for the Cincinnati neighborhood libraries reflect the organizational role of the librarian, who was charged with control of the collections, control of behavior in the public areas, and fulfillment of the needs of library patrons. Reading rooms for children were separated from those for adults. To encourage varied reading choices through browsing, open shelving was designed for periodicals and popular books.

Edward Tilton (1861–1933) was a nationally known library designer and a favorite of the Carnegie Foundation organization. Born in New York City, he studied at the École des Beaux-Arts and worked briefly with McKim, Mead & White. During a short partnership with William A. Boring, the firm designed the Ellis Island immigration station (1899).

Edward L. Tilton
Corryville Branch Library, 1906–7
Short Vine and Daniels streets

The Corryville Branch Library (originally the North Branch) expresses Carnegie architectural standards, with the librarian's charging desk at center stage, the homey fireplace in the original children's room, and the open bookcases. Design followed function, and sometimes emphasized institutional hierarchy, as is the case here where the glass dome hovers like an aureole over the librarian's charging desk.

Gruen Watch Co.

The two buildings of the Union Institute's Cincinnati campus face one another across McMillan Street on the western edge of Walnut Hills. They occupy steep, irregular sites (now above Interstate 71) and are set among artistic plantings and stone retaining walls. The design of the Procter & Collier building, which went up five years after Gruen, was intended to harmonize with the widely admired watch factory. The owners of both companies had a common desire to move their specialized skilled-labor firms to small plants set in grounds sufficient for landscaping and parking. Public transportation by trolley and personal transportation by automobile allowed industries such as these to be of, but not in, downtown Cincinnati.

Dietrich Gruen and his sons Fred and George moved from Columbus to Cincinnati, where they started a business in the basin. In 1913, they purchased property on what was then called Nanny Goat Hill to build a watch factory. Because the Gruen family's company made "high grade watches following Swiss models," the factory was patterned closely after a Swiss building. Completed in 1917, it cost $50,000.

Designed by Cincinnati architects Guy C. Burroughs and John Henri Deeken, the structure's variegated profile and fine materials give it a hand-crafted Arts and Crafts (or Craftsman) flavor. The exterior walls are of deep red tapestry brick, with stucco and half-timbering. The gambrel roof shimmers with green-glazed tile. The double front door has a glass inset, which resembles a pair of drooping eyes; it is a memorable Art Nouveau-like motif.

Inside, the dark wood paneling, exposed beams, and doorframes contribute to the Craftsman effect. The second-floor workrooms were open and lit by large windows. The watchmakers' tables were placed so that the workers were not crowded and all had good light for their delicate work. Like the owners of Rookwood Pottery, who believed they were applying art to industry, the Gruens established a functional and aesthetic work environment. There was an employee dining room and kitchen on the second floor, and outdoor gardens were created for relaxing breaks.[23] An addition to the east covers much of the property. It interferes with the most picturesque of the building's elevations, which are revealed in historic photographs.

John Henri Deeken (1888–after 1951) studied at the University of Cincinnati, but architecture was not taught there until 1922, after this project was completed. His partner, Guy C. Burroughs (1881–1936), had studied architecture in Chicago. Together or separately, the pair designed a number of buildings, including numerous houses and estates in Indian Hill, in a sophisticated style that suggests the shared aesthetic of the late English Arts and Crafts movement and the American Craftsman architecture and interior design movement.

Procter & Collier Advertising Co. Building (Beau Brummell Ties)

Time Hill/Union Institute
Deeken & Burroughs *(opposite)*
Gruen Watch Co., 1916–17
401 East McMillan Street,
Walnut Hills

Elzner & Anderson *(below)*
Procter & Collier Advertising Co.
Building (Beau Brummell Ties), 1921
440 East McMillan Street,
Walnut Hills

The Union Institute, an educational institution that awards advanced degrees for nontraditional college studies, purchased these two distinctive hilltop properties on the 1990s. They were authentically restored with the aid of historic photographs.

Procter & Collier Advertising Co. was the "captive" advertising agency for Procter & Gamble. The firm had sales offices in prime locations in New York, Los Angeles, and Chicago. A. O. Elzner and George Anderson, architects of the Ingalls Building, designed the Procter & Collier Cincinnati building, which was the company headquarters and printing plant. The picturesque design was developed in fieldstone, stucco, and half-timbers. The agency's copywriters stated that the building was a "structure in keeping with the new idea of civic beauty" and boasted that it was "one of the most attractive architectural studies in Cincinnati." The architects described their design as "Early Tudor."[24]

In 1936, the company sold the property to the manufacturer of Beau Brummell ties. The architecture and location also became an element in that firm's sales campaigns. The company told prospective customers that its products were manufactured in a "landscaped retreat high on a hilltop," adding that "with the inspiration of these beautiful, modern daylight studios . . . Beau Brummell stylists create America's smartest neckwear for men."[25]

MSA Architects directed the careful restoration and renovation for the Union Institute. Natorp, the original landscaper, restored the gardens.

Joseph G. Steinkamp & Brother
Xavier University Campus, from 1915
3800 Victory Parkway, Evanston

Xavier University's first administration building was named Hinkle Hall for Mrs. Frederick W. Hinkle, a major donor. Her portrait hangs in the entry foyer. The campus was reconfigured in the 1990s.

McGill Smith Punshon
Academic Mall, 1995–98

Xavier University Campus

Xavier University, which began as the Athenaeum of Ohio, was part of the St. Francis Xavier Church complex on Sycamore Street. The church, St. Xavier High School, and Xavier University trace their Jesuit origins to the work of the Reverend John Anthony Elet, who came to Cincinnati in 1840. When Elet became president of the Athenaeum, a boys' school founded by Bishop Edward Fenwick in 1831 was transferred to the Jesuits.

In 1911, recognizing that "it was time to prepare for moving from the inner city to the outer city," the college acquired twenty-six acres from the Avondale Athletic Club. The Athletic Club was adapted for the lower school, known as Xavier Academy. The ballroom of the clubhouse was divided into classrooms, and part of the banquet hall became the chapel. Much to the students' delight, the bowling alleys remained intact during the renovation. The same year, 1911, Xavier became a university when it opened the Xavier School of Commerce, Accounts, and Finance. Other vocational schools followed. Women students were admitted in 1918.[26]

In 1913, in preparation for the seventy-fifth anniversary of the Jesuits taking over the school in 1840, the Alumni Association commissioned Joseph G. Steinkamp and Brother to draw up long-range plans for the development of the Avondale campus. The plan positioned the academic department east of Victory Parkway (then called Northside Avenue). The athletic facilities were assigned to the west, between Dana Avenue and Winding Way.

The Stone, Webster Construction Co. and the Leibold-Farrell Building Co. erected the Steinkamps' first two structures, the administration and science halls, in 1919–20. The pair of octagonal towers that frame the entrance to Hinkle Hall are said to have been modeled after the castle of St. Francis Xavier's family in Navarre, Spain.[27]

The Xavier University buildings are strung out along the ridge above Victory Parkway. Although their elevated position gives the campus a somewhat fortress-like character, the pale stone and matching buff brick is welcoming rather than forbidding. The Steinkamps' Xavier buildings have parapets, which are either crenellated or plain. An occasional buttress or other medieval element enlivens the rather austere massing. Grouped rectangular windows are accented by larger Tudor-arched openings. The original buildings have been beautifully restored and landscaped.

Additions to the XU campus have continued to use the pale, monochromatic palette and the brick and stone building materials. The effect of the ensemble is peaceful and dignified. It evokes the contemplative mood of English college settings, quite unlike the lively but challenging cacophony of the University of Cincinnati campus. The well-kept grounds and park-like setting make XU a quiet oasis in the midst of the city. Academic and athletic activities have been placed in discrete clusters. The bulk of the mammoth new Cintas Center, intended primarily for basketball and large-group meetings, is gracefully nestled into the base of a newly graded hill east of the old campus.

Like other urban universities competing for quality students in the twenty-first century, Xavier University has understood the power of an attractive campus to make a positive first impression. In a 1994 design competition, XU awarded the commission for the redevelopment of its campus mall to McGill Smith Punshon, a local firm that traces its roots to 1856 and designer-engineers Joseph Earnshaw and Thomas B. Punshon.[28] For XU, reclaiming green space was a top priority. Public streets that dissected the campus were vacated to establish the Residential and Academic malls, which encompass 8.6 acres and include a number of smaller courts, gardens, and walkways. The project, which was implemented between 1995 and 1998, enhanced XU's image and established a sense of place that students and faculty value. The campus mall redevelopment won a local AIA honor award in 1999.

Shortly after the turn of the last century, Cincinnati's leading bankers and entrepreneurs turned to Burnham and Root's successor firm, D. H. Burnham & Co. of Chicago, to design a series of high-rise office buildings downtown.

By the 1880s, Chicago had supplanted Boston and New York as the center for innovative architecture. After the Chicago fire of 1871, the city experienced a population and building boom much like Cincinnati's in the 1840s. Aspiring architects migrated to Chicago, and people began to talk about a "Chicago school of architecture." Although he lacked a formal education in architecture, Daniel H. Burnham (1846–1912) was a talented designer. He trained under William LeBaron Jenney (1832–1907), the engineer-architect who experimented successfully with steel-frame construction for "elevator buildings" in the 1880s. In 1873, Burnham formed a partnership with another talented engineer-architect, John Wellborn Root (1850–91). Their early buildings were spare and functional.

In less than six years, Burnham and Root moved from the masonry bearing walls of their Monadnock Building to the steel skeleton of the Reliance Building. In the process, they created the flat-topped, steel-frame design model for the Chicago-style skyscraper. After Root's premature death in 1891 and the Columbian Exposition of 1893, Burnham reverted to the vocabulary and form of the classical column—base, shaft, and capital. Applied to the tall slab building, the base became the foundation, the shaft a stacked floors of offices, and the capital an attic story with a large cornice. Burnham & Co. employed this design device for its four Cincinnati skyscrapers. Three of the buildings—Union Savings & Trust (Bartlett Building), First National Bank (Fourth and Walnut Centre), and Fourth National Bank—lie on Fourth Street between Walnut and Vine streets. The fourth, the Traction (Tri-State) Building, is at Fifth and Walnut streets.

The first high-rise bank that Burnham designed in Cincinnati was for the Union Savings & Trust Co. The president, Jacob G. Schmidlapp, was a philanthropist as well as a banker. Deeply interested in architecture and housing reform, he had formed the Cincinnati Model Home Co. to build small apartment buildings for the working poor in places such as Norwood and Oakley. In addition to a banking floor and bank offices, the Union Savings & Trust Building was to have 407 office rooms for rent, yielding a projected income in excess of $10,000 a month. Ground was broken in October 1899, and about 500 men worked on the construction for more than a year.

At sixteen stories, Schmidlapp's bank was the tallest building in the city, usurping the honor from James McLaughlin's Johnston Building one block north.[29] Dark-gray bricks are laid in vertical piers that express the steel frame behind them. The windows are arranged in the Chicago style: three windows are grouped horizontally; the large center window is a fixed pane, and the two sidelights are sash windows. The base was altered when a large addition was put on the west side in 1927. At that time an entrance was enlarged and another added, along with the splendid vaulted ceilings, metal door ornaments, and sculpted eagles. These additions are crafted in the sleek, elegant Art Deco manner of the 1920s.

While the restrained classical character and tripartite form of the three other Burnham skyscrapers relates them to the Bartlett Building, the buildings vary in materials and decoration details. The former First National Bank Building is pale-gray brick with delicate monochromatic scroll ornament in the attic story. Horizontal ribbons of terra-cotta mark the floor divisions. Exterior walls gain interest from undulating bays, a device that Burnham & Root had employed in their Monadnock and Reliance buildings in Chicago. The exterior base and elegant entry lobby have been restored.

The rugged character of the former Traction Building suggests the vigor and enterprise of the street railway operation. The applied pilasters of the base make the only minimal allusions to classical ornament. The decked office midsection is composed of dark-red brick set in wide joints to give the appearance of rusticated stone. A decorative terra-cotta cornice visually rewards the viewer who follows the thrust of the tower skyward.

The former Fourth National Bank has a precious, gem-like character. Pink polished marble columns in the base and a heavy decorative cornice contribute to the lyrical quality of the design. In 2005, Cole + Russell Architects restored the exterior and renovated the interior for condominium residences.

D. H. Burnham & Co.
Union Savings & Trust Co./Schmidlapp/Bartlett Building, 1901–2
Fourth and Walnut streets
West wing by Graham, Anderson, Probst & White of Chicago, 1927

The Union Savings/Bartlett Building is the most powerful of Burnham & Co.'s Cincinnati skyscrapers.

Union Central Life Insurance Building (PNC Tower)

When the Chamber of Commerce building burned in 1911, Union Central Life president Jesse Redman purchased the ruined building and its valuable real estate. The insurance company held a competition (as the Chamber of Commerce had done earlier) to select the most suitable architect and design for this prominent corner. The commission went to the New York firm headed by Cass Gilbert in association with Garber & Woodward of Cincinnati.

Gilbert was a Zanesville, Ohio, native who had moved to Minneapolis as a youth. Most of his monumental early works, such as the Minnesota State Capitol and New York Custom House, were in the Beaux-Arts Classical style. His pre-1900 high-rise office buildings were similar to Burnham's bank skyscrapers and Elzner & Anderson's Ingalls Building.

Frederick W. Garber (1877–1950) and his brother-in-law Clifford B. Woodward (1878–1954) practiced together in Cincinnati from 1904–33. Both were educated at the Cincinnati Technical School, worked as draftsmen for Elzner & Anderson, and attended a two-year course in architecture at MIT. Garber won a Rotch Scholarship, which took him to Europe to study and travel.

In the exterior design for Union Central Life, the architects used the now-standard convention of the tripartite form: a heavy rusticated marble base, a glazed-brick tower shaft, and a heavy cornice capped by a little Grecian temple. The temple's Ionic colonnade and pyramidal roof resemble reconstructions of the Hellenistic tomb (after 353 BCE) of King Mausolus of Halicarnassus, which is known from remnants collected by the British Museum in the mid-nineteenth century. The materials for the exterior and the gilded interiors are sumptuous. The height of the building and its rich finishes make a powerful impression. Nonetheless, in 1911, this was a conservative design for Gilbert.

By 1905, American architects and critics had concluded that the round arches and post-and-lintel construction of Romanesque and Renaissance forms did not work well on towering structures, which called for vertical emphasis. In 1909, Gilbert had responded with an innovative scheme for the Woolworth Building in New York City. His soaring Gothic design complemented the vertical thrust of the fifty-five-story steel-frame structure. Gilbert's application of the Gothic aesthetic was widely acclaimed as an ingenious solution to the skyscraper design problem, and it was adopted by American architects at least through the 1922 Chicago Tribune Tower competition. Since construction of the Woolworth was almost simultaneous with that of the Union Central Life building, it is puzzling that Gilbert used the older, less-satisfactory Chicago-school formula in Cincinnati.

Gilbert scholar Sharon Irish dismisses the Union Central Life as "not a remarkable Gilbert building except in scale." She compares it to the Woolworth and concludes that although Union Central's tower is clad in white terra-cotta, "that is where its similarity . . . ends. There is none of the flame-like verticality of the Woolworth Building."[30]

Cincinnati architectural historian Walter E. Langsam speculates that the discrepancy between Gilbert's handling of the Cincinnati design and several other of his contemporaneous projects confirms the Garber and Woodward family anecdote that gives the actual design credit to the local firm. According to family tradition, Garber was hiking in Italy when he encountered a fellow American (an architect in Gilbert's office), with whom he struck up a friendly conversation. Later, after designing their competition entry for the Union Central building, Garber and Woodward asked the Gilbert firm to lend its name to their project, which won.[31]

Gilbert was definitely involved in developments after the commission was awarded. One of the puzzles in preparing the site was the removal and reuse of fragments from the Richardson building. Gilbert proposed to Oberlin College that the stone be incorporated in a chapel project there. About the same time, Garber and Woodward suggested that the remains be reused for a proposed Cincinnati Astronomical Observatory in Western Hills.[32]

In 1927, Garber & Woodward designed an annex for Union Central, replacing Isaiah Rogers's famed Burnet House that fronted on Third Street. And in 1939, the insurance company purchased and demolished the adjacent Electric Building on Fourth Street. Frederick W. Garber and Associates designed an addition to the main building on this site. Its purpose was a modern banking room for Central Trust Bank, which already occupied the ground level of the main building.[33]

Union Central Life left the downtown in 1964, three years short of its centennial, to build a new headquarters in the suburban city of Forest Park. Central Trust Bank (later PNC Bank), purchased the Fourth Street buildings. The PNC name was installed in neon on the tower.

Cass Gilbert with Garber & Woodward
Union Central Life Insurance Co. Building (PNC Tower), 1911–14
1 West Fourth Street
Annex by Garber & Woodward, 1927

In 1914 and for a few years after, the thirty-four-story tower was the tallest building in the United States outside New York City. Company advertisements hailed it as the "Office Beautiful."

Elzner & Anderson with the Ferro Concrete Construction Co.
Ingalls Building, 1902–4
6 East Fourth Street

Elzner & Anderson staked its reputation on the Ingalls Building, which was not only the first, but, at 210 feet, the tallest reinforced-concrete skyscraper to be built. Skeptics thought the frame would not bear the loads, and the city delayed issue of a building permit for two years.

Ingalls Building

Shortly after construction began on the first two Burnham buildings, railroad magnate Melville E. Ingalls (1842–1916) commissioned the local firm of Elzner & Anderson to design the sixteen-story Ingalls Building. The design is visually similar to that of the Burnham towers, but structurally more innovative—the Ingalls was the first reinforced-concrete high-rise office building in the world. This was a radical alternative to traditional masonry bearing walls or the newer Chicago steel-frame method. Elzner's development of the construction technology employed for the Ingalls project was a logical evolution of his pioneering design for the fireproof, cast-iron frame Neave Building (demolished for Tower Place garage) a decade earlier.

Constructors used the Ransome system, named for Earnest L. Ransome, who in 1884 patented a system for reinforcing concrete by using twisted steel rods. In the Ingalls Building, steel bars, stirrups, and hoops provide the necessary reinforcement for the concrete. The building was constructed in layers, one story being completed every two weeks. This daring engineering feat was wrapped in a conventional, Beaux-Arts Classical, buff-brick exterior to make it stylistically acceptable to the public.[34]

Born in Maine and educated at Harvard Law School, Ingalls had come to Cincinnati from Boston in 1871 on railroad business. A farsighted entrepreneur, he consolidated the "Big Four" railroad system in offices here, and then made Cincinnati his base for a number of business ventures throughout the region. Ingalls, Indiana, bears his name.[35]

At the time of construction, Ingalls was president of the Merchants National Bank, which had offices and banking services in the building. Building was a passion with Ingalls—he said that he built the $400,000 concrete tower as an "everlasting monument to Cincinnati, her progress and her enterprise."[36] He was quick to recognize talented local architects, especially those who had expertise in the latest building technology. At a time when other Cincinnati bankers turned to the more prestigious Chicago firm of D. H. Burnham & Co., his selection of Elzner & Anderson was vindicated by the success of the Ingalls Building. Ingalls was involved with the modern development of the Homestead Resort, a railroad hotel, in Hot Springs, Virginia. And in 1907, he built the popular Sinton Hotel in Cincinnati opposite the Ingalls Building. The Sinton was designed by local architect Frank M Andrews (1867–1948), whose work included the Seelbach Hotel in Louisville.

Ingalls was one of the city's most civic-minded residents. Although unsuccessful as the Citizens/Democrat candidate for mayor in 1902, he was an acclaimed volunteer executive. A founder of the Art Museum, he served as president during the time the Museum and Academy opened and the Schmidlapp wing was built. He was the major contributor to the building fund for the Cincinnati Country Club (also designed by Elzner & Anderson) and the Linton Unitarian Church (the work of James McLaughlin).

Alfred Oscar Elzner (1862–1933) was a Cincinnatian of German ancestry. He trained at MIT and in the office of H. H. Richardson near Boston and came home in 1886 to supervise construction of Richardson's Cincinnati Chamber of Commerce Building. Elzner practiced on his own until he was joined in 1897 by George M. Anderson (1869–1916), a member of a prominent Cincinnati family. Anderson was the first native Cincinnatian to earn a diploma (in 1895) from the École des Beaux-Arts in Paris. His brother was an officer in the Ferro Concrete Construction Co. (now Turner Construction Co.). The architects and Ferro Concrete jointly developed the technology used in the Ingalls Building.

Elzner & Anderson's later work is distinguished by its strong sense of structure and clarity. The American Book Co. Building (1904) on Pike Street facing Lytle Park is theirs, as is the Procter & Collier plant (1921) on McMillan Street. The partners designed a number of superior houses in upscale neighborhoods, primarily in a Colonial Revival manner, and they contributed designs for institutions and housing to the Mariemont development.

Hebrew Union College campus

A. Lincoln Fechheimer
Hebrew Union College campus, 1907 and later
3101 Clifton Avenue, Clifton Heights

Fechheimer arranged the buildings on the HUC campus somewhat asymmetrically along a ridge, looking down on Clifton Avenue.

Hebrew Union College–Jewish Institute of Religion (HUC) is the intellectual and spiritual center of Reform Judaism in the United States. It is a graduate school of theological studies for men and women who are training to be rabbis, educators, and community workers.

An informal coalition of Cincinnati rabbis founded the college in 1875. The first classes were held in the basement of the Mound Street Temple. When the student body grew, the board purchased a Sixth Street mansion, which served as the college for thirty years.

The inclined railroads of the 1870s and electric streetcars of the 1880s had made commuting to the suburbs easier. Cincinnati College had moved from Over-the-Rhine to a new campus in Burnet Woods in 1896. HUC joined the movement to the hilltops in 1905, when college trustees purchased Clifton Heights property in an area of parks, hospitals, and educational institutions.

A competition to design the campus and its individual structures was held in 1907. The award went to A. Lincoln Fechheimer (1876–1954), who had become a fine architect despite having been born deaf. His entry was in association with Harry Hake. The Fechheimer family had a long relationship with Reform Judaism in Cincinnati, so it was not surprising that young Fechheimer sought the commission. He had excellent credentials, having attended Columbia University and then the École des Beaux-Arts in Paris (the second Cincinnatian to do so, after George M. Anderson of Elzner & Anderson). Fechheimer graduated from the École in record time and with high marks.

Fechheimer's designs are in the Tudor tradition. The administration building established a style model that subsequent buildings followed. Most of the structures are two or three stories high, with raised basements and cross-gables or wall-dormers breaking the slate roofs. The buildings are faced in dark red brick laid in a staggered Flemish bond and trimmed in stone. The brickwork creates a lively pointillist staccato pattern that unifies the complex. The Cecil W. Herman Learning Center, almost midpoint in the aligned buildings, is distinguished by a pair of octagonal towers flanking a recessed Tudor-arched entry.

Fechheimer's sometime partner, Benjamin L. Ihorst (b. 1887), was involved in later buildings for the campus. Dormitories for on-campus living and the fine Freiberg Gymnasium, which opened in the 1920s, contributed to student health and morale. A library building was erected in 1931. The Klau Library holds the largest collection of Judaica and Hebraica outside of Jerusalem.

Unlike the neighboring University of Cincinnati campus, which has expanded into Burnet Woods and surrounding neighborhoods, Hebrew Union has remained mostly within its original boundaries. The notable exception is at the southern border, where HUC incorporated the former Masonic building. This handsome building was remodeled and enlarged in a modernist fashion by Osher and Dvoredsky and named Mayerson Hall for donors Rhoda and Manuel Mayerson. The building houses the Skirball Museum of Hebraica, the Center for Holocaust and Humanity Education, the Center for the Study of Ethics, the Archaeology Center, a lecture hall, and classrooms that are used for community outreach programs, including the Academy of Adult Interfaith Studies.

HUC has the largest collection of Jewish ceremonial objects in the United States, and select examples are beautifully displayed and interpreted. Permanent exhibitions focus on the Jewish community in local history, concluding in a sensitive thematic essay about survivors of the Holocaust.

Carl Strauss and other architects designed a number of later alterations to the campus. In 2004–5, David Scott Ross of Cole + Russell designed the Edwin A. Malloy Building, an addition that houses the American Jewish Archives. A key feature of the addition is a curved wall clad in Jerusalem stone. The center is named for the internationally renowned scholar Dr. Jacob Rader Marcus (1896–1995), who became a professor at HUC in the 1920s.

Following the HUC commission, Fechheimer and Ihorst designed Wilson Auditorium (1930) on the UC campus, the Wise Center Building in Avondale (ca. 1928), several important buildings for the zoological gardens, and (with P. L. McCoy) the classically detailed Dale Park School in Mariemont (1924–25).

Cole + Russell
Edwin A. Malloy Building, 2004–5

The curved wall is Jerusalem Stone.

Woodward High School

Around seventy years after it was built, Woodward High School became the home of one of the Cincinnati Public Schools' most attractive magnet programs, the School for the Creative and Performing Arts. Woodward was selected in part because it was one of the most handsome school buildings in the city.

In the early years of the twentieth century, art and aesthetics were considered essential to a well-rounded education, so Cincinnati Public Schools' building programs called for beautiful as well as functional designs. Rookwood Pottery fountains graced the hallways, panel paintings by local artists were hung in hallways and classrooms, and murals with historical themes were commissioned for libraries. The quality of the buildings, along with the breadth of the curriculum, attracted dedicated teachers and loyal students. Students contributed to funds to augment the art collections, and they became familiar with Cincinnati art and artists. The schools inspired pride of place in the city, and students and parents took pride in the public schools to a degree not seen before or since.

Special classrooms and buildings for manual (or hand) work and outdoor activities, such as gardening, supported the notion that opportunities to learn the simple moral virtues by contact with nature and through agricultural work had been lost to city life, especially within the tenement districts. Along with architecture and art, nature and gardening were thought to be civilizing forces that would teach young people to be well-rounded, responsible citizens.

Woodward was designed by Gustave W. Drach (1861–1940), one of Cincinnati's major turn-of-the-century architects. His work is characterized by a creative application of Beaux-Arts principles. He was frugal with applied ornament, preferring to add visual interest through the skillful combination of richly colored structural materials.

The school building's monumental five-story block is distinguished by a bold rusticated ground floor and an attic story topped by a heavily bracketed cornice. Slight shifts of surface plane, multiple quoins (alternating stone bands at the corners), a double-height entrance arch, and materials of contrasting warm and cool colors provide visual delight.

Drach was trained at the old 1850s Woodward High School (on the same site as the present building), the Ohio Mechanics Institute, and the Massachusetts Institute of Technology School of Architecture (1881–83). He worked in Boston for Cummings & Sears and in New York City for Herter Brothers before returning to Cincinnati to work briefly with architect George W. Rapp. In 1885, he set up his own firm, which endured until his death in 1940. His office was in the Union Savings & Trust bank building at Fourth and Walnut.

Gustave W. Drach
Woodward High School, 1908–10
Sycamore and 13th streets, Pendelton/Over-the-Rhine

The muscular character of Drach's architecture arises out of his preference for solid materials and massive walls.

Hughes High School

Under the boss political system, which held sway in Cincinnati from around 1885 until the early 1920s, machine politicians controlled Cincinnati public schools building projects. After many architects complained about the "system," the Board of Education was persuaded in 1906 to conduct a national competition for the new Hughes High School. To the dismay of all the local firms, the competition winner was John Walter Stevens (1856–1937), an architect from St. Paul, Minnesota, who had experience designing education buildings for Carleton College, the University of Minnesota, and the state reform-school system. Much of Stevens's work, which included numerous commercial buildings and warehouses, was in the Minneapolis-St. Paul area. Harry Hake (1871–1955) was the local architect, and Edward Hannaford was the local engineer.

Endowed by a bequest, the original Hughes school was built in the 1850s at Fifth and Mound streets downtown. In moving Hughes from the basin to the hilltops and in adopting a generous budget for the project, the school board signaled that this would be an important and progressive school, one that symbolized a new era in education. Stevens's design made the architectural statement the board wanted. Sited at the western terminus of Calhoun Street atop one of the city's highest hills, the castle-like edifice dominated its immediate neighborhood and echoed the Tudor-inspired Hebrew Union College buildings on Clifton Avenue to the north.

Stevens gave the massive walls a monolithic look by using only burgundy brick and having it laid in stretcher bond with dark grout in tight joints. The edges of the windows and the tall crenellated tower were lavishly articulated with stone and dark ivory-colored terra cotta, which trims the brick block like piped-butter frosting on mocha chocolate cake. The strong vertical of the 145-foot-tall tower invited schoolchildren to look upward, where terra-cotta gargoyles lurk under the heavy cornice. The interior appointments include artistically molded Rookwood tile fountains and architectural faience trim. The "modern" strip windows filled the demand for well-lit classrooms. The exceptionally large and beautifully proportioned auditorium has a graceful, curving balcony.

Local architects Rudolph Tietig (1877–1958) and William H. Lee (1877–1952), who were both educated at Cincinnati Technical School and MIT (1898), designed an addition in the same materials on the west side. A major renovation by Cincinnati-based Cole + Russell was begun in 2005 under a district-wide financial and programmatic plan sponsored by the state of Ohio and Cincinnati Public Schools.

J. Walter Stevens
Hughes High School, 1908–10
Clifton Avenue and West
McMillan Street, Fairview

This impressive structure anchors a busy uptown crossing.

Pugh Power (later Polk, now Park Place at Lytle) Building

The City Beautiful movement had a positive effect on corporate building programs. In news releases and publications, proud executives applied the terms "Factory Beautiful" and "Office Beautiful" to their company's new architect-designed buildings and the innovative technology that made them work. Management's regard for aesthetics arose in the context of a new concern for employee welfare.

Around the turn of the last century, efficiency experts began telling factory owners and office managers that contented employees turned out better products. The employee in a pleasant work environment was presumed to be more productive, less likely to unionize or strike, and more inclined to remain longer with the company. He might even be satisfied with minimal wages. The Factory Beautiful theory had a trickle-down component: improved facilities accelerated mass production, lowered prices, and raised the standard of living for all Americans. At least that was management's theory.[37]

In the first decade of the twentieth century, a number of aesthetically appealing and functional buildings went up in downtown Cincinnati and in suburban industrial parks. Northern Kentucky architects Dittoe and Wisenall designed the Pugh Power Building, named after Achilles Pugh (1805–76), a Pennsylvania Quaker who founded a printing company in 1830 and in 1836 began publication of the *Philanthropist,* an Abolitionist newspaper. Built in two sections, the Pugh is said to have been the largest reinforced-concrete building in the world at the time it was completed. Architectural critic Montgomery Schuyler praised the "straight-forward cage" (presumably that portion of the building above the Neo-Baroque first story) of the Pugh, which he preferred to the more "architecturesque" elevator buildings—the skyscrapers at Fourth and Walnut streets by D. H. Burnham & Co.[38]

Louis G. Dittoe (1867/70–1947) was educated and later taught at the Ohio Mechanics Institute. He worked briefly for S. Hannaford & Sons. From around 1893 until 1909, Dittoe was in partnership with Bernard T. Wisenall (d. 1942). The pair exhibited several buildings at the Cincinnati chapter, AIA fourth exhibit (1908) at the Cincinnati Art

Dittoe and Wisenall
Pugh Power (later Polk, now Park Place at Lytle) Building, 1904–5; 1909
Lytle Park

In 2005, the building opened as Park Place at Lytle, a luxury condominium development by the Miller-Valentine Group. GBBN Architects directed the imaginative renovation, which made use of the sturdy steel frame and large windows. The obelisk in the lower left of the photograph is a "city gateway" sculpture from the mid-1990s.

Museum. Dittoe was architect and superintendent of construction for the Ohio Exposition of 1910, and president of Cincinnati AIA, 1917–19.

During this period, investors began to build speculative office or manufacturing towers on the perimeter of the downtown business district. Because modern, well-designed buildings attracted the best-paying tenants, architects were called upon to design a number of these large, self-contained power buildings for potential tenants with light-manufacturing operations who preferred not to depend solely on CG&E. The earlier Textile Building on West Fourth Street, designed by Gustave Drach, had been a speculative building for the clothing industry. Like the Pugh, the Harry Hake–designed Power Building on East Eighth Street promised to deliver uninterrupted electricity through its own generators.

Samuel Hannaford & Sons
U.S. Playing Card Co., 1901
Robertson Avenue and Beech Street, Norwood

The card plant has large windows to provide ventilation and good light. Construction is reinforced concrete with buff-brick facing.

United States (U.S.) Playing Card plant

The U.S. Playing Card plant in Norwood is a prime example of the Factory Beautiful movement. U.S. Playing Card was (and is) the largest producer and distributor of playing cards; it supplies most of the world's casinos. The company, which was incorporated in 1881, still manufactures one of its earliest products, Bicycle brand cards, which feature the image of the then-popular high-wheeled bike.

Around 1900, management decided to move the card operation and its printing division from downtown to the small city of Norwood. Taxes were low, a railroad line was nearby, and an abundance of inexpensive land allowed the company to locate a low-rise plant in an attractive green park. The concept was similar to the one that had led Procter & Gamble to build Ivorydale on the outskirts of Cincinnati and St. Bernard in the 1880s.

Low walls enclosed the front lawn, contributing to the private park environment. Early photographs show fencing around the grassy lawn that marks the long approach to the plant, suggesting the park was intended for viewing, not recreation. The card plant offered indoor amenities, including employee lounges, dining rooms, and social clubs, all of which appealed to its numerous female workers. The restaurant in this "model plant" seated 1,368 people.

European modernist architects admired American factory architecture, which had always been much more utilitarian than public architecture—a trait that continued into the early 1900s. Hannaford's monumental design for the "card plant," as employees called it, emphasized clean, generous lines. Walter Gropius, a leading exponent of International Modernism, photographed this complex around 1910, around the time he was practicing with Behrens in Berlin and well before his tenure at the Bauhaus or at Harvard University. The central clock tower, which dominates the card plant façade, was originally lower and less prominent.

When Norwood was incorporated as a village in 1888, it was a middle- to upper-middle-class residential suburb. Early residents were initially unhappy when industry began moving into the community around 1898. But the Factory Beautiful movement assuaged their fears, and civic leaders ultimately applauded the expanded tax base.

Hamilton County Memorial Hall

Memorial Hall is an exceptionally fine and well-preserved example of the kind of Beaux-Arts Classical memorials that appeared in the United States immediately before and after World War I. The Soldiers and Sailors Memorial Building (more commonly known as Memorial Hall) was built south of the former College of Music and Music Hall, in an area that residents then regarded as a performing arts district.

The building has exterior walls of pale, smooth stone, but it is much more elaborate and baroque in presentation than the austere courthouse. Engaged and coupled Corinthian columns—a typical Beaux-Arts device—articulate the symmetrical façade. Six standing sculpted figures, attired in military or pioneer uniforms, adorn the frieze. Quotations from Lincoln's Gettysburg Address are carved in an attic-story panel. Heavy iron doors and recessed panels molded in a scroll pattern supply contrasts in material and pattern.

The lavishly decorated interior remains essentially intact. One of the most remarkable features is the wall treatment of muted ground colors overpainted in conventionalized designs. Military artifacts and documents are displayed in antique exhibit cases scattered throughout the first and second floors. The second-floor auditorium is a semicircular space surrounded by a curving corridor, a design device borrowed from French Renaissance interiors. A proscenium arch embellished with patriotic and moralizing words—Martyrdom, Manliness, and Equity—frames the shallow stage. An American eagle carrying the flag is painted on the ceiling above the stage. Boxes at the rear of the hall contain the original Thonet Bentwood chairs. All of the original electric chandeliers and sconces are in place.

The concert hall has perfect acoustics and sight lines. The intimate space, functional qualities, and historical ambience make it a favorite place for small concerts and meetings.

Samuel Hannaford & Sons
Hamilton County Memorial Hall, 1904–8
Washington Park

Memorial Hall is a public building owned by Hamilton County.

Hamilton County Courthouse

Inspired by the city's recent action on the much-discussed idea to drain the canal and build a subway topped by a parkway in its bed, Hamilton County commissioners decided to add a new and larger courthouse to a planned jail (the jail levy had been approved in 1911).[39] The Philadelphia firm of Rankin, Kellogg & Crane was selected to design the building. The architects and client chose the Beaux-Arts Classical style for the monumental building, perhaps because that style suggested dignity, justice, law, and order. After voters approved a levy in 1915, a construction contract was awarded to the Charles McCaul Co. Construction progressed slowly during the war. The new courthouse, with a jail in the attic story, was dedicated in October 1919.

The principal designer, John H. Rankin (1868–1952), had taken the two-year architecture course at MIT and then worked for the New York firm of Boring & Tilton, the designers of Ellis Island. Rankin had useful connections—he came from a distinguished old family and his father was a judge in Philadelphia. His firm worked primarily in the stripped classical manner popularized by French architect Paul Cret (1876–1945), who taught architecture at the University of Pennsylvania. Cret's work and theories were known through his independent commissions and consulting projects in the eastern and midwestern United States and Europe.

Rankin's cubic plan looked back to the 1850s courthouse, which had been partially destroyed in the riot of 1884. Constructed of smooth, pale

Rankin, Kellogg & Crane
Hamilton County Courthouse, 1915–19
Main Street and Central Parkway
Renovation:
GBBN, 2000

The 1893–1919 period ended as it had begun, with a return to classicism and a reliance on Beaux-Arts principles of planning.

New Hampshire granite and Bedford limestone, the new courthouse has an austere, dignified character. The horizontal massing adds weight and gravitas. The colossal orders of engaged columns, which unite the three-story middle section of offices and courtrooms, have come to symbolize the justice system in Hamilton County. Images of the orders appear regularly in law-related publications.

The original fireproof interior is just as imposing as the exterior. A grand two-story entry lobby, embellished with marble and bronze, runs the length of the Main Street façade. In a deliberate attempt to impose dignity on courtroom proceedings and reinforce the authority of the law, the original marble courtrooms were designed with high ceilings and with elevated benches for the presiding judge. The law library collection, which at the time was supposedly the most complete in the nation, was placed in a splendid library. In the original building there were two open courtyards, one of which has been covered. The courthouse public spaces have been beautifully lighted and the finishes restored by GBBN Architects.

View of Cincinnati from Union Terminal

Between the end of World War I and the Great Depression, Cincinnati modernized its government, its transportation systems, and its city center. Cincinnati became the first major city to adopt a comprehensive master plan, and the planned "new town" of Mariemont was developed. Several buildings from the period—Union Terminal and the Carew Tower, in particular—became local icons and nationally recognized architectural monuments of American modernism. They defined the character of the city and the region: urbane, sophisticated, and rich in history.

6

Modernism and Reform in City Building

1920–33

THE 1920S BEGAN on a positive note. Cincinnati's population growth between 1900 and 1920 had been a healthy 20 percent. An Ohioan was once again in the White House: Warren G. Harding, the Marion newspaper owner and Republican U.S. Senator, promised to restore prewar "normalcy." The national and local economies boomed.

Prohibition, which began in May 1919, put a damper on Cincinnati's entertainment industry. And yet swank "private" clubs and the bootleg industry prospered. Motion pictures, radio, live bands, and motoring contributed to the free-spirited life of the Jazz Age. Construction, which had all but stopped during World War I, resumed in earnest. Before the full force of the Great Depression hit in 1932, Greater Cincinnati's built environment had changed dramatically.[1] What's more, many of the new structures—buildings, bridges, and highways—had a new look, the streamlined look of the modern machine age.

A New Image for Cincinnati

New forms in architecture often grow out of new ways of thinking about the world. For Cincinnati, the 1920s were a time when changing perceptions about the city as a metropolitan community spawned new ideas about urban planning and architectural design.

Harry Hake
Cincinnati and Suburban Bell Telephone Co., 1930
Seventh and Elm streets

The Hake firm specialized in architectural design for public and commercial buildings. In this trim, compact building, which has been acclaimed for its Art Deco details, the function of housing tall electronic equipment dictated the form and vertical structural expression. The exterior walls presented an ideal surface for applied decoration. Cincinnati Bell's communication mission is symbolized in a high-relief frieze with carved French telephones and headphones.

Local political reforms were a catalyst for change. While boss rule had brought a new order and delivered an increased array of city services, including a municipal university and hospital, modern schools, and efficient waterworks plants, it had done so with bonded money in order to keep taxes low. By 1922, Cincinnati was on the verge of bankruptcy. Interest payments nearly equaled income, and the Ohio Legislature had capped the tax rates for municipalities. Safety services had been cut in half. City streets were in such disrepair that one automobile driver responsible for a traffic fatality was exonerated by a pothole alibi.[2]

When World War I ended, political reforms moved to the top of Cincinnati's civic agenda. Although George Cox was gone, the Queen City was still run by machine politics at a time when the Ohio cities of Dayton and Cleveland had installed model reform governments. Lincoln Steffens, a muckraking journalist writing for *McClure's Magazine,* had branded Cincinnati the "worst-governed" and Cleveland the "best-governed" cities in the nation.[3] From that time, control of the mayor's office, and with it city services, had moved in see-saw fashion from the machine to reform governments. In the 1920s, Cincinnati finally changed the perception of municipal corruption by adopting a new charter and city-manager form of government.

The new profession of city planning intrigued those who were concerned about inner-city housing problems, congestion, and metropolitan growth. Alfred Bettman, an attorney and civic leader, had assembled a small group of concerned men and women who formed a volunteer planning advisory committee, initially to address tenement-house reform.[4] In 1922, Bettman's planning advisory group retained a New York City firm, Technical Advisory Corporation (TAC), to study Cincinnati's urban conditions in the context of the metropolitan area.

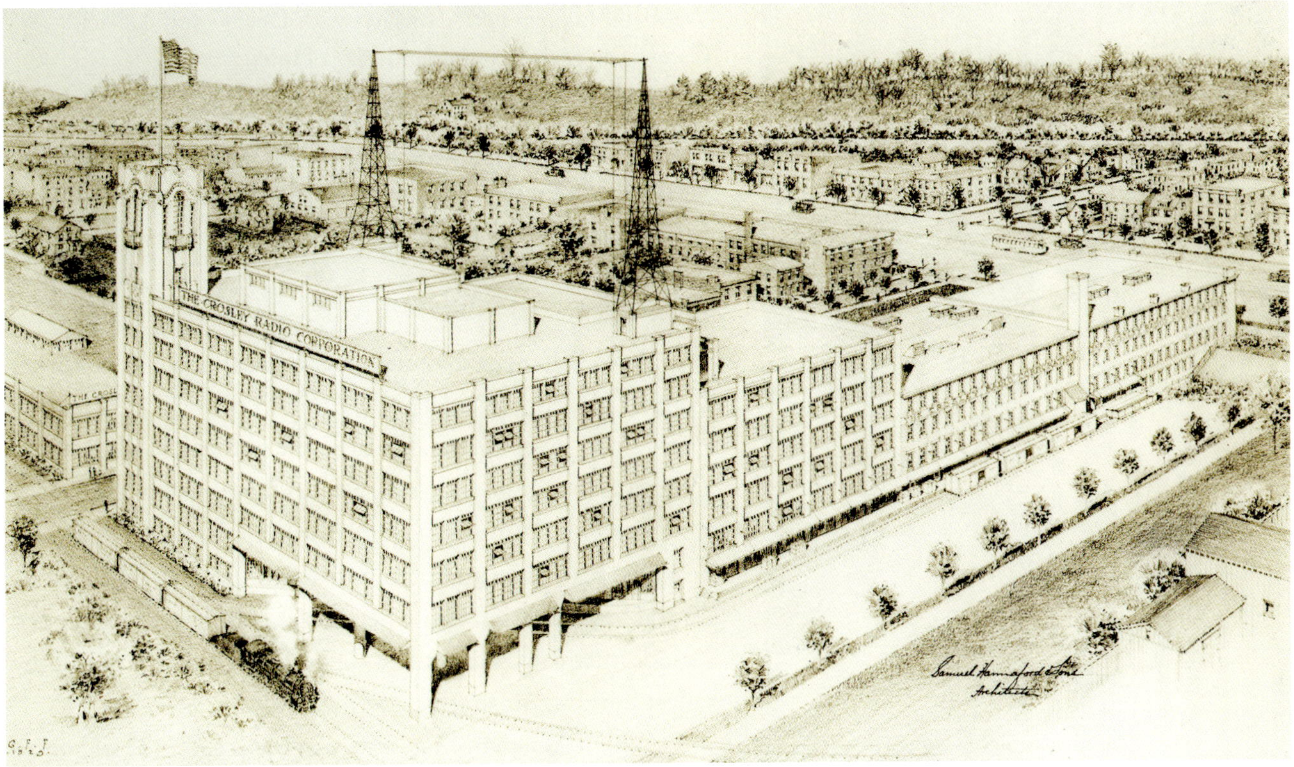

S. Hannaford & Sons
Crosley Radio Corp., 1929
Arlington Street and Colerain Avenue, Camp Washington

In 1922, Cincinnati inventor Powell Crosley founded the powerful WLW radio station, in part to supply programming for the radios he designed and manufactured. With the most powerful signal available, WLW became known as the "nation's station." This rendering for the modernistic facility, which was built in Camp Washington, envisions new and modern developments rising around historic church steeples and the company's plant and headquarters. The drawing is signed "G.F.F. 1929." G. F. Frankenberger (1890–1963) was with the Hannaford firm from 1923 to 1933.

At the same time, Victor Heintz, the statewide organizer in the Harding presidential campaign, took on Cox's successor, "Boss" Rudolf Hynicka. Heintz, a Fairview resident, founded a new organization named Cincinnatus. Composed largely of affluent attorneys and business leaders living in the silk-stocking hilltop neighborhoods of Clifton, East Walnut Hills, and Hyde Park, Cincinnatus initiated a political movement that by 1925 produced a new city charter government. Reforms included a small, at-large council with a mayor elected from its members, civil service, and a professional city manager.[5]

The business elite did not stop there. They used the new reform mentality to effect public improvements and the modernization of transportation systems that had been talked about for decades. Dixie Terminal and Cincinnati Union Terminal were just two of the results.

W. W. Ahlschlager & Associates with Delano and Aldrich
Carew Tower and Netherland Plaza Hotel, 1929–32
Fifth and Vine streets

The interesting massing of the Carew Tower and Netherland Plaza Hotel complex is visible from several sides. The tower is the tallest building in the city and in southwestern Ohio.

John J. Emery, a young and sophisticated New Yorker from an old Cincinnati family, came to town in 1924 to look after family investments. He brought innovative ideas about architecture and governance. Emery became involved with the Charter Committee (eventually becoming president), and he called for public and private redevelopment of the shabby central basin district. Using personal funds, Emery developed a modernistic skyscraper, the Carew Tower, which is still the tallest building in southwestern Ohio.

The TAC planning firm assigned Ladislas Segoe to write *The Official City Plan of Cincinnati, Ohio,* which council adopted in 1925.[6] Cincinnati made history by becoming the first major U.S. city to officially adopt a comprehensive plan. The city had had earlier plans for specific functions, such as parks, sewers, and boulevards, but the comprehensive plan integrated all the separate functions of city management into one plan.

It was no surprise that the planners identified congestion as a major problem. It had long been common knowledge that most of the tenements in the basin, where more than one-third of the population lived, were substandard housing. Segoe, who became a Cincinnati resident, encouraged community leaders to think of the city and its environs as an organic entity, with the central business district as its heart. Using a metropolitan analogy that argued for planning beyond political boundaries, he reasoned that a healthy organism depended upon the well-being of its extremities. The Charter Committee embraced Segoe's theory and, in 1931, persuaded Hamilton County officials and a few independent government entities in the county to adopt a limited regional plan.

As a therapeutic measure, Segoe urged segregation of life functions, with the basin dedicated to business and the expanding suburbs becoming a haven for residential use. The new legal tool of zoning facilitated rational land use. An able attorney, Bettman won approval of the principle in the Ohio Supreme Court and the U.S. Supreme Court. The city then passed a zoning code that put it on the cutting edge of city planning. The move was a timely one—the automobile, which had appeared on Cincinnati streets as early as 1891, was changing the way people thought about cities, suburbs, and community.

Automobiles, Parkways, and Bridges Encourage Decentralization

Since at least the 1860s, affluent Cincinnatians had been moving their residences to streetcar and railroad commuter suburbs. In the 1920s, the personal automobile encouraged professionals and the wealthy to build family houses in the unincorporated rural townships. Popular magazines and real estate promotional brochures extolled the benefits of working in the city while living in the "country."[7]

In the 1920s and early 1930s, Cincinnati and Hamilton County governments facilitated automobile traffic by building an extensive network of parkways and bridges, finally implementing some of the recommendations of the 1907 Kessler plan and the 1925 Segoe plan. These convenient connectors, forerunners of the beltway, spawned new residential developments and facilitated mobility among population centers. Planners expected improved roadways would bring traffic and people into the central city for business, shopping, and entertainment, but people also used the arteries to move away from the city.

Many of the viaducts and parkways were distinguished by their streamlined, modernistic designs. The eastern suburbs and villages beyond the city were connected to downtown by the Columbia Parkway (1927–30), which ran in a scenic ribbon from downtown to Mariemont. The Eighth Street Viaduct

Folwell Engineering and McGougal Construction
Western Hills Viaduct, 1932

At 3,300 feet, this is Cincinnati's longest viaduct. It spans the Mill Creek Valley, connecting Central Parkway to Harrison Avenue. The bow-shaped viaduct was part of the massive engineering project for Union Terminal that created a modern railroad and automobile traffic system. At the time, the arch and the viaduct were praised for their "modern structural design" and "Spartan simplicity."

Garber & Woodward with S. Hannaford & Sons
Vernon Manor Hotel, 1923–24
Walnut Hills

This comfortable residential and transient hotel was modeled after the Earl of Salisbury's Hatfield House (1611) in Hertfordshire, England, which was set in a "great park" designed by John Tradescant the Elder. Garber & Woodward's adaptation was in keeping with the hotel's parklike context adjacent to the Hauck estate and its extensive botanical gardens.

(1910, replaced by present bridge in 1928) had provided an essential connection to Price Hill. The Western Hills Viaduct (1930–32, replacing the 1908 Harrison Avenue Viaduct), which was part of the Union Terminal master plan, gave Westwood improved access to Central Parkway and the medical and educational institutions of Clifton. Central Parkway, which followed the bed of the former canal, was finally completed (without the partially constructed subway) in 1928. (Cincinnati voters approved a rapid transit bond issue for the subway in 1916, and the canal was drained in 1919. When construction funds were exhausted in 1927, the city abandoned the project. The bonds were finally retired in 1966.)[8]

Varied Architectural Styles Reflect Surroundings

In the 1920s, Greater Cincinnati residents began to see themselves as part of a metropolitan community rather than of a particular city or suburb. While boundaries blurred between the city and its suburbs, stylistic distinctions between urban

Louis E. Jallade
Mariemont Chapel,
1923–27
Mariemont

Charles Livingood, who directed the design and construction of Mary Emery's "new town" of Mariemont, requested a church based upon English Norman models. Local craftsman Otto Kadon supervised the expert stonemasonry. The church was nondenominational and intended to be more of a symbol of the community than of religion.

and suburban architecture became more pronounced. The taste for historicism remained strong in designs for suburban factories and housing developments, although clients and architects were becoming increasingly conscious of the costs of custom design work and the applied ornamental details that "period" styles required. Streamlined versions of historical styles, which grew in popularity because they were economical, soon became stylish.

Picturesque buildings with English Jacobean or Tudor styling were popular in the hilltop neighborhoods and the outlying villages and townships. Garber & Woodward used an English country house as the model for the Vernon Manor apartment hotel, which was built in an old city neighborhood that was changing from residential to institutional. The appeal of the English countryside and historicist architecture was expressed in the planned "new town" of Mariemont, which was patterned (loosely) after the Garden Cities and suburbs of England.

Mariemont was not the only planned community outside Cincinnati. In 1923, a number of wealthy families formed the Camargo Realty Co. to design a country club and divide farmland into estate-size lots in what became the Village of Indian Hill (now a city that prefers to call itself a "village"). Although not as tightly controlled as proprietary Mariemont, Indian Hill was an Ohio pioneer in zoning and land-use planning.

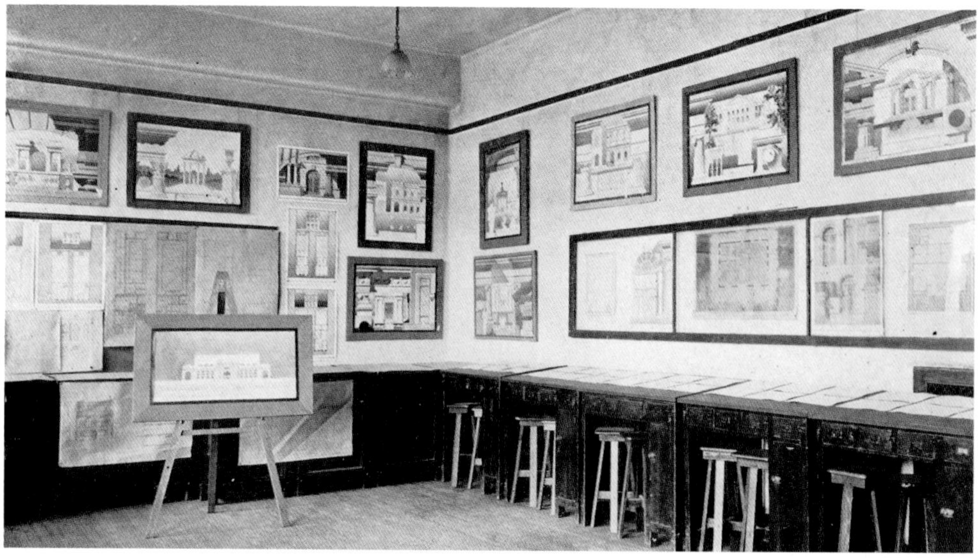

Architectural Drafting Room, Ohio Mechanics Institute

In the twentieth century, Cincinnati educational institutions that offered courses in architecture included the Ohio Mechanics Institute, Cincinnati Technical School, and the University of Cincinnati. A number of local architects concluded their training by enrolling in a two-year course at the Massachusetts Institute of Technology.

University of Cincinnati Introduces Architectural Education

When the School of Design broke away from the city university in 1886 to become the Art Academy, the university discontinued all fine and applied art and architecture courses (the school had offered limited "special studies" in "architectural instruction"). Dean Herman Schneider, who created the renowned cooperative work-study programs for the university, introduced the first program in architecture in 1922, and in 1925 he established the department of Architecture and Applied Arts. In 1946, when the department became the College of Applied Arts,[9] Ernest Pickering, who had taught at the school since 1925, was named dean.

Dean Pickering believed that an introduction to the history of architecture was an essential part of an architect's education. He presented students with a range of style options that could be used to enhance the "meaning" of a building, but he emphasized that a building without a style, one that embodied what he called "non-traditional modernism," could acquire meaning and aesthetic qualities through its proportions and massing.[10] The notion that an architect could design a significant structure with no identifiable historical style had gained acceptance in Europe. Once this principle became widely accepted in the United States, the answer to the question "In what style shall we build?" could be "In the style (or nonstyle) of our time."[11]

Traditional and Modernist Design

Even after the Crash of 1929, construction projects continued, fueling the local economy by keeping the building trades at work. Several of the largest urban commissions were designed in streamlined, modernistic styles that we now call Art Deco or Art Moderne (the terms were coined years later). In the 1920s and 1930s,

Fellheimer & Wagner
Cincinnati Union
Terminal, 1931–33

Area residents followed construction of the giant (109 feet high) arch and half-dome of the railroad terminal. The building was regarded as an exceptional example of architecture and engineering.

these structures were often described as "modern" (for the technology) in plan, function, and systems, and "modernistic" (for the style or "look") in architectural design.[12]

Contemporary writers noted that the new architecture reflected the spirit of the machine age and of Cincinnati's newly progressive community. For architecture patrons and Cincinnati boosters, "Modernism" was a positive term with promotional as well as aesthetic value.[13]

Not everyone subscribed to the streamlined, modernistic style. Most architects and clients continued to prefer buildings with historical and classical styling to the progressive (or faddish) styles of Deco and Moderne. And the time-honored École des Beaux-Arts practice of beginning with the "Plan" continued in this period. The Beaux-Arts traditions of symmetry, hieratic axes, and rational massing of enclosing elements were at the heart of the plans for Carew Tower and Union Terminal.

The tradition of using classical orders and ornament continued to be favored for corporate headquarters and for public buildings. But following a trend observed a decade earlier in the Hamilton County Courthouse, the massed forms and classical orders were often simplified or stripped down. The Dixie Terminal Building, Walnut Hills High School, and Cincinnati Gas & Electric Company headquar-

Tietig & Lee
Doctor's Building, 1923

The unrealized plan of Presidents' Square envisioned an ensemble of office towers with ornate façade decoration in the Venetian Gothic Revival manner.

ters, all by the local firm of Garber & Woodward, were costly and emblematic buildings in a spare classical mode that displays a contemporary sensibility.

Architects of the period often used a historical or eclectic mix of styles to embellish a project. The Allyn Company developed a plan for Garfield Place that would have produced an enclave of towers wearing historicist Gothic Revival façades in the manner of the company's lone prototype for the complex, the Doctor's Building.

Planning Was Cincinnati's Greatest Achievement

By the 1920s, Cincinnatians had abandoned the race for urban supremacy, even in the region and the state. Chicago, St. Louis, and Cleveland had more citizens, territory, and major corporations and taller, more monumental buildings. Civic leaders of the period turned inward, intent on fine-tuning the institutions already in

Ladislas Segoe (1894–1983)

Ladislas Segoe, 1894–1983

Ladislas Segoe, a former Hungarian army officer, used his engineering studies and experience with transportation systems to fashion a way of thinking about regional planning. In 1926, Segoe became the first planning engineer for Cincinnati. In the 1920s and 1930s, Segoe's work in the area included plans for Mariemont, traffic plans for Cincinnati Union Terminal and Western Hills Viaduct, and the site plan for the federal greenbelt town of Greenhills, north of Cincinnati. Segoe also wrote the revised Cincinnati city plan of 1948,[14] and he taught the first planning course at the University of Cincinnati.

When the decision was made to connect I-75 and I-71 via Fort Washington Way (a mistake that is only now being corrected), Segoe became disenchanted with Cincinnati city government and downtown merchants. His recommendations for a pedestrian-friendly downtown connected to the riverfront ignored, Segoe refused to take any more work from Cincinnati. But he continued to live in the city and maintained a downtown office for his international planning practice.

The practice of professional city planning within an independent department of Cincinnati's city government endured until 2003, when the planning function was drastically curtailed and folded into the department of community development.[15]

place. They set realistic goals for community building based upon the needs of the metropolitan area. The City of Cincinnati, with its traditions of learning and high culture, was the heart of the model that emerged.

Segoe's 1925 plan summarized and guided public policy for the next two decades. As mentioned, it was the first comprehensive plan adopted by a major city. Cincinnati was also the first major city to develop its capital budgets in concert with planning.[16]

The reengineering of the city by means of a comprehensive, metropolitan master plan guided by a charter, city-manager form of government was one of Cincinnati's greatest achievements. The city is a recognized pioneer in planning practices, and Bettman's legal victories in the Ohio Supreme Court and the U.S. Supreme Court have had an enduring life. They made case law that became the basis for national zoning codes and planning practices in urban areas.

Winston Churchill, touring the United States in 1932, was favorably impressed by Cincinnati's superb natural setting and modern architecture: "Cincinnati, I thought, was the most beautiful of the inland cities of the Union. From the tower of its unsurpassed hotel the city spreads far and wide its pageant of crimson, purple and gold, laced by silver streams that are great rivers." His hotel room in the Netherland Plaza had a modernistic bathroom fitted with yellow tile and streamlined fixtures, which he greatly admired and supposedly measured to re-create in his new town house in London.[17]

Cincinnatians were pleased with Churchill's praise for the beauty of their natural and built environment, and they were proud that in the 1920s the sobriquet of "worst-governed" city in the nation was exchanged for that of "best-governed."[18]

Lockwood, Greene & Co.
Cincinnati Enquirer Building, 1926–28
617 Vine Street

Both the Enquirer and the Times-Star buildings have simplified forms developed from smooth limestone blocks. Later generations have described the forms and rich applied ornament as "Art Deco."

Cincinnati Enquirer Building

The 1920s were the glory days of journalism in the United States. The growth of an educated, prosperous middle-class encouraged consumerism, which in turn bolstered the advertising industry. Radio (which Powell Crosley pioneered in Cincinnati) was in its infancy, and television was in the future. Newspapers were the primary advertising vehicles. Most urban centers had several daily papers, which enjoyed a steady stream of income from advertisers and an avid reading public.

The *Chicago Tribune* initiated the trend to erect monuments to journalism. The *Tribune*'s 1922 competition for design of its headquarters attracted international entries from the world's most prestigious architectural firms. The extensive coverage that the *Tribune* gave the competition resulted in an extraordinary amount of media attention to architectural design.

The winner was the Gothic design of the New York firm Howells & Hood. Eliel Saarinen's simplified, modernistic design won second prize and was ultimately the more influential. Significantly, when the *New York Daily News* selected Howells & Hood in 1929 to design its tower, the result was closer to Saarinen's *Tribune* submission than to their own. Architect John Mead Howells called the style of his design for the *Daily News* building "American Vertical," explaining that "the simple composition of verticals, which some like to call 'modernistic,' seemed appropriate for steel-cage construction." We would now call this design Art Deco, but no matter what the style was called, subsequent newspaper headquarters built in the late 1920s tended to follow the modernism of the Daily News Building rather than the Gothicism of the Tribune Tower.[19]

Cincinnati had three daily papers: the *Post*, the *Enquirer*, and the *Times-Star*. The *Enquirer* and the *Times-Star* erected new downtown plants in the 1920s. They were modern facilities, combining editorial, advertising, printing, and distribution functions. The *Times-Star*, which was owned by city boosters Charles and Anna Taft, selected the local firm of S. Hannaford & Sons. The *Enquirer* selected a national architect, Lockwood, Greene & Co. of Philadelphia. This prominent architecture and engineering firm specialized in newspaper offices and printing plants. Their clients included the *New York Times* and the Baldwin Piano Co. of Cincinnati.

At its opening in 1928, the Enquirer Building was described as "a soaring structure of fourteen stories, modern to a degree unparalleled in Cincinnati." It created a new image for the venerable newspaper, which had been founded in 1841 and had published the nation's first Sunday edition in 1854. (The *Enquirer*'s printing operation has since moved to Queensgate, and its editorial offices are at Third and Elm streets.)

Some writers have described the Enquirer Building as the first major structure in the city to have Art Deco styling. Although the materials and some of the styling have associations with Art Deco, the building has the flavor of a premodern period. The exterior is an eclectic mix of heavy little balconies, curious gargoyles, and multi-light arched windows, all suggesting a loose interpretation of late-Gothic sources. The iconography of the sculptural program alludes to the practices of reading and writing. The figures appear to be modeled after prophets in medieval manuscripts and athletes in Greek temple friezes. By contrast, the Times-Star program features figures from recent history.

The façade has a sparkling, painterly quality. Its small-scale decorative patterning and elegant demeanor make the Enquirer Building a suitable companion to the Second Empire Cincinnatian Hotel, its neighbor to the south. The interior public spaces are ornamented with rich marble and metallic materials in a sophisticated black-and-gold palette that looks fresh and new.

Mariemont

When Thomas Emery died suddenly in 1906, his wife, Mary, was left with an estate estimated at thirty-five million dollars. The sixty-two-year-old widow decided to memorialize her husband and their deceased children with bricks-and-mortar philanthropic projects. The Emery family fortune had been acquired through the manufacture of candle and glycerin products (later chemicals) and real estate development. Downtown Cincinnati and streetcar routes leading to hilltop suburbs were studded with handsome modern flats that the development and realty company Thomas Emery's Sons built and rented to working- and middle-class people. As a benefactor of Christ Church Episcopal, which operated a settlement-house-type mission, Mary Emery was certainly aware of the shortage of affordable housing in the inner city. In 1910, she informed her chief assistant, Charles Livingood (b. 1866), that she wished to make a new town the centerpiece of her many philanthropic ventures.[20]

Livingood, who had been a friend and classmate of an Emery son at Harvard University, became the visionary and decision maker for the large, complicated project. He traveled to England to visit the Garden Cities of Port Sunlight and Letchworth, and he met the leading planning practitioners at conferences in the United States. After careful study, John Nolen (1869–1937) of Boston, who had given the keynote address at the first National Conference of City Planning in Washington, DC, in 1909, was Livingood's choice to plan the new town. Nolen was assisted by Philip Foster and Justin Hartzog, who also became important planners. Livingood was a member of the design team, contributing numerous ideas and wielding veto power. He selected the architects for Mariemont's "Places" (or approved Nolen's suggestions) with great care. Livingood left the choice of period style to each architect, but it was understood that the style selected would be traditional and the works would be harmonized.[21]

Nolen, a student of Frederick Law Olmsted Jr. at Harvard University, was America's premier city planner. His eclectic blend of formal and informal planning principles was realized in Mariemont, which Nolen worked on from 1921–25. Emery had specified that her town was to be a model for subsequent reformers, so Nolen labeled it a "national exemplar." He envisioned a complete town that would exemplify "how well people of moderate means can live." Mariemont was inspired somewhat by the English Garden City movement, which was based upon the theories of Ebenezer Howard. But Nolen incorporated his own ideas and experience in town building in the United States. The European Garden City advocates were initially responding to economic concerns, and to a lesser extent the quest for community (they called it "fellowship"). Nolen's town-making philosophy was rooted in the notion of community as a producer of "local happiness."[22] Howard and the founders of the English Garden City were motivated in part by antipathy toward the city, but Mariemont's planners had a metropolitan vision. Advertisements stressed that residents could easily have regular economic and cultural interaction with the city of Cincinnati.[23]

Nolen emphasized efficient transportation routes and walking paths. Although most roads were straight, they frequently radiated from small parks or roundabouts. Lots for single-family houses were small, and multifamily buildings were clustered, saving ground for green space and communal vegetable gardens. For aesthetic reasons, all utilities were buried underground. Nolen's plan allowed for the automobile, but he and Livingood did not foresee that it would become indispensable, even to Americans of limited means.

Livingood envisioned a Norman English village church as the centerpiece of the community. The commission went to Louis E. Jallade (1876–1957), a New York architect who had designed a YMCA building for Emery in Newport, Rhode Island. Jallade was sent to England to study authentic examples. There he purchased roof stone from a damaged ca. 1300 Cistercian tithe barn to use in the Mariemont church. The

church's roof was constructed with a "sagging" indentation to give the desired antiquarian finish.

The inn (1925), designed by the Cincinnati firm of Zettel & Rapp, anchors the town center.[24] (The original conception called for a much larger building, in a V-shaped plan with long wings.) A sunken garden behind the inn was a popular summer dining room. The garden was located on the site of the present parking lot, one of a number of indicators that the town plan did not anticipate the number of automobiles Americans would own. Planners assumed that a portion of the residents would use public transportation to commute to jobs and cultural events in the city, so the rental units have communal garages. Mariemont was designed as a walking community, and it still works that way for those who choose to travel by foot.

The high-quality design and custom construction costs drove Mariemont housing beyond the reach of wage-earners. (Some disappointed aspirants to suburbia complained bitterly when rent rates were announced.) Mariemont became a haven for young professional families and retirees, and it has remained a highly desirable community. It continues to be an exemplar: Nolen's planning theories are admired by Andres Duany and other New Urbanists.[25]

John Zettel (1881–1950) and
Walter L. Rapp (1878–1974)
Mariemont Inn
Wooster Pike
Southeastern Hamilton County

The architects' original conception was for a much larger building in a V-shaped plan with long wings. Livingood, who described the principals as his "friends," most likely specified the Tudor Revival elements in the building.

Fellheimer & Wagner with Roland Wank and Paul Cret
Cincinnati Union Terminal/ Cincinnati Museum Center, 1931–33
Ezzard Charles Drive, West End

Renovation:

E. Verner Johnson and Glaser & Associates, architects; Messer-Cargile, construction manager, 1986–90; Bentley-Meisner Associates, landscape architects

The Cincinnati Commercial Club and Chamber of Commerce promoted construction of the landmark building as a demonstration of the city's modernity—and perhaps because it was good for business.

Union Terminal was a much-discussed and long-overdue reform. Most major U.S. cities had consolidated passenger and freight operations decades before with grand center-city Beaux-Arts railroad terminals. But because Cincinnati's terminal was a latecomer, it was located on the outskirts of the central business district and finished in a modern rather than a traditional style. The complex became an internationally celebrated icon of the emerging modern style. In his book *Architectural Design,* University of Cincinnati architecture professor Ernest Pickering used a photograph of Union Terminal to illustrate what he described as "non-traditional modernism."[26]

The terminal building was at the heart of a massive public and private transportation and development project. The seven participating railroads paid most of the more than $40 million cost of the complex; the city contributed funds for land acquisition and infrastructure. The site location and some of the program were based upon earlier studies by Cincinnati railroad engineer C. A. Wilson.[27] Business and community leader George D. Crabbs and Chief Engineer Henry M. Waite spearheaded the project.

Members of the architect-engineering-design team were nationally recognized specialists. The architect-engineers, Alfred Fellheimer (1875–1959) and Steward Wagner (1886–1958), organized the complex yet efficient circulation patterns of the terminal. Fellheimer had extensive relevant experience, including work on Grand Central Terminal in New York. The transportation circulation paths were layered rather than winding—stairways were to be found only in the private office and operations areas. Fifty years later, architect-educator John Hejduk (1929–2000) maintained that there was still much to be learned from the layered plan: "I was amazed by the incredible way the circulation worked. The train came in, you went up the stairs, down a concourse, then there was a whole series of levels for buses, taxis, and other transportation."[28]

As originally projected in elevation drawings, the plan called for a conventional arched entry and reception area, with the ornamental interior design in a somewhat modernized classical mode. Beaux-Arts-trained proto-Modernist Paul Cret (1876–1945) of Philadelphia was brought in as a consultant on aesthetics. Cret seems to have encouraged Fellheimer & Wagner to alter their design to create a more dramatic half-dome portal and to emphasize the dome motif in streamlined, modernistic ornamental details. Fellheimer & Wagner's young engineer, Roland Wank (1898–1970), who had recently returned from a tour of European Modern architecture, also has been suggested as a contributor to the change to "Modernism," as contemporary accounts described the final style.

The firm had the engineering skills required to create the highest half-dome in existence: eight arched trusses, the largest weighing 380 tons, support the dome. It became the symbolic gateway to the city. To complement the dramatic rotunda, the interior designers erased the classical swags on earlier renderings, clearing wall space for colorful, realistic murals of everyday life in Cincinnati factories. The circular patterns of the rotunda were repeated in bands of color

Sculptor Max Keck's bas-relief sculptures on the façade, symbolizing the relationship of Transportation to Commerce, are executed in a breezy Art Deco manner.

The Winold Reiss murals are notable for their brilliant color and abstracted realism.

on the ceiling and in terrazzo inlays on the floor. Aluminum was used lavishly for signage, decorative banding, doors, and furniture and to sheath the exterior dome. The furnishings were changed from heavy wooden benches to sleek leather settees and chairs; the typography of the directional signage became Moderne. Internationally known muralists were called in.

One theory about the modernization of the decorative scheme is that the project managers were told it would cut costs. But it is difficult to imagine that construction of the massive half dome, the extensive use of artists and craftsmen for the murals, and the custom leather and chrome furnishings presented a savings over the original program of more modestly massed spaces, simple molded ornamentation, and bare wooden benches. The dedication book published by the Cincinnati Chamber of Commerce may be closer to the true motives of the committee and designers when it states that ultimately a classical style was considered "inappropriate" for the machine-age building. In the "absence of the usual architectural embellishments such as columns, moldings and pilasters," the designers made use of the "texture and color" of the materials—mosaics, leather, metal, and marble—to secure "pleasing effects."[29]

Although the design took a modernist turn, the building plan continued to rely on Beaux-Arts axiality, symmetry, and processional spaces like the Netherland Plaza. It was thoroughly modern in its systems, including an elaborate switching network operated from a tower, which allowed the operator panoramic views of the tracks. The architect-engineers —experts in station construction— were doubtlessly aware of Eliel Saarinen's Helsingfors/Helsinki Railroad Station (1914), which had made an international impact. Cincinnati's terminal, with its massive sculpted masonry bulk over an ingenious steel frame, bears a striking resemblance to the Helsinki exterior.

All of the furniture was custom-designed and crafted in fine woods, leather, and aluminum. Some of the original furnishings survive in the concourse-level boardroom and in the Amtrak waiting room, which features wall coverings of stylized engine motifs carved in wood veneer by Pierre Bourdelle. The Moderne signage and metal work attest to the exceptional integration of architectural form and decorative detail throughout the project.

New York artist Winold Reiss (1886–1953) designed the spectacular 105-foot-long rotunda murals, which synthesize American and Ohio Valley history. Other Reiss murals portraying Cincinnati industries lined the former concourse; they are now displayed in the Cincinnati/Northern Kentucky International Airport. Most of the scenes were adopted literally from photographs taken expressly for the commission. In the tradition of Renaissance muralists, Reiss enlarged and scored the photographic prints, making cartoons for the mosaic artists. Other murals include portraits of the men who spearheaded the project, which included acres of outlying buildings and the Western Hills Viaduct. Reiss, a recent German immigrant, was fascinated by the raw character of America: its laborers, Native Americans, and African Americans, and its modern jazz. He may also have been a party to the decision to change the decorative scheme from traditional to modern.

Cincinnati Union Terminal holds a special place in the collective memory of the city and its hinterlands. Thousands of skilled workers from the building trades were involved with the construction, as a series of photographs of proud tile-setters, stonemasons, and ironworkers attests. Many more people had memories of the terminal in the 1940s during World War II, when it reached its peak as a transportation hub. It was the major point of departure for hundreds of thousands of military personnel from the Midwest. Passenger rail traffic declined throughout the nation at the close of the war, when people turned to the personal automobile for day trips and the airplane for longer journeys.

The original concourse was demolished in 1973 and the fourteen murals in that section were moved to an addition to the Greater Cincinnati airport, then under construction. Union Terminal reopened as an attractive but short-lived shopping and entertainment center in 1980.

Threatened by demolition, the terminal was one of several sites considered by the Cincinnati Historical Society and the Cincinnati Museum of Natural History when they conducted a search for shared museum space. E. Verner Johnson, a Boston-based museum architect who was the consultant for the two institutions, recommended the terminal, describing it as a "jaw-dropper of a building." Johnson observed that the vast spaces, the symmetrical design, and the original plan, which was based on the function of moving large numbers of people through space, invited programming for two distinct but complementary museums.[30]

Johnson worked with local architect Glaser & Associates to preserve the historic public areas and the vehicular ramps, where exhibits were built to suit the irregular spaces. A joint venture by Messer Construction Co. and minority partner William Cargile resulted in Messer-Cargile, the construction manager for this ambitious project. Most of the major exhibits are underground in what was an excavated but undeveloped parking garage space. Funding came primarily from generous private gifts, which were supplemented by construction bonds authorized by Hamilton County voters and the State of Ohio in 1986.

The complex, which incorporated the Cincinnati Historical Society Library and Museum, Cincinnati Museum of Natural History and Science, an Omnimax theater, and more recently a Children's Museum, opened as the Cincinnati Museum Center in 1990. Amtrak trains relocated to the terminal from a small station on River Road.

Designated a National Historic Landmark and National Civil Engineering Landmark, Union Terminal is a unique architectural monument, one with the power to represent a place and to engage a diverse community.

French artist Pierre Bourdelle carved colored linoleum to creative fantastic murals for the ladies' lounge. The flora and fauna images and the sinuous lines have a turn-of-the century Art Nouveau flavor.

H. Eldridge Hannaford for S. Hannaford & Sons
Cincinnati Times-Star Building, 1930–33
800 Broadway

The Times-Star Building's sculptural program may be read from all sides. From the entry on Broadway to the relief sculpture associated with the newsboy entrance on Eighth Street and the printing plant docks that open to Eggleston Avenue, the figural and abstract designs surprise and delight.

Drawing of interior signed and dated "H. B. Wuebling 11/28/1930."

The American eagle was a favorite symbolic and decorative motif of the era. Harry B. Wuebling was a draftsman.

Cincinnati Times-Star Building

The *Times-Star* newpaper facility was the crowning achievement for Samuel Hannaford's successors. Eldridge Hannaford (1892–1975), a grandson of the firm founder, was the principal designer of this monumental complex. The building is composed of interwoven three-dimensional blocks with the strong vertical elements that John Mead Howells, architect of the Chicago Tribune and New York Daily News towers, recommended for skyscraper design. Ferro-Concrete Construction Co. was the contractor for the building, which was a challenging project because of the heavy printing presses located in the eastern section.

The simplified forms have faint allusions to classical fluted columns, but they are handled with fluidity and geometric precision. The tower is a distinct unit, giving the impression of a true skyscraper. The upper part of the tower, with an airplane beacon in the shape of an urn, is the most complex of downtown's several skyscraper pyramids.

The sculptural program by Ernest B. Haswell and Jules Brys is rich in literary, historical, and mythological references to journalism and learning. It offers the viewer a measure of the mystery and visual delight found in a medieval church. The canted corners of the tower project three-dimensional figures in a manner that recalls Bertram Goodhue's popular Nebraska State Capitol (ca. 1922). Large bas-reliefs below the statuary contain profile portraits of printing icons, including Franklin and Gutenberg. Carved panels of shields guarded by winged lions adorn the lower levels. Decorative Art Deco zigzags are carved into stone walls and cast in metal for window grills.

A colossal round arch flanked by bolder pylons frames a portal of lavish carved stone, which opens into a Norman-coffered lobby. The building materials are notable for their exceptional quality and beauty. The high ceiling is studded throughout with countless gilded eagles, in a lavish tribute to the United States and the patriotism of the Taft family.

On the lobby wall, Anna (1852–1931) and Charles (1843–1929) Taft are honored with portrait heads cast in metal high relief. One of the couple's bequests established the Cincinnati Institute of Fine Arts and made the Taft Museum, along with its outstanding collections, a gift to the people of the city. Charles died while the newspaper building was under construction, and the immense tower office intended for him was occupied by his nephew Hulbert Taft. Taft descendants built a communications and entertainment empire, which became Taft Broadcasting. The *Times-Star* merged with the *Cincinnati Post* in 1958, and in 1974 the *Times-Star* name was dropped from the masthead.

The building is owned by Hamilton County, which has assigned it to the Juvenile and Domestic Relations Courts and affiliated agencies.

The sculpture is by Ernest B. Haswell and Jules Brys. The figures on the tower represent speed (for news), truth, progress, patriotism, and learning, symbolized here by the cloaked female holding a book.

St. Monica Roman Catholic Church

New sacred architecture of the 1920s usually acknowledged historic traditions, but some of the edifices have stripped-down silhouettes and abstracted ornamental details. Edward J. Schulte (1890–1975) and Robert E. Crowe (1881–1944) became partners in 1921. The firm designed the church and rectory for St. Monica's parish in Fairview Heights, a middle-class neighborhood that was then one of the most Catholic wards in the city. This handsome church served from 1938 as the Archdiocesan Cathedral before the seat was returned to St. Peter in Chains downtown following its modernization by Schulte in the mid-1950s.

The parish was organized in 1910. The present church, dedicated to the mother of St. Augustine, was constructed entirely with donations from parishioners. The church was built at a cost of $250,000, and dedicated in December 1928. At the request of the pastor, the architects used Early Christian church architecture—in particular, Sant' Apollinare in Classe, Ravenna—for inspiration. The apse mosaic in the interior of the sixth-century Italian basilica was a model for the apse mural in St. Monica.

Crowe & Schulte were masters at coordinated decorative ensembles, and the St. Monica complex is remarkable for the integrity of its interior and exterior programs. The design is all of a piece—its gently molded stone surfaces and gem-like stained glass are tightly orchestrated. St. Monica's sand-colored profile is smooth and rounded. The attenuated, manneristic sculpture of the church façade contributes to the building's "traditional modernism" styling.[31]

Roman Catholic church architecture never abandoned the medieval tradition of using the visual arts to complement a structure designed for worship. Clement Barnhorn, assisted by his pupils Clothilde Zanetta, Carolyn Zimmerman, and Ruth Kerr, created the sculpture for the façade. In 1936, Carl Zimmerman and Charles Seyffer, of the faculty at the Cincinnati Art Academy, did many of the paintings, including the tree of life mural in the apse and probably the stenciling on the walls. The artists adopted the brilliant color palette of reds, blues, and greens found in Byzantine mosaics. The prismatic stained glass, also in brilliant primary colors, is by the Zettler workshop in Munich.

Many congregations in the Catholic Archdiocese engaged Crowe and Schulte or Schulte alone to design their parish church. Among the best known are St. Cecilia in Oakley, St. Catherine in Westwood, and Christ the King in Mount Lookout. The partnership of Schulte & Crowe ended in 1933.

Crowe & Schulte *(above)*
St. Monica Roman Catholic Church, 1926–27
328 West McMillan Street, Fairview Heights

The parish enlisted teams of local artists, who worked for more than a decade to complete the elaborate program of art and interior decoration.

St. Monica, interior with apse mural *(above, far right)*

The Ravenna basilica of Sant' Apollinare in Classe was a design source for the building and the apse mural.

Paramount Theater

Cincinnati's grand movie palaces were located downtown between Fifth Street and Sixth Street. The Albee Theater on Fountain Square was the public favorite, and its demolition provoked widespread protests. The downtown movie theaters attracted their largest audiences on Saturday nights; during the week, people tended to patronize the lesser entertainment venues in the hilltop suburbs. Architect Edward J. Schulte designed this theater and office complex for Mrs. Howard Wurlitzer at Peebles Corner, Walnut Hills. (The theater has been demolished, but the central office section survives.)

Peebles Corner was a streetcar junction, and this historic district was one of the oldest and busiest hilltop neighborhood centers in the city. The second-run, 1,100-seat movie house boasted the area's "first push-button screen widener." A three-story cylindrical corner tower takes advantage of the splayed angle of two major streets and creates an effective neighborhood landmark. The lavish interior was thoroughly eclectic, with exotic Mediterranean features, a true "pleasure house of the people."

Schulte's office was in this handsome complex, which has Art Moderne characteristics. His library contained a book about the architecture of Bertram Goodhue, one of the most talented of the American traditional modernists, and many of Schulte's designs (such as this one) are suggestive of Goodhue's work. Further attesting to his interest in the latest fashions, Schulte's library also contained the popular book *The Metropolis of Tomorrow* (1929),[32] written and illustrated by Hugh Ferriss, an architectural renderer, whose sfumato drawings of the skyscrapers he envisioned for the future city captured the imagination of several generations of architects. Just as the architectural photography of the 1920s influenced new architectural designs, Ferriss's architectural renderings were widely admired and influential in this period. Schulte's soft-edged works are suggestive of Ferriss's mannerist, sfumato style.[33]

Thomas W. Lamb
Albee Theater, 1925 (demolished)
Fifth Street

The exotic interior decoration of the Paramount was almost as lavish as that of the Albee. The interiors of both theaters have been demolished. The Palladian arch of the Albee has been incorporated into the Convention Center.

Crowe & Schulte
Paramount Theater Building, 1931
900 East McMillan Street, Peebles Corner, Walnut Hills

Movie theaters were often designed in modernistic styles that uplifted people dispirited by the Great Depression.

Garber & Woodward with John Russell Pope
Cincinnati Gas & Electric Co. (later Cinergy Headquarters Building), 1928–30
139 East Fourth Street

Stout Doric columns create an impressive entry to the building.

The pyramidal top is a local landmark that inspired the architects of the Times-Star and Procter & Gamble buildings.

Cincinnati Gas and Electric Co. (now Duke Energy Building)

Compared to New York City or Chicago, Cincinnati was late in recognizing the pioneering efforts of contemporary European practitioners of the International Style. Throughout the 1920s and into the 1930s, local corporations and public entities continued to favor traditional styles. However, in the hands of a new generation of architects, classical forms became more streamlined and applied ornament was reduced or eliminated. In line with the persistent Beaux-Arts tradition, sculpture and murals were often integral to the architectural design.

The erection of handsome traditional structures, such as Cincinnati Gas & Electric's corporate headquarters in the heart of the city's central business district, reinforced the pride local business leaders took in being known as "solid Cincinnati."

CG&E moved from West Fourth to this new headquarters on East Fourth in 1930. The fledgling company's first office had been designed by James W. McLaughlin in the tradition of a crisp Renaissance palazzo. This handsome new building underlined the company's rise to a major regional power company. Its style conforms to current architectural theory that the vocabulary used in designing the façade and the massing of the wall units ought to signal the function of the building, describing the character of the occupying entity and the activities that would occur within. In effect, the designer's job was to invest the building with "meaning" by providing visual clues to its role in the life of the community.

John Russell Pope (1874–1937), a New York architect known for his work with the National Gallery and Jefferson Memorial in Washington, DC, designed the exterior. Its updated neoclassicism is in the tradition of Pope's work in the East. The firm of Garber & Woodward was responsible for the program and the massing. The pyramidal top echoes that of the former Union Central Life Insurance Building two blocks to the west, which Frederick Garber designed earlier with assistance—perhaps on the façade and interior—from Cass Gilbert. These two buildings provided inspiration for the Cincinnati Times-Star Building and, ultimately, the twin octagonal towers of the Postmodern Procter & Gamble headquarters.

Sculptor Harry Easton designed the gas-lit stone urns that top the twelfth-story recesses and illuminate the upper stories. The David Hummel Building Co. was the constructor.

The timeless appeal of the building has carried over into the twenty-first century. The building has been renovated and restored, and Cinergy, CG&E's successor, was headquartered here. In 2006, the name was changed to Duke Energy.

Carew Tower Netherland Plaza Hotel Complex

The Carew Tower complex replaced an Emery hotel, arcade, and shopping complex. It expressed the taste and vision of developer John J. Emery Jr. (1898–1976), who was interested in art and architecture and carefully followed the design and construction process of his building projects.[34]

The hotel's scale and opulence reflect the heady optimism and fun-loving spirit of the age. When the Netherland Plaza opened in 1931, contemporaries marveled at the rich, fantastic interiors. The facility also won praise for the ultramodern quality of the plan and the mechanicals. The complex included what was then a state-of-the art parking garage. The pale gold brick exterior of the Carew Tower is an unusual hue for skyscraper construction.

In the dedication booklet, architect Walter W. Ahlschlager (d. 1965) described the innovative multiple-use structure as a "city within a city." Ahlschlager, who practiced primarily in Chicago and New York, claimed that the complex was the "last word" in modernity.

William K. Delano (1874–1960), principal of the elite New York firm of Delano & Aldrich and a contributing architect, has been described as the aesthetic adviser, responsible for the massing of the tower and the geometric exterior design. A friend of Emery, he had designed his contemporary Indian Hill residence, Peterloon, in a traditional Georgian Revival style. Emery was most likely familiar with the handsome skyscraper Delano & Aldrich designed for Brown Brothers in New York City, which appears to be a prototype for the massing of the Carew Tower. The constructor, the Starrett Corpo-

W. W. Ahlschlager & Associates
with Delano & Aldrich
Carew Tower-Netherland Plaza
Hotel Complex, 1929–31
Fifth Street between Vine and
Race streets

The spatial experience of the complex's interior flows from the Race Street entrances up into a grand central lobby, which has been converted to a high-ceiled dining area.

Apollo mural

The cross-landing has a barrel vault with silvery paintings of Diana and Apollo to symbolize arrival and departure. The paintings and decorative arts in the hotel are by anonymous artists and craftsmen, unlike those at Union Terminal, where the artists were recognized and celebrated in the dedication book.

ration, was well known for its grandiose schemes, including an early 1920s proposal for the "tallest building in the world" in New York City, which went unbuilt.[35]

The architects used Beaux-Arts principles in planning the form, interior volumes, and massing of their building, but then they (or their interior designers) turned to contemporary French Art Deco sources to create the desired atmosphere of elegance and modernity.[36]

The Art Deco style was popularized in 1925 with the *Exposition des Arts Decoratifs* in Paris. Publications from the fair supplied a ready made decorative vocabulary for copyists of the latest Paris fashions. The Netherland Plaza's interior designers were especially influenced by the metalwork of Edgar Brandt and Raymond Subes and the Wiener Werkstaette, which was displayed at the Paris Art Deco exposition and well documented in publications. Light fixtures throughout the hotel consist of cut metals in gold and silver, with a flame-like upward flair. Indirect lighting is also used effectively: There is a recessed oval light well in the ceiling of the Hall of Mirrors, and the side walls of the Pavilion Caprice have portholes that emit indirect light. Other Art Deco motifs, some drawn from nature and primitive cultures, appear as art and ornament throughout the public areas of the Netherland Plaza. They contribute to the aura of elegance and exuberance.

The grand lobby has been converted into an open dining room and bar. While much of the polyglot decorative scheme works to fine effect here, the fussy French Rococo murals seem at odds with the simpler forms derived from ancient civilizations. Perhaps they are the designer's ironic comment on the likes of Marie Antoinette (and hotel guests) playing in a faux-primitive setting. At the north end of the room, a short flight of stairs rises to a wall fountain of Assyrian character.

Behind the fountain, a processional space leads to a room that was originally the Restaurant Continentale. Equipped for ice-skating shows, the Continentale was a fashionable dining destination in the 1930s and 1940s. The Hall of Mirrors Ballroom on the third floor and the Pavilion Caprice above it have long been the center of Cincinnati social life.

This was the second hotel built in Cincinnati by the Emery family; Thomas Emery's Sons had developed the Palace, which is now the Cincinnatian. In 1946, John J. Emery Jr. built the Terrace Plaza Hotel, which was also a work of modern art.

When the hotel was renovated in 1982–83, the Emery family commissioned a luminous mural of the city skyline by Tom Bacher, an internationally acclaimed Cincinnati artist.

Garber & Woodward
Dixie Terminal, 1913–21
49 East Fourth Street

From the vaulted interior visitors may view the Suspension Bridge and Kentucky skyline.

Dixie Terminal

Behind the traditional façades of many 1920s buildings lay interior spaces and systems that reflected the latest thinking and technologies. The Dixie Terminal was modern in rationale, consolidating an essential transportation function into a regional system. The building was designed as a streetcar and bus terminal that would connect Ohio with its Kentucky neighbors—hence the name "Dixie." Cincinnati's Taft family was involved with the financing, and two Taft brothers, Councilman Charles "Mr. Cincinnati" Taft and Senator Robert "Mr. Republican" Taft, had their law offices here.[37]

Despite the lively Rookwood tile entry portal, the Dixie Terminal exterior conveys an expression of bland propriety. The restrained Renaissance motifs of the façade may well reflect the Tafts' conservative taste in architecture, just as the building's regional function testifies to their progressive interest in efficient metropolitan transportation.

The firm of Garber & Woodward seems to have inherited several important clients, including the Taft family, from Elzner & Anderson, the well-connected firm in which Frederick Garber and Clifford Woodward trained before they attended MIT. In this relatively early project for their firm, Garber and Woodward demonstrated the ability to exploit the emotive qualities of enclosed space that characterizes much of their work. Some of the firm's other remarkable interiors are in the Cincinnati Gas & Electric Building, Union Central Life tower and annex, and Walnut Hills High School.

Dixie Terminal reflected the traditional Beaux-Arts styling of the grand rail terminals of New York City, Cleveland, and Columbus, Ohio. The Dixie was the last transportation terminal in Cincinnati to be designed in a classical mode. It looks back to McKim, Mead & White's design for Pennsylvania Station (1902–10) in New York City, where McKim's soaring coffered vaults were modeled after the ancient Roman Baths of Caracalla. Dixie Terminal is built more to a human scale, but the interior is still in the grand manner.

The high-vaulted ceiling, decorated with blue and gold cherubs, makes this a favorite downtown interior. The south wall has been opened up with a large window to allow a view of the Roebling Suspension Bridge and the new Freedom Center Museum on the riverfront.

The patterns of the Rookwood tile entry are more "modern" in design than the architecture and interior decoration of the building.

Garber & Woodward
Walnut Hills High School, 1931
3250 Victory Parkway, Evanston

Garber & Woodward had Greco-Roman and Jeffersonian models in mind when they designed the building for this college preparatory school.

The circular library with Corinthian columns and an oculus in the rotunda is one of the most revered spaces in Walnut Hills High School.

Walnut Hills High School

The opening of Walnut Hills High School's new campus was described as being of "more than sectional importance." Top students from all parts of the city were invited to enroll in the six-year college preparatory program, which had a Latin requirement and Greek elective. Since it was a preparatory school, providing a classical education, classical forms must have seemed appropriate to the architect and the client.

Walnut Hills High School rises on a gentle hill in the manner of an ancient temple on an acropolis, leading a contemporary news reporter to praise its "Grecian simplicity." (The design vocabulary actually suggests Roman versions of Greek forms filtered through federal America.) The imposing formal entrance leads to a portico and dome inspired by Thomas Jefferson's designs for the University of Virginia library and his home, Monticello. The architects designed a circular library with Corinthian columns and located it in the rotunda, as Jefferson had in Virginia. At the time, it was believed to be one of the "most modern" school libraries in the United States.[38] More than fifty years later, dedicated alumni contributed generously to the library's restoration.

The Cincinnati Public Schools system expanded geographically and academically in the 1920s as the population moved outward from the core and more students attended high school. Walnut Hills High School and Western Hills High School (constructed 1925–28) in Price Hill were collectors of students from broad geographic areas. Walnut Hills, which was limited to college preparatory studies, was the prototype magnet school for the entire city. Western Hills was a general studies school that served the city neighborhoods of Price Hill and Westwood. For more than a decade, it also admitted noncity students living in the unincorporated areas of Delhi Township and Green Township. Also designed by Garber & Woodward, the "West High" building was less elaborate than Walnut Hills, but it made a serious statement through its Renaissance-inspired details and stately library. As in the other district high schools, the library was singled out for special treatment.

At Western Hills, the walls were decorated with handsome murals by local artist E. A. Volkert. Before West High was built, high school students in the western suburbs and townships traveled by foot and streetcar to Woodward in the basin, and after 1908, to Hughes in Clifton Heights. With the construction of Walnut Hills and Western Hills high schools, the Cincinnati Public School board adopted the public policy of providing metropolitan service. At the time, city school leaders pledged to serve expanding populations in the county, even though they were beyond Cincinnati's political borders. In the 1940s, that policy was retracted and western township residents were denied admission to CPS unless the unincorporated areas agreed to annexation by Cincinnati. When voters rejected that proposal, the Oak Hills School District was organized in the townships.[39] At that time, a number of outlying communities expressed their desire to establish identities separate from the city by incorporating as villages or establishing local tax districts for education and parks.

Depression-era federal financing under the Works Progress Adminisration and other agencies enabled Cincinnati to fulfill its plans for public improvements such as Columbia Parkway, in the foreground, which hugs the hillsides as it winds its way along the Ohio River.

7

The Depression Era

Public Works Provide Essentials and Amenities, 1933–44

THIS CHAPTER BEGINS with the onset of the Great Depression and ends with the expansion of the economy driven by the war effort. The federal government financed most of the architecturally significant work. Among such projects were several post offices, Lunken Airport, park buildings and parkways, public housing, and a new town—Greenhills. Although times were tough, some corporations were able to grow. Among companies that produced buildings of note were Ohio National Life Insurance, Cincinnati Milling Machine, and Wright Aeronautical. Entertainment in the form of motion pictures was also thriving, as exemplified by the 20th Century Theater.

During the 1930s and early 1940s, the economy and building activity were dominated by the Great Depression and World War II. The economic downturn was not as sharp in Cincinnati as in other places because the city's industrial base was more diversified, and bank failures were limited. Some businesses, such as Crosley Radio, Procter & Gamble, and Cincinnati Milacron, prospered during the Depression. A few, such as Ohio National Life Insurance and a local Coca-Cola franchise, took advantage of depressed construction prices to build new corporate and industrial buildings. Nevertheless, the loss of nearly 59,000 industrial jobs and 41 percent of all its wage-earning jobs by 1933 dealt a severe blow to the city's economy, and the construction industry was forced to depend on federal support to a great degree.

Ten weeks after the inauguration of Franklin Delano Roosevelt in 1933, the first Federal Emergency Relief Act provided $500 million for public work programs, to be carried out with the active cooperation of state and local governments. The Public Works Administration (PWA) undertook major building projects, including post offices, courthouses, and dams, that historically had been the responsibility of the federal government. The PWA also spurred construction of massive housing projects to correct slum conditions in the inner cities and create new "communities" in the suburbs. The Civil Works Administration (CWA) employed over 23,000 people in Hamilton County in building roads, sewers, and other public projects.

The Works Progress Administration (WPA), best known of the New Deal agencies, replaced the CWA in 1934 and continued until 1943. During those years, 8.5 million people performed nearly 10 billion hours of WPA work for nearly $9 billion in wages. At its peak, the WPA provided relief to over 3 million people—a third of the nation's unemployed. About three-quarters of WPA projects involved constructing buildings and roadways. The local Civilian Conservation Corps (CCC) camp based in Mount Airy Forest employed hundreds of young African American men in building infrastructure such as dams, roads, and trails and in planting trees.

Most of the projects were planned and sponsored by cities, counties, and other public agencies, which contributed a 10- to 30-percent match toward the total project costs. Armed with its 1925 plan, Cincinnati rapidly took advantage of federal funding to build parkways, viaducts, and recreation and park projects, including the 1,500-acre Mount Airy Forest. The total infusion of federal funds into the Cincinnati area amounted to about $100 million. Government-funded building projects also employed local architects. Large-scale public housing projects Laurel Homes (1936–38) and Lincoln Court (1940–42) were divided among teams of architects to spread the benefits as widely as possible.

In view of the poor economic conditions and suffering of the population, the exuberant forms and ostentatious ornament of the prosperous 1920s now seemed excessive to designers and the public alike. There was also hope that science and technology would lead to economic and social progress and a growing faith in the machine as the means by which this would be accomplished. The practical innovation in the 1920s of aerodynamic streamlining for automobiles, ships, railroad locomotives, and airplanes was applied in the 1930s to consumer goods such as refrigerators, clocks, and radios. Architects also adapted it to buildings, giving them a forward-looking appearance with streamlined profiles, rounded corners, horizontal bands of windows, and sleek new materials such as glass block, aluminum, chrome, and plastics.

At the same time a Modern or International style of architecture was emerging. The movement was advanced in the United States by a critically important exhibition at the Museum of Modern Art in New York in 1932. Co-curated by Philip Johnson and Henry Russell-Hitchcock, the exhibit, entitled "The International Style: Architecture since 1922," helped to define the principles of Modernism. Its principal tenets were rejection of historical styles, emphasis on pure utilitarian functionalism, and treatment of buildings as enclosed spatial volumes rather than as opaque decorated enclosures.

The broader implications of this radical new approach to design were introduced in the United States during the late 1930s by designers and intellectuals who immigrated to escape Nazi persecution. Its two leading proponents were Walter Gropius (1883–1969), who came to head the architectural school at Harvard, and Ludwig Mies van der Rohe (1886–1969), who taught at the Illinois Institute of Technology (IIT) in Chicago and designed its campus. Both had served as director of the Bauhaus School in Germany, and they imported concepts and methods directly from it. More nuanced and adaptable versions of Modernism were also available through the influence of Alvar Aalto (1898–1976), a Finnish architect who briefly joined the faculty at MIT, and his friend and compatriot Eliel Saarinen (1873–1950), who developed the Cranbrook Academy of Art outside Detroit.

"Modern" architects responded to the need for flexible interiors and the new technologies of construction with exterior surfaces that were thin, flat, continuous, and without ornament. This approach corresponded well with the need for efficiency of design during difficult economic conditions, but high style Modernism would not be widely embraced in the United States until after World War II.

Responsibility for the design of federal buildings had rested with the U.S. Department of the Treasury since the creation of the Office of the Supervising Architect in 1852. Although the American Institute of Architects (AIA) perennially argued that private architects would do a better job than government employees, the desire for standardization of design and greater efficiency made in-house production of architectural work desirable. James A. Wetmore (1863–1940), who served as acting supervising architect from 1915 to 1933, reasserted the role of the office in designing all government buildings during his tenure.

Because Wetmore was an attorney rather than an architect, the design of federal government buildings was actually directed by Louis A. Simon (1876–1958), who was superintendent of the architectural section from 1905 to 1933 and followed Wetmore as supervising architect from 1933 to 1939. A well-respected and conservative designer who received his training at MIT, Simon favored classical forms as the most representative of American democracy. During the Depression, these forms persisted in government buildings, but their massing was simplified and their surfaces were flattened, resulting in a sort of "stripped classicism" or "Depression Modern."

Beginning in 1930, emphasis on the role of federal projects in generating work increased, and the supervising architect's office elected to hire private architects for a few of the larger projects. For example, the U.S. Postal Service Main Office (originally known as the Dalton Street Annex) was contracted to Samuel Hannaford &

James A. Wetmore, Supervising Architect
Samuel Hannaford & Sons, Consulting Architects
U.S. Postal Service Main Office, 1932–33
1623 Dalton Street, West End

Built only a few years apart, this building and the downtown Post Office, both designed by Samuel Hannaford & Sons, bear a strong similarity to each other and to other Federal architecture of this period. Completed in 1933, the building's simple block massing, symmetrical composition, and flat walls are relieved by ornamental flourishes, including bas-reliefs of American eagles over the doorways, bronze doors, and elaborate hanging bronze lamps.

Louis A. Simon, Supervising Architect
Samuel Hannaford & Sons, Consulting Architects
Federal Courthouse, former U.S. Post Office and Courthouse, 1937–39
550 Main Street

The courthouse is an excellent example of a monumental public building of the New Deal era. Originally a post office as well as a courthouse until 1995, the building was designed by the locally prominent Samuel Hannaford & Sons under the supervision of Louis A. Simon. The old lobby, running through the building from Walnut to Main Street, was richly outfitted with Rookwood tile, bronze writing tables, and brass light fixtures.

Sons as consulting architect. Built in 1932–33, at the transition between the Hoover and Roosevelt administrations, the building is an excellent example of Depression Modern, with its smooth sandstone walls punctuated by elongated recessed window openings creating the effect of a colonnade on the long façade. Rather than interrupt the front elevation with a central entrance in the Beaux-Arts tradition, this design locates the entrances in the end bays, thus increasing the building's monumentality and emphasizing regularity rather than symmetry. Pylon-shaped light standards and bas-reliefs of American eagles dramatize the doorways. Other decorative elements include bronze doors and grilles, marble floors and wainscoting, and elaborate Moderne light fixtures.

The reinforced-concrete structure stands on thousands of forty-foot-long piles in response to the unstable soil conditions in the Mill Creek basin. Special floodgates in the basement protect the building and its contents. The building was located near Union Terminal's mail-handling building to facilitate moving mail by railroad. By the 1960s, however, most mail moved by truck and air, prompting the construction of an adjoining truck terminal. In the 1980s, the Annex became the Main Post Office and all administrative offices were moved here.

Louis A. Simon,
Supervising Architect
Thomas Harlan Ellett,
Consulting Architect
U.S. Post Office and
Courthouse, 1939–40
Scott Boulevard at
Seventh Street
Covington, Kentucky

This handsome building by New York architect Thomas Harlan Ellett reflects the preferred treatment for government buildings of the New Deal era, with its flat roof and smooth limestone walls, embellished with bas-reliefs.

The former U.S. Post Office and Courthouse on Fifth Street and the Main Office on Dalton Street bear a strong similarity to each other and to other Federal architecture of this period. As with the 1932–33 Dalton Street building, responsibility for the downtown structure, built in 1937–39, was shared by Louis A. Simon, then supervising architect of the treasury, and Samuel Hannaford & Sons as consulting architect. The limestone building displays a similar monumental but understated façade, with the entrances in the end bays. Classical ornament is limited to belt courses and moldings with Greek motifs. On the interior, the amply proportioned post office lobby ran through the building from Walnut Street to Main Street, functioning like an indoor street. It was also richly outfitted with Rookwood tile, bronze writing tables, and handsome brass light fixtures.

With the installment of Roosevelt as president, government agencies were reorganized and new ones established. In 1933, the supervising architect's office was renamed the Public Works Branch and transferred to a newly created Procurement Division, which was to oversee all the federal government's properties, facilities, machinery, equipment, stores, and supplies. When Henry Morgenthau Jr. became secretary of the Treasury in early 1934, he continued the policy that all federal buildings (with a few exceptions) be designed under the supervising architect. Most federal buildings were small and not economical for private architects to handle, but a few larger building projects were assigned to individual consulting architects who were assigned to Washington, DC, on a temporary salaried basis to produce the design as well as the working drawings and specifications. The expectation was that outside architects would provide fresh ideas but greater efficiency would result if the work were performed under the supervision of the trained personnel in the supervising architect's office.

This courthouse replaced Alfred B. Mullett's elaborate French Second Empire Post Office, built in 1876–83, which the federal agencies had outgrown by the 1920s. The new building provided double the amount of usable floor area. By 1950, the federal courts had once again outgrown their space, and additional offices were provided in the John Weld Peck Federal Building across Main Street, built in 1962–64. In 1995, the post office moved out of its grand public space to a skywalk space at 525 Vine Street so that the entire building could be used as a courthouse.

The Covington post office was the result of a rare national competition. As stated above, during the mid-1930s federal architects designed all the public buildings except for a few that were drawn by temporary consulting architects. However, in May 1938 Morgenthau announced two competitions to test the practice of hiring more private practitioners. One contest was for the design for a prototypical small post office. The other was for a $450,000 post office and courthouse building in Covington, Kentucky. As with the small post office project, Louis Simon's office undertook the working drawings and specifications.

The Covington competition, which attracted over 650 entries, yielded designs that reflected the architectural tastes of the era; most were conventional, but a few were "modern." The winning design, by New York architect Thomas Harlan Ellett (1880–1951), reflects the preferred treatment for government buildings of the New Deal era: a sort of pared-down classicism with smooth limestone walls. Ellett's training at the University of Pennsylvania and the American Academy in Rome and experience in the office of McKim, Mead & White in New York had disposed him to traditional forms. Covington's post office and courthouse building, completed in 1939–40, resembles Cincinnati's contemporaneous federal buildings but on a smaller scale.

Ellet's design is enhanced by the incorporation of artwork inside and out. Sculptures of pinecones and needles cap each pilaster, and two stone carvings surmount the entrances. The bas-relief over the north entrance, by French-born New York artist Carl Schmitz (1900–67), titled *Horsebreeding*, depicts a farmer with his arm around a foal, representing the protection provided by the courts to those seeking justice. Above the south entrance, a bas-relief by Danish sculptor Reinhold Hirlund, titled *Tobacco,* features a young woman and her younger brother in a tobacco field. At the south end of the lobby stands a powerful statue by the Austrian-born sculptor Romuald Kraus (1891–1954) of a woman with her arms raised, titled *Justice.* Kraus, who was best known for another statue of Justice in the Newark, New Jersey, federal courtroom, taught at the Cincinnati Art Academy before going to the University of Louisville in 1947, where he taught until his death in 1954. Many New Deal buildings were enriched by murals and sculptures funded by the WPA and PWA as a way to generate employment for artists.

Kruckemeyer & Strong
Lunken Municipal Airport, Administration Building, 1936–37
Wilmer Avenue and Airport Road, East End

The Administration Building reflects the streamlined aesthetic, with stepped massing and flat planar walls, clad in brick and limestone. The two-story lobby is dramatized by a gallery and two colorful murals enabled by the WPA Federal Art Project. The architects for the terminal had been involved with planning the airport since 1928.

Lunken Airport

Lunken Airport, Cincinnati's first municipal airport, was dedicated in 1930. It was built in an area historically known as Turkey Bottom, which was mostly cornfields except for a portion that had been used as a polo field around the turn of the twentieth century. The polo grounds were first used as an airfield during World War I. After the war, Edmund H. Lunken, president of the Lunkenheimer Valve Co., and U.S. Army Major E. L. Hoffman envisioned a permanent airfield there and formed the Lunken Airport Co. in 1922. The site was preferred to Grisard Field in Blue Ash because it offered easier access to downtown and proximity to major thoroughfares and railroads.

The stepped massing and flat planar walls of brick and limestone of the Administration Building reflect the streamlined aesthetic. The two-story lobby is dramatized by a gallery and two colorful murals produced by the WPA Federal Art Project. The architects for the terminal were Kruckemeyer & Strong. Edward H. Kruckemeyer (1886–1965) and C. R. Strong (1890–1968) had been involved with planning the airport since 1928 and had designed a wide range of buildings in the Cincinnati area, including factories, hospitals, and the large housing developments Winton Terrace and English Woods for the Metropolitan Housing Authority.

By 1925, the first runway was completed, the polo club barn was converted to a workshop, and two hangars were moved there from Grisard Field. The airport was leased to the Embry-Riddle Aviation Corp., which was taken over by American Airlines in 1930. Charles A. Lindbergh landed the *Spirit of St. Louis* at Lunken Field, fresh from its record-breaking flight across the Atlantic. In the late 1920s, Ed Lunken agreed to donate the facility to the city if it would commit to expanding and improving it. A bond issue was passed, and in 1928 the city purchased additional lands to enlarge the airport. New hangars and aids for night navigation were installed as well. The federal WPA program funded further improvements, including the Administration Building, which is still in use today. The WPA also converted 200 acres of land northwest of the airport into a recreation area that included a golf course, tennis courts, running and bicycling paths, and playground.

Unfortunately, the building was completed just before the 1937 flood, which destroyed or damaged many Art Deco interior details. These were not replaced when the terminal was rebuilt before World War II. Despite this loss, the building still conveys the ambience of the New Deal era. The murals—one depicting mankind bending under the weight of gravity and the other man freed to fly by aviation—were painted by William Henry Gothard (1908–68), who later became the chief conservator at the Cincinnati Art Museum.

To the east on Airport Road are three brown brick aircraft hangars in the Art Deco style. Hangar 1, the easternmost of the three, was built in 1929. It features a terra-cotta frieze depicting airplanes. The two other hangars are similar in design, with broad bands of steel window sash in the center flanked by decorative brickwork in a chevron pattern at the corners.

Lunken Field served as the local airport for mail until 1947, when the commercial passenger flights were transferred to Boone County, Kentucky. Growing corporate and private plane traffic has kept Lunken active.

PWA/Associated Architects, including Frederick W. Garber; Harry Hake; Potter, Tyler & Martin; Samuel Hannaford & Sons
Laurel Homes, 1936–38
Ezzard Charles Drive, West End

Laurel Homes was the city's first attempt to replace urban blight with modern, sanitary, low-rent apartments for low-income tenants. The layout of the site, eliminating streets to create superblocks and clustering units around courtyards to provide open space, represented a radical departure from the historic development pattern.

PWA/Associated Architects, including Frederick W. Garber; Harry Hake; Potter, Tyler & Martin; Samuel Hannaford & Sons
Lincoln Court, 1939
West End

Landscaping and sculpture were added to give Lincoln Court a sense of place and community.

Laurel Homes and Lincoln Court

After its creation in September 1933, the Cincinnati Metropolitan Housing Authority (CMHA) quickly advanced a plan for "slum clearance." Previous planning by the City Planning Commission and Better Housing League had already envisioned new public housing in the West End, where conditions were notoriously dismal. Residents were packed in at more than five times the city average density, and mortality rates were two to five times higher than in the rest of the city. Most living units had inadequate sanitation; 60 percent still shared outdoor privies. "More than 70 percent of the murders in the city occurred in the basin, particularly in the West End, as did more than 75 percent of the aggravated assaults."[1] The coincidence of population density with poor health, substandard sanitation, and high crime rates convinced city officials that replacing blighted housing with modern, sanitary, low-rent apartments for low-income tenants was imperative.

Using federal funds, the city bought and cleared a thirty-one-acre site just east of Union Terminal, between Lincoln Park Drive (now Ezzard Charles Drive) and Liberty Street and Linn and John streets. The 1,039-unit apartment complex, known as Laurel Homes, was completed in 1938. It was the city's first and largest attempt to improve living conditions in the inner city, and the second-largest housing project built by the PWA in the United States. It was also segregated; African Americans were excluded. They protested; two years later another 264 units were added to Laurel Homes, and in 1941 the 1,015-unit Lincoln Court was completed—all reserved exclusively for blacks. The late Theodore M. Berry, Cincinnati's first African American mayor, described Laurel Homes as "one facet in the emergence of unified action to pursue economic and social justice for blacks."[2]

Laurel Homes illustrated the prevailing concepts about housing in the 1930s. The PWA emphasized standardization of design, low density, communal values, social and recreational opportunities, ample automobile parking, and attention to health, light, and air. The new housing consisted of flat-roofed, two- to four-story brick buildings in a variety of right-angled shapes. The architecture was functional, modern, and uniform. The more significant aspect was the layout of the site. Streets were mostly eliminated to create two superblocks, which enabled pedestrians to circulate free of automobile traffic and increased available open space. The buildings were arranged in formal groupings around courtyards. Altogether the buildings occupied only 24 percent of the property; the remainder was devoted to green space with plantings, a park, and a playground. The openness was enhanced by burying all utilities underground. For the sake of efficiency, a single steam-heating plant provided heat. A community building on the playground and retail buildings on Linn Street rounded out services to this new neighborhood.

Design work for Laurel Homes and Lincoln Court was divided up among several architectural firms in an effort to employ as many different firms as possible. Led by Frederick W. Garber, the associated architects included many of the leading firms in Cincinnati: Charles Cellarius; Potter, Tyler & Martin; Samuel Hannaford & Sons; Tietig & Lee; and Rapp & Meacham. Although there were many architects involved, the character of the components was so uniform that one building was indistinguishable from the next.

In recognition of its local and national historic significance and a desire of the community to mark the fiftieth anniversary of the complex, Laurel Homes was listed in the National Register of Historic Places in 1987. In 1989, it was also locally designated a historic site by City Council. Normally local designation would ensure preservation. In this case, however, the complex was razed in 2000 and replaced by a new mixed-use, mixed-income development of town homes known as City West, which attempts to restore the physical and social fabric of the historic neighborhood that previously existed there. It is ironic that the solution proposed for the social problems of the 1930s—a superblock composed of apartment buildings surrounded by greenspace—came to be seen as the source of social problems in the 1990s. City West, a Neo-Traditionalist and New Urbanist development funded by the federal Hope VI program, consists of owner-occupied and rental buildings that front on a grid of traditional streets.

Greenhills

Roland A. Wank and G. Frank Cordner
Greenhills Community Building, 1936–38
Enfield Street, Greenhills

Along with Greendale, Wisconsin, and Greenbelt, Maryland, Greenhills was one of only three federal Greenbelt communities built. Planner Justin Hartzog, who laid out Greenhills, had assisted John Nolen in planning Mariemont. The curving streets of the subdivision followed the topography of the land. The farmland north of the town was preserved as open space. The Greenhills Community Building is typical of public buildings created under the WPA program. The original principal architect, Hungarian-born Modernist Roland A. Wank, had worked for the New York firm of Fellheimer & Wagner on the design of the Cincinnati Union Terminal and served as chief architect for the Tennessee Valley Authority (TVA). He continued as a consultant after G. Frank Cordner replaced him as principal architect.

In 1935, the Resettlement Administration began a program to build new towns across the country. Championed by Rexford Tugwell, a member of Roosevelt's "brain trust" and administrator of the Resettlement Administration, the movement in new town planning was sparked by the Garden City concept, promoted in England by Ebenezer Howard in the 1890s and early 1900s and realized in a modified version in Mariemont by John Nolen in the 1920s. The aim of the Depression-era new towns project was to provide work for the jobless, support the construction industry through purchase of materials, and lessen crowding in the inner cities by relocating lower-income residents. The new towns were intended to serve as models of modern planned communities and good housing design. The unique feature of these towns was the Greenbelt, a ring of undeveloped green space surrounding the town, meant to separate the town from surrounding built-up areas, reserve land for expansion, and provide for the health and recreation of the residents.

Cincinnati was one of only three cities selected for the first phase of Greenbelt communities, along with Greendale, Wisconsin, and Greenbelt, Maryland. Greenhills was begun in December 1935 with the purchase of 5,930 acres of farmland, and ground was broken almost immediately. The first families moved into Greenhills in the spring of 1938. The town was laid out by Justin R. Hartzog, who had been involved in planning Mariemont. He preserved most of the site's natural character; the curving streets of the subdivision followed the topography of the land, and the best farmland north of the town was preserved as open space. This land was transferred to the Hamilton County Park District and named Winton Woods Park in 1939.

Greenhills was a complete community. It had a modern sanitary and stormwater sewage system, retail center, community center, swimming pool, athletic fields, and playgrounds. In 1940, the Hamilton County Park Board leased 900 acres of land and developed an eighteen-hole golf course. The architecture of the homes, shops, and community buildings was modern. Although the houses are plain, with flat roofs and little decorative detail, they were built with high-quality materials—steel casement windows, copper plumbing, hardwood floors, and stainless-steel sills—for durability and easy maintenance. The retail district, consisting of a row of shops with a shared parking lot, was one of the earliest shopping centers of its type in the Cincinnati area.

The Community Building has some fine examples of public art by local artists who were employed by the WPA. In the Pioneer Room is a mural painted by Paul Chidlaw (1900–89), a native Cincinnati artist and teacher who was described as "Cincinnati's leading modernist" by

Richard Zoellner
Life along the Ohio River, 1938
Greenhills Community Center

Richard Zoellner (1909–2003) was known for his New Deal murals, such as this group in the library of the Greenhills Community Center depicting historical scenes of industry and commerce on the Ohio River. From 1933 to 1942 Zoellner completed a number of public commissions, including murals for the Cincinnati Zoo as well as U.S. post offices in Cleveland, Georgetown, Hamilton, Medina, and Portsmouth, Ohio.

Owen Findsen, art critic for the *Cincinnati Enquirer.* In the library, a frieze by Richard Zoellner (1909–2003) depicts the Ohio River's role in the development of Cincinnati and the surrounding river valley. One scene portrays the great flood of 1937. Born in Portsmouth, Ohio, Zoellner was a graduate of the Art Academy of Cincinnati. In the mid-1940s he joined the art faculty at the University of Alabama Department of Art, where he taught painting and printmaking for thirty-three years. A third mural, 180 feet long and covering three walls in the cafeteria, by Leo Murphy (1906–80), has been painted over. Murphy painted portraits of socially prominent Cincinnatians and taught at the Art Academy of Cincinnati.

The initial residents of Greenhills were limited to those with an income between $1,000 and $2,500 per year, a level that eliminated the unemployed and very poor. In fact, many of the early residents were the workers who built the town. Apartments were open to whites only, who lived in the Cincinnati area, had a steady job, and were inclined to abide by a thirty-page booklet of rules to prevent blight. Even with these exclusionary and paternalistic regulations, there was a long waiting list to get in.

Despite the success of the three Greenbelt towns, the federal government abandoned construction of any further new towns because of the great cost and shifting priorities as the nation prepared for war. After World War II, when the federal government transferred the Greenbelt communities out of federal control, Greenhills was the first to go. In December 1949, the residents formed the Greenhills Home Owners Corporation, which bought the 610-acre tract occupied by the village. Many tenants then bought their apartments or town homes. Today there are nearly 4,400 residents, including many third- and fourth-generation descendants of the original "pioneers." Of the original 5,930 acres belonging to Greenhills, 2,045 acres are now in Winton Woods county park, approximately 530 acres are within the corporate limits of Greenhills, and 3,400 acres were eventually sold to the Warner-Kanter Co. for the development of Forest Park, another planned community. Greenhills has been listed on the National Register of Historic Places since 1989.

Fechheimer & Ihorst
Ault Park Pavilion, 1930

Ault Park pavilion was constructed in a grand Renaissance-inspired design.

R. Carl Freund
Trailside Nature Museum, 1939
Burnet Woods

Completed in 1939 with PWA funding and CCC labor, the Trailside Nature Museum was designed by R. Carl Freund. Despite alteration of the building's original flat roof to a pitched roof in 1975, the design is an intriguing fusion of rustic and Wrightian features, with its rough stonework, horizontal emphasis, irregular plan, and cedar log pergola at the entrance. Other unusual design elements are prominent horizontal bands screening the window on the façade and rounded corners.

Cincinnati's park system was shaped by the vision of George E. Kessler (1862–1923) laid out in his 1907 plan, *A Park System for the City of Cincinnati.*[3] Kessler pointed out the need to relieve crowded conditions and traffic in the city and the importance of securing land before it was developed. He promoted the potential of hillside parks to provide distant views and create desirable residential neighborhoods. Kessler also recommended parkways and boulevards to connect the parks with each other and the residential districts with downtown.

The fact that these projects were already planned gave Cincinnati an advantage in applying for federal assistance. The New Deal enabled construction of Columbia Parkway and left Cincinnati's parks with a permanent legacy of attractive amenities. Nearly half of the 130-plus structures existing in Cincinnati parks today were built during that period, and many of them were designed by the talented architect R. Carl Freund (1902–59). A native of Wisconsin and a graduate of the University of Cincinnati, Freund began his career in 1920 as a draftsman for Fechheimer & Ihorst. He also worked for Zettel & Rapp, John S. Adkins, and Crowe & Schulte.

In 1930, shortly after the onset of the Depression, Freund began contract work for the Cincinnati Park Board. Altogether, Freund designed thirty-seven buildings in Cincinnati's parks during a period of almost thirty years. Up to the 1930s, the design of Cincinnati's park buildings was formal, with symmetrical layouts and Renaissance-inspired pavilions such as those in Mount Echo Park (1928) by Rendigs, Panzer and Martin and Ault Park by Fechheimer & Ihorst (1929–30). At the beginning of his career, Freund also tended to use revival styles, as seen in the Tudor Revival comfort station (1930) in Seasongood Square on Reading Road in North Avondale.

During the 1930s, however, Freund's interest in integrating buildings with nature became more pronounced. In Mount Airy Forest, he applied the rustic style advocated by the National Park Service as the most appropriate for wilderness settings. Shelters, pavilions, and comfort stations were typically built of local fieldstone with exposed log framing and shingle roofs, such as the Oval Shelter (1931) in Mount Airy. The influence of Frank Lloyd Wright is clearly evident in Freund's later work, particularly the Trailside Nature Museum (1939) in Burnet Woods, the open shelter in Mount Echo Park (1940), Oak Ridge Lodge (1948) in Mount Airy Forest, Bellevue Hill Park Pavilion (1955), and the Administration Building (1955) in Eden Park.

R. Carl Freund
Mt. Echo Open Shelter, 1940
Mt. Echo Park

Sitting on the brow of Mount Echo, this imaginative open shelter offers a panorama of the Ohio River valley. This unusual structure consists primarily of a low-hipped roof supported only by two massive stone chimneys. The twisting corbeled brick chimneys are a playful element reminiscent of Elizabethan chimney pots. Built in 1940 under the WPA program, this shelter vividly reflects the influence of Frank Lloyd Wright in its design, including the long horizontal lines, low cantilevered roof, use of natural materials, and prominent fireplaces.

Cincinnati Zoo

Rescued from debt by local philanthropists Anna Sinton Taft and Mary M. Emery in 1917, the Cincinnati Zoo was purchased by the City of Cincinnati and transferred to the Cincinnati Park Board in 1932. During the Depression, the Zoo began a period of progress and growth enabled by funds from private donors, particularly Mrs. Julius Fleischmann, and also from the federal WPA and PWA programs.

The Zoo adopted a plan of capital improvements, including "new state-of-the-art exhibits, visitor facilities, paved parking, new water mains, building repair, and hundreds of new trees and shrubs." The new displays, beginning with a moated Monkey Island in 1930, featured "barless and cageless" naturalistic settings landscaped by Carl Kern, who also created the rocky landscape of Krohn Conservatory.

The Zoo's architects during the 1930s were Fechheimer & Ihorst, whose partnership lasted from 1926 to 1946. The firm is best known for its original design for the Tudor Revival Hebrew Union College campus and the fine Renaissance-inspired Ault Park Pavilion (1930). Its design of the Wilson Auditorium at the University of Cincinnati displayed the firm's ability to employ Art Deco massing and allegorical sculpture, which it developed further in its projects for the Zoo, including the Reptile House.

When it was completed, the Reptile House was rated one of the most modern buildings for the exhibition of animals in the world. It provided variable air conditioning to create environments suitable for all sorts of reptiles, including alligators, crocodiles, turtles, and snakes. The Reptile House was a low, symmetrical building with stepped cubic massing. It was faced with stucco, trimmed with limestone, and decorated with bas-relief panels over the doorways. The fireproof structure of masonry, clad in stucco and trimmed with stone, cost approximately $135,000, a very large sum at the time.

Inside, the convincing displays were set among rocks, sand, or pools and conformed to the conditions required for each type of reptile. The displays featured dioramas painted by five artists working for the WPA's Fine Arts Program: Leo Murphy, Mathias Noheimer, Richard Zoellner, Paul Chidlaw, and Dorothy Blodgett. Unfortunately but understandably, these dioramas were painted over when the Reptile House was converted into an aviary by architects Carl A. Strauss and Ray E. Roush Jr. in 1961–62.

Fechheimer & Ihorst
Former Reptile House, Cincinnati Zoo and Botanical Garden, 1936–37
3400 Vine Street, Avondale

The Reptile House was rated one of the most modern buildings for the exhibition of animals in the world. Architects Fechheimer and Ihorst employed Art Deco massing and allegorical sculpture.

Lazarus Department Store

The original late-1870s department store building was an innovative design by James W. McLaughlin, one of Cincinnati's most skillful nineteenth-century designers. The building pioneered the use of a steel skeleton, which enabled large windows to display wares. The building's enlargement and exterior updating in 1936–38, which nearly doubled its size, was intended to stimulate trade and bring buyers to the lagging downtown. The Lazarus family, who had acquired the store from the Shillitos in the late 1920s, selected Potter, Tyler & Martin, a local firm with Modernist experience, to provide a more fashionable, up-to-date image.

George F. Roth Jr. (1905–89), a younger member of the firm, designed an eight-story addition on the west end of the building and completely renovated the original building. G. Marshall Martin (ca. 1898–1964) and his fellow partner Russell Potter had been associated with Harry Hake's firm before going out on their own in 1933. Martin was trained at the University of Pennsylvania, where he came under the influence of Paul Cret, the Beaux-Arts-trained proto-Modernist who served as consultant for Union Terminal. The firm was renamed the Roth Partnership in 1979 after the death of the other three original partners.

The renovation blended old and new elements together with a new streamlined exterior, featuring rounded corners and horizontal bands and combining traditional and novel materials in unexpected ways. The use of granite, marble, and limestone provided a variety of color and texture to the sculpted cladding, which exhibits stylized Mayan motifs. Over each of the main entrances is a handsome marquee of bronze and nickel, appointed with a bronze electric clock. Glass block was used in the men's clothing department "to provide daylight examination of fabric and color." The interior was modernized and the original skylighted atrium was floored over.

In 1946, the same firm added a new service building on the Elm Street end. When the Lazarus store closed in the 1990s, Towne Properties and PDT Architects rehabilitated and converted the building to housing and office use, reopening the spectacular atrium. Known as the Lofts at Shillito Place, it opened in 1999.

Potter, Tyler & Martin
Former Lazarus Department Store/John Shillito Department Store,
Renovation/addition, 1936–38
151 West Seventh Street

The Lazarus family, which had acquired the John Shillito Department Store in the late 1920s, selected Potter, Tyler & Martin to provide a more fashionable, up-to-date image to stimulate business at the end of the Depression. The use of granite, marble, and limestone provides color and texture to the stone cladding, which is sculpted with stylized Mayan motifs.

Frederick W. Garber
United Way/Community Chest/Red Cross Building
(formerly Ohio National Life Insurance Co.), 1933
2400 Reading Road
Walnut Hills

At a time when only a handful of new office buildings was being built, Ohio National Life Insurance Co. took advantage of rock-bottom prices to expand. It purchased a four-story industrial structure from the Globe Register Co. and hired architect Frederick W. Garber to remodel it. Garber reclad it in limestone and added a massive square tower at the southeast corner using a blend of classical and Art Deco details.

United Way/Community Chest/Red Cross Building (formerly Ohio National Life Insurance Co.)

Like the former Shillito/Lazarus Department store, this building is a Depression-era remodeling of an earlier building, in this case a four-story concrete and brick industrial structure originally built for the Globe Register Co. In 1932, the building was purchased by the Ohio National Life Insurance Co., allowing it to double its office space. A neighboring warehouse and two frame structures were also acquired and demolished to provide room for expansion and parking.

An article in the *Commercial Times-Star* on May 27, 1932, described the purchase as one of the largest of the year. This was remarkable, as economic conditions enabled only a handful of new home-office buildings to be constructed at the time. Nevertheless, Ohio National was able to launch the project by taking advantage of rock-bottom prices and grow to a $200 million company by 1933 through reinsurance consolidations with other companies.

Architect Frederick W. Garber reclad the building in limestone and added a massive square tower at the southeast corner containing the new entrance, elevators, stairway, and restrooms. The front of the building was reoriented from Reading Road south toward downtown. The projected design was symmetrical, with identical wings flanking the tower. The east wall was faced with brick rather than stone in anticipation of a matching addition, but when the building was remodeled in 1951, the building was extended to the north rather than to the east.

This building was one of Garber's first commissions after he began practicing alone near the end of his life. For most of his career, from 1904 to 1932, Garber was associated with Clifford B. Woodward. Until Woodward's death in 1932, the two partners were inseparable in their education, careers and private lives. They attended MIT together and worked as draftsmen for Elzner & Anderson before establishing their own firm. For many years, the brothers-in-law lived and actively participated in the community affairs of Glendale, Ohio, where one of their first commissions, a house for William Cooper Procter, was built in 1904.

The work of the Garber & Woodward firm was generally traditional in style. The Ohio National building is a careful blend of classicism and Art Deco details. Its flattened rectilinear forms, smooth walls, fluted pilasters, and simple parapet suggest muted classical forms. The tower, with a four-story recess with a bas-relief at the top, curved windows, and ornamental metal work, reflects a more exuberant modeling and decoration. Garber described his approach to the design as "the simplest architectural expression, which . . . by its solidity and strength is indicative of an insurance company."[4]

In 1959, the building was purchased by the Community Chest for $1.3 million, thanks to a gift from the Cincinnati Milling Machine Co. (later Cincinnati Milacron) and the family of its founder, the late Frederick A. Geier and his widow, Juliet E. Geier. Mr. Geier had also been instrumental in founding the Community Chest in Cincinnati, and the building is dedicated to his memory. Ohio National moved to a new building on William Howard Taft Road in 1960, when it celebrated the fiftieth anniversary of the company. In 1996, the company moved to Blue Ash.

20th Century Theater

During the Depression, motion pictures were a popular and welcome diversion from the worries of everyday life. During the 1920s, the design of movie theaters had evolved into a new building type as architects created enormous motion picture palaces with ornate, exotic, and atmospheric architectural expressions. By the late 1930s, however, theaters were updating to the latest styles and technology to attract attention.

On opening day, August 1, 1941, the 20th Century Theater was acclaimed as "the most modern theater in Cincinnati; the finest suburban theater in the entire Midwest; a super deluxe colossal in every respect."[5] With its sculptured massing, rounded marquee, undulating wall, and soaring sign, it exhibits the most flamboyant use of streamlined Moderne architecture in Greater Cincinnati. Smooth terra-cotta in eye-catching colors of magenta, mauve and blue dramatizes the asymmetrical façade. The sign tower, which carries the name of the theater in large neon letters, is nearly eighty feet high. The heavy glass front doors were designed to open with a fingertip. Original interior innovations included indirect lighting, spring-back, cushion-armed chairs, improved acoustics, loveseats, and air conditioning.

The theater's original owner, Willis Vance, owned numerous theaters in the area, including the Ohio in Norwood, the State in Newport, and the Guild in Walnut Hills. The 20th Century Theater was built by F&Y Building Service of Columbus, Ohio, and designed by architect Fred W. Stritzel, who was employed by the company from 1934 to 1943. The booming motion picture business enabled companies like F&Y to focus exclusively on theater architecture and construction. Organized in 1920, F&Y was very prolific during this period, building theaters all over Ohio, West Virginia, Kentucky, and Indiana. Other designs by Stritzel are the Sunset (1941) in West Price Hill, Westwood (1940), Ridge (1942), and Mariemont theaters.

In 1983, the 20th Century closed after a decade of showing second-run movies. After interim uses as a flooring store and a church, the building was renovated and reopened in 1997 by an Oakley entrepreneur who converted the theater to a cabaret-style concert hall. The theater still retains its original doors, marquee, poster windows, ticket booth, and terra-cotta, and provides an important anchor of activity on Oakley Square.

20th Century Theater, 1941
3021 Madison Road, Oakley

The 20th Century Theater, hailed as the finest suburban theater in the entire Midwest upon its opening, exhibits flamboyant use of streamlined Moderne architecture, with its sculptured massing, rounded marquee, undulating wall, and soaring sign. It was the first air-conditioned theater in Cincinnati.

Coca-Cola Bottling Plant

When the Coca-Cola plant was completed in 1938, it was one of the most modern plants in the Midwest. Like the other commercial buildings mentioned above, the local Coca-Cola bottling facility signified the emergence of the local economy from the depths of the Depression. It was a triumph of American enterprise and imagination. For investors William O. Mashburn Jr. and J. Cromer Mashburn, this impressive new facility realized their dream of a greater and more beautiful plant and a tribute to their father, who worked for the company in Atlanta thirty years before coming to Cincinnati and understood its economic potential early on.

Architect John Henri Deeken (1888–1974), who practiced locally from 1907 to 1948, was best known for his Tudor Revival and Neo-Georgian mansions in Indian Hill. In his design of the Dana Avenue plant, however, Deeken made a stylistic departure from his more conservative residential work. Reflecting an Art Moderne influence, the building presents a sleek limestone façade with its central entrance emphasized by a three-story cylindrical tower with a tiered top. Other Moderne details include horizontal bands of windows with grouped aluminum sash alternating with glass block, chevron motifs, and swooping aluminum railings. The interior features marble and olive-wood paneling, stainless-steel trim, and geometric light fixtures. Terrazzo floors with rings of green, red, and cream are used throughout the public spaces.

The streamlined modern architecture helped to promote the image of Coca-Cola as an efficient manufacturing operation.

The spectacular two-story entrance lobby is dramatized by semicircular stairways that wind up the front wall, which is decorated with a mural by John Holmer Jr. The mural portrays people enjoying bottles of Coca-Cola under umbrellas, in soda shops, at work breaks, and at local recreational spots: Old Coney Island, Sunlite Pool, and River Downs Race Track. There are also scenes of men and women working in the plant itself. The murals express the social importance of work as well as the enjoyment of increased leisure time enabled by it.

In 1986, Coca-Cola moved to a new facility at Duck Creek Road. The building was purchased and rehabilitated as the headquarters of F&W Publications, then owned by Richard and Lois Rosenthal. After F&W was sold in 1999, Xavier University purchased the building.

John H. Deeken
Former Coca-Cola Bottling Plant, 1938
1507 Dana Avenue, Evanston

Architect John H. Deeken used streamlined styling to create the image of an efficient manufacturing operation. The building presents a sleek limestone façade with banded windows and a central entrance emphasized by a three-story round tower.

Austin Co. and Paul Philippe Cret, design consultant
Cincinnati Milling Machine (Cincinnati Milacron) Engineering and Services Building, 1941 (demolished 2001)
Marburg Avenue, Oakley

The threat of war in Europe led Cincinnati Milacron, a world leader in the production of machine tools, to enlarge its Oakley plant. The new Engineering and Services (E&S) Building, which housed the corporate offices, was completed in 1941. Designed by Paul Philippe Cret with the Austin Co., it was an elegant, streamlined yet monumental design characteristic of "Depression Modern" industrial buildings of the period. Its U-formal composition and low, horizontal form reflect the trend toward expansive suburban campuses built for industry beginning in the mid-twentieth century.

Cincinnati Milacron Engineering and Services Building

The vast expansion in the late 1930s and early 1940s of the company formerly known as Cincinnati Milling Machine until 1970, and then as Cincinnati Milacron, signaled the recovery from the Great Depression and the industrial mobilization for World War II. A world leader in the production of machine tools, the company had moved to Oakley to a new plant designed by Detroit-based architect Albert Kahn with local firm Rapp, Zettel & Rapp and built in stages from 1907 through 1915. The new complex was as self-sufficient as possible, with its own foundry to produce castings, a power plant to provide electricity, steam, and compressed air, its own water plant, and a railroad line and station to transport employees to and from work.

During the 1930s, domestic sales dropped, but overseas and export business helped keep the company afloat. By the late 1930s, impending war in Europe led the company to plan for expansion. The plant expansion was designed in 1941 by the Austin Co. and built by the Ferro Concrete Construction Co. (now Turner Construction), which had first gained renown for its role in the Ingalls Building (1903), the world's first reinforced-concrete skyscraper. Defense work kept the company busy throughout the war.

The renowned architect Paul Philippe Cret, who a decade earlier had consulted on the Union Terminal, assisted the Austin Co. with the Engineering and Services (E&S) Building, which housed the corporate offices. It was an elegant, streamlined, yet monumental design that was characteristic of "Depression Modern" industrial buildings of the 1930s and early 1940s. A five-part, U-shaped formal composition, its low, horizontal form and flat roofs reflected the trend toward expansive suburban campuses built for industry beginning in the mid-twentieth century. The building's orange brick façade was articulated by setbacks, and the entrance was emphasized by a broad flight of steps, framed by sleek light standards on stone pylons.

The Cleveland-based Austin Co. was one of the most important innovators in the construction industry during the mid-twentieth century. The Austin method of "undivided responsibility," the standardization of factory construction, the company's contribution to Depression Modern design, and the development of the controlled-conditions plant are among its noteworthy achievements and propelled the company's growth. In the Austin method, the client contracted with one organization that handled all the activities of design, engineering, and construction. This process brought together engineering and architectural design in order, it was thought, to ensure speed, efficiency, and economy.

Cincinnati Milacron passed from the hands of the Geier family in 2000 and shortly afterward divided into two companies: Cincinnati Machine, which was purchased by Unova and moved to Kentucky, and Milacron, which focused its business on plastics. The plant in Oakley was demolished in 2001 to make way for a big-box retail shopping center.

Albert Kahn Associates
Wright Aeronautical Corp. (now General Electric Aircraft Engines), 1940–41
Evendale

Upon its completion in 1941, Wright's new plant in Evendale was the largest defense project in the aircraft industry. The machine-shop assembly building alone provided more than thirty-seven acres of unobstructed floor space. Designed by Albert Kahn (1869–1942), the building is an expression of modern functionalism, a steel-framed, single-story workspace with a two-story office extension presenting a formal façade to I-75.

Wright Aeronautical Corp. (now General Electric Aircraft Engines)

Another major industrial investment occurred in 1941, when Wright Aeronautical Corp. completed construction of a huge new defense plant in the upper Mill Creek Valley. A site just north of Reading was chosen because space for large-scale manufacturing in the city was limited by the 1930s. The area around the plant was still occupied by farms and residences for working-class families, but it rapidly evolved into an industrial center, which was incorporated as the village of Evendale in 1953.

The plant's designer was Albert Kahn (1869–1942). Known for his pioneering designs for the Ford Motor Co., Kahn built about two thousand factories between 1900 and 1940. At its peak in the late 1930s, Kahn's firm employed a staff of over 600 and produced nearly a fifth of all architect-designed industrial buildings in the United States. The firm's standardization of factory and other facility design allowed it to produce a huge volume of military projects during World War II. Other local projects by Kahn include factories for Ford in Walnut Hills (recently renovated) and Chevrolet and Fisher Body in Norwood (demolished).

Kahn played a pivotal role in the evolution of the industrial building type, initially in the development of the multistory concrete-frame structure and later in the design of single-level factories with steel frames. His first plant for the Ford Model T, built in 1909 in the Detroit suburb of Highland Park, was a reinforced-concrete building several stories high. His next plant for Ford abandoned the multistory factory concept in favor of a single-story building. The early factory was vertically organized; materials and parts were lifted to the upper floors and gradually lowered as they were assembled until they emerged as in complete cars at the ground floor. Once electric motors were introduced to manufacturing, gravity was less of a factor and work was reorganized on a single level. To light the interiors of these vast horizontal work areas, Kahn used sawtooth light monitors and continuous bands of metal windows on the exterior. His approach to the design of industrial buildings was revolutionary. While nineteenth-century architects wrapped industrial buildings in decorated façades and traditional forms, Kahn was more concerned with the function of the space than with architectural style.

The Evendale plant was part of a massive expansion of Wright's manufacturing facilities aimed at meeting the war effort. The plant in Cincinnati manufactured Cyclone 14-cylinder radial air-cooled engines for military airplanes. Cincinnati offered familiarity with industrial processes, accessibility to transportation, and plentiful sources of fuel, power, and water, as well as skilled workers because of the local machine-tool heritage. Upon its completion, the Wright plant was the largest defense project in the aircraft industry, covering over two million square feet of floor space, or about fifty acres. The machine shop and assembly building alone provided more than thirty-seven acres of unobstructed floor space.

The building is an expression of modern functionalism and one of the last built under the supervision of Kahn, who died in 1942. It consists primarily of a steel-framed, single-story workspace surmounted by a sawtooth roof of skylights. The exterior elevations are articulated by continuous horizontal bands of steel windows and buff brick masonry. A smaller, flat-roofed office extension of similar design on the west end with a colonnaded entrance pavilion provides the building's public face along the highway. The plant was acquired by General Electric in 1949 to manufacture jet engines and continues in operation to this day.

The Terrace Plaza Hotel, Cincinnati's first major postwar building, developed by Thomas Emery's Sons and designed by Skidmore, Owings & Merrill, represented the modernization of downtown.

8

Modernizing the City, Post–World War II

1945–64

CINCINNATI'S GREAT ECONOMIC growth after World War II enabled the city to modernize its infrastructure and architecture. The 1944–48 Metropolitan Master Plan envisioned the city as a commercial center surrounded by residential suburbs and connected by a network of highways. The ascendancy of the automobile and the lure of a better life in suburbs spurred the creation of shopping malls such as Swifton Commons and new housing in communities such as Forest Park. Modernism was fully embraced, beginning with the Terrace Plaza Hotel downtown and followed by public buildings such as the public library, park pavilions, firehouses, and schools, as well as churches and corporate headquarters.

Like the rest of the country, Cincinnati experienced great economic growth and expansion after World War II. Pent-up demand from years of a depressed economy and war rationing created a huge market for consumer goods. There was also an enormous need for housing. Families who had doubled up during hard times were eager to set up their own households, and the return of war veterans created a wave of marriages and births that put further pressure on the housing market.

To help meet the demand for housing, the government underwrote construction of vast developments of moderately priced homes. The Federal Housing Administration (FHA) guaranteed loans to builders, and federally insured mortgages for homebuyers required only small down payments and offered low, fixed-interest rates. Growth was further encouraged by government investment through the Federal Highway Act of 1956 in a new interstate highway system that connected cities and provided easy access to suburban neighborhoods.

In Cincinnati's Metropolitan Master Plan, released in segments between 1944 and 1948, planner Ladislas Segoe envisioned a new urban form, with downtown as a civic and commercial center within a network of limited-access highways and surrounding suburbs. Two major highways were planned: the Millcreek Expressway (I-75), winding through the industrial corridor along the Mill Creek toward Dayton; and the Northeastern Expressway (I-71), running through the Deer Creek Valley toward Columbus. These highways were linked by a series of connectors: at the riverfront by Fort Washington Way, named after Cincinnati's original military outpost; by the Norwood lateral highway about 15 miles north; and by a cross-county highway, now known as the Ronald Reagan Highway, still farther north.

The central riverfront, which had deteriorated after the devastation of the 1937 flood, was seen as potentially valuable land because of its convenience to downtown. The 1939 Redevelopment Plan for the Central Riverfront began to address issues such the declining property-values, blighted buildings and traffic snarls. After a hiatus caused by World War II, the 1948 master plan recommended complete clearance and redevelopment of the riverfront for a broad range of civic and recreational uses. In place of industries, produce warehouses, and deteriorated housing, the plan envisioned new buildings for municipal courts and public safety departments (police, fire, and traffic) a new state office building, convention center, hotels, museums, shops, apartments, parks, bus terminal, heliport, and a new multisports stadium to replace the outdated Crosley Field in the West End. Along the north edge a library, natural history museum, and historical museum were envisioned.

As time passed, however, one after another of these envisioned facilities was built elsewhere. Cincinnati Gardens, a new 8,000-seat arena and auditorium, was developed privately and opened in 1949. Its location on Seymour Avenue between Bond Hill and Roselawn was considered more central to the new suburbs and accessible than the riverfront. Other facilities were scattered around downtown. The Natural History Museum was built on Gilbert Avenue in 1955–57; the Convention Center opened at Fifth and Elm streets in 1967 and expanded to the west in 1985–87; the bus terminal moved to Gilbert Avenue in 1970; and a new building for city offices was built near City Hall in 1987–88. In the meantime, the area west of the Suspension Bridge became an expanse of parking lots with a few produce markets. It was not until 1970 that a new stadium, coliseum, and luxury high-rise housing were finally completed in the area east of the bridge.

As for downtown, postwar planners believed that it would become more exclusively devoted to commerce and civic uses. Housing was considered undesirable for downtown and more happily situated in outer neighborhoods. The plan proposed no new housing in or near downtown except for a few apartment towers on the river. The West End, with its concentration of dense and dilapidated housing, was to become an industrial park because of its proximity to downtown and access to river, rail, and highway transportation. Gradually much of this old residential neighborhood was erased through urban renewal and interstate construction.

The postwar baby boom stimulated a wave of new single-family home construction in the suburbs, especially in the unincorporated areas west and northwest of the city, including Delhi, Colerain, and Springfield townships. There were also new multifamily, medium-density housing developments for lower-income residents, such as English Woods, Valley Homes, and Winton Terrace. Development was further spurred by the construction of a ring highway, Interstate 275; the first section of which was built in 1958–61. The expressway's greatest impact was on Forest Park and Colerain Township, where new residents, businesses, and industries were attracted by the combination of plentiful land and easy access to the highway system.

Forest Park, a complete new town, was built in the mid-1950s on farmland that was once part of Greenhills. After the war, the federal Public Housing Authority, preparing to dispose of undeveloped portions of the Greenbelt towns, hired Justin R. Hartzog, the chief planner of Greenhills, to create a preliminary plan for a second new town named North Greenhills. In 1952, the land was purchased by the Cincinnati Citizens Development Committee, a group of corporate leaders who supported the goals of the 1948 master plan and wanted the project completed.[1] A private developer, the Warner-Kanter Corp., took over in 1954. Marvin L. Warner and Joseph H. Kanter, both natives of Alabama, established themselves among Cincinnati's greatest entrepreneurs. After the war, the two formed a partnership to build low-cost federally insured apartments in the Birmingham area, and then expanded into the Midwest. Warner-Kanter, which envisioned a modern middle-class American utopia, renamed the new town Forest Park to distinguish it from the low-income image of Greenhills during the New-Deal era. Yet they were committed to creating a complete community, with shopping, recreational facilities, churches, schools, offices and light industries, and they donated land for civic and social purposes. Miss America served as the official hostess at the public opening in 1956. Today Forest Park is the third-largest city in Hamilton County and takes pride in the cultural, racial, and socioeconomic diversity of its 20,000 residents.

With the development of new residential areas came suburban shopping centers and new corporate campuses. The Jonathan Woodner Co., a New York-based developer, announced plans drawn by Ketchum, Gino & Sharp in 1953 for the Swifton Shopping Center on a forty-one-acre tract at the southeast corner of Reading Road and Seymour Avenue on the northern edge of Bond Hill. Envisioned as Cincinnati's first regional shopping center, it featured a Rollman's department store and fifty-four smaller shops in an "ultramodern" design, clustered around a landscaped open-air plaza with covered sidewalks and surrounded by parking for 3,000 cars. Swifton Village, an adjoining apartment complex for 4,500 residents, was expected to generate a steady stream of customers. Neighborhood opposition triggered

Swifton Shopping Center, 1956
Reading Road, southeast corner of Seymour Avenue, Bond Hill

Completed in 1956, the former Swifton Shopping Center in Bond Hill was envisioned as Cincinnati's first regional shopping center. It featured a department store and smaller shops clustered around a landscaped open-air plaza with covered sidewalks and surrounded by parking. This photo shows the courtyard after renovation by PFB Architects in 1985.

by concerns about traffic congestion delayed construction until 1955, when a New Orleans firm took over the project. Unfortunately, the desired regional market never materialized at this location; it was simply too far from the nearest highway interchange, and the low income levels of the surrounding neighborhoods made it minimally viable for retail. (Now known as Jordan Crossing, the mall has been renovated several times and largely converted to educational, church, and office uses.)

In the same year that Swifton Shopping Center opened, it became outmoded by the first enclosed, climate-controlled shopping center: the Southdale Mall near Minneapolis. Conceived by Victor Gruen, an Austrian-born architect who became a leader in shopping-center design, this new mall was considered a marvel in its day. The same model was followed in Tri-County Mall, which was developed in the early 1960s at the interchange of I-275 and state route 747. When the site was selected, the area was still rural in character, but highway access and its enclosed mall design have made it a successful retail location for thirty-five years.

Corporate offices and manufacturing plants flourished after the war in a time of renewed optimism and continued confidence in progress through technology. In 1948 alone, there were thirty-eight new industries established in Cincinnati, with over a thousand employees. Some were gigantic, such as the new aircraft gas-turbine division of General Electric north of Lockland at the former Wright Aeronautical aircraft plant. In that same year, over eighty companies expanded their facilities, including American Tool Works Co., Cincinnati Chemical Co., Cincinnati Gas & Electric, Crosley Motors, Hilton Davis Chemical Co., Procter & Gamble, and Westinghouse Electric & Manufacturing Co.[2]

Confidence in the ideals of progress and technology during the postwar era was expressed in these and other major commissions through the rising popularity of architectural forms originated in Europe during the Modern Movement of the 1920s and 1930s. What came to be widely known in America as the "International Style" (after a Museum of Modern Art exhibition co-curated by Philip Johnson and Henry Russell-Hitchcock) was initially derived from the rational industrial process and so was a perfect fit for these new factories.

Progressive designs during the the 1950s and 1960s, the heyday of Modernism in America, were based on functional analysis and structural efficiency, as well as purely aesthetic intentions, such as reflective transparent surfaces, asymmetrical abstract volumes, and an absence of traditional ornament. By purifying architecture around these key principles, Modern architecture hoped to provide inexpensive housing and solve urban and social problems while providing a more open and clean image for the built environment. There was little building for civilians during the war, so the initial impact of this new thinking was felt in the design of war-industry housing in the early 1940s. After World War II, however, a more mature and doctrinaire version of this aesthetic ideology took hold, proliferating in commercial and institutional architecture, and to a lesser degree in housing.

Commercial and corporate architecture in the Modern mode became an increasingly important tool for public relations. Well beyond its origins as an efficient design and construction methodology, and beyond its idealistic wish to solve social problems, it was now adopted by corporate America and other large patrons as a form of advertisement, a superficial expression of progress, idealism, enlightened thinking, rationality, and control. Like their predecessors in the 1910s and 1920s, local corporations, government, and institutions of the 1950s and 1960s preferred a more conservative blend of traditional forms with a modern surface treatment.

In the Cincinnati area, the Natural History Museum (1958) at 1720 Gilbert Avenue by Cordes, Pressler & Hauck (vacated in 1990 and demolished in 2002 to make way for WCPO-TV) was a formal composition of simplified classical forms in a smooth stone skin. A new Christ Church (1957) was built, designed by architect

Potter, Tyler, Martin & Roth
Former Ohio National Life Insurance Co. Building, 1961
William Howard Taft Road

Completed in 1961, the former home office building of Ohio National Life Insurance Co. presents a three-part massing with smooth limestone walls articulated by varied vertical groupings of windows. While modern, the design was intended to convey the traditional dignity of this financial institution.

David Briggs Maxfield of Oxford, Ohio, with traditional gabled massing and flat façades (It has since been remodeled twice to make it still more traditional.) Public buildings of this period tended to be conservative, including the appealing but backward-looking Art-Moderne North Avondale School (1949) by E. C. and E. T. Landberg and the rectilinear Cincinnati Police Headquarters at 310 Ezzard Charles Drive (1955). There were a few exceptions, however, that expressed a more full-blown International style, such as Woodward High School in Bond Hill (1953) (demolished in 2005) by Charles Cellarius, with its horizontal lines and window bands, and the Ninth Street Fire Station at Broadway (1951) by Woodie Garber, with its transparency and bold geometry. Procter & Gamble's 1956 headquarters by Voorhees, Walker, Smith & Smith and Ohio National Life Insurance's headquarters at the southwest corner of William Howard Taft Road and Highland Avenue by Potter, Tyler, Martin & Roth also presented a restrained approach to Modernism. The John Weld Peck Federal Building (1962) by Potter, Tyler, Martin & Roth and Harry Hake & Partners is a modular composition in stone with a grid of narrow windows nearly flush with the wall surface—free of ornament as the International style dictated, but also without any of the style's soaring dynamism or progressive idealism.

Among the most daring designs in Cincinnati in the period in the Modern style were the Terrace Plaza Hotel (1943–48) by Skidmore, Owings & Merrill (SOM); the Cincinnati Public Library (1954, 1983) by Woodie Garber; the Bellevue Hill Park Pavilion (1955) by R. Carl Freund; and St. John's Unitarian Church (1959) by John M. Garber. But more experimental approaches were not always successful. The Kroger Co. headquarters (1954) was downtown's first skyscraper with a lightweight curtain wall. It was designed by Wyatt C. Hedrick (1888–1964) of Fort Worth, Texas, who operated a nationwide architectural practice from 1925 through the 1950s. Originally clad in a blue-and-white checkered pattern, the Kroger Building was more tastefully redressed in conventional horizontal metal bands by GBBN in 1980. The alteration was inspired more by economy than by aesthetics.

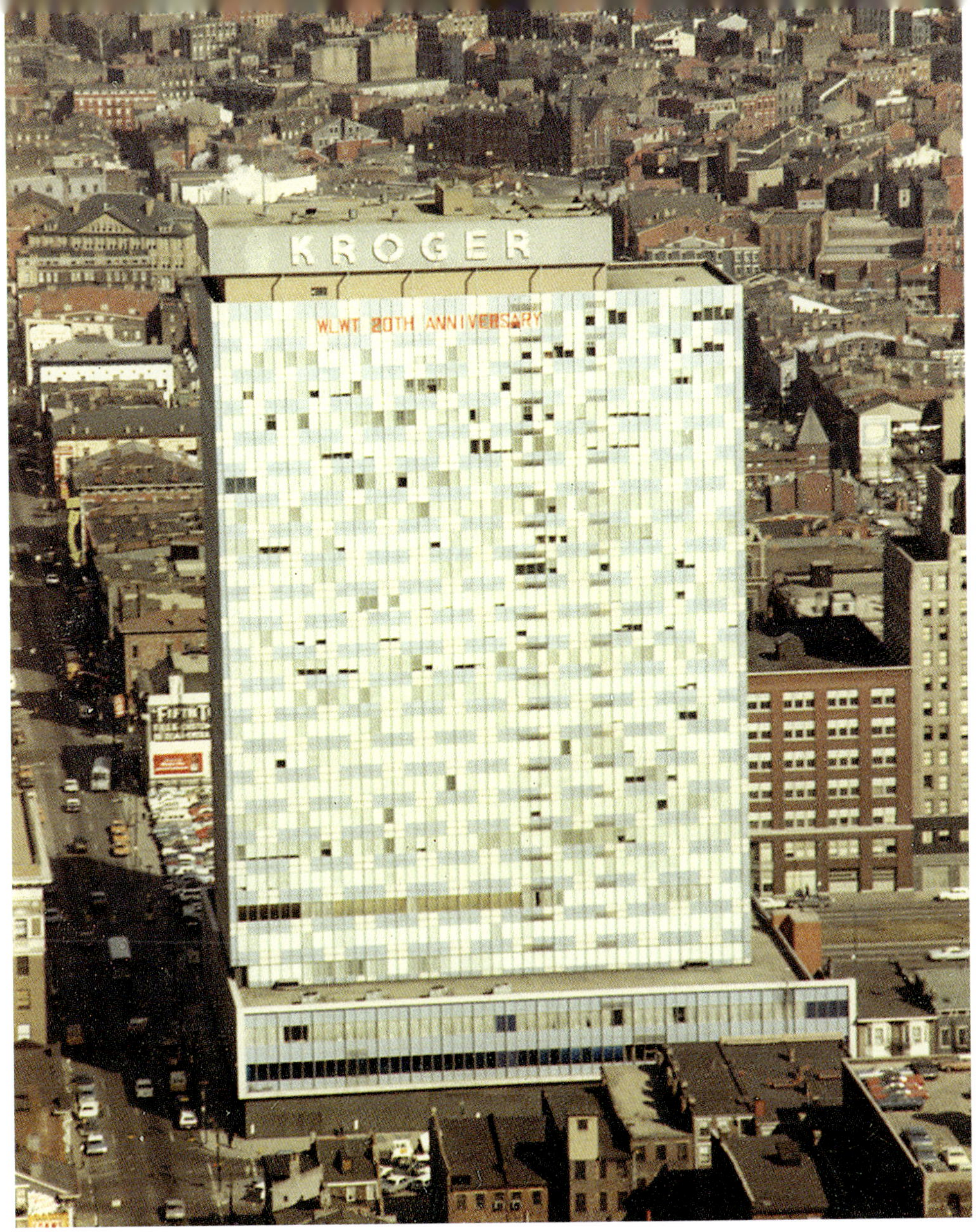

Wyatt C. Hedrick
Kroger Co.
Headquarters, 1954
Renovation:
GBBN, 1980
1014 Vine Street

The Kroger Co. headquarters by Wyatt C. Hedrick of Fort Worth, Texas, was downtown's first skyscraper to exploit a lightweight curtain wall. In 1980, it was reclad by GBBN.

In the late 1950s, some corporations began to move out of the center city to the suburbs and beyond, just as their clients and workers were doing. Relocating enabled them to obtain larger building sites at lower cost and with access to highways. The Gibson Greeting Card Co. moved to suburban Amberley Village, and Union Central Life Insurance relocated to a rural setting in Forest Park for its sprawling new headquarters. Their new buildings adopted the ground-hugging and land-consuming horizontal massing, smooth surfaces, and window bands typical of this period.

As one would expect, the University of Cincinnati was very receptive to the Modern aesthetic. Procter Hall (1968) by Woodie Garber, Siddall Hall (1964) and Calhoun Hall (1967) by Tweddel, Wheeler, Strickland, Beumer, and the original French Hall (1953) and Dabney Hall (1960) by Potter, Tyler, Martin & Roth are examples. The most successful are the first two portions of the College of Design, Architecture, Art and Planning (DAAP): the Alms Building (1952) and the original DAAP Building (1958) by James E. Allan. Allan, a graduate of UC's College of Engineering, practiced from 1946 to 1969 and taught at the UC Evening College

James E. Allan
Alms Building, 1952; DAAP Building, 1958
University of Cincinnati

The Alms Building (1952) and the original DAAP Building (1958) of the College of Design, Architecture, Art and Planning were designed by James E. Allan, a graduate of UC's College of Engineering. Taking cues from the most influential European design school, Walter Gropius's Bauhaus at Dessau, Germany, of 1926, the asymmetrical massing of Alms is broken into individual geometrical components. Yet the use of red brick mitigates the starkness of Modernism.

from 1932 to 1963. Taking cues from the most influential European design school, Walter Gropius's Bauhaus at Dessau, Germany, of 1926, the asymmetrical massing of Alms is broken into individual geometrical components. Rather than relying on a regular pattern of fenestration, windows relate to the interior spaces. The entire north wall is transparent, providing northern light ideal for drafting. Stairways with brightly painted pipe railings are revealed behind glass for their full height, adding interest to the exterior.

Cincinnati's leading Modernist was Woodward "Woodie" Garber (1913–94). In contrast to his father, Frederick W. Garber, whose firm Garber & Woodward was known for its traditional designs, Woodie embraced the new. After training at Cornell and working for John Russell Pope, SOM, and his father's firm, he established his own office in 1953. He helped shape the Architectural Foundation of Cincinnati, and was presented with a President's Award from the American Institute of Architects in 1982 in recognition of his influence on local architecture.

Woodie Garber was a remarkable innovator who at times attracted exceptional publicity for his unbuilt projects—schemes often beyond the conceptual reach of his patrons or the city. In the mid-1940s, he designed a glass-sheathed, reinforced-concrete skyscraper tower on Lytle Park for Schenley Industries, a speculative endeavor to persuade the company to move its corporate headquarters from New York to Cincinnati. According to a twelve-page cover story in the inaugural issue of *Progressive Architecture* in 1945, this frankly modern structure would have been the first sealed, climate-controlled building and the first office tower without permanent interior partitions. The building site was directly across the street from the Taft Museum and occupied by two houses at the time. Senator Robert A. Taft Sr. opposed the project, and the site was incorporated into Lytle Park when it was reconstructed in the 1960s after the tunnel for I-71 was built underneath. It is revealing that this design by a native-born local architect was not built, despite the attention and praise it received in a national magazine. Garber's later work is slightly more conservative—thoroughly modern, but not groundbreaking and often somewhat eccentric.

Skidmore, Owings & Merrill
Former Terrace Plaza Hotel, 1943–48
Sixth Street

The former Terrace Plaza Hotel was Cincinnati's first major downtown construction project after World War II. It was an innovative mixed-use complex employing Modernist design principles.

Terrace Plaza Hotel

Cincinnati's first major downtown construction project after World War II was the former Terrace Plaza Hotel (1946–48), one of the first hotels built in America after the war, and maybe the first Modern hotel ever. Commissioned by Thomas Emery's Sons, the Terrace Plaza was an innovative, mixed-use complex combining hotel, office, and retail space in a formula similar to that of the Emerys' Carew Tower/Netherland Plaza Hotel. The project began with leases for J. C. Penney's and Bond's, a stylish apparel store.[3] The Emerys, wanting a decidedly Modern building, selected Skidmore, Owings & Merrill (SOM) in the belief that SOM's lack of previous hotel design experience would foster novel solutions. It did.

The Terrace Plaza was one of the early successes that helped SOM become the preeminent American architectural firm of the post–World War II era. The firm was founded in 1936 in Chicago by three midwesterners, including University of Cincinnati graduate Louis Skidmore; the New York office opened in 1937. Committed exclusively to Modern design, SOM solidified its reputation with New York City's Lever House (1951–52), one of the world's greatest early Modern skyscrapers. SOM became a full-service design firm, combining architectural, engineering, planning, interior, and environmental design and project-management services.

The Terrace Plaza's novel design featured a slim eleven-story hotel tower on top of a mostly windowless seven-story retail and office block. The most distinctive aspect was the placement of the hotel lobby on the eighth floor. Using the zoning setbacks required, the designers created a rooftop terrace at this level that offered outdoor dining in the summer and ice-skating in the winter. There were three glamorous restaurants, including the Skyline Room off the lobby and the legendary circular Gourmet Room, cantilevered provocatively from the penthouse. The building incorporated many advances in design and technology. It was one of the first in the nation to use fully automatic elevators and the first hotel in Cincinnati to offer television sets. It represents only the second known use of thin face brick in stacked bond, in which the vertical joints run continuously, indicating that the brick is not structural.

The Terrace Plaza initiated SOM's interior design department, founded by Benjamin Baldwin, the "dean of interior designers."[4] Stainless steel, marble, leather, and textured fabrics distinguished the public areas. All hotel furnishings were custom-designed, including Thonet molded wood furniture, monogrammed Rookwood ashtrays, china, uniforms, matchbook covers, and even labels on bourbon bottles in the bar. Motorized beds converted into couches, and desks doubled as bars or luggage racks. Movable partitions enabled conversion of two or more rooms into a suite. Specialized lighting included spotlights for reading, makeup lights for bathrooms, and filtered floodlights to enhance colors and textures.

Works by major modern artists enlivened the public spaces: a mobile by Alexander Calder hung in the hotel lobby; a "crazy modernistic mural" by Joan Miró covered the curved wall of the Gourmet Room, and Saul Steinberg's witty drawings of Cincinnati landmarks, one of only six murals by the renowned *New Yorker* cartoonist, sparked up the Skyline Restaurant.[5]

William S. Brown was SOM's partner-in-charge for the project, and the renowned Gordon Bunshaft is credited as the designer, but Louis Skidmore also had a hand in it, and much of the work was done by Natalie de Blois (b. 1921).[6] In a field then dominated by men, her work may not have received full credit.[7] Joining SOM in 1944 with an architecture degree from Columbia University, de Blois designed numerous projects for the firm, including the Pepsi-Cola and Union Carbide buildings in New York. She received a Fulbright Fellowship for study at the École des Beaux-Arts in 1951–52 and was named a Fellow of the American Institute of Architects in 1974.

While the building's original form remains largely unchanged, the original marquee, stylized signs, and furnishings are gone. Expansive windows on Vine and Sixth streets were bricked up above the first floor to reduce glare in the Bond's interior. Retail spaces have since been subdivided and storefronts changed. The artworks were given to the Cincinnati Art Museum in 1965, after the Emery family sold the Terrace to the Hilton Hotels Corporation. Nevertheless, the building remains a local landmark of postwar Modernism.

Woodie Garber & Associates and Samuel Hannaford & Sons, associated architects
Cincinnati Public Library, 1955
800 Vine Street
Additions:
Architekton and F. W. Pressler & Associates, 1982
Shepley Bulfinch Richardson & Abbott and Gartner Burdick Bauer-Nilsen (GBBN)

With its initial completion in 1955, the Cincinnati Public Library's Main Branch was the first such building to be built in the nation after the war. Featured in Time *and* Life *magazines, it was widely recognized for its contemporary design and use of an open plan. It was Garber's single most important executed project.*

Cincinnati Public Library

When the original portion of the Cincinnati Public Library's Main Branch opened in 1955, it was the first postwar main library building in the United States. Featured in *Time* and *Life* magazines, it was widely recognized for its contemporary design and use of open space. Designed by Woodie Garber & Associates with working drawings by Samuel Hannaford & Sons, it was Garber's single most important executed project. The library was organized around subjects in an open plan intended to flex with changing needs, in what library director Carl P. Vitz envisioned as "a department store of knowledge."[8] The exterior design expressed the functions of the spaces inside, with windowless brick expanses and window bands corresponding to floors occupied by closed stacks and open reading rooms. The former Rare Book Room, perched on the roof at the southwest corner, was a distinct rectangular volume with floor-to-ceiling windows. It had vertical stainless-steel louvers to control the light levels.

The main entrance to the library, set back in an angled recess at the southwest corner, was dramatically transparent, with glass windows that sloped outward at the bottom. The brick veneer on the exterior was pulled back from the corners, exposing the thinness of the material and expressing its use as a skin rather than a weight-bearing material. The windows were double-glazed, with heat-absorbing glass for the exterior and inner panes of clear plate, sandblasted on the sealed side to control sky and sun glare. The rectilinear mass of the building was relieved by a serpentine garden wall at the southeast corner, reputedly inspired by Jefferson's garden wall at Monticello, but maybe more by Alvar Aalto's undulating Baker House dormitory at MIT (1946–49).

On the third-floor terrace were reflecting pools and a sculpture by Harry Bertoia (1915–78), an Italian-born artist associated with the Cranbrook Academy of Art. The selection of Bertoia was another example of how current Garber was in his approach to design. In 1953, Bertoia had just received his first major corporate commission from Eero Saarinen for the General Motors Technical Center in Warren, Michigan. In the coming years, his pieces would appear in public places and corporate spaces all over the country.

In 1979–82, a somewhat awkard addition to the library by Architekton and F. W. Pressler & Associates was wrapped around it on the north and east, expanding the library space to Walnut Street, thus forming one of the largest public library buildings in the United States at the time. The 1955 building was reorganized and remodeled to create one integrated facility. An impressive atrium was created, providing natural light into the building and giving users a view of all five floors of the building, including closed stack areas. Several original touches, such as the serpentine brick wall surrounding the garden, the Venetian glass tiles on the columns, and the central service core remain, while the Rare Book Room was converted to a meeting space now known as the Huenefeld Room.

In 1997, the Main Library was renovated again when an addition was built across Ninth Street, connected with a three-story, metal-clad pedestrian bridge. This work was designed by the Boston firm Shepley Bulfinch Richardson and Abbott and local architects Gartner Burdick Bauer-Nilsen (GBBN). The Boston firm is the successor of H. H. Richardson, who was renowned for his Romanesque Revival libraries. The addition responds to the 1950s-era building in fundamental ways—height, material, and floor levels—but it appears more traditional, particularly in the way the two-story square brick columns divide the window bays, in contrast to the thin pipe columns that punctuate the continuous window bands of the older building.

PROCTER & GAMBLE CO. HEADQUARTERS

In 1956, Procter & Gamble built its first corporate headquarters downtown at the corner of Sixth and Sycamore, not far from the Gwynne Building, the company's previous location. Designed by Voorhees, Walker, Smith & Smith, this eleven-story limestone, granite, and marble office building has a regular rhythm of nearly square windows. At the top is a recessed penthouse articulated by pilasters, similar to the attic story of a Greek temple. The regularity, simple massing, and solidity of the building express a sense of competence and conservative calm in contrast to the flashier steel and glass structure commissioned by Lever Brothers, one of Procter & Gamble's competitors. The interior was painted "eye-ease green," and the offices were created with movable metal partitions for complete flexibility.

Voorhees, Walker, Smith & Smith (VWSS) was a New York firm that began in 1885. With rotation of partners over time, it became Haines Lundberg Waehler in 1968, and it is now known as HLW. The firm's first major commission was the Metropolitan Telephone Building, followed by the New York Times Building, the city's tallest structure in 1905 and the icon of Times Square. Ralph T. Walker, who joined the firm in the 1920s, created a series of striking and expressive skyscrapers, including the Barclay-Vesey Building for the New York Telephone Co.

In 1937, the firm designed the nation's first modern research laboratory for Bell Telephone at Murray Hill, New Jersey, based on the flexible-modular concept. In response to tremendous demand in the decade after World War II, the "staid, staunch firm" of VWSS designed a vast number of laboratories and other buildings for telephone and other industries such as Ford, General Electric, International Business Machines, General Foods, Union Carbide, Westinghouse, and Dupont.[9] This experience made them a natural choice as architects for P&G's new headquarters at this time.

In 1972, Skidmore, Owings & Merrill extended the building east to Broadway. The entire half block south of it was cleared and extensively landscaped. SOM, which gained international recognition with the completion of Lever House in New York in 1952, was among the most inventive and active proponents of the Miesian approach. The firm produced many more variations on glass towers for corporate headquarters all over the nation. By 1970, it had 1,000 architects and offices in Chicago, New York, San Francisco, Portland, and Washington, DC. SOM had designed a steel-and-glass tower for this site, but it was not to be. Instead, a nondescript conference and data center and garage were built on the north side of Sixth Street. The plaza was redesigned in 1985 by local landscape architects Bentley-Meisner after construction of the latest twin-towered office building by Kohn Pederson Fox. Cincinnati-based BHDP, in collaboration with CUH2A, recently updated the interior, providing a contrasting new steel-and-glass entrance.

Voorhees, Walker, Smith & Smith
Procter & Gamble Co. Headquarters, 1956 *(section on left)*
Additions to right:
Skidmore, Owings & Merrill, 1972; Kohn Pederson Fox, 1982

With its simple massing, solidity, and regularity of window openings, Procter & Gamble's first downtown headquarters building, designed by Voorhees, Walker, Smith & Smith of New York, expresses a sense of competence and conservative calm.

St. John's Unitarian Universalist Church

The congregation of St. John's seized the opportunity to embrace a dramatic design for their new building on Resor Avenue in Clifton. This church represents a radical departure in image and location for the congregation, which had worshipped in a Gothic-style red brick building at the northwest corner of Elm and Twelfth streets in Over-the-Rhine since the end of the Civil War. The new sanctuary has a strikingly modern design, its façade striated with slender steel spires, yet it was also contextual in scale and setback with the neighboring houses. The church was built in two phases; beginning in 1952 with a nondescript, flat-roofed church service unit without a sanctuary. In 1959, the worship space was added on the front, framed by a steep single-gabled roof soaring up toward the south. The space is spare, with bare brick walls, burnished concrete floor and metal deck ceiling, but inspiring in its spaciousness and sensitivity to light. A concrete screen across the front blocks out the view of the more mundane surroundings, while a horizontal band of glass at the top of the wall draws attention upward and frames a dramatic and ever-changing piece of the sky.

The chief designer, architect John M. Garber of Garber, Tweddel & Wheeler, described the building as "heliocentric" because he arranged openings in the façade to direct beams of sunlight into the sanctuary. On Christmas, Easter, and the summer solstice, the sun hits a twelve-foot-high golden wall sculpture composed of a myriad of metal rods and flakes, by Harry Bertoia. A window band across the top of the front wall allows the sun to reflect from the ceiling during the Christmas season. The chapel features a bold abstract and colorful painting by Hugo Webber, which was a gift from Garber and art patron George S. Rosenthal.

Garber (1922–88), a graduate of Yale College and the Harvard Graduate School of Design, was a man of diverse talents. He practiced architecture, taught at the University of Cincinnati and Columbia University, and also sculpted in wood.[10] From 1959–63, he was associated with Cincinnati architects Richard Tweddel and Richard Wheeler, whom he met at Harvard. Tweddel and Wheeler were fellow faculty members at UC, and Tweddel also taught at Miami University. After St. John's, the firm's best-known commission was the Oratory at Grailville, a spiritual retreat for women in Loveland, Ohio, completed in 1962.

John M. Garber
St. John's Unitarian Universalist Church, 1952–59
320 Resor Avenue, Clifton

Architect John M. Garber gave this church a strikingly individual design. In place of a traditional steeple, slender steel spires striate the façade. Its setback and scale allow it to fit well into its residential context.

Christ Church

David Briggs Maxfield
Christ Church, 1956–57
318 East Fourth Street

The case of Christ Church, one of Cincinnati's oldest and most prestigious congregations, vividly illustrates the prevailing local attitudes about Modern architecture in the postwar period. By 1937, parish leaders had concluded that they needed a new building. Their Gothic Revival church, built in 1835 and designed by Henry Walter, was seen as functionally obsolete and unfashionable. (In contrast, the Greek Revival St. Peter in Chains Cathedral, also by Walter, would be rehabilitated.) Thanks to a gift made by philanthropist Mary Emery, the interior had been redecorated in 1890 by Tiffany Studio in New York, but the decor, particularly the iridescent purple and gold tile, was considered garish by many.

The new church was conceived as a memorial to Dr. Frank H. Nelson, who served the church as rector for over forty years and had an enduring dream of a new church building. There was a strong commitment to remaining downtown. "While other parishes have chosen to move from the center of the city, Christ Church is determined to stay here, ministering to the needs of the entire community and in particular, to the bottoms area," said the Reverend Nelson Burroughs.[11] The project was delayed by war, but in 1946 a committee hired the Finnish-born architect Eliel Saarinen's firm to design a new complex.

Eliel Saarinen (1873–1950) moved to the United States in 1923, after winning second place with his influential entry in the international competition for the Chicago Tribune Tower. He is best known for designing the campus for the Cranbrook Academy of Art and School, where he lived from 1928 until his death

The chapel at Christ Church still retains some of the original decorative scheme by the Tiffany Studio in the 1890s.

in 1950. Eliel Saarinen's son, Eero (1910–61), was also an important architect of the next generation. Eliel had recently designed the First Christian Church (1940–42) in Columbus, Indiana, which was nearby and widely published. This was the first of many contemporary buildings in Columbus and one of the first churches of modern design in the nation. A geometric composition of direct simplicity, it is a rectangular volume with a freestanding, sheer-walled clock tower.

Eliel Saarinen's design for Christ Church, which strongly resembled a larger, urban version of the First Christian Church in Columbus, was shown to the congregation for the first time in early 1949. The new building would be a rectangular block built of pinkish Minnesota stone facing Fourth Street (as had the old church), with a large square tower at the corner rising more than eighty feet. A new entrance courtyard on the site of the old church building would link the new church, chapel, and parish house. The project also called for resurfacing the parish house to match the church and completely renovating the interior.

A lifetime member described the Saarinens' design as honest and daring, but there was an uprising of virtually the whole parish against the design. Saarinen was asked to scale down his proposal and reorient the front to Sycamore Street. Eliel Saarinen submitted revised plans, but they lacked the majesty of the original scheme, and he died shortly afterward. Meanwhile, his design for Christ Church Lutheran in Minneapolis was completed in 1949. With its simple, rectilinear forms in an asymmetrical composition, it was very similar to his plan for the Cincinnati church, which was never built. The church building committee rejected the design.

In 1951, it was decided to begin again. David Briggs Maxfield (1906–71) was selected from among more than seventy architects in North America and England to do a new design. A specialist in church architecture, Maxfield was based in Oxford, Ohio, where he was a member of Miami University's architecture faculty from 1930 to 1951. In addition to Christ Church in Cincinnati, he designed four other churches for the Episcopal Diocese of Southern Ohio, including St. Paul's Episcopal in Oakwood. He also created chapels at Miami, Ohio State, and Ohio universities.

About six hundred people viewed a presentation of Maxfield's plans in the spring of 1954, and support was near-unanimous. The design received national attention in *Time Magazine*. The style was described as a modern interpretation of Gothic, with simplified massing and a high degree of transparency. The front was dominated by a giant stained glass window by Robert M. Metcalf of Antioch College, said to be one of the largest in the country.[12]

The old church was finally razed in August 1955, and the cornerstone of the new church was laid in June 1956. Naturally, a number of parishioners mourned the passing of the old church and wished it could have been duplicated. Many others struggled in various ways with the time-bound relationships between traditional form and spiritual experience, or those between specific stylistic symbols and their denominational identity. There continued to be debates about the interior decoration of the new church, and the beautiful windows from the old church were preserved and reinstalled in the new church.

The new building was completed in 1957 for a little over $1.5 million. Maxfield apparently solved the circulation problems, but ironically the design fell short in terms of liturgical function. The building has been renovated several times since it was completed. In 1982, the mechanical systems were updated and the interior redecorated. Designer and artist William Schickel of Loveland, Ohio, simplified the space and provided a new color scheme. In the following decade, however, there was a wish for a warmer ambience, which resulted in another extensive renovation of the church and adjoining spaces, this time by Philip Markwood of Columbus, Ohio. Completed in 1998, this renovation made all facilities of the church handicapped-accessible and revised the church interior with an attractive neo-Gothic motif, executed in wood. The exterior was reconfigured to make it more transparent and compatible in design with the 1908 Parish House.

While some may wish that the Saarinen plan had been executed, the building is considered viable for the congregation's current needs. It is instructive to reflect on how this building has been affected by the prevailing taste of the times and on the challenges sixty years ago (and even today) in embracing radical new approaches to architecture. The story of Christ Church is perhaps particularly instructive about how decisions on architectural style, tradition, and innovation are tied up with the self-image of a given institution and how it sees itself across time as well as within the ongoing community.

Bellevue Hill Park Pavilion

R. Carl Freund
Bellevue Hill Park Pavilion, 1955
Ohio Avenue and Parker Street, Fairview

This design by R. Carl Freund reflects the influence of Frank Lloyd Wright's late work in the use of bold geometric forms, cantilevered roof, and decorative treatment, yet with its own flair, so well suited to the site and the playfulness of a playground.

Parks provided a more playful venue for modern architecture. An excellent example is the whimsical park pavilion that stands on the edge of Bellevue Hill, where an inclined railway once climbed. The site was formerly occupied by Bellevue House, a hilltop resort, beer garden, and dance hall, which served beverages made by Christian Moerlein's brewery located at the bottom of the hill in Over-the-Rhine. After the incline was rebuilt in 1880 to accommodate streetcars, it was no longer necessary for travelers to transfer and the Bellevue House declined. The incline stopped operating in 1927, and the site lay fallow until 1936, when some of the land was acquired by the Cincinnati Park Board. The park was enlarged and the pavilion was built in 1954–55. The architect was R. Carl Freund (1902–59), a University of Cincinnati graduate and designer of numerous park buildings, schools, and church-related structures.

In contrast to its natural setting and earlier rustic park buildings, this pavilion reflects a futuristic aesthetic. It consists of a circular domed core with a flat cantilevered roof extending over a kidney-shaped recessed bandstand and dance platform. Three mushroom-shaped reinforced-concrete pergolas, each with a canopy of open grillwork supported by a cluster of columns, are reminiscent of Wright's Johnson Wax Co. Administration Building (1936–39) in Racine, Wisconsin. The pergolas look as if they could twirl in the air like skirts. The Bellevue Hill Park Pavilion and the Park Board Administration Building (1955) in Eden Park, the last park buildings designed by Freund, are among his best. Both reflect the obvious influence of Frank Lloyd Wright's late work in their use of bold geometric forms, overhanging eaves, and decorative treatment and in the way they take advantage of their natural settings.

Gibson Greeting Card Co.

Reflecting the 1950s movement out of downtown to the suburbs, the Gibson Greeting Card Co. left its 1921 building at 223 West Fourth Street and moved to Amberley Village. Beautifully set on a multi-acre campus, its new corporate headquarters, completed in 1957, exhibits many of the characteristics of the period. It has a low, ground-hugging profile with horizontal banded steel windows. Perforated steel awnings shelter the first-floor windows, while the second floor is set back in a loggia punctuated by short, square steel columns. The massing is symmetrical, with a stepped roofline and multiple setbacks from the front. The central entrance is recessed and faced with polished pink and gray granite, sporting the Gibson logo over the doorway. The east wing includes a dining room (or meeting hall) with a curved wall. (Gibson vacated the building in 2001, after the business was sold.)

The Gibson Building was designed by the Cincinnati architecture and engineering firm of A. M. Kinney. Founded in 1929, A. M. Kinney has been steered by the same family for three generations. The firm began by specializing in professional mechanical engineering services and expanded into architecture during the Second World War. It was the largest design and engineering firm in town during the 1950s through the 1970s. Some of the firm's other local projects include UC's Crosley Center (1969), the largest continually poured, reinforced-concrete building in the world, and the Ohio Environmental Protection Agency's A. W. Breidenbach Environmental Research Center (1975). Both are in the raw concrete mode of the Brutalist style popular with progressive designers in Britain and Europe in the 1950s and 1960s, characterized by strong, exaggerated, bulky forms and raw treatment of materials, especially unfinished concrete.

A. M. Kinney
Gibson Greeting Card Co. plant, 1955–57
2100 Section Road, Amberley Village

The former Gibson Greeting Card Co. plant in Amberley Village reflects the movement of industry out of downtown to the suburbs and the application of modern design to corporate architecture in the 1950s.

Harley, Ellington & Day (now Harley Ellis Devereaux) and Cellarius & Hilmer
Union Central Life Insurance Co. Headquarters, 1959–64
1876 Waycross Road, Forest Park

Union Central Life Insurance Co. celebrated its centennial by departing from its iconic downtown tower to this formal modern corporate campus in the suburbs.

Union Central Life Insurance Co.

With the approach of its centennial in 1964, John Lloyd, CEO of Union Central Life Insurance, sought a new image for the company. Its previous headquarters, at the southwest corner of Vine and Fourth streets, was the tallest building in Cincinnati when it was built in 1911–13. But by mid-century, different trends took hold. Lloyd's decision to build a new headquarters departed dramatically from the company's past by leaving downtown for a 190-acre site in the distant suburb of Forest Park and abandoning a traditional white tower for a long, low building of gray granite in the modern mode. Set way back from the road in an expansive lawn, the building is horizontally oriented in sympathy with its setting. The three-story main building is nearly the size of one downtown block. The façade is formal, with a central entrance pavilion, and has an executive penthouse on top. The windows are shielded from direct sun by a perforated stone screen set a few feet in front of the façade. Brises-soleil (sunshades) screen the windows on the upper floors. In front is a 120-foot granite tower that houses the company chimes, which were relocated from downtown. Describing the Union Central Life building on the occasion of the ribbon-cutting on April 27, 1964, the *Cincinnati Enquirer* praised its modern design and its spacious amenities for employees, including the dining room, lounges, and an auditorium.

Attention was also given to aesthetic elements. For the cafeteria Cincinnati artist Lumen Martin Winter created a Venetian-style glass mosaic depicting the Cincinnati riverfront in the early 1900s, with the old Union Central tower. In the lobby is Winter's 3,000-pound bronze abstract screen depicting the *Seven Needs of Man*. The dining room features a forty-foot long abstract painting. The headquarters even had a meditation room with a stone mosaic in which chunks of smoky quartz and other semiprecious stones were designed to focus rays of overhead light on a simple altar. Internationally known for his huge sculptures and mosaic murals, Winter created a giant mural of Venus and Apollo for the Top of the Fair in the Heliport and administration building for the 1964–65 World's Fair in New York City. His first mural was a 1600-square-foot fresco on the interior walls of the Friars Club in Clifton depicting the Ohio Valley and events of World War II.

The Union Central Life Insurance building was designed by Harley, Ellington & Day of Detroit and Cellarius & Hilmer of Cincinnati. Harley, Ellington & Day began in 1908 in Detroit, where their early projects included the Stroh Brewery and White Chapel Mausoleum, important Detroit landmarks. The firm served the region's top corporations, including the Ford Motor Co., General Motors, Chrysler Corp., Michigan State University, and Detroit Edison. Recent mergers created Harley Ellis Devereaux, one of the nation's largest planning and design-and-build services firms, with offices in Detroit, Chicago, Cincinnati, and Los Angeles. Perhaps because of the Detroit connection, the Union Central Life Insurance complex shows some similarity to the General Motors Technical Center, a complex of low steel-and-glass buildings carefully arranged in a vast acreage of flat land. Built in 1948–55 in Bloomfield Hills and designed by Eliel and Eero Saarinen, it featured sculpture by Bertoia.

The local firm of Cellarius & Hilmer served as architects of record for the project. Charles Cellarius (1891–1973) was known as a conscientious interpreter of traditional styles, particularly Georgian Revival, as seen in the Bond Hill School (1932). As supervising architect for Mariemont, he designed the Dale Park Fire Station and a group of houses on Beech Street. Many of his commissions were educational buildings for Berea College, Ohio University, Ohio State University, Miami University, and the University of Cincinnati (UC). His streamlined design for Woodward High School (demolished), completed in 1952 in Roselawn, was indicative of his shift toward Modernism. Herbert F. Hilmer, who is known for designing the Wrightian Faculty Club at UC (also scheduled for demolition), became his younger partner in 1956.

City view from Mount Adams

During this period, implementation of the 1964 plan for Cincinnati transformed the central business district through the construction of contiguous blocks of large, tall buildings. A number of architectural projects—Riverbend, the Playhouse in the Park, Greater Cincinnati International Airport, and Procter & Gamble headquarters—brought national attention to the area.

9

Toward the Bicentennial

New versus Old, 1964–88

CINCINNATI EMERGED FROM the postwar period with its downtown lively, most of its historic building stock intact, and a ring of thriving neighborhoods within the city limits. The downtown core had five major department stores (Shillito's, Pogue's, McAlpin's, Rollman's, and Mabley & Carew), dozens of specialized shops, numerous good restaurants (Pigall's, the Gourmet Room, and the Maisonette all had national reputations), and more than half a dozen fine historic office buildings. In order to build on this legacy, civic leaders did what they had been doing in Cincinnati since 1925, when their predecessors adopted the first comprehensive city plan in the nation—they put together a plan for optimal development.[1]

By the late 1950s, however, when preparation for the 1964 Downtown Plan began, planners could see that the suburban expansion encouraged by the 1948 Regional Plan was having a deleterious effect on the central business district, as peripheral growth was doing everywhere in the United States. Growth was occurring at the edges of the city but not in the core, so civic leaders devised a plan to redevelop downtown block by block, hoping to make it more attractive. At that time, "more attractive" meant "new." There was little appreciation of the city's historic building stock, which seemed old-fashioned compared with the steel-and-glass towers going up in New York, Chicago, and other cities. Although a few modern buildings had recently been built in Cincinnati, the most innovative one, the Terrace Plaza Hotel, had a brick veneer façade that blended in with nearby buildings. The

1964 Downtown Plan

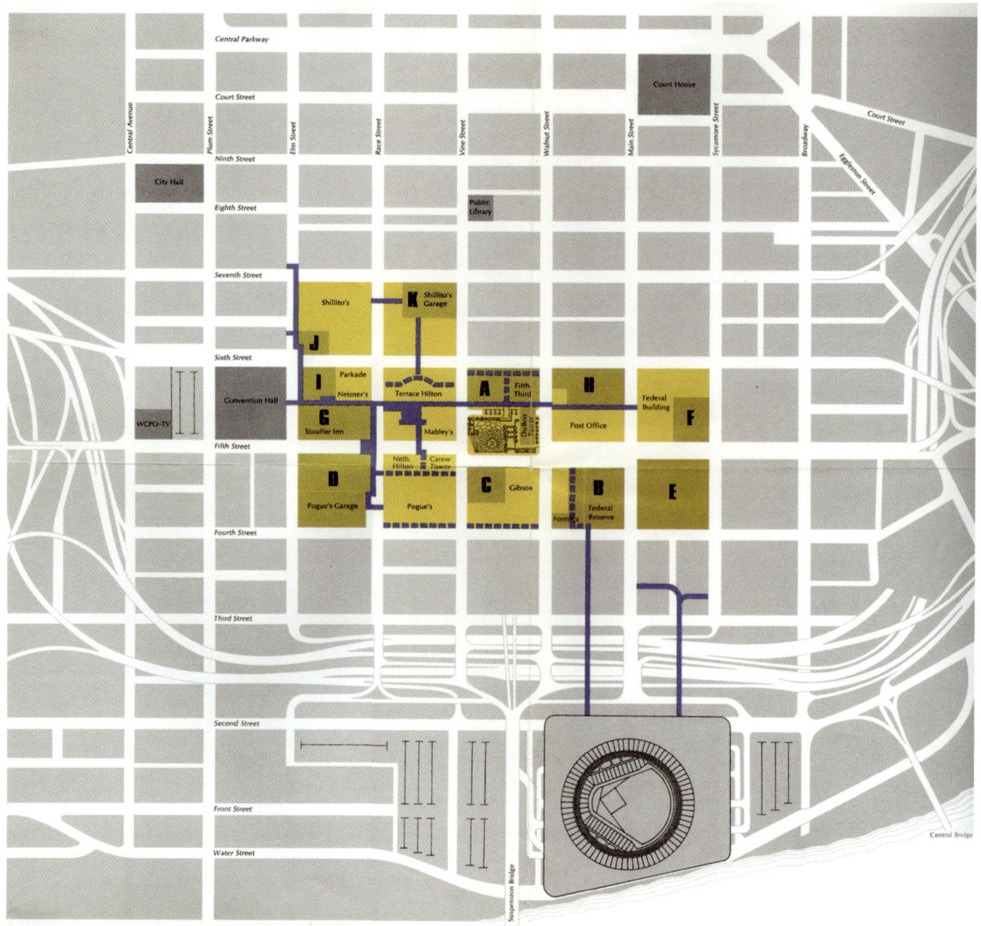

only office tower made of expressly modern materials, the Kroger Co. headquarters, was several blocks north of the city center and, unfortunately, the building was a particularly bad example of its type, clad as it was in an awkward checkerboard of light blue-and-white porcelain enamel panels.

Besides a commitment to rebuild most of the underdeveloped blocks in the center of the city, the 1964 plan contained two important ideas. The first was to prohibit surface parking lots in the core, a provision that kept Cincinnati from looking like an asphalt wasteland as many other cities did. The second was to create a second-floor system of "skywalks," meant to offer the kind of easy access between stores that suburban malls provided. The skywalks gave the downtown a distinctive image and were popular with tourists. But, though this effect may not have been obvious when they were envisioned, they cast shadows on the sidewalks and streets below, making the traditional urban pedestrian experience less pleasant than it had been. And since many of the links in the system ran through office buildings and stores, when any of those places were under construction or closed, a part of the system was cut off. The skywalk system was discontinuous in a way city streets are not.[2]

Another result of the 1964 plan was that because the city was rebuilt block by block (or partial block), rather than on individual building lots or combinations of

David L. Niland

No Cincinnati citizen had a greater impact on the city's physical environment in the 1960s, '70s, '80s, and thereafter than David L. Niland. Although his own architectural work is largely confined to private houses, he served on the city's Urban Design Review Board throughout the period and was its most influential and articulate critic. A professor at the University of Cincinnati's College of Design, Art, Architecture and Planning in charge of the sixth-year architecture program throughout this period, Niland's influence was so great that students used to call the final year the "David Niland School of Architecture." The only Cincinnati architect whose work was published internationally, he made important contributions to the art of architecture in the area of handicapped accessibility, an area that became important during this period as a result of the passage of the Americans with Disabilities Act, which affects almost every aspect of design. In two important houses, for the Irwin Hanensons in Bond Hill and for the Hugh Hawkins family in Indian Hill, Niland proved that aesthetics not only need not suffer but can actually be advanced in buildings designed for clients who depend on wheelchairs.

lots that had to be acquired one by one, the scale on city streets grew larger. Not only were many buildings taller, but they also had larger footprints, often encompassing what had been alleyways, and thus lacking the human scale compatible with street life. At first this bigness seemed desirable; in America, bigger is usually considered better. But after a number of massive blocks had been built, people began to discover the pleasures of smaller-scale older buildings with more refined detailing.

In the beginning, however, people felt the excitement of the new, which suggested rebirth of the city center. To ensure quality as well as quantity of new development and some visual coordination, the 1964 plan contained a provision for an urban design review board composed of architects and civic leaders, four serving at a time, to evaluate new projects as they were proposed for blocks designated for redevelopment. This board had a significant, if subtle, impact on the quality of design downtown.

Salmon P. Wallace
Provident Bank, 1967
Fourth and Vine streets

The first modern office tower in the city's traditional financial district, the Provident Bank Building replaced a hotel that had been a center of local social activity for decades. Unwittingly, it ushered in an era when downtown would be devoted more completely to business.

The first modern skyscraper in the middle of downtown Cincinnati did not fall under the board's jurisdiction, however, as it was built for a site that was not part of the plan. The Provident Bank Building of 1967, designed by Salmon P. Wallace of Dallas, went up on the southeast corner of Fourth and Vine streets, where the Sinton Hotel had been located, in the heart of the Fourth Street financial district. The nineteen-story, blue-glass-walled tower with projecting vertical aluminum mullions took its place rather quietly in the cityscape. The next year, the bank and its building were purchased by financier Carl Lindner's American Financial Corp. holding company.

In 1968, a modest modern high-rise hotel, designed by Bill Brown of the local architectural firm Architekton, was built for Stouffers at the corner of Sixth and Elm streets. In 1977, when it was being managed by Clarion, it received an addition to the north, designed by David Beers of Welton Beckett's New York office. It is now called the Millennium.

Fountain Square Redesign Creates New Image for City

The big change in downtown Cincinnati came in 1969, however, when the city's historic center, Fountain Square, which had been an elliptical island surrounded by traffic, was redesigned. The square became a large, stone-paved, pedestrian plaza with the historic Tyler Davidson Fountain bubbling in the center. The thirty-story Dubois (now Fifth Third) Tower edged the east side, somewhat dwarfing the Fountain, and a low-rise block housing the headquarters of the Fifth-Third Bank, stores, and a parking garage defined the northern edge along Sixth Street. The square was designed by RTKL of Baltimore, while the vertical-striped office tower and six-story low-rise block were by Harrison & Abramovitz of New York. The completion of the new Fountain Square represented the first successful implementation of the 1964 plan, which had labeled each block to be redeveloped with letters of the alphabet A through K. Fountain Square, which was bounded by Fourth and Fifth and Vine and Walnut streets, had been designated Block A.

Developer Towne Properties was awarded Block B. Before the year ended, part of Block B, which was catty-corner from Fountain Square (between Fourth and Fifth, Walnut and Main streets), started to take form when the elegant, travertine-clad, fourteen-story Formica Building opened. The downtown plan was even being implemented in alphabetical order. Though this alphabetical progression would not continue for long, every designated block was eventually redeveloped. The 1964 plan was probably the only city plan in history to be not only adopted as law, but actually carried out in detail. Although the Formica Building's east-west connections to the skywalk system would not be functional until Block C was rebuilt in 1981, the building's interior first-floor north-south arcade was lined with shops

Harry Weese & Associates
Formica Building, 1969–70
Fifth Street between Walnut and Main streets

Combining an office tower with a retail shopping arcade and new galleries for the Contemporary Arts Center, the Formica Building brought a variety of types of activity to its site as well as north-south and east-west interior connections between blocks.

which linked Fourth and Fifth streets. Upstairs were new second-story, skylighted, cruciform galleries for the Contemporary Arts Center, which overlooked Fountain Square and Government Square. (Government Square was an open space south of the Federal Building, where all city buses docked beside glass canopies, designed by Champlin Haupt in 1971, and where it was possible to change from one line to another.) The Formica Building complex was designed by Harry Weese & Associates of Chicago; architect T. C. Chang was the partner in charge.

The rest of Block B was completed in 1972 with the opening of a new icy white marble Federal Reserve Bank. The design, by the third-generation Cincinnati firm Harry Hake & Partners, was altered considerably by the government client. The result was a building that hovered between a stylized classicism and a fussy modernism, without much conviction about either. The bank included an almost-enclosed garden that was the antithesis of lively, inviting Fountain Square. The fine stele-like fountain is by the sculptor Oliver Andrews.

Work had already begun on a more confident building that would open in 1974 on block H between Fifth and Sixth, Walnut and Main streets. Built by the Western-Southern Life Insurance Co. for the Southern Ohio Bank, the structure, which is known as the 580 Building, inventively incorporated the skywalk system. The owners agreed to keep this taupe brick-floored, brick-walled, air-conditioned passageway open twenty-four hours a day since it served as the building's internal spine and connected it with Fountain Square. Designed by RTKL partner Mario Shack with Bill Jackson of Harry Hake & Partners, the building contained a dramatic skylighted, four-story banking room, elevators for the two sleek fourteen-story, dark glass-walled office towers, and an underground garage.

RTKL with Harry Hake & Partners
Southern Ohio Bank, 1972–74
Sixth and Walnut streets

The chunky Southern Ohio Bank building continued the masonry tradition of downtown Cincinnati but applied the handsome modern taupe-colored brick to large-scale abstract forms and complemented them with dark glass curtain walls. It also absorbed the skywalk system inventively.

New Development Takes Its Toll on Historic Buildings

Three years later, in 1977, planning began in earnest for the redevelopment of Block C (immediately south of Fountain Square). Although considered prime for redevelopment, the block contained the grand 1,000-room Gibson Hotel and the glamorous, classical Albee Theater, both of which had closed but would have to be demolished before rebuilding could occur. The virtues of the hotel, with its generous lobby and elegant meeting rooms, were not widely recognized at the time, but the glorious Albee, which had a gigantic Palladian arch on the façade, struck a chord, and a preservation battle was fought to save it. Although the battle was lost, the arch was preserved and incorporated into an addition to the convention center. The $38 million, 460-room Westin Hotel, which was built on the site of the

Caudill Rowlett Scott (CRS) with Baxter, Hodell, Donnelly & Preston and Wilson Associates
Cincinnati Convention and Exposition Center expansion, 1983–87
Addition to Dr. Albert B. Sabin Convention Center by Harry Hake & Partners, 1967
Palladian Arch from the Albee Theater by Thomas Lamb
Fifth Street between Sycamore and Elm streets

The new two-block-long Cincinnati Convention and Exposition Center preserved a bit of local history when the architects incorporated an elegant marble Palladian arch from the façade of the grand Albee Theater, which was demolished to make way for the mixed-use Fountain Square South.

Albee, has none of the grandeur of the old Gibson, but it was considered more desirable because it was new. And because it was smaller and taller (at seventeen stories), there was room on the site for a twenty-nine-story office building for the First National Bank (later called Star Bank, now US Bank). The pink granite-clad complex was designed by Abramovitz-Harris-Kingsland with Poor, Swanke, Hayden & Connell, both of New York.

Although programmatically it was to be more like the mixed-use Carew Tower complex directly to the west—with an office building, hotel, garage, and shopping arcade all connected inside—planners had hoped that the mixed-use structure would contain a grand interior public space, sort of an open-air Fountain Square. The angular new complex, however, had neither the elegance of that historic grouping nor the inviting publicness of Fountain Square. In fact, the main public area was empty and rather dark. The shops were confined to the edges. And the only place to sit down was at an expensive café operated by the hotel. In hindsight, it seems strange that planners did not envision Block C as an extension of the Carew Tower Arcade and absorb the lessons it had to teach. But at the time, historic architecture was little appreciated. Anything new and different, it was assumed, would be better than the tried and true. One thing the complex did provide was a second-level connection to the Formica Building complex next door, as well as another large underground parking garage.

Abramovitz-Harris-Kingsland Poor, Swanke, Hayden & Connell, and KZF
First National Bank (now US Bank) Building and Westin Hotel, 1977–81
Fifth Street between Vine and Walnut Streets

The First National (now US) Bank Building and Westin Hotel surround an atrium that was intended to be an interior public space similar in function to Fountain Square. The complex contains retail stores, restaurants, and underground garage.

Skidmore, Owings & Merrill with Baxter, Hodell, Donnelly & Preston
Central Trust (now PNC) Center, 1978–79
Fifth and Main streets

The Central Trust Center was the first new skyscraper in Cincinnati to depart from the rectangular shape of early modern towers and adapt a shape tailored to the site. It frames Government Square and steps back at the top and bottom to meet the street and sky.

Late Modern Departures from the Modernist Box

In 1978, work began on two more interesting buildings, the Central Trust Center (now PNC Center) on Block E, across Main Street from the new Federal Reserve Bank, and the new headquarters for Federated Department Stores on the northeast corner of Block K. The creamy travertine-clad Central Trust Center steps back at the base and at the top and folds around the corner of Fifth and Main streets to frame Government Square. The complex was designed by Richard Keating (then of the Houston office of Skidmore, Owings & Merrill) with Jim Donnelly of Baxter, Hodell, Donnelly & Preston of Cincinnati. The developer was Houston-based

RTKL
Federated Department Stores Headquarters, 1978–80
Seventh and Vine streets

The Federated Department Stores headquarters tower began construction while it was still being designed—on top of an existing parking garage, which had a chili parlor on the ground floor. Still, the tower turned out to be one of the most elegant office buildings in the city.

Gerald Hines, known for his buildings of quality. Because a concern with energy savings was emerging, the windows, set in thick frames above tinted aluminum insulated panels, filled only 40 percent of the wall surface, instead of the 60 percent common in skyscrapers of the immediate postwar years. The building also had lush plantings and significant original works of art: a color field mural by Ellsworth Kelly behind the tellers' stands and a kinetic George Rickey sculpture outdoors on the prominent urban corner. (The Kelly was later removed and donated to the Cincinnati Art Museum, which traded it for another work by the same artist.)

The Federated headquarters was built on top of a parking garage on the northwest corner of the downtown core at Seventh and Vine streets. It is as notable for the way it was built as for the design itself. The then relatively new fast-track "design-build," system was used, in which the building is under construction while it is still being designed. The building is a sleek white metal-skinned tower with a chamfered top that was obviously inspired by Hugh Stubbins's much-heralded Citicorp Center in Manhattan, which also had an aluminum skin and triangular top. Federated's cladding was painted white and its top was pleated, while silvery Citicorp had a tilted flat surface. The design team, headed by Ed Haladay of the Atlanta office of RTKL and the Henry C. Beck Construction Co. of Dallas, was selected in a limited competition. Here, too, energy savings was a major concern. The decision to build the fourteen-story tower on top of a seven-story parking garage was made because of the site's proximity to both the center of the city and Shillito's, the company's main store in Cincinnati, and because Federated already owned the land.

Central Trust and Federated both represent departures from the plain, rectangular, glass-walled slab towers that had become the norm in the 1950s (though only one, the twenty-four-story Kroger Building, had been built in Cincinnati). In 1981, GBBN Architects was hired to reclad the eyesore, replacing the blue-and-white porcelain enamel panels with alternating bands of stainless steel and glass. In an attempt to distinguish them from the norm or respond to their specific sites, all the office buildings that went up in downtown Cincinnati in the 1980s had dynamic shapes. Ironically, two speculative office buildings built in 1982 by different architects and developers ended up looking like twins. The one on the northwest corner of Fifth and Sycamore streets, on Block F (which was first called Columbia Plaza, then Prudential and, finally, the Chiquita Building) was rotated on its site to form triangular plazas on the outer and inner block corners. That twenty-nine-story, 590,000-square-foot tower is essentially a slab. But because it is set at an angle (it actually aligns with the bend of the river) and its ends form triangles, the building seems to have a dynamic polygonal shape, which somewhat masks its size. The thin lines between the dark glass window bands and the rosy precast concrete panels also bring down the scale of the tower designed by Alfonso Varela of 3D International of Houston, which was completed in 1985.

3DI
Chiquita Building, 1982–85
Fifth and Sycamore streets

Originally built on speculation, this tower became the home of a major local corporation. By simply rotating the building on its site and triangulating the end walls, the architects managed to give it a distinctive and identifiable form.

The Cincinnati Commerce Center (initially called the Linclay Building) on the northwest corner of Sixth and Vine is also sheathed with narrow bands of dark windows and precast panels, rotated on its site, and twenty-nine stories tall. It, too, has setbacks at the top and a decorative corner plaza with a prominent sculpture at the base (though this one has a colonnade and some retail space on the ground floor), and its precast panels are deep tan stippled concrete. It was designed by Gin Wong of Los Angeles with Hixon Architects and Engineers of Cincinnati. The fact that two large speculative office buildings were built at roughly the same time was a testament to confidence in downtown Cincinnati's future, not just on the part of civic leaders but also of investors. The Cincinnati Commerce Center was not even built on one of the blocks designated in the plan, but on the site of the old Palace

RTKL
Hyatt Regency Hotel, 1982–84
Fifth Street between Race and Elm streets

This modern hotel tower curves to offer river views to more of the rooms. It also has all the elements of a modern commercial hotel: a light-filled, multistory atrium and easy access to luxury shops, a parking garage, and the convention center.

Movie Theater, which had been surrounded by stores and restaurants in low-rise buildings and was therefore not considered "blighted." But the site was deemed economically desirable by the private sector when there seemed to be a market for new office space.

Although most new construction was for office buildings, a new Hyatt Regency Hotel and Saks Fifth Avenue store went up in 1982–84 on Block D, on Fifth Street between Race and Elm streets. Though they were built at the same time as part of the same development parcel, along with a city garage that had shops at the base, the three designs were not well coordinated. The twenty-two-story, orange-brick-clad Hyatt, which is curved on one side and V-shaped on the other, was designed by RTKL of Baltimore. Saks was designed by Robert J. Bridges Associates of New York, a firm that had designed other Saks outlets, mostly in suburbs. The city garage was by Hefley/Stevens and ATA Team Associates, both of Cincinnati.

Skidmore, Owings & Merrill
Atrium One and Atrium Two, 1980–85
Fourth and Main streets and Fourth and Sycamore streets

The architects of these two massive office towers saved energy and created a sense of community inside by arranging the office floors around light-filled central atriums.

The arrival of Saks was considered a coup by Cincinnati officials and a boon to well-off shoppers, but the design of the 75,000-square-foot, two-story store with chamfered corners would have been more at home outside the city than it was on its urban site.

In 1980, the first of a pair of two even bigger buildings went up on Fourth Street, where Cincinnati banks, stockbrokers, and law firms had traditionally been located. They were called Atrium One and Atrium Two because their office floors were built around gigantic central atriums in order to have fewer outer walls and therefore conserve energy. Atrium One, at the corner of Fourth and Main streets, was built for Cincinnati Bell by the Hunt Development Co. of Indianapolis. Atrium Two, which extends the block to Fourth and Sycamore streets, opened two years later. Both Atriums were designed by the Chicago Office of Skidmore, Owings & Merrill. Bruce Graham, architect of both the John Hancock Building and the Sears Tower in Chicago, was the partner in charge. Their size is not immediately apparent. Atrium One, at twenty stories, has more office space than the forty-eight-story Carew Tower. But their massive scale is more in tune with the architect's hometown than with Cincinnati.

New Building Designs Change Character of the City

The appearance of all these big buildings changed the character of downtown Cincinnati. Where once there had been little coffee shops, shoe repair shops, family-owned stores, and movie theaters, now there were long, barren walls. When retail stores did appear at the bases of the new buildings, they were usually pharmacy or fast-food chains that could afford the higher rents, and the retailers often turned inward, opening onto lobbies rather than sidewalks. The high-priced, code-mandated "retail" spaces often remained vacant for years. The absence of street life, the change in scale, and the absence of meaningful decoration on building surfaces eventually led to a certain disillusionment with modernism, not only in Cincinnati but all over the country, and fostered an appreciation of old buildings and the new "Postmodern" buildings that had some of the characteristics of historic ones.

Postmodernism Makes an Impact

Cincinnati not only still had a number of fine late-nineteenth- and early-twentieth-century buildings, which lent themselves to what was then called "adaptive reuse" (conversion to new purposes), but was also the site of one of the most important and successful buildings in the Postmodern style, the Procter & Gamble Building by Kohn Pedersen Fox (KPF) of 1982–85. The prominent up-and-coming New York firm had designed several well-received Late Modern buildings, such as 333 Wacker Drive in Chicago, that had unusual shapes derived from their sites, as the Chiquita Building and the Cincinnati Commerce Center did, though those were less bold and artful. But the P&G commission—which involved adding to a conservative limestone building that, though built in 1956, was more classical than modern—posed a different kind of contextual challenge. When the architects came to Cincinnati, they were surprised to see a number of historic towers with attractive pyramidal tops, such as the Central Trust (Union Central Life, now PNC) Tower, Cincinnati Gas & Electric, and the Times-Star Building, so they decided to pick up on the larger urban context. They built two low-rise blocks of offices, similar in style to their neighbors, if somewhat more open and lively, placed them perpendicular to one another so that they would edge the site, and added a pair of towers at the corner. They devoted the rest of the block to an elliptical drive-in turnaround and a formal garden with trellises along the sidewalks to maintain the street line.

It was a dramatic and unprecedented scheme, one that brought their careers to a new level, put Cincinnati on the architectural map, and furthered the popularity of the Postmodern movement in architecture. With the building at around the same time of the Riverbend Music Center for outdoor performances, commissioned by the trustees of the Cincinnati Symphony Orchestra from Princeton, New Jersey, architect Michael Graves, two important examples of the style, both of which were widely published, were located here. Although Postmodernism did not, of course, immediately supplant abstract, angular Late Modern architecture—one characteristic of late twentieth and early twenty-first century architecture is that several styles have usually been popular at the same time—it did gradually make an impact.

In 1983, Philip R. Duke & Associates and Chelsea Moore Development Co. announced plans for a sleek twenty-three-story tower with an eight-story atrium over the skywalk at 525 Vine Street, across from Fountain Square. Designed by Michael Moose, a gifted young architect recently arrived in the city as a chief designer for the established Cincinnati firm of Glaser & Myers (now Glaserworks), 525 Vine was sheathed in bands of gray-green precast concrete and glass, stepped back on the southeast corner, and raised on pillars that created a two-story space at the base to connect the street and skywalk levels. It was the first tall building downtown designed by a local architect since 1931, when the Times-Star Building was on the boards.

Five years later, Moose designed Centennial Plaza, on the western edge of downtown, in a restrained version of the Postmodern style, with relatively small windows and a collection of separate, relatively low (eight- to eleven-story) buildings grouped around a formal plaza that contains the somewhat classical *Cincinnati Venus* by Jim Dine. The style and character of the buildings was appropriate for the site between Central Avenue and Interstate 75, west of City Hall and St. Peter in Chains Cathedral. It is beyond the Central Business District but not quite in Queensgate, so it was designed to be an enclave into itself.

Around the same time, Central Bancorporation (the old Central Trust Bank, now PNC) built another tower on the east side of its site, at 255 Fifth, also with Gerald D. Hines Interests. The Chemed Center, too, was a simplified version of Postmodern classicism. Designed by David Childs of the New York office of Skidmore, Owings & Merrill, the thirty-two-story tower steps back at the top in the Art Deco manner, creating a kind of pyramidal effect on the eastern side of downtown the way the Carew Tower does on the west side, and visually pulling together the cluster of new flat-roofed and old capped towers around it, while relating all these to the P&G complex across the street. The Chemed Center meets the street with a dignified, traditional loggia that was inspired by the one on the CG&E Building but resembles the entrances to P&G and to Michael Graves's Humana Building in Louisville. The last major building to be designed in the spirit of the 1964 plan brought its objectives full circle, from old to new and back again.

Although the block strategy of the 1964 Downtown Plan had the effect of enlarging the scale of downtown Cincinnati, it was the remodeling and expansion

Harrison & Abramovitz
Dubois (now Fifth Third) Tower, 1969–70
Fifth and Walnut streets

This classic modern office tower, a rectangular slab with a flat top and vertical bands of windows to emphasize its height, was designed both to provide a tall accent in Fountain Square as well as modern office space. Located near the top, the Banker's Club has dining rooms with fine city views.

Elzner & Anderson with Ferro-Concrete Construction Co.
SHV Headquarters (formerly American Book Co.), 1903–4
Fourth and Pike streets
Renovation:
PDT, 1981

This building, which resembles an Italian Renaissance palazzo, is actually an unusual early example of the use of reinforced concrete. It also set a precedent later, when the light industrial structure was converted to office use at the beginning of the historic preservation movement.

of the 1966 Cincinnati Convention Center designed by Harry Hake & Partners that most dramatically altered the cityscape. The geometrically patterned, shiny black-and-rose granite walls represent a dramatic improvement of what had been one of the city's eyesores, with its mud-colored pebbly aggregate walls beneath an awkward pointed arcade. And the incorporation of the elegant old white marble Palladian arch from Thomas Lamb's beloved Albee Theater adds a sense of history. Although it provides convention space within walking distance of hotels, stores, and restaurants in a way few of its competitors do, the two-block-long structure, which required the closing of Plum Street and rerouting traffic, disrupts the core.

Tietig & Lee
Coffered ceiling at the old Federal Reserve Bank, 1927
Fourth and Race streets
Renovation:
A-E Design and decorator Tana Hendrix, 1982

After stark modern office buildings had become the norm for several decades, older ones with elegant historic detailing like this began to be appreciated again. The coffered ceiling here had been designed for the Federal Reserve Bank by the Cincinnati architects Tietig & Lee.

Historic Preservation and Adaptive Reuse

It is less surprising that Postmodernism gained a foothold in a conservative city such as Cincinnati than it is that Cincinnatians, who have always been proud that their city has a longer and richer history than most of its Midwestern neighbors, took some time to fully appreciate their architectural heritage.

The first signs of interest in historic buildings came from nonprofit institutions such as the Academy of Medicine, which moved into the classical nineteenth-century Captain Pearce town house at 320 Broadway in 1960. Then, in 1977, The Willa K. Butterfield Senior Center renovated the Renaissance Revival Fechheimer mansion, which had been built by Samuel Hannaford on Garfield Square in 1861–62. The mansion had been the home of the Cuvier Press Club from 1937 to 1973. In 1976, after the club had moved to the Fourth and Race Tower, the city acquired the property and remodeled it with a $1.2 million grant from the federal Department of Housing and Urban Development. Architects David Lee Smith and Donald Stevens designed the renovation.[3]

A few years later, individual companies began to realize that they could create more interesting and economical office space by converting old commercial buildings than by building anew. If the old buildings were located on the edges of downtown, that was not necessarily undesirable; most workers arrived by car and parking could be provided more economically there.

In 1980, Freedman Advertising purchased an 1882 mixed-used commercial building next to City Hall. Jones and Speer Architects removed the pizza-parlor-Tudor siding that a restaurant had installed, reopened the original big glass ground-floor windows, and painted the brick exterior taupe, brown, and orange, in a Postmodern version of a Victorian color scheme. Freedman not only acquired expansion space, but also got a stone church next door as part of the deal—and historic preservation tax credits.

SHV, the Dutch conglomerate that had acquired the David J. Joseph Co., purchased the old American Book Co. building, next door to the Taft Museum in 1981, and architect John Bammerlin of PDT converted it into handsome new offices. The Italian palazzo-style commercial structure, which had been built by the Ferro-Concrete Construction Co. in 1903–4, had high ceilings, solid walls, natural ventilation, and, according to the architect, "column spacings that were quite advantageous."

That same year, one of the city's grandest skyscrapers, the thirty-four-story Central Trust Tower (formerly the Union Central Building) at Fourth and Vine streets, was renovated, partly because it was losing tenants to the new office buildings and partly because its owners had begun to recognize its aesthetic value. The building had been designed by the New York architect of the Woolworth Building, Cass Gilbert, with the Cincinnati firm Garber & Woodward. In 1982, the old Federal Reserve Bank Building at Fourth and Race streets was restored as local headquarters of the Columbus-based Huntington Bank by architect Sam Boulmetis of A-E Design and decorator Tana Hendrix of Huntington. (Actually, even before the bankers discovered the magnificent 1927 Tietig & Lee first-floor banking rooms with blue-and-gold coffered ceilings and walnut wainscoting, a Bonnie-and-Clyde-style theme restaurant called the Last Picture Show had found the bank's subterranean vaults.) The banking room is now a posh bar, the Federal Reserve. The building's owner, Lanny Holbrook, has his law and business offices in the tower room once occupied by the Cuvier Press Club.

The next year, a developer, Robert Chavez, acquired the old French Bauer Ice Cream Factory at the corner of Court and Elm streets and, also using historic preservation tax credits, converted it to office space. Chavez hired Centerbrook, an architectural partnership that Charles Moore had founded in Centerbrook, Connecticut, as Moore Grover Harper. Centerbrook transformed the gutsy old factory, which originally had little office space, into a sleek but intentionally quirky Postmodern structure by creating a stepped-up atrium and covering the entire exterior

Centerbrook Architects with Rabun, Hatch, Portman, McWhorter
Court Street Center (former French Bauer ice cream factory), 1986
Court and Elm streets

This old ice cream factory on the edge of downtown was converted to a stylish Postmodern office building for rental and occupancy by Chavez Properties, the owner and developer. The project succeeded at least partly because the architects felt free to adapt it playfully and stylishly and because the rules governing preservation tax credits in place at the time allowed free interpretation of that kind.

with colored reflective glass. The architects worked with Rabun, Hatch, Portman, McWhorter of Atlanta after Chavez Properties of Cincinnati brought in Affiliated Properties of Atlanta. The building, renamed the Court Street Center (now the home of Turner Construction), was completed in 1985. The same year, the 1931–33 Times-Star Building at Eighth Street and Broadway was redesigned for new owners, Burke Marketing Services Co., by Basil Carter and Associates of New York.

The most exciting downtown preservation project of the 1980s was the $20 million renovation of the sumptuous Netherland Plaza Hotel, which had opened in 1932. The 1981–83 project was guided by Richard Rauh Assocs. of Atlanta, interior designer Rita St. Clair of Baltimore, and Rabun Hatch and Dendy of Atlanta for Dunfey Hotels of Hampton, New Hampshire, and the Emery family, who had built the Art Deco hotel. The Netherland was not only a part of the Carew Tower Arcade complex—along with a three-story shopping arcade, garage, and a forty-eight story office building—it was also one of the grandest hotels in the nation. And after the new hotels that had opened in Cincinnati failed to dazzle, it looked better than ever.

Between 1985 and 1987, an even earlier Emery hotel, the more modest Cincinnatian on the northwest corner of Sixth and Vine streets, was remodeled. This time, instead of restoring the 1882 interiors that had been lost over the years, the architects decided to do a playful Postmodern scheme, more like the approach used at the French Bauer factory than the restoration of the Netherland. Gary Edwards of Edwards Design in Washington, DC, worked with architect Elmer Burger of Williams Trebilcock Whitehead of Pittsburgh, Messer Construction Co., and KZF of Cincinnati to transform the dowdy 149-room hotel into an up-to-date fantasyland. The architects did preserve a decorative mahogany staircase with white marble steps, but they emphasized the eight-story atrium surrounded by bay-shaped balconies and cascading ivy. They filled the atrium with pyramidal towers made of openwork grids and brought the interior to life with a Postmodern color scheme of periwinkle, terra-cotta, mahogany, and camel.

Unintended Consequences of the 1964 Plan

Before the city's bicentennial celebrations began in 1988, the entire 1964 plan had been implemented. But success in city building is never simple. Every change has unintended consequences, and factors that could never have been foreseen can undo even the best-laid plans. When the L. S. Ayres department store suddenly closed during the bicentennial year, the skywalk system, which had been a major provision of the 1964 plan, started to unravel just as it was completed. The Indianapolis-based store had replaced the local H&S Pogue, which had originally occupied the space south of the Carew Tower Arcade on Fourth Street but later expanded into the space north of the arcade formerly occupied by Mabley & Carew. At that point, Pogue's (and then Ayres) opened to both Fourth and Fifth streets, providing a connection for the entire block. Because there were skywalk connections on both sides as well as on the eastern and western ends of the arcade, Ayres had become the heart of the system. When the store closed, those arteries were abruptly severed. Enclosed connections from store to store or building to building really did tie the downtown together, but since they were dependent on private ownership, the system proved vulnerable to the winds of economic and social change.

During the years when the plan was being put into effect, downtown shopping continued to decline despite the mall-like environment that had been created. Eventually all but one of the downtown department stores that were thriving when planning began had closed. Shillito's (renamed Lazarus and then, in 2005,

Macy's) survived on a much reduced scale in a different location: at Fountain Place, a complex that is a very much reduced version of a project that represented another disappointment for downtown planning in the late 1980s. With much fanfare, the city's Department of Economic Development first announced a developer's competition in 1986 for a mixed-used complex on the site north of Fifth Street and west of Fountain Square. It was to have shopping, a major hotel, and an office building taller than the Carew Tower. Negotiations went on for three years. At least four developers expressed interest and submitted schemes by Kohn Pedersen Fox of New York, Murphy/Jahn of Chicago, Hellmuth Obata Kassabaum (HOK) of St. Louis, and 3DI of Houston. But the project was never built; local leaders were unwilling to accept a scaled-down scheme or one that would be built in stages, even though by 1986 the hotel occupancy rate was very low, the need for office space had been met, and retail activity was declining.

Nothing planners could have done would have changed the fact that residential growth was occurring at the edges of the city, and with it, suburban shopping malls were attracting larger and larger shares of the market. But the building of new office buildings on the northern and eastern edges of downtown, several blocks from Fourth and Race streets, where stores had traditionally been located, also meant that office workers were farther from downtown merchants than they had been before, so noontime shopping errands became rare.

More importantly, new buildings did not stimulate growth downtown. They may have somewhat stemmed the tide of movement toward the suburbs, but they did not prevent it. And even though its planners had created a more attractive downtown than those in many other cities, Cincinnati did not substantially grow during the years of successful building. The metropolitan area did grow, slowly, but the city itself actually declined in population between 1964 and 1988—and continues to do so. More troubling, for those who see growth as a sign of vitality, Cincinnati, from 1850 on, has steadily declined in size relative to other American cities. It went from the sixth-largest city in the United States to sixteenth in 1920 and forty-fifth in 1990. Size and relative size have little to do with quality of life. Who, after all, would argue that Palm Beach, Florida, does not provide a better living environment than Las Vegas, Nevada (even though Las Vegas is many times its size and the fastest-growing city in the United States today)? But civic leaders, almost everywhere, confuse growth with prosperity and well-being.

A New Plan for 2000

In 1981, when it became obvious that the goals of the 1964 plan had been achieved, or were about to be, planners and civic leaders set about making a new plan. Significantly, even though the problems were different than they had been thirty years before, the Plan for the Year 2000 did not contain any radical new ideas. With all the new office buildings and without the department stores, the movie theaters, and all the restaurants that had prospered in the immediate postwar years, downtown was no longer lively, especially after dark. The solution proposed—in Cincinnati as in every other city that was experiencing the same phenomenon—was downtown housing. If more people lived downtown, the argument ran, there would be excitement similar to that of New York, Chicago, San Francisco, or Boston, where urban living was customary. In Cincinnati, unlike those cities, there was a substantial amount of impressive, inexpensive housing stock near downtown. That was one of the things that made the city attractive to newcomers and a comfortable place for citizens of all income groups to raise families. Some debate took place about the validity of building downtown housing, and some new middle- and upper-income housing was planned and built. Rental apartments went up at Lytle Place and on Garfield Square, and condominiums, such as Adams Landing and Park Place at Lytle, were built beginning in the 1980s. But only now, in the twenty-first century, is downtown residential development becoming economically viable. Downtown Cincinnati in 2006 remains essentially what the 1964 plan helped it become, a central business district.

Preservation in In-Town Suburbs

The first major renovations of historic houses in Cincinnati's hilltop or in-town suburbs came during the 1950s, in the working-class community of Mount Adams, a hilltop neighborhood that had dramatic views of the Ohio River and of the skyline and was within walking distance of downtown. Gradually, Mount Adams's simple frame row houses (and the few brick ones) were turned into stylish apartments, first for artists and actors and then for prosperous young professionals. Trendy bars and cute shops opened, and Mount Adams became a center of wholesome nightlife. A few new apartment buildings were constructed more or less in character with the old, certainly with more originality than those in other areas. Then, in 1964, a twenty-four-story building with modern luxury apartments, Highland Tower, was built near the crest of the hill, assuring the neighborhood's future as a bastion of the upper middle class, but also undermining its funky, individualistic character to some extent. In 1973, a much more indigenous and original new housing complex was built on the east side of Mount Adams. The Cloisters Condominiums, designed by Hardy Holzman Pfeiffer of New York, were shed-roofed, cedar-sided town houses perched on stilts and angled to take advantage of views and echo the scale of nearby dwellings.

Other in-town residential neighborhoods where the housing stock had been well preserved began to experience change in their shopping districts as supermarkets and drug stores moved to nearby strip malls and houses were modernized or

Paul Muller & Associates
Renovation of Esquire Theater, 1987–90
Ludlow Avenue, Clifton

At a time when neighborhood movie theaters were closing all over the country, members of the Clifton community got together, bought theirs, and had it stylishly converted to an art cinema with several small theaters. The survival of the Esquire provided not only a place for neighbors to meet for casual entertainment, but an anchor for a truly functional and fun-filled business district.

upgraded. Each neighborhood took on a slightly different character. Northside became offbeat, so bookstores, little galleries, and coffeehouses opened. Hyde Park became luxurious, so fancy dress stores and antique shops moved in around its charming elliptical "square." Corryville developed lively restaurants, photographic supply stores, and other outlets geared to the nearby university community, and they flourished through the 1980s.

The most impressive neighborhood-preservation effort occurred on Ludlow Avenue in Clifton, where nearby residents fought to preserve their supermarket,

Hyde Park Square
Erie Avenue between Edwards Road and Michigan Avenue

The fountain-filled esplanade in the middle of Hyde Park Square recalls the original form of Fountain Square downtown. It serves as a place for neighbors out for a walk to meet and a verdant plaza for surrounding shops.

grocery store, and movie theater while patronizing new restaurants, artistic clothing stores, historic ice cream parlors, and bakeries. First, the old Ludlow Garage, which had serviced automobiles for decades, was converted to an informal concert hall by entrepreneur Jim Tarbell, who went on to become a restaurateur and later a Cincinnati councilman. Then, in 1981, the garage interior was turned into a shopping arcade designed by Architekton, ArchitectsPlus, and Hefley/Stevens Architects. Finally, a group of Clifton residents formed a corporation that bought the Esquire Theater and created an art house cinema. The corporation helped preserve the neighborhood business district as an entertainment area as well as a shopping venue. The Esquire Theater was inventively redesigned by architect Paul Muller & Associates and remains one of the few ventures of its kind in the country.

While most growth was occurring in the suburbs and exurbs—in many cases encouraged by corporations that advised new employees to live there—many of Cincinnati's hilltop neighborhoods not only remained popular but became more desirable. Houses in Hyde Park, East Walnut Hills, Mount Lookout, and Clifton commanded prices higher than those in most suburbs. One reason was that a significant segment of the Cincinnati establishment had never moved out. Another was that people came to appreciate large, well-built, historic houses, many of which were on lots even larger than suburban properties. But not all neighborhoods prospered equally, and some, such as Hyde Park, which in the early twentieth century had had a mix of income groups, became exclusively the haven of professionals and businesspeople. Even modest houses were expensively maintained or renovated. In other communities, grand houses were insensitively divided into apartments. The separation of the population into income groups that was occurring in new subdivisions on the periphery was also taking place incrementally and privately in the city.

One factor that averted a complete exodus to the suburbs was the Cincinnati Public Schools system. During this period, CPS oversaw the maintenance of good neighborhood schools and the creation of magnet schools. Walnut Hills High School, the citywide college preparatory school, where students continued to achieve and to earn high test scores, enabled the city to compete for residents with the more prosperous suburbs.

RTKL
Fountain Square, 1966–69
Proscenium stage added by Baxter Hodell Donnelly Preston, 1985
Fifth Street between Vine and Walnut streets

The redesign of Fountain Square was the first visible manifestation of—and a central element in—the 1964 Downtown Plan. It was intended to make the city's symbolic center more accessible to pedestrians, and for decades it functioned very successfully as a meeting place.

Fountain Square, 1966–69; Proscenium Stage, 1983–85

Few cities have a discernible center, a unique public place that serves as a symbol and that everyone recognizes as its heart. Cincinnati's Fountain Square is one. It offers an opportunity to simply wander, meet informally with friends, or gather for civic events. It has been the city center since 1870, when a local hardware merchant, Henry Probasco, donated the Tyler Davidson Fountain to the citizenry in memory of his business partner and brother-in-law. City officials agreed to create a paved esplanade for it on the site of the old butcher's market on the north side of Fifth Street between Vine and Walnut. The tree-lined 60-by-400-foot esplanade was designed by William Tinsley.

At that time there was little traffic. But by the 1950s, when the ideas behind what became the 1964 Downtown Plan were being discussed, the streets around the esplanade were becoming so busy that they were difficult to cross. Americans were beginning to travel to Europe in numbers, and many returned impressed by the big public squares they had seen, especially the Italian piazzas where local residents and tourists gather to sip coffee or drinks at all hours of the day. Fountain Square was designed to function as that kind of space, even though, in the United States, public and private space are more clearly defined, lingering in cafés is not customary, and the weather is rarely conducive to outdoor dining. Nevertheless, Fountain Square, as redesigned by Richard Chalmers of RTKL of Baltimore between 1966 and 1969, did attract large crowds at lunchtime, even though, with only occasional and expensive table service on the periphery, people had to bring their own sandwiches. But because the new square was easy to reach and had numerous nooks and crannies and a number of places where strollers could wander in and out casually, the square had visitors throughout the day and often in the early evening hours. The esteemed city planner and planning historian Edmund Bacon of Philadelphia called it "the most successful public square in America."[4] Fountain Square received a national Honor Award from the American Institute of Architects, the first earned by a Cincinnati project.

As the square became popular for public events, city officials decided that a podium of some kind was necessary for ceremonies. In 1985, a proscenium stage designed by Cincinnati architects Baxter, Hodell, Donnelly & Preston (now BHDP) was added. The stage was removed in 2005 and the entire square was rebuilt according to a design by Cooper Robertson & Partners of New York. The fountain was moved north and a bower of trees was added.

The square's most important function is to serve as a center, an organizing device for the downtown core. It was the first block redeveloped in the 1964 plan, framed by the Fifth-Third Center, the first outdoor segment of the skywalk, and the Dubois (now Fifth Third) Tower. Although the square has changed with the times, its centerpiece, the Tyler Davidson Fountain, remains the symbol of Cincinnati, shown on postcards and in television newscasts the way Times Square is in New York.

Hardy Holzman Pfeiffer
Robert S. Marx Theater at the Cincinnati Playhouse in the Park, 1967–68
Eden Park

The architects of the Robert S. Marx Theater made a virtue out of a minimal budget. They created the most avant-garde theater in the country with bare concrete walls, exposed lighting systems, and air-conditioning ducts used as decoration. Hugh Hardy went on to design the Cloisters in Mount Adams for Towne Properties.

The Cincinnati Playhouse in the Park, 1967–68

When it opened in 1968, the Robert S. Marx Theater at the Playhouse in the Park was the most avant-garde building in Cincinnati and, arguably, the most up-to-date theater design in the United States. The 672-seat theater was built as an addition to the small, nonprofit professional repertory theater created in 1960 in an historic shelter house in Eden Park, which abuts the then-fast-changing hilltop neighborhood of Mount Adams.

The Marx Theater had exposed concrete-block exterior and interior walls, only one layer thick, on top of a steel frame. It featured the country's first asymmetrical thrust stage, with seating surrounding the areas where the action usually takes place. It was designed to provide the acting company maximal flexibility. Actors could enter from twenty-four different points, numerous lighting effects could be provided, and at every point the audience was brought into the theatrical experience. There were clear sightlines from almost every seat. Even the costume shop was exposed to the outside through gigantic windows. The idea was to involve the audience and make it part of the theatrical experience by stripping away mystery and pomp and, in the words of the time, "letting it all hang out."

Air-conditioning ducts, lighting, and the sound system were left exposed as elements of the design—a complete functional openness that was both in style at the time and dictated by a minimal budget of less than $1 million (an amazing $1,443 per seat). The funds had been raised solely from private donations. The budget allowed only a minimal lobby, where decoration was provided by ventilation ducts and air diffusers treated as works of sculpture in stainless steel (that, too, was the style of the time). It was not simply supposed to *be* functional, it was supposed to *look* functional. The tall, narrow, irregularly shaped lobby was further enlivened by exposed vertical fluorescent lights and forty-foot-tall mirrors. Sound absorption was provided by colorful carpeting laid on both floors and ceilings. Inside the theater itself, the only soft elements were upholstered seats and stair carpeting. The plaza outside was illuminated by airport runway lights.

The theater was designed by the young, up-and-coming firm of Hardy Holzman Pfeiffer Associates. One of the partners, Hugh Hardy, while he was trying to decide whether to go into architecture or theater after college, had worked for the architect Eero Saarinen on the Vivian Beaumont Repertory Theater at Lincoln Center. Hardy became an architect and went on to become one of the most active and innovative theater designers in the country. His firm was responsible for Orchestra Hall in Minneapolis, the Brooklyn Academy of Music, and the New Amsterdam and New Victory Theaters in Times Square. One of his first commissions came from a college friend, Brooks Jones, who, as the artistic director of the Shelterhouse Theater, invited him to convert the historic park building into a performance space. Its success, both architecturally and aesthetically, led to the offer to design the Marx Theater, which has many of the features of Saarinen's Lincoln Center theater, albeit on a smaller, low-budget scale with a fresh, even more direct, behind-the-scenes quality. When the Marx opened, *Progressive Architecture* magazine raved, "Cincinnati One-Ups Lincoln Center," referring not to Saarinen's progressive design but to the then-out-of-style pompous marble concert halls on the main plaza by Philip Johnson, Wallace Harrison, and Max Abramovitz.

Only steps from the Cincinnati Art Museum, the Murray Seasongood Pavilion band shell, and, at the time, the Cincinnati Historical Society and Cincinnati Museum of Natural History, the Playhouse helped make Eden Park a cultural center.

In 1980, Cincinnati's Architects Team Associates (ATA) added the large lobby that the Playhouse had never had, creating a bridge to the original Shelterhouse Theater over the original plaza. In the 1990s, Glaserworks removed an unsightly administrative building next to the Shelterhouse and added a dining area, rehearsal hall, restrooms, and offices in a design that reflected the daring modern aesthetic of the Marx Theater and celebrated the historic Shelterhouse as a jewel.

The Procter & Gamble Headquarters Building, 1982–85

It is difficult to imagine how shocking the model of the Procter & Gamble Building was when it was first unveiled, with great fanfare, on April 10, 1982. A press conference for 8 a.m. had been called only the night before. When reporters arrived, they found a table with a blue satin, pleated cover, much like a fancy bedspread, surrounded by chairs, TV cameras, and stone-faced officials. What could merit all this? When the crowd arrived and the cover was removed, the reason for the mystery was obvious. The company was unveiling a design for a new building like no one there had seen before, presented in handsome, hand-colored models and hyperrealistic photomontages showing it already in place. The crowd was speechless. No one knew what to make of it. This writer returned to her desk at the *Cincinnati Enquirer* to prepare a review, and when it was coming out of the printer, reporters congregated to read what she had to say as the words were appearing on the page. Never before had most of them expressed the slightest interest in architecture, but this was something new—or old? Why? What did it mean?

It meant that not only the general public but also some talented avant-garde architects and their clients had become disillusioned with bland, abstract modern architecture. And it meant that the idea that a building should relate to its context was being taken to the next level. Not just the same materials were being used, not only were there gestures to define the block, but the forms of historic structures were being employed, inventively but unmistakably, by ambitious young architects.

The case of the Procter & Gamble Building was somewhat unusual, for the new 800,000-square-foot office building was an addition to an unusually conservative one that the company had erected in 1956. P&G had hired the New York commercial firm of Voorhees, Walker, Smith & Smith and built a mundane eleven-story limestone slab, which looked like a government office building with a colonnade on top.

Sixteen years later, in 1972, to expand its headquarters, P&G brought in Skidmore, Owings & Merrill, the firm that designed Lever House, the headquarters of its main competitor, Lever Brothers. With an architect (Charles Luckman) as president, the company had built the first corporate curtain wall skyscraper, a daring green-glass tower on Park Avenue in New York City, designed by SOM partner Gordon Bunshaft. But for P&G, the Skidmore architects could not figure out what to do, so they simply duplicated what was already there, continuing its bays down to the end of the block.

Kohn Pedersen Fox (KPF) had a much more inventive approach. It freely used the semiclassical language of the original to create a pair of low-rise buildings on the north and east edges of the adjoining city block. The place where the buildings joined was marked with a pair of capped towers, a two-story octagonal entrance pavilion on the inside corner, and a three-story auditorium and cafeteria pavilion on the outside corner. The new rectangular wings echo the shapes of the old and maintain the same 120-foot width, but they are slightly lower and stepped down at the top to provide clerestory windows.

KPF also added more columns to the base of the old building and moved the entrance from Sixth Street on the north to Fifth Street on the south, reorienting the complex to the city's symbolic center, Fountain Square. And because of the way the towers were capped, even the Times-Star Building at Broadway and Eighth streets is brought into the downtown ensemble.

The towers are slightly separated to suggest a gateway. As the architects, Eugene Kohn and William Pedersen, remarked at the time, a pair of towers has more impact than a single one, especially in a cityscape that already has several pyramidal ones. The L-shaped complex not only creates the illusion of an entryway from the highway, but also frames the northwest edge of downtown. It helped extend the central business district two blocks east.

The two-block site was largely filled with a formal garden, which is outlined with pergolas along the sidewalk. Designed in collaboration with Bentley Meisner, landscape architects, of Cincinnati, the gardens provide a different kind of outdoor

experience than Fountain Square or any other urban plaza. They are open to the public as well as to P&G employees.

The building also symbolizes the conservative, stolid company impressively. Symbolism, along with reintroduction of ornament and respect for the urban context, were the major goals of the Postmodern movement in architecture, which amounted to a critique of abstract, box-like International style modern architecture. The Procter & Gamble Building is a prime example of the style.

Kohn Pederson Fox
Procter & Gamble Headquarters, 1982–85
Addition to former headquarters by Voorhees, Walker, Smith & Smith, 1956, and SOM, 1972
Fifth Street between Main and Sycamore streets

The architects of the Procter & Gamble Headquarters responded imaginatively to the challenge of adding an addition to the bland existing limestone building by creating one of the best examples of Postmodern Classicism in the United States. The two-block-long structure frames a formal garden that is open to the public.

Michael Graves Architect with Carl Strauss and Ray Roush
Riverbend Music Center, 1982–84
Coney Island Amusement Park on the Ohio River

This outdoor pavilion built for the Cincinnati Symphony Orchestra provides covered seating in an open-walled structure with river views and open-air seating on an earth berm inspired by ancient Greek and Roman amphitheaters. Framed by a pergola painted in earth tones and intended for outdoor eating, the complex elicits a full range of sensual pleasures.

Riverbend Music Center, 1982–84

The Cincinnati Symphony Orchestra's decision to build a summer pavilion on the grounds of an old riverside amusement park, Coney Island, and to hire the architect Michael Graves to design it meant that Cincinnati would acquire one of the most unusual and interesting structures of the Postmodern era. It also meant that Cincinnatians would once more have the opportunity to attend outdoor summer concerts on a regular basis. The Cincinnati Summer Opera had performed in an open-walled pavilion at the Cincinnati Zoo for more than fifty years before its trustees decided to relocate to Music Hall. Though occasional concerts took place at various band shells, there was no regular venue. Part of the impetus to create a permanent outdoor home was a labor contract that required the orchestra to employ musicians year round, but symphony supporters also hoped summer concerts would expand audiences.

One symphony trustee, C. Lawson Reed Jr., had a serious interest in art and architecture as well as in music. He had built a house and a factory for his company, Xomox, with the respected Cincinnati architects Carl Strauss and Ray Roush Jr., for whom Michael Graves had worked when he was a student in the co-op program of the School of Architecture at the University of Cincinnati. Reed also served on the Board of Trustees of the Whitney Museum in New York, where Graves had recently been commissioned to build an addition (which was never built). Reed urged his symphony colleagues to hire Graves to design the symphony pavilion with his old friends Strauss and Roush as collaborators.

Graves, who teaches at Princeton University and has a serious interest in and broad knowledge of architectural history, came up with a design that drew from ancient Greek, Roman, Italian Renaissance, and modern sources. The pavilion itself, composed of a broad, sloping roof supported on exposed steel truss towers, is modern. The semicircular, sloped earth berm in front of the pavilion resembles Greek and Roman amphitheaters (but can accommodate 10,000 people). The pergola that surrounds the berm and the flat painted classical statues that dance across the roofline are Postmodern references to an indoor theater that the Italian Renaissance architect Andrea Palladio built in Vicenza, Italy, which itself was inspired by amphitheaters from ancient Greece and Rome. The hefty draped acroteria figures were created by New York artist Edward Schmidt.

The pavilion is sited at the river's edge, with the rear wall of the stage open to permit views of the river behind the performers. Because it is in a floodplain only about one hundred feet from the water, the building had to be made of materials that could be cleaned after flooding, and it has to be thoroughly washed down from time to time. But the romantic siting makes the effort worthwhile.

The shape of the $7.9 million pavilion, which seats 4,500, was created to offer excellent natural acoustics for orchestral music. But to pay for the structure, the symphony had to adapt it for the electronic amplification required by the popular music groups who lease it for concerts of their own.

The structure is painted in earth tones—buff, dark brown, blue-green—typical of the Italian countryside, which served as the architect's inspiration. But the music center is a very personal response to an unusual design problem adapted to a unique site in a location that has provided memories of romantic summer nights to Cincinnatians for generations.

Carl Strauss and Ray Roush
Xomox Corp. Plant, 1968–69
4444 Cooper Road, Blue Ash

The architects designed this sleek, sophisticated factory building for one of their most loyal and most aesthetically adventurous clients in an outer suburb where serious architecture is a rarity. Later the client, C. Lawson Reed Jr., invited them to design the Riverbend Music Center with Michael Graves.

Zion & Breen
Serpentine Wall at Riverfront Park, 1977
Entrance at Yeatman's Cove by the Public Landing

Undulating along the edge of the Ohio River beneath Riverfront Park, the Serpentine Wall offers outdoor seating for public events and direct access to the river itself. Because of its gigantic scale, it is visible from afar, although people meandering along it appear to be tiny dolls.

Glaser Associates with M. Paul Friedberg & Partners
Bicentennial Commons at Sawyer Point Park, 1988
with gateway sculpture by Andrew Leicester and Garth Rockcastle
Pete Rose Way and Eggleston Avenue

Visitors to the many activities available at the Bicentennial Commons receive history lessons in the most playful and imaginative way. Passing through the Gateway Arch, they encounter a gigantic flood column, waltz around the Flying Pigs, and view the Ohio River in miniature. As they play along the river banks, they cannot forgot that the water forged the city's history and determined its site.

The Cincinnati Riverfront, 1968–88

It was during the late 1960s and 1970s that the riverfront, which had been changing for decades, finally began to take on the appearance of its new role as a recreational area. Planners had been talking about transforming what had become a shabby, underused industrial area since the great flood of 1937. They had incorporated provisions for a park and stadiums into the plan made in the aftermath of the flood and into the 1948 Master Plan for Metropolitan Cincinnati, but it was only when Riverfront Stadium was built in 1968 that there were visible signs of change. The enormous stadium, designed by Heery & Heery of Atlanta, was built to replace the Reds' historic Crosley Field in the West End and to provide a venue for professional football. In 1973, the stadium was joined by the Riverfront Coliseum and Plaza, designed by Cincinnatian Gary Lesniewicz. This arena was to be used for professional ice hockey as well as for concerts and other public events that still take place there today. Three years later, Yeatman's Cove Park opened just west of the L&N Bridge, not exactly where the first settlers had landed (that site was under Riverfront Stadium) but nearby and adjacent to the new Public Landing and its parking areas.

The most impressive element in the new series of parks is the powerful concrete, serpentine wall, designed by Robert Zion of the New York-based landscape architects Zion and Breen and completed in 1977. It meanders horizontally for several hundred feet and serves as a retaining wall while providing access to the river, seating for events, and an edge to the river that reads from the other side, nearby bridges, and tall buildings in the downtown. Because the steps are several times larger than those in a normal staircase, the thirty-five-foot-tall Serpentine Wall mediates between the scale of the Ohio River and that of the human activity above. The marvelous tubular waste cans, other furnishings, and light fixtures in the park area are oversized too. They have a suitable nautical character and were designed to withstand flooding, which reaches their level about every ten years.

Over the next decade, facilities such as a boathouse for the Cincinnati Rowing Club and a fishing pier were added to the riverfront park system, while a growing interest in history and ways to depict it were developing within the disciplines of art and architecture. It was just in time for the bicentennial celebrations, when the city decided to give itself a new $14 million, twenty-two-acre park east of the arched brick railroad trestle for the L&N Bridge (with $8 million in private contributions and a $300,000 grant from the Greater Cincinnati Foundation). Bicentennial Commons at Sawyer Point was designed by Glaser Associates (now Glaserworks) according to a plan by Paul M. Friedberg & Associates of New York and named for the philanthropist and former U.S. Secretary of Commerce Charles Sawyer. The Commons playfully recounts the history of Cincinnati while providing a number of delightful places to unwind. These include the earth-bermed and tent-covered Procter & Gamble performance pavilion, a children's play area, a dining plaza, volleyball and tennis courts, and a river walk, as well as idyllic plantings by landscape architect Eric Doepke. The unique feature in the park is an environmental sculpture by British-born, Minneapolis-based artist Andrew Leicester and the Minneapolis architect Garth Rockcastle. A modern version of the Ishtar Gate to Babylon, it consists of a series of curved outdoor rooms flowing into one another like galleries in a museum. The first, which forms an arc at the drop-off point, replicates an old canal barge. Visitors then pass through a canal boat lock, which is set into a serpentine earth berm reminiscent of the Indian mounds near Cincinnati. At the top of the mound, where the first dramatic view of the river appears, is a miniature Ohio River with Pittsburgh at one end and Cairo, Illinois, at the other. In the middle is the Queen City's crown, with a 115-foot-tall flood column with an ark on top. It is surrounded by the Flying Pigs (a colonnade with piglets on top) symbolizing the old meat-packing industry for which Cincinnati was once known. Some city council members disapproved of reviving the Porkopolis image. The issue was debated in the council chamber, where members of the art community arrived wearing pig-nosed masks to support the sculpture. It was approved; public opinion was with the playful piglets.

Elzner & Anderson
Cincinnati Zoo Elephant House, 1907
Renovation:
Glaser & Myers and THP Limited, 1982
Eden and Clifton Avenues, Avondale

The romantic Elephant House, an early example of the use of reinforced concrete, is only part of the Zoo's unusual collection of significant buildings. The Cincinnati Zoo contained naturalistic environments for animals long before they became popular elsewhere.

The Cincinnati Zoo, 1875–2005

After the energy crisis of 1974, conservation movements gathered steam worldwide. Zoological gardens, which had grown up in the nineteenth century as parks where animals were displayed as curiosities, began to be seen as protectors of the species they had inherited. (The New York Zoological Society even changed its name to the New York Conservation Society.) Interest developed in creating environments for the animals that were as similar as possible to those they experienced in the wild. The Cincinnati Zoo, however, had been showing its animals in naturalistic habitats for over half a century. The second-oldest zoo in America, it opened in 1875 with a German animal trainer, Sol Stephan, on the staff. He remained until retiring at 88 in 1937. Stephan brought Carl Hagenbeck (1844–1913) from Steilingen, Germany, where he had created the first naturalistic environments for the animals, instead of the tiny cages used in most zoos of the time. (The Hagenbeck Tierpark on the outskirts of Hamburg is still owned by the Hagenbeck family, which started out training animals for circuses. The Tierpark is still regarded as one of the leading zoos in the world.) Hagenbeck's African Veldt in Cincinnati, which did not open until 1933, long after his death, is a large, cageless area where zebras, wildebeasts, ostrich, elands, and African cranes wander freely. It was one of the first exhibits of its kind in the world. The animals are so comfortable in it that they have been able to reproduce naturally, creating a self-perpetuating display.

The Cincinnati Zoo also contained some romantic buildings, such as the Elephant House with its "Moorish" domes, which suggest that the places where the animals came from are strange and exotic. But the Zoo had also installed numerous environments, such as the barless, moated lion, tiger, and bear grottoes, before the conservation movement took hold. Even in the postwar period, when technology was valued more than a naturalistic approach, the Cincinnati Zoo built a domestically scaled brick aquarium, designed by Carl Strauss and Associates, who also created the dramatic Walk-Through Flight Cage in 1961–62. This huge metal net draped far above the treetops not only allowed birds to fly free, but also enabled zoo visitors to join them (on foot).

In the 1970s, when Glaser & Myers Architects were employed to build new exhibits and update some of the old ones, they had an impressive tradition to build on. In 1978, they created a Gorilla Environment that put the animals on a kind of stage, but one geared to the apes' natural needs. In 1982, with THP, Glaser & Myers renovated the concrete-domed Elephant House, which had been built by concrete pioneers Elzner & Anderson in 1907. (Even animals in Cincinnati benefited from the historic preservation movement.) Over the years, the firm has created a host of new exhibits linked by verdant plantings that separate one display from another while making each one seem to be in the wild. The task has not been easy—the Zoo occupies a site that encompasses only sixty-four acres, many of which are devoted to parking and back-of-the-house services that visitors never see but that are essential for the kind of research and animal care that is a primary task of a modern zoo.

Heery & Heery
Greater Cincinnati International Airport, 1973–74
Renovation of and addition to Kenton County Airport, 1943, with new Main Terminal by Fisk, Rinehart & Hall, McAllister, Stockwell, ca. 1965
Kenton County, Kentucky

A frank, straightforward, and artful use of modular parts helped turn this confident expansion of what had been a one-room airport into an international hub. The Greater Cincinnati Airport today provides direct access to cities around the world.

Greater Cincinnati International Airport, 1973–74

No building changed the destiny of Cincinnati during the 1970s and '80s as completely as an unusually modest one that was almost out of sight, thirteen miles from downtown, across the bridges in Kentucky, and rarely considered a work of architecture. And yet, when it was being built, it was featured in *Architectural Record* magazine twice (in 1973 and 1974), and, the magazine reported, "delegations are coming from all over the world to study the Cincinnati approach." The days of exuberant architecture expressing the wonder of flight, such as Eero Saarinen's TWA Terminal at JFK and Dulles Airport, were over, and the age of architecturally ambitious airports in Asia had not yet begun. The emphasis in airport design at this time was on efficiency, economy, and expandability. The Greater Cincinnati Airport exhibited all three. It also looked clean, fresh, and welcoming. It was designed —with the active participation of the airport's director of planning, Robert Keefe, who argued for a coordination and minimal commercial intrusion—by Heery & Heery of Atlanta, the architects who had designed (the later demolished) Riverfront Stadium.

The architects involved were Ennis Parker, Ray Graves, and Mack Scoggin. Scoggin went on with his wife, Merrill Elam, to become one of the most respected architects of the next generation. Walking distances were about half those at other large airports. Terminals were largely composed of prefabricated components—precast, prestressed concrete floor plates and long-span steel trusses—assembled on-site. The ten gates in the original 1943 Kenton County Airport and its 1965 addition by Fisk, Rinehart & Hall, McAllister, Stockwell were retrofitted to create Terminal A for $2.5 million, while the new Terminals B and C, with eight gates each, were built for about $6 million apiece. But what was most impressive was the way the components were assembled, integrated, and used to create an unusually appealing environment, uncluttered by big airline logos or other advertising and opened with window walls to the activity on the runway.

The airport's attractiveness and efficiency and the availability of nearby land for expansion were significant factors in Delta Air Lines' decision to make Cincinnati a hub. That decision not only led to extensive economic development but also gave Cincinnatians easy access to the rest of the world at a time when globalization was becoming a major force in everyday life. When the airport became a hub, the short walking distances evaporated, as did the clean lines and controlled commercial activity. Instead of a row of concourses along the airport roadway, directly adjacent to the drop-off points and parking lots, Delta built two additional concourses perpendicular to Terminal C and the airport drives. Each one had at its center an aboveground shopping mall, seemingly detached from the land. The walking distances grew so long that subway trains and moving sidewalks had to be installed. Nevertheless, becoming a hub helped put Cincinnati on the aerial map.

The downtown skyline reflects a $2 billion transformation of the riverfront. A series of ambitious projects at the turn of the twenty-first century included reconfiguring Fort Washington Way and constructing two stadiums and the National Underground Railroad Freedom Center. A multiblock, mixed-use development known as the Banks and a fifty-acre riverfront park would complete the transformation.

10

Dynamic Mix of New and Old

1989–2006

At the turn of the twenty-first century, Greater Cincinnati's accomplishments in architecture, historic preservation, and planning were characterized by the revitalization of downtown and Over-the-Rhine; the redevelopment of the Ohio and Kentucky riverfronts; a phenomenal expansion of arts, education, and cultural institutions; and an emerging perception of the importance of regional cooperation. The processes of design and development have been shaped by teams of national and local architects and directed and supported by public entities or private development organizations. During this period, public and private stakeholders contributed substantially to furthering the goal of creating a dynamic, diverse, sustainable, and stimulating environment.

Revitalizing Downtown with Arts, Entertainment, Residents, and Visitors

Cincinnati's Bicentennial celebration in 1988 reconfirmed the importance of the riverfront and its connection to the central business district, a concept that had appeared as early as 1948 in the metropolitan master plan. Government and civic leaders continued to express concern about the vitality of the central business district as residents and businesses spun away from the urban core. By 1990 the city's population, which had peaked in 1950 at 503,000, was down to 331,294. Downtown office and hotel development were strong, and the convention center had been expanded in 1987. But retail, entertainment, and housing were lagging and the redevelopment of the western riverfront had stalled. In 1989, City Council appointed a committee of corporate leaders chaired by Nelson Schwab Jr. to assess progress on the Cincinnati 2000 Plan for downtown, which had been published in 1982. The review reconfirmed the goals of the plan, emphasizing the vision of round-the-clock activity created through a mix of uses, especially retail, arts, and entertainment. The housing goal was adjusted downward to a more realistic 4,000 units. There was also renewed resolve to redevelop the rest of the riverfront, build new stadiums, and plan further growth of the convention center.

A key recommendation of the Cincinnati 2000 Plan Review Committee was to create a private, nonprofit organization to monitor downtown's progress and work with city government to see that development goals were met. Downtown Cincinnati Inc. (DCI) was formed in 1993 with initial city funding until a business improvement district was implemented. DCI was directed by Rick Greiwe, who saw downtown revitalization as a continuation of the Bicentennial's mission, and chaired by David Phillips, a retired executive from Arthur Anderson. In 1984, Phillips had chaired a commission of business leaders who analyzed the management of every department in Cincinnati City Hall and made a hundred recommendations to tighten the budget.

DCI began by producing Vision 2020, which was developed with widespread public input and provided a framework for strategic planning and decision-making about downtown. Vision 2020 acknowledged that suburban growth was threatening downtown as a center for white-collar jobs, shopping, and entertainment. It also established DCI's mission as promoting downtown as the vital heart of the region, attracting new tenants, residents, and visitors and maintaining a clean and safe environment. DCI has served to revitalize downtown, especially in the areas of safety, housing, transportation, arts, and entertainment.

Nevertheless, development of new office space downtown had slowed; only four office towers have been completed since 1989. Duke Realty and Manuel Mayerson completed the thirty-five-story Scripps Center on Third Street at the corner of Walnut in 1989. The design by Hoover & Furr of Houston, with Glaser & Associates as architect of record, created a curved glass façade overlooking and evoking the curve of the river. The other three sides were precast concrete with punched openings.

Central Bancorporation (now PNC) and Houston-based Hines Interests completed the thirty-two-story Chemed Building at 255 East Fifth Street in 1991. Skidmore, Owings & Merrill's tasteful scheme was designed by David Childs of the New York office. The last major building to be designed in the spirit of the 1964 plan, it steps back at the top in the Art Deco manner, creating a kind of py-

Skidmore, Owings & Merrill
Chemed Building, 1991
255 East Fifth Street

As one of the newer high-rise office buildings, the Chemed Building exemplifies a more traditional approach from the prestigious firm of SOM, historically known for Modernism.

ramidal effect similar to Carew Tower. In 1992, Duke Realty completed a building at 312 Elm Street, later renamed the Enquirer Building. Space Design International (now FRCH) designed this boxy tower to be exactly 312 feet tall.

That was the end of the downtown office boom, which had reached a crescendo in the early 1990s with grand plans for an unbuilt forty-nine-story tower on the west side of Fountain Square, discussed in chapter 9. Instead, a new team of developers (Towne Properties, Duke, and Belvedere) built the three-story Fountain Place, which opened in 1997. Anchored by a downsized Lazarus (now Macy's) department store, with blue-chip retailers Tiffany, Brooks Brothers, and Palomino Rotisseries and Bar, the structure was designed by Cooper Carry of Atlanta and BHDP to support the future addition of a tower, pending suitable economic conditions. Since then, Eagle Realty, the real-estate arm of Western-Southern Life Insurance Co., constructed the fifteen-story Queen City Square by Hellmuth, Obata & Kassabaum in 2005 at Broadway and Third Street.

To meet the housing goals of the Cincinnati 2000 Plan, the city contracted with Towne Properties to build the Garfield Place Housing project, possibly the first new residential buildings built downtown in at least fifty years. The multiblock project was conceived by former city council member Arn Bortz, who, in the 1980s, joined the Towne Properties firm established by his brother Neil Bortz, Marvin Rosenberg, and Lambert Agin in 1961. Towne had led the back-to-the-city movement of the 1960s with the development of residential units in Mount Adams. Arn Bortz began a downtown residential initiative with the Gramercy and the Greenwich, two low-rise new apartment buildings on Garfield Place flanking Piatt Park. (The park was redesigned by Bentley-Meisner, landscape architects.) The historically inspired six-story units were designed by the New York firm

Gruzen Samton Architects, with PDT, architect of record
Greenwich Apartments, 1996
Garfield Place at Piatt Park

For more than three decades, Towne Properties has developed attractive housing through renovation and new construction, drawing young professionals to downtown Cincinnati, Covington, and Mount Adams. The new Gramercy and Greenwich Apartments frame Piatt Park, recalling the town houses that once existed there, but with a modern flair at the roof line.

Gruzen Samton, and Tom Tilsley, PDT Architects, served as architects of record. Towne followed this with the conversion into loft-style apartments, designed by PDT Architects, of the 1897 Groton office building at Race and Seventh streets by Crapsey & Brown with a matching 1925 addition by Harry Hake, and the former Lazarus/Shillito department store building.

The city was also eager to capitalize on renewal of the riverfront at the foot of Mount Adams. A narrow, mile-long site known as Adams Landing was envisioned with a hotel, offices, and 1,250 units of high-end housing. William Turnbull Associates and KZF Design created a master plan for a dense, urban village like a terraced Italian hill town. William Turnbull Jr. (1935–97) was a San Francisco-based architect who specialized in difficult or sensitive sites. He and Cincinnati architect Robert Doran, then with KZF Design, worked together as lead designers. Because of high cost and rocky market conditions, the ambitious plan was downscaled, redesigned, and broken into phases. The first phase, a condominium tower known as Adams Place, opened in 1993. Reflecting its context, the building's brick skin provides a historical reference and domestic character, and its stepped top echoes the city skyline. Irrigated terraces by landscape architect John Bentley provide a veil of greenery.

While Adams Place is now a very desirable place to live, the urban condominium concept was slow to catch on and caused the original developers to default. The second developer hired Duany Plater-Zyberk, the creators of Seaside, Florida, to draw up a smaller New Urbanist scheme, but it also was too dense and expensive to build. After the second developer defaulted, the city assigned the project to Towne Properties in 2001. A revised master plan by RTKL and Urban Design Associates called for the creation of five villages. Twain's Point, the first village of twenty-six traditional-looking town houses by PDT Architects, opened in 2005.

William Turnbull Associates and Doran Studio, with KZF Design, architect of record
Adams Place, 1993
Riverfront

Adams Place was the first phase of the larger Adams Landing project, meant to capitalize on its riverfront location at the base of Mount Adams. Robert Doran, the principal designer, began the project while he was with KZF Design and completed the design after establishing the Doran Studio, collaborating closely with William Turnbull all the while.

The next phase of mid-rise apartment buildings, known as Foster's Point, was designed by Cole + Russell.

Since 1993, the market for condominiums had swelled by 2005 to nearly 2,500 condos either built or under development in the basin. Most are being created through the conversion of office and retail buildings in a major shift of land use downtown. Daniel Burnham's 1902 Fourth National Bank Building at 18 East Fourth Street is being redeveloped by JFP Properties, with plans by Cole + Russell. Miller-Valentine Group converted Dittoe & Wisenall's 1905 Pugh/Polk Building, adjacent to the Taft Museum of Art, to 113 units known as Park Place at Lytle, designed by GBBN. Muller Architects designed the $20 million renovation of the former McAlpin's department store. The site includes two buildings: the 1850s former Shillito's building by James W. McLaughlin and the 1873 Mitchell & Rammelsberg furniture store by Walter & Wilson, which will be converted to retail space at the street level and sixty condos above. In the West End, the New Deal-era public housing projects Laurel Homes and Lincoln Court were razed and replaced by traditionalist row houses under the Hope VI program of the U.S. Department of Housing and Urban Development.

Cesar Pelli Associates, with GBBN, architect of record
Aronoff Center for the Arts, 1995
700 Walnut Street

The $82 million center draws audiences from the metropolitan area for Broadway shows and other arts and entertainment presentations. The design successfully marries contextual brick and transparency that enlivens the street.

During the 1970s and 1980s, downtown Cincinnati lost all its theaters, including the landmark Shubert, Palace, and Albee, and the central business district was at risk of becoming an office compound used solely during the day. Realizing belatedly that arts and entertainment are critical components of urban life, city economic development officials designated a block at Seventh and Walnut streets as an arts and entertainment district. State Senate President Stanley J. Aronoff orchestrated state funding for construction of the Aronoff Center for the Arts as a home for Broadway shows. Private donors, including Procter & Gamble, Fifth Third Bank, Mickey and Stanley Kaplan, and Alice and Harris Weston, were inspired to join the effort to revitalize the CBD with a fine performing and visual arts complex. Completed in 1995, the center was designed by the celebrated Cesar Pelli Associates with GBBN. In turn, this spurred the creation of a "Backstage" entertainment district surrounding the Aronoff Center, with whimsical streetscape improvements by Michael Schuster & Associates and new restaurant and retail spaces by Towne Properties.

The new millennium brought a wave of other ambitious arts projects. The Contemporary Arts Center, by the Pritzker Prize-winning architect Zaha Hadid, with KZF Design as architect of record, was described by the *New York Times* upon its 2003 opening as "the most important American building to be completed since the end of the Cold War."[1] In the same year, the Cincinnati Art Museum completed the $10 million Cincinnati Wing renovation by KZF Design. In 2004, the Taft Museum of Art reopened after a rigorous renovation and respectful addi-

KZF Design
Cincinnati Wing, Cincinnati Art Museum, 1963, 2003
Eden Park Drive

The entrance hall to the Cincinnati Wing, created through the reconfiguration of the 1963 Adams-Emery Wing of the Cincinnati Art Museum, is dramatized by a huge window that provides vistas of Eden Park and the distant cityscape. The nude marble figure of Eve Disconsolate by Hiram Powers stands silhouetted against the window. Former museum director Timothy Rub and Jim Cheng, project architect, collaborated to create an elegant series of galleries where about 400 works by local artists are displayed and interpreted.

tion by Ann Beha Architects of Boston, with KZF Design as associate architects. Reed-Hilderbrand Landscape Architects, also of Boston, redesigned the expanded gardens.

To attract out-of-town visitors, the city also aimed to expand its convention business. Completed in mid-2006, the long-awaited $180 million expansion and technological upgrading of the Cincinnati Convention Center, with nearly 200,000 square feet of exhibition space, enabled the city to host over 75 percent of the conventions and meetings booked in the nation. Because of the mammoth scope of

Ann Beha Architects, with KZF Design, architect of record
Taft Museum of Art, 2004 (formerly Baum-Longworth-Taft residence, 1820)
316 Pike Street

The Taft Museum of Art completed a $22.8 million renovation and expansion in 2004. While the historic museum building, with its world-class permanent collection, was refurbished with historically appropriate finishes, the rear addition provides a new entrance, parking, and spaces for programs and services, including a new gallery for special exhibitions. The new wing takes a respectful backseat to the historic former Baum-Longworth-Taft residence, and the new gardens include a terrace for outdoor dining and special events.

the project, three local firms—GBBN, BHDP, and Cole + Russell—formed a partnership to serve as the architect of record. LMN of Seattle was the design architect, and the interior design firm was Sussman/Prejza of Los Angeles. The boxy metal-and-glass addition leans out over Central Avenue and seems to burst out of the shell of the more polished and polite 1980s renovation. Taking advantage of its high visibility at downtown's western gateway, a grid of angled metal panels spells out "CINCINNATI" and adds texture to the building.

Gustave W. Drach
Hale-Justis Apartments, c. 1905
20 East Central Parkway
Renovation, 2001
Francis P. Russell

Center City Properties created thirty luxury lofts in this former industrial building, the former home of the Hale-Justis Wholesale Drug Co.

Opportunities and Setbacks for Over-the-Rhine

In the early 1990s, city leaders finally realized that the fate of downtown was inextricably linked to Over-the-Rhine. Cincinnati's most important historic neighborhood and one of the largest collections of brick Italianate architecture in the nation, Over-the-Rhine continued to be the site of a long-standing contest between advocates of low-income housing and advocates of market-rate development. A fierce battle had been fought over its listing in the National Register of Historic Places in 1983 because of the fear of gentrification. But by 1993, when City Council designated Over-the-Rhine as a local historic district, both sides agreed that this action was essential to put the brakes on demolition of its precious historic building stock. In 2002, city planning director Elizabeth Blume brought opposing sides together to agree on a future direction, which was outlined in *The Over-the-Rhine Comprehensive Plan* in 2002, produced by consultants Ken Cunningham & Associates and the University of Cincinnati Community Design Center.[2]

Private investment in Over-the-Rhine's historic buildings had been going on for decades, beginning with individual pioneers who invested in row houses around the old Woodward High School and art galleries, bars, and high-tech industries along Main Street. The pace picked up rapidly in the mid-1990s. The University of Cincinnati launched the rehabilitation of the former home of OMI College of Applied Science, which had been vacant since 1988. After an earlier plan by Morphosis to adapt it as a new home for the Contemporary Arts Center was scrapped, the early-twentieth-century Jacobethan-style building by Samuel Hannaford & Sons was converted into the loft-style Emery Apartments, named after philanthropist Mary Emery, founder of Mariemont, who had provided the funds for the building in 1910. Designed by GBBN and developed by Mansur Real Estate Services of Indianapolis, the renewed building opened in 2001. It became home to a creative class of tenants, a bustling café, and the Niehoff Urban Design Studio, operated by

Glaserworks
Market Shed
Findlay Market
Over-the-Rhine

The shed is a restatement of an old farmers' market. It is painted the colors of fruits and vegetables.

the University of Cincinnati. The Emery Theatre, the former auditorium for the school and once a world-class concert hall, still awaited restoration.

Civil disturbance in 2001 triggered by the death of a fleeing unarmed young African American man at the hands of police dealt a severe blow to the arts and entertainment scene, causing several businesses to close. Fortunately, many civic leaders and self-styled New Urbanists never lost faith in Over-the-Rhine as a model for diversity and urban living. Even as the city and the county as a whole continued to lose population, the number of residents downtown grew as young singles snatched up rehabbed units in Over-the-Rhine and empty nesters committed themselves to downtown condos. As 2005 began, the total number of units between the two areas was within reach of the 4,000-unit goal. The demand led to dozens of historic housing conversions in OTR, including the Hale-Justis Building, the American Building, and the old Ahrens-Fox fire engine factory on Fourteenth Street.

Over-the-Rhine has also attracted investment in some high-profile commercial projects. The city turned over the management of the historic Findlay Market to a private, nonprofit corporation and pumped millions into improvements. Designed by Glaserworks, the phased project included renovation and expansion of the market house, rehabilitation of brick row buildings on Elder Street for a mix of market-related uses, a new parking lot, and a new open-sided shed for tailgate vending by farmers from the region. The market project is expected to spur further investment in renovations around it.

Parsons Brinckerhoff,
Chan Krieger,
Hargreaves Associates,
and KZF Design
Fort Washington Way,
2005
Riverfront

The $300 million reconstruction of Fort Washington way not only reconnected the Cincinnati's central business district to the riverfront, but created new public space. The crossings were treated as gateways with artistically designed bridges and streetscapes.

Corporations tempted to flee to the suburbs looked to the city for incentives to remain. To induce the Kroger Co. to stay downtown, the city agreed to build a $12 million, 950-car parking garage at Vine and Central Parkway. The development team of Al Neyer Inc. and R. M. Kimbler Interests chose Arquitectonica of Miami and DNK Architects of Cincinnati to design this four-story concrete structure. The breezy contemporary design features a colorful glass elevator/stair tower on Central Parkway and attempts to echo its brick surroundings with red metal screens in the openings. The city also helped finance twenty-five new live/work residential units on the east side of Vine Street abutting the garage. This development addressed a number of concerns, including the need to improve Vine Street and increase market-rate housing in the area. The housing also provided more gravity to this gateway intersection and gave the garage a more pedestrian scale compatible with the block opposite.

Reconnecting the City to the River

Cincinnati's riverfront, the subject of a series of ambitious plans, changed considerably at the turn of the twenty-first century with the reconstruction of Fort Washington Way and construction of two stadiums and the National Underground Railroad Freedom Center. A twelve-block, mixed-use development known as "the Banks" and a fifty-acre riverfront park would complete the transformation. Altogether this represents the investment of about two billion dollars, expressing enormous faith in the future of the riverfront.

Since its completion in 1961, Fort Washington Way had been a wide gulf separating downtown from the river. After receiving an "F" safety rating in the early

1990s, this heavily used highway connector was completely reconstructed from 1998 to 2000, including new surface boulevards flanking the highway and six new bridges connecting downtown with the riverfront. On the south side below Pete Rose Way is a new transit center, which currently serves buses but is planned to handle commuter and possibly intercity trains in the future. The upper level could carry a light rail transit line. This award-winning project, carried out by Parsons Brinckerhoff, Chan Krieger of Cambridge, Massachusetts, Hargreaves Associates of San Francisco, and KZF Design, treated the crossings as gateways with artistically designed bridges and streetscapes. The improved Fort Washington Way accommodates an increased number of vehicles per day on the highway and enabled the city to reconnect to sixteen acres of land along its riverfront.

Riverfront Stadium (1970) brought the Cincinnati Reds and Bengals together, but as the new millennium approached, both teams insisted upon their own arenas. The doughnut-shaped stadium represented efficiency, economy, and modernity, but it compromised the intimacy of scale desired for baseball. The demand for luxury boxes by both the Reds and Bengals made the stadium outmoded. After vigorous debate about locating a new baseball park on Broadway Commons at the edge of the Pendleton portion of Over-the-Rhine, voters finally passed a countywide bond issue to build two new stadiums on the riverfront in 1996. First up in 2001 was the new 65,000-seat Paul Brown Stadium, a daring, jagged and soaring contemporary design. The nostalgic 40,000-seat Great American Ball Park followed in 2003. Both projects are funded by a countywide sales tax collected by Hamilton County.

Next was the question of how to fill the gap between them. Mayor Roxanne Qualls appointed a new Riverfront Advisory Committee, tapping Jack Rouse, designer of theme parks and museums, as chair. The group came up with a plan for the Banks, which included twelve blocks of housing, hotel, retail, and office space on a platform of parking garages totaling as much as $175 million in development. In 1999, the Port of Greater Cincinnati Development Authority was reactivated to implement the plan for the Banks. The National Underground Railroad Freedom Center won the coveted and symbolic central site at the north end of the Roebling Bridge.

Despite the progress in drawing new residents downtown, pressure grew to ease regulations and reduce red tape in the development process. Under the direction of planning director Elizabeth Blume, the zoning code was streamlined to make it simpler to use, and Mayor Charlie Luken appointed a task force to advise on the best way to speed development in the city. Among their more controversial recommendations was relocating the economic development staff into the city manager's office and creating the Department of Community Development and Planning, thus eliminating planning as a separate function of government.

Another key outcome was the creation of a new private development corporation, Cincinnati Center City Development Corp. (3CDC for short). This nonprofit organization was charged with enhancing downtown Cincinnati's position as a regional center of high-value employment, housing, arts, culture, and entertainment with support from the downtown business community. 3CDC decided to focus initially on three areas: Fountain Square, the Banks, and Over-the-Rhine. Its first project, a $40 million renovation of Fountain Square designed by Cooper Robertson of New York, included relocating the Tyler Davidson Fountain to the square's center, planting clusters of street trees, eliminating the skywalk, and repairing the city-owned garage underneath the square.

Capital Program for Cincinnati Public Schools

In 2003, Cincinnati Public Schools (CPS) launched a ten-year, one-billion-dollar capital program to rebuild its schools with local, state and federal funding. Led by Michael L. Burson, facilities director, the program was based on a facilities master plan, itself almost a decade in the making. Many older school buildings had fallen into disrepair; even newer schools built in the 1950s through the 1970s were judged incapable of retrofitting with air-conditioning and wiring for communications technology. In addition, the student enrollment had waned and shifted away from the urban core, leaving CPS with surplus capacity. Concepts about education had also changed; the new base model called for "pods," or groups of four classrooms clustered around a common space.

The plan took into account an inventory by the Cincinnati Preservation Association that identified thirty-four schools as listed or eligible for the National Register of Historic Places. CPS used this information, backed by the community's desire to keep some of its architecturally significant buildings, to appeal to the Ohio Schools Facilities Commission to waive a rule requiring that renovations exceeding two-thirds of the cost of a new building be replaced. Initially, only sixteen of the district's eighty-two schools would have been saved. The final plan called for downsizing to sixty-six schools, including thirty-five new buildings and thirty-one renovations. Redundant buildings were to be made available for redevelopment. This massive public works campaign has involved most large local architectural firms and resulted in some creative contemporary architecture.

In September 2005, Pleasant Hill Elementary School by Burgess & Niple (B&N) was among the first to welcome students and teachers to a new facility. The "standards-based model" for design of CPS departs from the centuries-old linear classroom organization by clustering four classrooms around a common extended-learning area. In addition to providing spaces conducive to education, many of the new schools are designed to function after hours as centers of community life.

One of the most innovative school projects is Riverview East Academy at 3555 Kellogg Avenue in Columbia Tusculum. This new 105,000-square-foot school, which opened in January 2006, is built atop steel-and-concrete pylons to elevate

SFA Architects and Alexander Camabeam & Associates
Riverview East Academy, 2006
3555 Kellogg Avenue, Columbia Tusculum

Planned with extensive community involvement, Riverview East catapults CPS into the twenty-first century. The school's unique form responds to its riverfront location and reflects its function as a community learning center, combining core academics with superb music, art, and science facilities, as well as health and social services and a police substation.

the building above the floodplain. Designed for 615 students in grades K–12, the building consists of three cubic modules connected by bridges, all clad in corrugated metal. One cube is the community building, with a gymnasium, a cafetorium, music rooms, a computer room, and a community/parent meeting room. The other two cubes for academics follow the favored arrangement of classrooms in pods. Lights turn on and off automatically, triggered by movement, for maximum energy efficiency.

SFA Architects and Alexander Camabeam & Associates enlivened the building inside and out with bright colors to emphasize the geometric components. The décor is inspired by the school's riverfront environment; the floor in the corridor displays a waving pattern representing the river's edge, and the bridges are painted bright blue with portholes. Riverview East Academy shares an interesting interplay of volumes, planes, and colors with SFA's design of Mayerson Academy and the adjoining board of education headquarters in Corryville, completed in 1992.

The University Leads the Rebirth of Uptown

While downtown Cincinnati has had its architectural triumphs, the University of Cincinnati (UC) has taken the lead in introducing signature architecture to the region. Beginning in the late 1980s, with strong leadership by President Joseph Steger; Dale McGirr, whose title was expanded to vice president for planning, finance and community development; Jay Chatterjee, then dean of the College of Design, Architecture, Art and Planning (DAAP); and Ronald B. Kull, university architect, the university embarked on a massive program of high-end patronage, commissioning new buildings by signature national architects teamed with leading local firms. Through the state's investment of a billion dollars and the leaders' advocacy of distinguished architecture as a means of enhancing the life of a place, the campus has been dramatically transformed.

Daniel Libeskind, with GBBN, architect of record
The Ascent, 2005–2007
Covington

This unusual, spiral-shaped tower will feature condominium homes within walking distance of Covington's historic district and downtown Cincinnati. Libeskind's design responds to the curvature of the cables of the Roebling Bridge and the multifaceted vistas of the riverfront site.

The largest single contribution to the success of this transformation has been the campus master plan by San Francisco–based Hargreaves Associates, which created a conceptual framework for both the existing infrastructure of the campus and ambitious new growth. The campus gains its integrity through its landscape—the spaces between buildings. Where the lack of a predominant architectural style or pattern previously created the impression of chaos, the reconfigured campus celebrates a diversity of daring designs united by a cohesive plan.

UC has also reached out to redevelop the area beyond its borders, convening nearby institutions—Cincinnati Children's Hospital Medical Center, the Cincinnati Zoo, the Health Alliance of Greater Cincinnati, and TriHealth—as working partners in the Uptown Consortium. The mission is to ensure that the uptown region is a safe, attractive, and livable community for its residents, employees, students, and visitors. The consortium is working with local neighborhood-based redevelopment corporations in Clifton, Avondale, Clifton Heights, University Heights, Fairview, Corryville, and Mount Auburn on $375 million of construction. Among the projects are the massive Calhoun Street Marketplace, which provided parking, apartments, condominiums, retail and town houses, and Stratford Village, a ten-acre site on Clifton Avenue that features fourteen neo-Tudor residential buildings in a pedestrian-oriented New Urbanist compound. Most of this new development tends to rely on traditionalist design to engender a sense of familiarity and comfort among users and to appeal to the parents of college-bound students.

A Dynamic Mix of Old and New

While the majority of recent signature architecture is clustered on the UC campus and downtown Cincinnati, quality design has occurred in other Cincinnati neighborhoods, the Northern Kentucky riverfront, and the suburbs. Works of originality such as the Lipson Alport Glass headquarters by Cooper Carry in Walnut Hills and Terry Brown's studio in Hyde Park have made their own idiosyncratic statements.

In Covington, Kentucky, millions have been invested in mixed-use development on the riverfront since 1990. The Corporex Corp., a major builder headed by William Butler, built RiverCenter with its two pedimented office towers by PDT Architects, a Marriott Hotel by KZF Design and PDT, Embassy Suites by KZF Design, and the fifteen-story Madison Place, with four floors of luxury town houses atop offices by GBBN. Butler aspired to bring world-class architecture to Kentucky with construction of the Ascent, a spiral-shaped condominium tower by Daniel Libeskind, master redesigner of the World Trade Center site, with GBBN as architect of record. Corporex was also a driving force behind the 200,000-square-foot

Studio of Terry Brown

Terry Brown
Studio of Terry Brown,
1992–2006
3331 Erie Avenue,
Hyde Park

Terry Brown is a disciple of Organic Architecture, as practiced by Herb Greene, Bruce Goff, and Bart Prince. Brown's approach to design blends Prairie School concepts, Secessionist ornament, and Native American themes. As Sidney K. Robinson, a professor of architecture at the University of Illinois in Chicago, describes it, "Organic architecture steps forward in a world of caution and compromise to take personal responsibility for its energy and its invitation to individual freedom."[3] Brown's work is the embodiment of that freedom—to the point where it has sparked controversies in the neighborhood and the city over the role and limits of individualistic architecture and the question of personal liberties in the built environment.

Brown's studio, which began as a modest early-twentieth-century dwelling of 1,100 square feet, slowly evolved over fifteen years. Brown added a lighthouse-like mushroom-shaped chamber on the front and molded the exterior with many layers of sculpted shingles.

Everywhere ornament seems to sprout from the surface; there are ceramic shells in the walls, colorful chunks of slag glass at the base, and ribbons of metal along the ridge. Skewed geometry is fundamental to the design—in the triangular windows, a stairway of circular steps, and the almond-shaped trellis. Brown uses forms and materials in original and unexpected ways, and the artistic effect is completely individualistic yet somehow internally harmonious.

Cole + Russell
Evendale Municipal Building, 1997
Reading Road, Evendale

When designing a new city hall for Evendale, architects Cole + Russell reorganized the existing collection of government buildings around a new commons area, creating a town square with a sense of place. The Municipal Building's central entrance diagonally faces the commons, dramatized by a curving colonnade. The building is an example of a design approach at which local architects have become very adept: combining traditional materials and forms with contemporary functions and technology.

Northern Kentucky Convention Center, completed in 2002. In the Riverside Historic District on the east side of the bridge, Towne Properties and Cole + Russell created a historically inspired block of apartments known as Roebling Row.

As Cincinnati's suburbs mature, local governments such as Mason, Erlanger, Evendale, and Springdale, Colerain, Delhi, and Deerfield have built new municipal buildings and firehouses that reflect their increasing stature as independent cities and urban townships. As exemplified in Evendale's new city hall, by Cole + Russell, the preferred approach for these new government buildings is a contemporary interpretation of traditional forms and materials, often working in the Wrightian Prairie style. Two private buildings in Blue Ash, Temple B'nai Tzedek by Jose A. Garcia and BHDP and the Design Center by ArchitectsPlus, stand out as distinctively modern designs. Michael McInturf, a Peter Eisenman disciple and project architect for the DAAP addition, has created a cutting-edge addition to the Cincinnati Country Day School in Indian Hill.

Architecture in Cincinnati appears to be shaped equally by the past and the future. The historic-preservation movement, which emerged in the 1960s in reaction to urban renewal and picked up momentum in the 1980s, has been enthusiastically embraced. Many firms have become extremely skilled at blending contemporary forms with historical references and creating compatible new additions to historic buildings. In their more cutting-edge creations, local architects have embraced concepts in common with their national counterparts. These ideas include interplay between interior and exterior spaces, rejection of rectilinear organization in favor of complex geometries, fluidity of spaces, use of folding planes, and the exploration of weightlessness.

ArchitectsPlus
Design Center, 2000
10816 Millington Court, Blue Ash

ArchitectsPlus took a contemporary approach in creating the Design Center after a tornado demolished its previous office building in 1999. Rick Koehler, one of the firm's founders, asked designer Christopher Kepes to create something that would make people smile as they drove by on I-71. The bold geometric shapes and primary colors are eye-catching. The building is like a sign, advertising architecture and related design services. In a largely conservative market, here the architects emerged from disaster with a free rein to do something progressive.

Initiatives for Sustainable Design

The 1990s brought a new sensibility about the value of "sustainable" design in architecture. Also known as "green" or "high-performance" design, in practice it means buildings are compatible with the environment of their sites, water is conserved and protected, indoor occupant health is enhanced, energy use is both minimized and locally created, and environmentally preferable building materials are selected.

In 1995, the Cincinnati chapter of the American Institute of Architects formed the Committee on the Environment, one of the earliest such committees in the United States. By 2002, the Cincinnati Regional Chapter of the US Green Building Council (USGBC) and Sustainable Cincinnati were organized. And in 2005, as a result of the Hamilton County Community Compass Master Plan, the Hamilton County Planning Commission formed a Green Building Committee to work with the other fifty-two jurisdictions in the county in planning for a more sustainable future.

In 2001, the University of Cincinnati began a sustainable design initiative for new buildings, which must meet the LEED (Leadership in Energy and Environmental Design) Silver rating level. Although internationally known architects have designed most of the new campus buildings, it has been the responsibility of the Cincinnati architects of record to organize and document the process for achieving environmental compliance. By October 2005, UC had registered its thirteenth LEED project, surpassing the achievement of any other university, institution, or corporation in the nation.

Other recent examples of sustainable design include the 2004 Northern Kentucky Water District building, which incorporates sustainable water-management techniques; the Cincinnati Zoo's 2005 education building, which is also a teaching example; and PNC Bank's seven new branches, which are models of commerce that openly speak to the connection of the workplace and the natural environment.

Leaving a Legacy of Fine Architecture and Planning

High-quality architecture, like all art forms, must have patrons who are willing to support experimentation. The more radical designs of local architects were possible because their clients gave them the freedom to explore new forms. In several cases, the patrons have been the architects themselves, but there are those exceptional clients—a Jewish congregation, a high-tech media producer, and a private school—who are open to progressive ideas. Through their early and sustained investments in new architectural ideas, Cincinnati's corporate and cultural leaders, and especially the University of Cincinnati, have made an enormous and lasting contribution to our community. In the last five years, Cincinnati has invested well over two billion dollars in many other projects in the core, especially in the art museums, sports arenas, convention centers, and educational facilities.

Initially there may have been a tendency for clients to accept highly innovative designs more freely from architects of world renown. And yet the involvement of these outsiders has helped to educate the public here, cultivating a clientele for new design concepts and creating more fertile ground on which to build. As a result of these efforts, there is now a growing realization that quality architecture and design, along with arts and educational institutions, have made Cincinnati a more desirable place for students, conventions, businesses, visitors, and residents alike. A dynamic mix of contemporary architecture and revitalized historic places has made the area a destination for design excellence.

Art Academy of Cincinnati

The relocation of the Art Academy of Cincinnati from its original home by James W. McLaughlin adjacent to the Cincinnati Art Museum on Mount Adams to Over-the-Rhine was a major boost for the historic neighborhood. The decision to move to Over-the-Rhine reflected the area's redevelopment as an arts district, anchored by Main Street art galleries and the Pendleton warehouse of artist studios on the east, Music Hall and Memorial Hall on the west, and Uptown Arts on the north. The new location was challenging, but like the new Aronoff Center for Design & Art at UC and the Contemporary Arts Center buildings, it was intended to stimulate a more urban, cutting-edge sensibility on the part of the students and faculty.

For its new home, the Academy doubled its space to 120,000 square feet by acquiring two buildings on Jackson Street: the 1910 John Shillito Co. furniture warehouse, most likely also designed by McLaughlin, and the 1923 former printing plant of the George Rosenthal Co. A new angled, metal-and-glass entrance and projecting neon letters spelling "A R T" up the side of the building hint at the transformation inside. The architects chose to cut through six floors to create an atrium, inserting a new monumental metal stair. The atrium links the buildings even though none of the floor levels were aligned, and it also provides a communal space. The industrial character created by the mushroom-shaped columns and raw concrete floors is appropriate for this cutting-edge art school. The building also obtained a high score in the LEED Green Building Rating System, a voluntary national standard for developing high-performance, sustainable buildings.

Design Collective and McGill Smith Punshon
Art Academy of Cincinnati, 1910, 1923; 2005
1220 Jackson Street, Over-the-Rhine

Design Collective, Inc. of Baltimore and the local firm of McGill Smith Punshon created an exciting new home for the Art Academy of Cincinnati from a pair of early-twentieth-century industrial buildings. A new six-story atrium joins the two buildings and creates dramatic interior views. The industrial character created by the mushroom-shaped columns and raw concrete floors is perfect for this cutting-edge art school.

Cesar Pelli Associates, with GBBN architect of record
Aronoff Center for the Arts, 1995
700 Walnut Street

At night, the dramatically lit transparent façade of the Aronoff Center lights up the street like a lantern and reveals the activity inside.

Aronoff Center for the Arts

With its 1995 opening, the Aronoff Center for the Arts anchored a new arts and entertainment district in downtown Cincinnati. World-renowned architect Cesar Pelli, the former dean of the Yale University School of Architecture, was the designer, and the local firm of GBBN was architect of record. Born and educated in Argentina, Pelli spent his early career with Eero Saarinen and Victor Gruen Associates. His best-known projects include the World Financial Center in Lower Manhattan, a residential tower for the Museum of Modern Art in New York, Canary Wharf in London, and the Petronas Towers at Kuala Lumpur in Malaysia.

The Aronoff Center exhibits Pelli's skillful ability to blend modern form with an enriched and engaging palate of materials and patterns, while also gesturing to the context. The complex is an assemblage of cubic volumes, each expressing the function within. The heart of the complex is the 2,700-seat Procter & Gamble Theater, inspired on the interior by Louis Sullivan's Chicago Auditorium (1888–90). The high, outwardly curving glass-and-steel façade enclosing the lobby is framed by masonry end walls. On the exterior, the 440-seat Jarson-Kaplan Theater echoes the form of the larger hall, but at a smaller scale, while the 250-seat black-box space on Main Street known as the Fifth Third Theater has simple, rectangular massing.

The walls were clad in brick, out of respect for the surrounding architectural fabric, perhaps even for Cincinnati's historic Music Hall, and, according to Peter Strange of Messer Construction, the builder, to respect Cincinnati's strong masonry tradition. Contrasting bands of teal green marble and a coursed sandstone base provide texture and round out the palette, which is repeated in the patterned brick plazas and finishes throughout the building. The complex interacts vigorously with its urban setting. Unlike many performing arts venues, which are raised above the street and set back, this building sits right on the sidewalk, with a small plaza at each corner. The lobbies extend across the Walnut Street façade, allowing one to walk through the building from plaza to plaza. The transparency of the façade and the activity in the lobbies invite passersby to come inside. In turn, patrons of the Aronoff Center can gaze from the lobby balconies at the lively Backstage district outside, with its theatrical streetscaping and renovated historic buildings.

Administrative offices, retail space, and an art gallery are located along the north side in a steel-and-glass wing in an understated modernist treatment that contrasts with the center's theater-related core. The Alice F. & Harris K. Weston Art Gallery, at the corner of Seventh and Walnut streets, also has a spectacular three-story lobby at street level, which draws people in, sometimes with large-scale and site-specific installations, and then downstairs into more intimate galleries below.

In the year the Aronoff Center opened, Pelli received the American Institute of Architects Gold Medal, the highest honor given in recognition of a significant body of work of lasting influence on the theory and practice of architecture. The Aronoff Center for the Arts has launched a new generation of signature architecture in downtown Cincinnati.

Lightborne Building

In the 1999 renovation of the former Excelsior Laundry plant on East Fourteenth Street, Ken Jones & Associates aimed to preserve this 1928 reinforced-concrete industrial building by Tietig & Lee and to contrast old and new in a way that would convey the essence of Lightborne, a motion-media design and production studio backed by investor and photographer Tom Schiff. The exposed brick walls and concrete floors are enlivened by fresh, new interventions. The mechanical and electrical systems are all exposed in tall steel-and-glass cabinets, which double as partitions for work spaces and showcase the role of high technology in the firm's work. Organic designs by local artists express a high degree of creativity. The stairway in the lobby, a free-floating abstraction of a whale spine, was created by a team of ceramic artist Michael Frasca and architects Jose A. Garcia and Ken Jones. Joe Deluca fashioned its undulating iron handrail. Artistic glass lamps by Jonathan Christie and James Mongrain provide accents of luminous color. Architect Terry Boling also contributed to the design.

Ken Jones & Associates
Lightborne Building, 1999
212 East 14th Street, Over-the-Rhine

The renovation of this 1928 industrial building for Lightborne, a motion design and production studio, contrasts new and old. The exposed brick walls and concrete floors are enlivened by organically inspired interventions by local artists. The stairway in the lobby, a free-floating abstraction of a whale spine, was designed by ceramic artist Michael Frasca with architects Jose A. Garcia and Ken Jones.

Lois and Richard Rosenthal Center for Contemporary Art of the Contemporary Arts Center

The Lois and Richard Rosenthal Center for Contemporary Art of the Contemporary Arts Center (CAC), completed in 2003, has brought worldwide attention to Cincinnati. Designed by internationally acclaimed architect Zaha Hadid, the center is her first commission in the United States and the first major American museum to be designed by a woman. Markus Dochantschi of New York was the project architect and KZF Design of Cincinnati was architect of record.

Born in Baghdad in 1950, Hadid was trained at the University of Beirut as a mathematician. In the early 1970s, she moved to London to study architecture, where she worked for Rem Koolhaas, the iconoclastic Dutch architect. Prior to the CAC commission, Hadid had made her reputation on radical designs that were mostly unbuilt. The selection committee whittled down 100 submissions to three—Daniel Libeskind, Bernard Tschumi, and Hadid—and went to see their work in Europe. Alice Weston, a member of the committee, said that seeing Hadid's Vitra Fire Station in Weil-am-Rhein, Germany (1990–94), was the deciding factor. "It was like walking into a piece of jewelry; the spaces were so beautiful."[4]

Hadid's CAC Building provides 87,000 square feet in six stories, plus a lower level, on a challenging corner site of only 11,000 square feet. It provides six times as much space as the CAC's previous home a block away in the Formica Building, including galleries, offices, a 300-seat performance hall, café, and shop. The playful Un-Museum, an interactive educational center for children and families, occupies the top floor. Because the site is so compact, "your journey through the building must be more vertical than horizontal," according to Hadid.[5]

In contrast to late-nineteenth-century traditional museums sited in a park or on a hill, the CAC is located at the corner of Sixth and Walnut, one of the busiest intersections in the city. The building stands right on the sidewalk, its glass wall jutting out and inviting the public in. The concrete sidewalk is drawn into the building and swoops up, becoming the full-height back wall in an effect Hadid calls the "urban carpet." Light strips introduce diagonal lines in the sidewalk outside and repeat throughout the building in the floors and ceilings, blurring the division between inside and outside, up and down, solid and surface.

Contemporary art is about pushing the envelope, and this building does that literally. The exterior is a pile of shifting slabs, colors, and materials—clear blue glass, raw concrete, and blackened aluminum. Some elements even project over the property line. The building is like a jigsaw puzzle of angled shapes; solids, and voids that are reflected in the volumes inside. Hadid chose to arrange the building by reversing the usual order of things and placing heavier materials on the top with lighter, transparent materials on the bottom. The structure appears to defy gravity.

According to KZF's Don Cornett, "Her design process is not linear; it's evolutionary. She revised it four or five times; she did thirty to forty models. Every component has some impact on the whole."[6] Every aspect is unique to this building and inspired by its location and function. The design is based on the grid pattern created by buildings on the surrounding blocks, but deconstructed and made perpendicular. Herbert Muschamp, then architecture critic for the *New York Times,* believes that "[a]s a pure virtuoso of design, she has no living rival."[7] In 2004, Hadid received the Pritzker Architecture Prize. Generally acknowledged as the world's most prestigious award for architecture, the prize honors a living architect whose built work constitutes a significant contribution to the built environment and to humanity.

The center's most striking feature is the atrium and its zigzagging black aluminum stairways. Each stairway is a bridge supported only at the ends, seeming to float in space. The stairs rise to a two-story gallery at the fourth floor, a sky lobby of sorts. As Hadid intended, "From the stairs, visitors can see each other moving through the building and interacting with the art. This way, the architecture facilitates the experience of art as a collective experience."[8] Views are framed by angular walls.

The CAC is a noncollecting institution, so the building was not designed around a permanent collection. The galleries vary in shape, size, and height and are thus easily adaptable for the size and media of contemporary art. In turn, there is opportunity for art to respond to the building. There is no doubt that the building itself is a work of contemporary art that perfectly fits its purpose. With significant funding from the city and state, but primarily from private donors, the project represents a major effort to establish Cincinnati as a serious center for the arts.

Zaha Hadid, with KZF Design
Lois and Richard Rosenthal Center for Contemporary Art, 2002
44 East Sixth Street

The center is the first U.S. commission of internationally acclaimed architect Zaha Hadid, and the first major American museum to be designed by a woman. The building is like a jigsaw puzzle of angled shapes; solids and voids are reflected in the interior volumes.

Zaha Hadid, with KZF Design
Lois and Richard Rosenthal Center for Contemporary Art
Interior view of atrium and stairway

The atrium and scissor-like stairway provide drama to the interior of the arts center, providing visitors vistas through the building and accentuating the experience of their procession through space.

NBBJ, with Glaserworks
Paul Brown Stadium, 2002

This 65,600-seat arena is a daring new landmark on the Cincinnati riverfront. Angled outer walls with different materials, layers, and textures break down the enormous scale and create a sense of motion. A pair of canopies cantilevers over the sideline seats like the soaring wings of a seagull. Openings at the corners of the stands create dramatic views of downtown and the river.

Paul Brown Stadium

Named after the former owner and manager of the Cincinnati Bengals football franchise, this 65,600-seat arena is prominently positioned at the west end of Cincinnati's riverfront. The stadium's designers, NBBJ's Sports and Entertainment division based in Los Angeles and Glaserworks of Cincinnati, created "a progressive new image, with jagged planes of glass, concrete, and steel,"[9] in contrast to the retro approach of the Great American Ball Park. To break down the enormous scale of the building, they divided up the slanting and angled outer walls with different materials, layers, and textures. Two canopies of translucent fabric cantilever over the upper tier of sideline seats like the soaring wings of a seagull. NBBJ was inspired by the look of the new Stadium Australia in Sydney, an open-ended, winged structure where the opening ceremonies for the 2000 Olympics took place. Night lighting amplifies the dramatic effect, changing the stadium "from a solid object into a series of backlit-semi-transparent scrims and overlapping grids."[10]

To make Paul Brown Stadium look light and "almost in motion," the architects borrowed another Australian form, the boomerang, to support the gull-wing roofs. The boomerang-shaped columns emphasize the outward flare at the top of the wall and make the design more sculptural than straight columns would. The wedge-shaped scoreboards of smooth and corrugated steel are also sculptural elements, crossing "as if they have collided in midair."[11]

The cast-concrete seating bowl has been cut open at the corners to create dramatic views of downtown and the river. Slicing the corners made good design as well as business sense because it allowed the team owners to increase the number of skyboxes and premium seats along the sidelines while dispensing with the less desirable corner seats. Glaserworks was mindful of how the building fit onto the site and within the urban context. Rather than forcing the stadium to line up with Fort Washington Way, the architects rotated it slightly to accentuate the views.

Great American Ball Park

Cincinnatians' pride in their baseball heritage shows in the Great American Ball Park, designed by HOK Sport of Kansas City and GBBN of Cincinnati. With 42,000 seats, it is more intimate and animated than the football stadium. In its idiosyncratic configuration and its associations with the history of the first professional baseball team, it looks back in many ways to historical Crosley Field in the West End. At the foot of Main Street, the ballpark is offset by two long, low brick blocks—the Reds Hall of Fame and Museum and an office building—creating a more human-scale, urban setting. Together these structures frame the green space known as Crosley Terrace, which is the approach to the main entrance. Statues of baseball heroes line the walkways. The lawn slopes at the same angle as Crosley's notorious left field. Inside is a nostalgic Sun/Moon Deck. A replica of the Longines analog clock above the scoreboard over left field also recalls Crosley Field. A gigantic Tall Stacks-themed feature in the outfield emits puffs of smoke after each strike and fireworks after each home run. One local architect compared the park's visual excitement to Barnum & Bailey's circus.[12] A limited foul territory allows fans to enjoy excellent views of the game. A notch in the stands between home plate and third base provides a glimpse from downtown into the ballpark. The stands in right field are lower to allow views of Northern Kentucky, the river, and barges floating by.

The ballpark embodies current design trends and borrows aspects from ballparks other than Crosley Field. It responds to the "retro-park" model set in 1992 by Baltimore's Camden Yards with its long brick warehouse framing right field. In its size and transparency it resembles Cleveland's Jacobs Field (1994). It is also quite similar in design to HOK's SBC Park in San Francisco, which offers views into the ballpark from a waterfront promenade and spectacular views of the Bay Bridge and the skyline. Some critics think that architecturally the Great American Ball Park lacks the "continuity, consistency, and unity of Paul Brown Stadium, Coors Field in Denver, and Camden Yards in Baltimore," but the intimacy of scale and the nostalgic décor more than make up for this in the minds of many baseball fans.[13]

HOK Sport, with GBBN, and Michael Schuster & Associates
Great American Ball Park, 2003
100 Main Street

At 42,000 seats, the Great American Ball Park is more intimate and animated than the previous stadium. From the stands, patrons enjoy breathtaking views of the river and barges floating by. The building's nostalgic trappings provide an amusement park-like experience of America's most popular professional sport, with its roots in the Cincinnati Red Stockings.

Symbolically sited at the north landing of the Roebling Suspension Bridge, which crosses the river that separated slavery and freedom, the Freedom Center is the centerpiece of the new Cincinnati riverfront. The $110 million facility, ten years in the making, was intended to be a safe house for lessons and reflections on the ongoing struggles for freedom.

Blackburn Architects of Indianapolis, the lead architects, and BOORA Architects of Portland, design consultants, worked in partnership with Alexander-Camabeam & Associates of Newport, Kentucky, architects of record, to create this center. Walter Blackburn died of cancer in 2000, after the design was complete but before construction began. His wife, Alpha, who has chaired the Indiana Civil Rights Commission since 1990, designed the interiors and carried on her husband's work. The exhibits were designed by Jack Rouse Associates, and Martha Schwartz was landscape architect.

The building's three pavilions are said to symbolize the three constitutional amendments that ended slavery: the Thirteenth, abolishing slavery; the Fourteenth, providing equal protection regardless of race; and the Fifteenth, providing the right to vote. They also express three themes: courage, cooperation, and perseverance. The spaces between the buildings represent winding pathways that run northward through the building. These recall the perilous journeys made by escaping slaves along the many roads to freedom. The rough stone walls seem timeless. The gently curved roof crowning the building is clad in copper, which blends with the warm-toned stone and gives the building richness.

In contrast to the opaque surfaces of the north- and south-running walls, the other elevations are largely transparent and create a lantern effect when the building is lit at night. The glass walls frame sweeping views of the river and Kentucky as well as downtown Cincinnati. A broad balcony overlooking the river features an eternal flame, representing the candles placed in the windows of safe houses to beckon fleeing slaves. The building is offset by landscaping that echoes the curving lines of the building in the brick-and-stone paving. On the south side, a mottled blue flagstone pathway accented with small boulders recalls the river.

The three lower floors are devoted to exhibits and public spaces, while the top two floors house spaces for research, education, and administration. A restored slave pen from a Kentucky farm is a powerful presence at the second level. The interior of the central pavilion is dominated by a circular core containing the elevators and a grand open stairway. The circle is an important motif for Alpha Blackburn, who sees it as a symbol of cooperation, inclusion, and creativity, reflecting the center's larger vision of freedom for all.

Blackburn Architects, BOORA Architects, and Alexander-Camabeam & Associates
National Underground Railroad Freedom Center, 2004
Central Riverfront

The centerpiece of the new Cincinnati riverfront, the Freedom Center is symbolically sited at the north end of the Roebling Suspension Bridge, which crosses the river that separated slavery and freedom before the Civil War.

Lipson Alport Glass & Associates Headquarters

While architects strive to express contemporary concepts, many still base their designs on Modernist principles and regional styles. The Cincinnati headquarters of Lipson Alport Glass & Associates (LAGA), completed in 2000, is an excellent example. The building is the vision of Stevan Lipson, and Atlanta architects Cooper Carry made it a reality. Founded in 1947, Lipson Alport Glass & Associates specializes in brand design, identity, and innovation. Its CEO believes the "building embodies design . . . [it is] a place of work that elevates and celebrates the process of creativity."[14] Lipson studied visual design at the Illinois Institute of Technology in Chicago, where he was steeped in the architecture of Mies van der Rohe on campus and exposed to the work of Frank Lloyd Wright.

Cooper Carry
Lipson Alport Glass & Associates Headquarters, 2000
Eden Park Drive

The Cincinnati headquarters of Lipson Alport Glass & Associates is an elegant interpretation of Modernism influenced by both early Frank Lloyd Wright and Mies van der Rohe. This angular and elegant assemblage of metal, stone, brick, and glass displays a strong horizontal emphasis, while at the same time its flaring roof makes it soar. CEO Stevan Lipson worked closely with architects Cooper Carry of Atlanta on this large infill project situated almost halfway between uptown and downtown.

Hargreaves Associates
University of Cincinnati
Uptown, Clifton Heights/Corryville

Hargreaves Associates' master plan for UC's west campus led to conversion of sprawling parking lots into a signature green space, which includes Sigma Sigma Commons and the Campus Green. The landscape design features a collection of braided pathways and geometric earthworks. Meisner & Associates was the local landscape architect for University Commons, the green pictured here. The Commons is bordered by Kingsgate Conference Center, the Vontz Center, and Procter Hall.

University of Cincinnati Master Plan

In the late 1980s, the University of Cincinnati (UC) hired Hargreaves & Associates to create a master plan for the campus. George Hargreaves, a young landscape architect and professor at the Harvard Graduate School of Design, had never designed such a plan before, but he and his colleague Mary Margaret Jones created a new vision for the campus. Adopted in 1991, the Hargreaves & Associates plan put forth three guiding principles. One, all new buildings needed to fit well with the existing fabric of the campus. Hargreaves characterized the clashing axes of previous construction as "force fields" that could inspire and shape new infill. In this way, the university could capitalize on the chaos of the past arrangements. Two, architecture should be used to create a meaningful and functional open space. It was essential to reclaim green areas to create a more suburban sense of place. Concentrating new buildings in a more urban density would leave more room for large unprogrammed areas essential for student life. Three, landscaped spaces—courtyards, plazas, and greens—should be linked like a string of pearls. The campus was envisioned as a series of indoor and outdoor spaces that would be connected and engaging for the users.

One of the most dramatic aspects in the renewal of UC's west campus is the transformation of sprawling parking lots at the north end into a central unifying green space. The first section of the new landscape was Sigma Sigma Commons, completed in 1998. The site is now defined on the south by the new Student Recreation Center located at the juncture of two axes on campus: one established by the grid of the academic ridge along Clifton Avenue and the other by the diagonal of Nippert Stadium. Hargreaves's design blended these two axes as well as the slope of the campus in a series of wedged berms. The tilted earthworks are crossed by walkways that carry through the topographical alignments of the campus. In the center, Hargreaves used stone steps to create an amphitheater, contrasting the rectilinear masonry elements with the softer earthen forms. A memorial light tower of brick and stone by the Boston-based firm of Rudolfo Machado and Jorge Silvetti provides a commemorative landmark at the edge of the central open space.

The next phase was the larger Campus Green, which extends north from Sigma Sigma Commons all the way to Martin Luther King Boulevard. Among the most prominent features of the landscape design are a collection of braided pathways and landscape features, strong and continuous enough to unify the otherwise incompatible geometries, levels, and forms of the campus; and a collection of sinuous and geometric earthworks, harking back to the prehistoric mounds and other forms that once marked this region as an important settlement for Native Americans. The braided pathways represent an ancient stream that once ran there. The north end of the Campus Green is punctuated by a ziggurat-shaped mound covered with vines and bordered with curving water-walls. Wedge-shaped terraces with seating and plantings line the eastern edge, continuing the motif established by Sigma Sigma Commons, and small lawns provide places for spontaneous recreation, helping to create a sense of place for people where there was once only pavement.

Peter Eisenman, with Lorenz & Williams
Aronoff Center for Design and Art, 1988–96
University of Cincinnati

Michael McInturf Associates, with GBBN, architect of record
Cincinnati Country Day School addition, 2002
6905 Given Road, Indian Hill

The addition to Cincinnati Country Day School reflects the influence of McInturf's mentor Peter Eisenman in its shifting planes and angles. On the exterior, the most prominent feature is the roof, which is folded into many planes, responding to the surrounding landscape. The roof rises in the center above the main entrance hall, from which all spaces flow.

Aronoff Center for Design and Art

Peter Eisenman's 1988 design for the Aronoff Center for Design and Art, an addition to UC's acclaimed College of Design, Architecture, Art and Planning (DAAP), kicked off the successful campaign of signature architecture on campus. Praising the building, which was completed in 1996, Herbert Muschamp, architecture critic for the *New York Times*, announced that this design "has opened the door for some of the most talented architects in the emerging generation."[15] Like Hadid's, Eisenman's work had been largely theoretical until the UC building and two other major commissions in Ohio—the Wexner Center for the Arts at Ohio State University (1989) and the Columbus Convention Center (1993)—established him as a leading practitioner. It was up to Dayton-based Lorenz & Williams to make Eisenman's concept buildable.

The site presented some supreme challenges. It was located at the highly prominent northwest corner of campus, and President Joseph Steger wanted to preserve a sense of openness there rather than build out to the street. But the existing group of buildings didn't leave much room. Eisenman's solution was to wrap the addition around the back of the buildings on the north, away from the main campus, and place it mostly underground.

Eisenman based his design on the chevron-shaped footprint created by the 1950s and 1970s DAAP buildings. He took this shape and used a computer to shift it north, turning and tilting it into a complex scheme. In the process, Eisenman created a transitional zone between the older rectilinear portions of the complex and a new serpentine addition. This zone, which became the concourse and atrium, functions as the heart of the building. The concourse constantly expands, contracts, and bends as it extends for the length of the building. Walls appear to tilt, and ceilings dive and rise precariously. Rooms are not rectilinear. Bridges and ramps offer unexpected views into spaces above and below. A palette of pastel colors relates the new addition to the planes of the old and emphasizes the constantly changing geometries. Critic Charles Jencks compared the effect to an "intermeshing of tectonic plates" and "an earthquake of forms."[16] The effect can be disorienting; users are kept guessing about how to find their way. Eisenman admits that he sought to "disrupt the physical sense of normalcy"[17] through unusual angles, segmented uneven walls and ceilings, and twisting corridors.

Computers were used to translate the design into three—or even four—dimensions. The development and proliferation of computer-aided design (CAD) in the 1990s has had a powerful and liberating effect. CAD became a tool to generate radical architecture, making it possible to build conceptions that otherwise could not even be drawn. Because of the shifting levels and angles, each point on the computer rendering had three coordinates. It was a challenge to ensure that lines generated by computer would actually meet up in space. Unlike a Modernist building, in which the form is integral with the structural system and overtly expressed, in this building there is no structure visible. The exterior is clad in EIFS, a synthetic material, and the interior with drywall, giving the building a sense of weightlessness.

And yet the new building fulfills its purpose, which is to bring together the college's four schools under one roof, physically as well as socially. It doubled the size of the library and provided a large auditorium as well as communal café space. The wide concourse through the core creates a sense of openness and intellectual exchange as intended; it doubles as an open classroom space where work in progress can be observed by passersby. This is not a building one simply walks through; it makes one think about architecture and challenges its occupants to take risks in their artistic projects.

Michael McInturf came to Cincinnati with Peter Eisenman as project architect and construction supervisor for the DAAP addition at UC. He decided to stay and joined the DAAP faculty. Eisenman's influence on McInturf's work can be seen in his Upper School addition to Cincinnati Country Day School.

Frank Gehry, with BHDP
Vontz Center for Molecular Studies, 1997–99
University of Cincinnati

Designed by the internationally renowned architect Frank Gehry, the Vontz Center is highly sculptural, with its bulging exterior walls. It was designed in part as a gateway to the medical complex and link to the west campus and surrounding neighborhood.

Vontz Center for Molecular Studies

The cutting-edge design of the Vontz Center for Molecular Studies represents the excellence of the UC Medical Center, which ranks in the top 25 percent of research-based academic health-centers in the United States. Designed by the internationally renowned architect Frank Gehry, the $46 million facility houses state-of-the-art cancer and neurosciences laboratories. The center was named in honor of local businessman and UC alumnus Albert Vontz Jr., who donated $5 million toward the project. The Cincinnati firm BHDP served as associate architect, and San Diego-based Earl Walls, noted for his work on Louis Kahn's sublime Salk Center in La Jolla, California, consulted on the design of the laboratories.

Like most of Gehry's work, the Vontz Center is highly sculptural; the underlying steel structure is virtually denied. The exterior walls bulge and curve, and the oversized, oddly angled gridded windows protrude or are recessed from the vast punched openings in the surface. The building's plan is simpler than it appears: it is roughly cruciform in shape, with lab blocks on the north and south and offices and auditorium to the east and west. A dramatic atrium at the center provides common space for collegial conversations and plenty of light, which streams through the skylight above. A twisting concrete stair rises through the middle of the atrium, providing engaging views of this grand space.

Winner of scores of prestigious design awards, including the 1989 Pritzker Architecture Prize, Gehry is known for wrapping his curvaceous buildings in metal. The Vontz Center is his first building clad in brick, which was chosen for the sake of local context and also economy. The columns of the reinforced concrete structural system conform to a regular grid that accommodates the lab modules, but the exterior is "a connected cluster of contoured masses."[18] To make bricks conform to the desired curve, they were prefabricated in panels, which were then assembled. Gehry's building is highly intuitive and subjective; he uses a series of sculptural models that he repeatedly reworks. The result is a highly idiosyncratic and spirited expression of creativity. The Vontz Center provides a fitting new icon at the gateway to UC's medical campus.

Michael Graves, with KZF Design
Engineering Research Center, 1992
University of Cincinnati

The Engineering Research Center, by illustrious UC alumnus Michael Graves, is strongly evocative of classical architecture, monumental yet warm in tone. It has a prominent presence on the Campus Green, and its orientation on axis with University Place strengthens one of the campus's most important entrances.

Engineering Research Center

The renowned Engineering Research Center was designed by world-class architect Michael Graves, a UC alumnus, with KZF Design, architect of record. Of all the recent buildings by signature architects on UC's campus, this is the most evocative of classical architecture. Although the building's overall volume is slightly off-center with the strong axis of University Place, the building's massing nevertheless firmly establishes that axiality, strengthening one of the campus's most important entrances. The narrow site forced the building upward to a height of eight stories. In contrast to the synthetically cloaked DAAP addition, this building is enriched with an elegant skin of Ohio sandstone, terra-cotta- and ochre-colored brick, and a prominent copper roof.

A loggia across the east side the building provides sweeping views of the campus green. The top of the building is capped by a two-story colonnade. The seventeen-foot drop from the plaza to the west and University Place is negotiated by a monumental stairway through the building. The barrel-vaulted copper roof is surmounted by five smokestacks that, like the porthole windows, evoke the grand steamships of an earlier day. The center hall at the first floor is dramatized by a vaulted ceiling with heavy brick arches. The interior is richly finished with quarry tile floors, wood seating, and wainscot. The articulation of the east elevation into four pavilions helps break down the building's mass and lets natural light into the elegant corridors, which are located at the perimeter.

Graves founded his architectural practice in Princeton, New Jersey, in 1964 and taught at Princeton University for almost forty years. His works range from major commissions such as the Public Services Building in Portland, Oregon, to whimsical designs for furniture, teapots, and other household items. Other prominent commissions in the region include the Humana Building (1982–85) in Louisville and the Riverbend Music Center (1983–84) east of Cincinnati.

By the mid-1970s, Graves was moving away from the pure white forms of orthodox Modernism, and gradually enriching them with color, symbolic allusion, complex layering, and experiments with materials. By 1979 (the year of his ground-breaking Portland Building), his style had matured into a consistent symbolic language of abstracted historically allusive forms and colors, with strong debts to Classicism and its proponents Claude-Nicholas Ledoux, Thomas Jefferson, and Aldo Rossi, among others. The Engineering Research Center is a perfect example of his developed style, and offers a rich playground of historical and allusive interpretation.

Henry Cobb, Pei Cobb Freed & Partners, with NBBJ
College-Conservatory of Music, 1991–99
University of Cincinnati

A concern for urban design inspired the $110-million transformation of the College-Conservatory of Music into a "campus village" of renovated and new buildings. The new entrance court and circular piazza provide a gracious public space and function as a single point of entry for all the venues within.

College-Conservatory of Music

The College-Conservatory of Music (CCM), acknowledged as one of the nation's top three conservatories of the performing arts and electronic media, has undergone a $110 million transformation. Dedicated in 1999, the new Conservatory complex is the culmination of an eight-year process. Henry N. Cobb, a founding partner of Pei Cobb Freed & Partners and former chair of Harvard's Graduate School of Design, working with NBBJ of Columbus, architect of record, "assisted Dean Robert J. Werner in propelling CCM forcefully into the twenty-first century," observed Joseph Power, the owner's representative for the university.

Cobb insisted on freedom from preconceived notions. The result was an enhanced "campus village" of renovated and new buildings. Memorial Hall, a run-down but handsome women's dormitory by Hake & Kuck (1924–25), was converted to faculty offices and practice rooms. The 1910 Schmidlapp Gymnasium by Garber & Woodward became the Dieterle Vocal Arts Center, keeping the historic character and creating an engaging interior. The 1967 Mary Emery Hall was reconstructed for administrative offices, classrooms, faculty offices, and a new electronic media center, with a new parking garage below to improve traffic flow and access. The Corbett Center for the Performing Arts was renovated into a richly appointed, first-class concert hall. The 1967 auditorium, one of Edward J. Schulte's last and few secular works, and the 1972 theater by Ming Cho Lee were also renovated. The ingenious and flexible Cohen Family black-box studio-theater and a beautiful and acoustically effective recital hall named after Dean Robert J. Werner were added at the north end and tied via a terrace to McMicken Commons.

Concern for urban design, in terms of how the pieces fit together and connected with the campus, was the driving concept for the Village. The pivotal component was a new entrance court and circular piazza, providing a single point of entry for all the venues within. The piazza functions brilliantly, with a central ramp allowing cars to come and go from the garage below without dominating the public space. Cobb's solution was distinctly Modernist, but contextual; the facility is a member of the chorus, not a diva. And yet the physical setting for CCM's activities now reflects their artistic excellence.

Main Street

An overriding goal of the master plan, according to its executor, University Architect Ronald B. Kull, is to generate a quality of life on campus that will attract students and activate the campus. To do this, the university borrowed a successful technique for revitalizing older downtowns, known as "Main Street." The approach involves mixing uses—residential, commercial, entertainment—to attract round-the-clock activity at the center of a community.

The concept was to cluster a variety of uses along a spine running diagonally southwest-northeast through the campus. Beginning at the McMicken Commons above Clifton Avenue, squeezing between Nippert Stadium and the Schneider Quadrangle, and ending at Campus Green along Martin Luther King Drive, Main Street comprises a pedestrian pathway and access to the buildings that frame it: University Pavilion, Tangeman University Center, the Joseph A. Steger Student Life Center, and the Student Recreation Center. Each of the buildings was designed by a different signature architect, but each was coordinated with the others to achieve an integrated whole. A local firm, Glaserworks, was instrumental in coordinating the work of the signature firms. The process was an extraordinary work of collaboration: all four architects designed their buildings to work together. At some places, the buildings are only thirty feet apart. Each building is unique, but each takes its place in the ensemble.

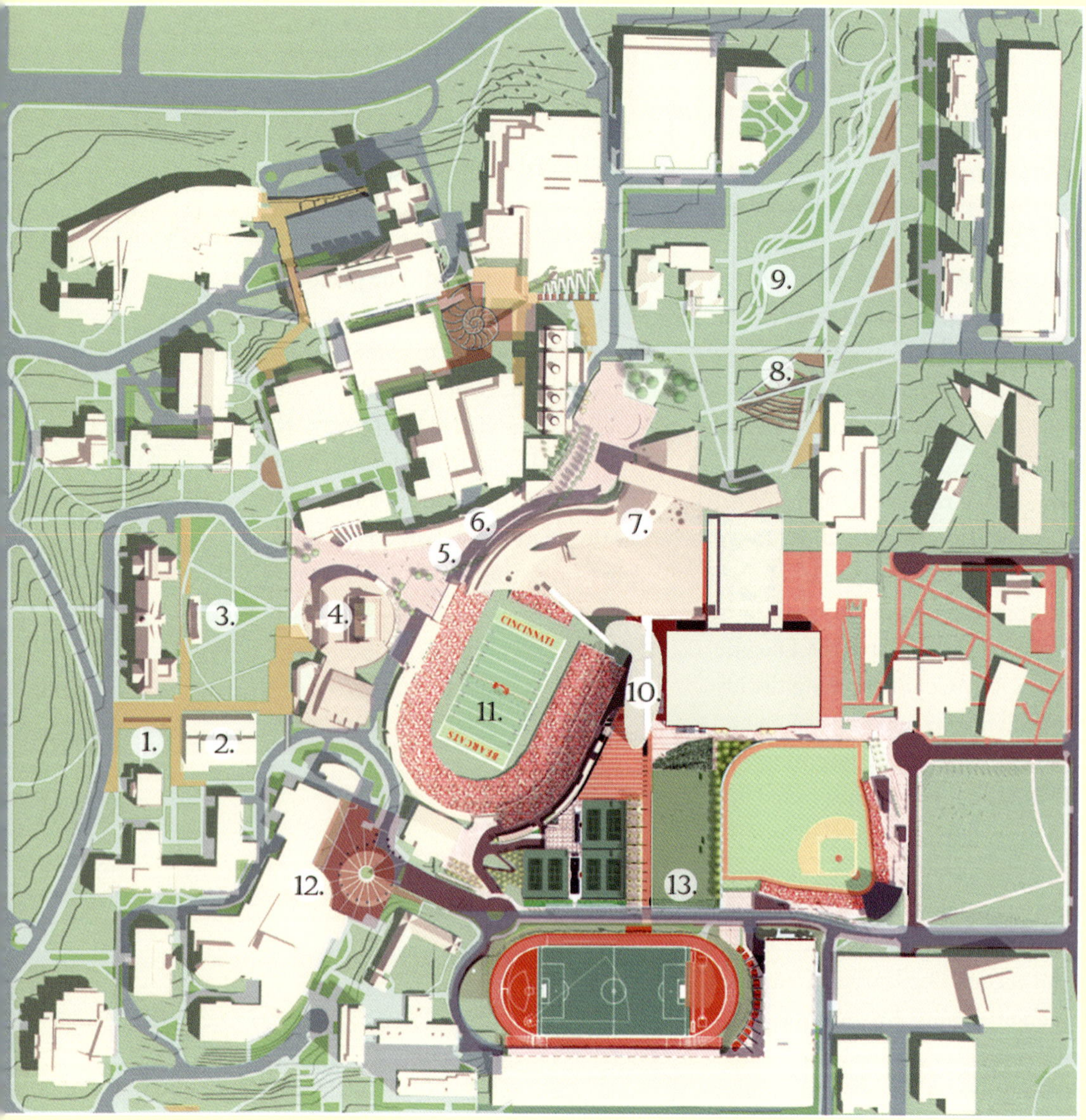

1. Fountain
2. University Pavilion
3. McMicken Commons
4. TUC
5. Pedestrian Way
6. SLC
7. Rec Center
8. Sigma Sigma Tower
9. Campus Green
10. R. E. Lindner Athletic Center
11. Nippert Stadium
12. CCM
13. Varsity Village

Leers Weinzapfel, with GBBN
University Pavilion, 2002
University of Cincinnati

Located on McMicken Commons, the new University Pavilion is eye-catching and innovative. The woman-owned partnership of Leers Weinzapfel is known for its lean modern approach, enriched by an exceptional refinement of detail. The transparent glass façade is welcoming and acts like a lantern when lit from inside at night.

University Pavilion

Located on McMicken Commons and visible from Clifton Avenue, the new University Pavilion by Leers Weinzapfel, with GBBN, architects of record, is an especially elegant, finely detailed, and gracefully proportioned facility. This "one-stop shop" houses all student administrative services, including admissions and enrolment, financial aid, scheduling, career development, and disability services. The top floor penthouse, where the offices for the president, vice presidents, and board of trustees are located, provides a sweeping view of the entire campus. Located on a steep slope, the building has entrances on three sides. The entry that faces Clifton Avenue, which is marked by a red rectangle and is heralded by a linear fountain designed by Hargreaves, acts as a front door for the university. A bridge connects the building to the College Conservatory of Music and the Tangeman Student Center.

The Boston-based partnership of Leers Weinzapfel, founded in 1982 by Andrea Leers and Jane Weinzapfel, has created buildings on numerous Ivy League campuses, including Harvard, MIT, Brandeis, and the University of Pennsylvania. Although the firm is known for clean Modernist designs, as seen in the University Pavilion, this six-story rectangular mass fits well with its more traditional neighbors. The glass façade overlooking the Commons is transparent and welcoming; it acts like a lantern when lit from inside at night. A multistory lobby with a grand open stairway extends across the front and animates the space. The planes of the walls are offset, and the roof seems to hover. The varying grids of the windows and masonry joints provide subtle rhythm and texture.

Tangeman University Center

The Tangeman University Center, by Gwathmey Siegel & Associates in partnership with the local firm GBBN Architects, represents a unique mix of old and new. Gwathmey Siegel & Associates is a New York-based architecture firm with an international reputation for excellence. A large part of their work consists of projects in campus settings and urban centers as well as additions to historic buildings. Partner Charles Gwathmey supervised the design of the UC project.

Preserving part of the original 1935–37 building by Harry Hake was a given in order to provide a continuity of image with the existing campus. The $50 million renovation and expansion maintained the Georgian Revival façade facing McMicken Commons as well as the gabled roof and crowning cupola but wrapped the remainder of the building in a new cylindrical addition. The architects gutted the old building and created a three-story atrium in the center with a central staircase and flanking balconies. A large portion of the slate roof surface was replaced with glazing that allows natural light to flood the stark, white atrium below. The heavy mass of the cupola appears to rest, improbably, on the glass surface of the roof.

On the Main Street level, a dining lounge offers students a retail food court and is surrounded to the east by a two-story glazed wall that overlooks the sports stadium. The second floor of the rotunda houses a conference center with flexible meeting spaces arranged around the new atrium. Beneath the new skylight at the McMicken Commons level of the atrium, an open amphitheater provides a place for informal meetings and performances. The south wing houses the relocated campus bookstore, an upscale dining facility, the central campus kitchen, and the Great Hall, a new 1,000-seat auditorium for events and ceremonies.

Gwathmey Siegel & Associates, with GBBN Architects, 2003–4

Charles Gwathmey opened up Harry Hake's 1930s student union building, allowing sunlight to flood the newly created three-story atrium. The Georgian façade was preserved and given a contemporary metallic edge.

Joseph A. Steger Student Life Center

Named for the former UC president who presided over the reshaping of the campus, the Joseph A. Steger Student Life Center winds its way down the hill at the center of Main Street. Designed by Mario Violich of Moore Ruble Yudell of Santa Monica in partnership with the firm's principal, Buzz Yudell, and Glaserworks, the $26.2 million Steger Center imitates a street in an old European hilltown, a narrow passage of low scale with densely packed nonaligned units. This 500-foot-long crescent-shaped building was chosen by the American Institute of Architects (AIA) as one of the world's eleven most notable buildings. The building represents a masterful solution to an extremely challenging building site with a sixty-foot grade change.

At 92,000 square feet, it is just one-third as large as the Recreation Center, but it plays a major role in enlivening the pedestrian passage along Main Street. The aim was to house uses that would maximize activity during all hours. The best alternative was a combination of retail computer lab, copy- and photo-processing center, fast-food restaurants) and student-related offices, including the UC Center for Community Engagement; Ethnic Programs and Services; Graduate Student Association; Office of Judicial Affairs, Student Activities and Leadership Development; Student Government; and UC Women's Center.

The Student Life Center is connected and responds to the 1925 Swift Hall to the north, by Harry Hake. Like Swift, Steger Center has brick at the base with horizontal window bands, but the upper floors are metal-clad rather than visible concrete. The mews—the space between the two buildings—is divided into many small landscaped terraces that step down the hill. The terraces provide many intimate places for sitting.

The design team used physical and virtual models to assess the relationship among the Main Street buildings and the space in between. This enabled them to envision the way the stair from the Recreation Center met the ground, the layout of the trees and lights along the street, and the quality of the views from the street into Nippert Stadium and other campus landmarks.

Moore Ruble Yudell, with Glaserworks
Joseph A. Steger Student Life Center (*left*), 2005
University of Cincinnati

The Steger Student Life Center is the spine of UC's new Main Street. This 500-foot-long crescent-shaped building connects with the older Swift Hall to create a galleria-like gateway and provides a mix of uses to enliven its spaces at all hours. The wayfinding system and its signage are by Kolar Design.

Thom Mayne, Morphosis, with KZF Design
Student Recreation Center, 2005
University of Cincinnati

The most complex building on the UC campus, the Student Recreation Center is actually made up of three buildings: the recreation center, a serpentine wing with six large lecture halls, and a bar-shaped wing of housing that straddles the other two elements. The curving classroom wing shown here seems inspired by the stadium it borders.

Student Recreation Center

Aside from the $103-million renovation of CCM, the $85-million recreation center is the largest investment ever in a single new building on campus. The project is the result of a close collaboration of Thom Mayne of Morphosis of Los Angeles and locally based KZF Design. Mayne had come to Cincinnati in the late 1980s to present a relatively restrained proposal for moving the Contemporary Art Center to the former OMI College of Applied Science Building, now the Emery Apartments. He achieved international acclaim in the mid-1990s, winning the prestigious Pritzker Architecture Prize in 2005. In terms of complexity, the Student Recreation Center exceeds even Eisenman's DAAP addition.

The 3.4-acre site is at the nexus of the athletic complex to the south, the academic ridge, to the west, the new green space to the north, and the residential complex to the east; the vast and complex recreation center knits them all together. Major pedestrian paths crossing the campus were incorporated into the new structure, creating yet deconstructing axes of orientation. The 353,000-square-foot structure is actually made up of three buildings: the underlying recreation center, a serpentine wing with six large lecture halls overlooking Nippert Stadium, and a bar-shaped wing of housing that straddles the other two elements.

The central building, defined by a wide, sweeping roof with a gentle curve, houses the first-rate recreation facilities, including an Olympic-size pool visible from outside. This enormous structure uses giant trusses to provide large expanses inside. The trusses are a starting point for angular and aerodynamic forms that shape and punctuate the rooms. The angular walls create spaces that give the impression of the interior of an ancient pyramid or being on the set of *Metropolis,* the classic 1927 science-fiction film.

The classroom building on the west side resembles a raised serpentine wing working its way up the hill. At first the classroom wing could be mistaken for part of Nippert Stadium; the outer wall leans out at the top like a grandstand. Its height is accentuated by a framework covered by a metal scrim resembling an airplane wing. Lit from inside, this form gives the building extra height and drama and helps animate Main Street. The third building, known as the "bar," is an angled nine-story, matte-gray, metal-clad box that hovers above the recreation center. The top four floors provide suite-style housing. Below are a reception area, administrative offices, racquetball courts, and more weight- and fitness-training areas. A convenience store and dining facility on the lower floors round out the services for residents.

The main entrance at the north end of the building has a multigabled roof, imitating the folds of the newly created landscape forms nearby. Although the housing bar is linear in contrast to the curving classroom wing, together they create a continuous "wiggle worm" that runs along Main Street. The bar also strengthens the southern edge of Sigma Sigma Commons. The complexity of the building is reflected in the visual interplay between the various levels. From the juice bar, one looks over the pools; from a large dining area known as the Marché (French for "market"), one looks over the stadium and cavernous gym, from Main Street one can gaze into the leisure pool. The interplay of spaces illustrates Mayne's penchant for manipulating the building volume by adding and subtracting pieces to create enlivening forms and views. Mayne also plays with seemingly random patterns. He punches the low-arched roof, as though it were Swiss cheese, with round skylights. On the housing bar, he runs irregularly spaced windows across the metal walls in shallow horizontal bands, suggesting a digital punch card.

Bernard Tschumi, with Glaserworks
Richard E. Lindner Athletic Center, 2005–2006
University of Cincinnati

Varsity Village and Richard E. Lindner Athletic Center

Glaserworks was also architect of record for Varsity Village. Varsity Village includes a new 3,028-seat baseball stadium, the Lawn, tennis courts, a brick-paved plaza, underground parking, and MRI facility, and the Richard E. Lindner Athletic Center. Designed by Bernard Tschumi, the Athletic Center is shaped like an apostrophe to fit on a very tight site between the Fifth Third Arena, the stadium, sports fields, and the new Student Recreation Center.

Bernard Tschumi, a Swiss-born architect and former dean of architecture at Columbia University, won the Grand prix national d'architecture in 1996. Tschumi garnered international acclaim in 1983 when he won the competition for Parc de la Villette in Paris. Tschumi was selected to design the Lindner Center chiefly on the basis of his design for Lerner Hall, a student center on the main campus of Columbia University. Lerner Hall honored its context—a McKim, Mead & White–designed master plan—and made a dramatic architectural statement by means of a mullionless, glass-fronted courtyard.

Tschumi enjoys the ambiguity of the relationship between the curvilinear plan of the Athletic Center and the orthogonal site in which it sits; he calls it "contextual free-form," and indeed, somehow this organic form does fit the context. The striking exterior is a sort of concrete honeycomb made up of welded steel V-columns that are clad in precast. The V-columns form a five-story-high truss that allows the curving exterior wall to span more than 140 feet across an existing below-grade mechanical room that could not be moved. On the interior, a five-story atrium links the north and south entrances and acts as a common space for all the center's activities. The atrium will hold a museum of UC sports memorabilia. A stair rises in a single width for the entire length of the atrium. The athletic offices are on the top floor, and training rooms are below ground. Although the center will be used principally by athletes, the new auditorium, classrooms, the UC Club, and the playing fields will be shared with students and faculty from the entire university. In addition to the uses listed above, the center houses the faculty club and Student Health services.

Bernard Tschumi describes the Athletic Center as "contextual free-form." The exterior—sort of concrete honeycomb composed of a diagrid of welded steel V-columns covered with curved precast concrete panels—functions like an exoskeleton, allowing long spans of open floor space inside.

Looking south from Garfield Place.

Epilogue

As an aspiring city in the Ohio wilderness, Cincinnati boasted many natural advantages: a location on a great river in what was to become the middle of the national population, fertile hinterlands, and an exceptionally beautiful setting amidst rivers and hills. As this book notes, from the city's earliest years, civic "boomers" attempted to guide its development. Among other techniques, they embraced quality architecture to foster pride of place in residents and to attract newcomers. Their methods worked. By the 1830s, talented designers had produced a distinctive urban place, and it led the nation in population growth.

With the twentieth century, Cincinnati's reliance on architecture and planning for economic development intensified. But cities rarely evolve logically, predictably, or entirely as planned. Even when implemented, architecture and land-use programs that focus solely on expediency and growth often produce unhappy results. There is a growing recognition that quality of life issues affect growth and community happiness.

While most indicators for the future are encouraging, population in the city proper has continued to decline. Meanwhile, preservation and revitalization of a local asset and national treasure—the Italianate Over-the-Rhine district—remains in doubt. Two nonprofit entities—the Corporation for Findlay Market and the Cincinnati Center City Development Corp. (3CDC)—are engaged in the district, which has demonstrated the potential to attract creative residents and businesses back to the core. 3CDC is also providing leadership for the renewal of Fountain Square and for completion of The Banks riverfront revitalization plan.

Architecture and planning cannot solve urban social or political problems, but they can be tools to craft designs for fitting and pleasing spaces and places that satisfy the human need for order, variety, and beauty.

In 2006, area residents have reason to be encouraged about their emerging built environment. Exciting new structures add distinction to downtown Cincinnati, Covington, and the university campus in Uptown. The Cincinnati CBD has been reconnected to the riverfront; cultural organizations have expanded their historic structures and missions; the public school system is implementing an extensive program of historic preservation and new construction; the handsome convention center expansion is an effective tool for those who sell the city; and the business community has coalesced around the need for speedy and dramatic improvements to the core and Over-the-Rhine. In addition, elected officials in Cincinnati, Hamilton

County, Northern Kentucky, and progressive urban townships are embracing quality design and planning as tools to preserve and enhance the natural and built environments.

The Ohio River nestled between the hills continues to be the thread that binds the historic communities together and makes each return to the city a sentimental journey home. The river and adjacent parklands have become magnets for leisure-time activities, such as the celebrated Tall Stacks river festivals and unbeatable Labor Day fireworks displays.

Attractions related to the river and new opportunities for downtown living are part of the excitement that is building in the city. Pedestrians delight in the Purple People Bridge walk to Newport and the new and challenging bridge climb. People are intrigued with downtown living, where attractive housing is within easy walking distance of the waterfront, parks, theater, bistros, and the city center.

The fall 2006 completion of a reconfigured Fountain Square, which will place the iconic Genius of Water fountain in a more intimate, parklike plaza, further evidences the rediscovery of urban values and local leaders' faith in the power of architecture and design.

Like Henry Probasco and his team, who created this Cincinnati symbol in 1871, today's patrons, designers, and public officials have collaborated to rejuvenate this gathering place in the heart of the city. So long as great art, architecture, and special urban places like this bring people harmoniously together, we may—and should —be optimistic about the future of this and other American cities.

Fourth Street Promenade

Notes

Preface

1. Writer's Program (Ohio), *Cincinnati: A Guide to the Queen City and Its Neighbors* (Cincinnati: Wiesen-Hart Press, 1943); Architectural Foundation of Cincinnati, *Architecture and Construction in Cincinnati: A Guide to Buildings, Designers, and Builders* (Cincinnati: Architectural Foundation of Cincinnati, 1987); Daniel Hurley, *Cincinnati: The Queen City* (Cincinnati: Cincinnati Historical Society, 1982); Geoffrey J. Giglierano and Deborah A. Overmyer, *The Bicentennial Guide to Greater Cincinnati: A Portrait of Two Hundred Years* (Cincinnati: Cincinnati Historical Society, 1988); John Clubbe, *Cincinnati Observed: Architecture and History* (Columbus: Ohio State University Press, 1992); Alice Weston and Walter E. Langsam, *Great Houses of the Queen City: Two Hundred Years of Historic and Contemporary Architecture and Interiors in Cincinnati and Northern Kentucky* (Cincinnati: Cincinnati Historical Society, 1997).

Chapter 1

1. There are numerous variants of the name. O-Y-O is preferred by www.ohiohistorycentral.org, the online encyclopedia of the Ohio Historical Society.

2. Richard Scamyhorn and John Steinle, *Stockades in the Wilderness: The Frontier Defenses and Settlements of Southwestern Ohio, 1788–1795* (Dayton: Landfall Press, 1986), 129.

3. For an interpretive overview of the period, see Daniel Hurley, *Cincinnati: The Queen City* (Cincinnati: Cincinnati Historical Society, 1982), ch. 1. Detailed accounts of the settlement of the Miami Purchase and early years of Cincinnati may be found in Henry A. Ford and Mrs. Kate B. Ford, *History of Cincinnati, Ohio with Illustrations and Biographical Sketches* (Cleveland: Williams and Co., 1881); Daniel Aaron, *Cincinnati, Queen City of the West, 1819–1838* (Columbus: Ohio State University Press, 1992).

4. Daniel Drake, *Natural and Statistical View, or Picture of Cincinnati and the Miami Country* (Cincinnati: Looker and Wallace, 1815); Benjamin Drake and Edward D. Mansfield, *Cincinnati in 1826* (Cincinnati: Morgan, Lodge and Fisher, 1827); and Charles Cist, *Cincinnati in 1841: Its Early Annals and Future Prospects* (Cincinnati: E. Morgan, 1841).

5. William Henry Harrison delivered a talk in 1837 before the Historical and Philosophical Society (founded 1831), which met in Cincinnati and was the predecessor of the Cincinnati Historical Society. The address was published in 1840. This passage is cited in Ford, *History of Cincinnati,* 16.

6. Henry D. Shapiro and Zane L. Miller, eds., *Physician to the West: Selected Writings of Daniel Drake on Science and Society* (Lexington: University Press of Kentucky, 1970), 140. Along with providing an excellent commentary on Drake's scientific and political views, this work is the best source for his extensive written works. It contains selections from his accounts of the city in 1810 and 1815.

7. Jacob Burnet, *Notes on the Early Settlement of the North-Western Territory* (Cincinnati: Derby, Bradley and Co., 1847), 434–437; and A. E. Jones, *Extracts from the History of Cincinnati and the Territory of Ohio* (Cincinnati: n.p., 1888) 40–41 (ca. 1878), citing Burnet's letter to Historical Society, 35.

8. Thomas Jefferson and members of the American Philosophical Society (founded 1743 in Philadelphia) encouraged studies and explorations, such as those conducted by Harrison and Drake, that might refute allegations by the French naturalist Georges-Louis Leclerc, Comte de Buffon (1707–88). Buffon argued that the American environment produced plant and animal life inferior to that of Eurasia. By way of proof, he cited the supposed absence of large mammals (hence the hunt for mammoth fossils) and the low virility of the people in the New World.

9. Drake and Mansfield, *Cincinnati in 1826,* 44–45.

10. Scamyhorn and Steinle, *Stockades,* 13, 29, 65, 81, 113.

11. Miller and Shapiro, *Physician,* 145.

12. Ibid., 27.

13. Ibid., 83.

14. Ibid., 84.

15. For a survey of the literature, see chapters 2–4 of Leland Roth, *American Architecture: A History* (Boulder, CO: Westview Press, 2001). Thomas Jefferson's theories about government and architecture set a standard for the new nation. Jefferson looked to the ancient world of republican Rome and democratic Athens for models, and he designed buildings for the University of Virginia and his house at Monticello in the classical tradition of ancient Rome. As secretary of state, Jefferson lived for a time in Paris, where he studied the Maison Carrée, a Roman temple at Nîmes. Like other learned men of his generation, he was familiar with the writings of Palladio, the Italian Mannerist architect, and Sir Christopher Wren, the great scientist and architect of seventeenth-century London. Jefferson was the friend and patron of Charles Bulfinch and Benjamin Henry Latrobe, who popularized the Neoclassical styles in America and who both contributed designs for the U.S. Capitol. The Greek temple style was the first classical fashion to be used widely across the country. It created a national idiom, which reached Cincinnati in the 1820s and blossomed in the 1830s.

William Henry Harrison was one of the most vocal advocates of U.S. aid to Greece during its battles for independence.

16. Beverley W. Bond Jr., ed., *The Intimate Letters of John Cleves Symmes and His Family* (Cincinnati: Historical and Philosophical Society of Ohio, 1956), 77.

17. Ford, *History of Cincinnati,* 77–78. The plan for Hygeia was published in England as an appendix to Drake and Mansfield's *Cincinnati in 1826.*

18. Shapiro and Miller, *Physician to the West,* 83.

19. Drake and Mansfield, *Cincinnati in 1826,* 29–35.

20. The first known local use of "Queen of the West" to describe Cincinnati is in a publication from 1819.

21. Scamyhorn and Steinle, *Stockades,* 15.

22. Sue Ann Painter, *William Henry Harrison: Father of the West* (Cincinnati: Jarndyce and Jarndyce Press, 2004), 30.

23. The reduced military unit moved across the Ohio River to new quarters in Newport Barracks.

24. John F. Edgar, *Pioneer Life in Dayton and Vicinity, 1796–1840* (Dayton: W. J. Shuey, 1896). Available at http://www.daytonhistorybooks.com.

25. Judith Spraul-Schmidt, "Exhibiting the Changing World through the Ohio Mechanics Institute: From Annual Fairs and Exhibitions to Grand Expositions, 1838–1888," *Ohio Valley History* 5, no. 1 (2005): 37–46. Spraul-Schmidt tracks the evolution of the organization's name from its 1828 origin as "Mechanic's" through "Mechanics'" in the 1850s and simply "Mechanics" from the 1870s, and argues that the 1870s form demonstrated that OMI had become a "modern institution."

Chapter 2

1. M. Joblin and Co., *Cincinnati Past and Present* (Cincinnati: M. Joblin and Co., 1872), 373–77.

2. Daniel Hurley, *Cincinnati: The Queen City* (Cincinnati: Cincinnati Historical Society, 1982), 33–34.

3. Young, as federal architect, was listed as the official designer, but according to Walter E. Langsam, the design fits within the development of local architect James Keys Wilson.

4. Alan I. Marcus, *Plague of Strangers: Social Groups and the Origins of City Services in Cincinnati, 1819–1870* (Columbus: Ohio State University Press, 1991), passim.

5. Charles Cist, *Sketches and Statistics of Cincinnati in 1859* (Cincinnati: n.p., 1859), quoted in Henry A. Ford and Kate B. Ford, *History of Cincinnati, Ohio with Illustrations and Biographical Sketches* (Cleveland: Williams and Co., 1881), 102.

6. A number of German American architects and engineers appeared in the 1840s and 1850s. Among those listed in the 1850s directories are Otto G. Leopold, Joseph Goettle, C. E. Schultz, Adrian Hegeman, and John Mierenfeld. German Americans, many of whom had trained in the fine polytechnical schools of Germany, tended to emphasize engineering.

7. For a thoughtful analysis, see Hurley, *Cincinnati,* 55–62.

8. Roger Fortin, *Faith and Action: A History of the Catholic Archdiocese of Cincinnati, 1821–1996* (Columbus: Ohio State University Press, 2002). Fortin's estimates from archdiocese records are slightly higher than those given by contemporary chronicler Charles Cist.

9. Cincinnati city directories, 1840–41, microfiche file, Cincinnati Historical Society Library.

10. The quarrying of materials by the congregation was a cost-cutting activity that was not unusual in the period. Stone was readily available from Isaac Graveson's firm about 1850 and from the David Hummel Co., which operates today as Hummel Industries. In good years, an average of 1,000 buildings went up in Cincinnati, and by 1859, 80 percent were constructed of brick or stone.

11. Blanche M. G. Linden, "Spring Grove: Celebrating 150 Years," *Queen City Heritage* 53 (1995): 8–12.

12. Since the 1820s, Cincinnati gentlemen with time and money had pursued horticulture, floriculture, and viticulture as educated amateurs. Interest in horticulture led to formation of a society and to the publication in Cincinnati of the *Western Horticultural Review* (1850–54) by Dr. John Aston Warder, an eminent physician and horticulturist. Warder developed extensive model gardens for his Clifton estate (purchased by Bowler), and then in North Bend, where a number of fine old trees and his house remain. As a member of the Cincinnati public school board, Warder traveled the country studying education methods and model schools in an effort to propose ideal architectural plans for local schools. Rebecca Goodman and Barrett J. Brunsman, *This Day in Ohio History* (Cincinnati: Emmis Books, 2005), 216.

13. Ford and Ford, *History of Cincinnati,* 96.

14. Leland Roth, *American Architecture: A History* (Westview Press: Boulder, 2001), 200. Like most claims of "first," this one must be strictly qualified. In the Cincinnati area, the planned suburb of Hygeia (ca. 1825), in what became Ludlow, Kentucky, was earlier, but its more formal paper plan was never realized. Cleves, in far western Hamilton County, was established in 1818 by William Henry Harrison. Influenced by Jeffersonian theory and a farmer's respect for nature, Harrison used a combination of grid and curved streets that accommodated a Native American earthwork in the undulating main street.

15. Howard followed the natural topography and favored a landscape system close to the "picturesque" aesthetic, which had a wild, untended look. Strauch, who followed with his "lawn landscape" plan, was inclined toward the aesthetic of the "beautiful," which required careful tending and pruning. See Linden, "Spring Grove," 16, 37.

16. Daisy M. Smith, ed., *A.B. Mullett Diaries &c: Annotated Documents, Research and Reminiscence Regarding a Federal Architect Engineer,* selected and interpreted by Suzanne Mullett Smith (Washington, DC: Mullett-Smith Press, 1985), 143; Antoinette J. Lee, *Architects to the Nation: The Rise and Decline of the Supervising Architect's Office* (New York: Oxford University Press, 2000), 68–76.

Chapter 3

1. Architect James W. McLaughlin was an aide to Major General John Charles Fremont; later he became an illustrator-journalist. Engineer William S. Rosecrans became a major general in the Army. Engineer Washington Roebling enlisted in the war as a private and returned a brevetted colonel.

2. When President-elect Abraham Lincoln stopped in Cincinnati on his journey from Illinois to Washington, DC, representatives of northern Kentucky had prominent roles in the grand parade and the speeches at the Burnet House hotel.

3. Geoffrey J. Giglierano and Deborah A. Overmyer, *The Bicentennial Guide to Greater Cincinnati: A Portrait of 200 Years* (Cincinnati: Cincinnati Historical Society, 1998), 261; Daniel J. Kenny, *Illustrated Cincinnati: A Pictorial Hand-Book of the Queen City* (Cincinnati: George E. Stevens and Co., 1875), passim. As part of his detailed descriptions and illustrations of the architecture of individual buildings, Kenny catalogs the existence and type of elevator.

4. E. F. Farrington, *A Full and Complete Description of the Covington and Cincinnati Suspension Bridge, with Dimensions and Details of Construction* (Cincinnati: J. P. Lindsay and Co., 1867), 16.

5. See David Ehrlinger, *The Cincinnati Zoo and Botanical Garden from Past to Present* (Cincinnati: Cincinnati Zoo and Botanical Garden, 1993); also Judith Spraul-Schmidt, "Designing the Late Nineteenth Century Suburban Landscape: The Cincinnati Zoological Garden," *Queen City Heritage* 51, vol. 1 (Spring 1993): 40–51.

6. Richard Morris Hunt and other École des Beaux-Arts graduates introduced French traditions to the United States. Robust versions of the Renaissance or Baroque Second Empire style (named for Emperor Louis Napoleon III) were widely admired in the United States. Technical achievements, represented here by John Roebling's revolutionary use of steel cable in the Suspension Bridge and the Cincinnati Observatory's "lighthouse in the sky," were ultimately more significant than style. They foreshadowed the future city, which would be based upon science and steel.

7. The American Institute of Architects was organized in New York City in 1857, but it was more than a decade before the AIA formed a national organization. The Cincinnati chapter, the second in the United States, was established in 1870.

8. Farrington, *Full and Complete*, 17.

9. James Marston Fitch, *American Building: The Historical Forces That Shaped It*, 2nd ed. (New York: Schocken Books, 1966), 155.

10. Farrington, *Full and Complete*, 16.

11. Harry R. Stevens, *The Ohio Bridge* (Cincinnati: Ruter Press, 1939), 180.

12. Joseph S. Stern Jr., "Lighthouses in the Sky," *The Cincinnati Historical Society Bulletin* 39 (1981): 231.

13. Giglierano and Overmyer, *Bicentennial Guide*, 214.

14. Zane L. Miller, *Visions of Place: The City, Neighborhoods, Suburbs, and Cincinnati's Clifton, 1850–2000* (Columbus: Ohio State University Press, 2001).

15. J. D. Forbes, *Victorian Architect: The Life and Work of William Tinsley* (Bloomington: Indiana University Press, 1953), passim.

16. Schmitt's earliest Cincinnati murals were painted in 1862 for St. Francis Seraph. Other works are in Immaculata and various churches in the tristate region. Wilhelm Lamprecht, the muralist for the Sisters of Charity Mother House, was also a member of the Altar Building guild. See Annemarie Springer, *Nineteenth Century German-American Church Artists*, ch. 3 (Bloomington, IN: Springer, 2001).

17. Stewart Brand, *How Buildings Learn: What Happens after They're Built* (New York: Viking-Penguin, 1994), 134.

18. Such mixed land use was common throughout the nineteenth century. By the 1860s, civic leaders were beginning to demand the removal to the periphery of unattractive as well as noxious industries. The issue came before council and the courts during removal of a market house to make way for the Tyler Davidson Fountain.

19. *Cincinnati Daily Gazette*, July 22, 1866.

20. Jayne Merkel, *Cincinnati Enquirer*, January 29, 1967.

21. Frederic Goss, *Cincinnati: The Queen City*, 4 vols. (Chicago: S. J. Clarke, 1912), 3:957–58, 272–73.

22. Owen Jones, *The Grammar of Ornament* (London: Day and Son, 1856; repr., New York: Portland House, 1986).

23. *Cincinnati Daily Gazette*, July 21, 1866; Kenny, *Illustrated Cincinnati*, 106.

24. The archeological phase of the Gothic Revival began in England and spread quickly to the United States. Historic restoration movements on the continent and in Great Britain fueled the revival. In France, the influential architect-engineer and theorist Viollet-le-Duc was restoring a number of the great medieval monuments; his influential work on Sainte Chapelle, the jewel of Paris, was completed by 1850. Augustus Welby Northmore Pugin designed a Gothic decorative scheme for the rebuilding from 1836 of the Palace of Westminster (Houses of Parliament).

25. Renewal took several decades. The massive federal building in the adjoining block was underway. Other monumental new buildings went up slowly around the square: McLaughlin's Carew Building in 1890 and his Rawson Building in 1893. Probasco hoped that the fountain idea would be multiplied until there was one in each ward. (The flower stand has been moved along with the fountain to the new square.)

26. William F. Poole, *The Tyler Davidson Fountain Given by Henry Probasco to the City of Cincinnati* (Cincinnati: Robert Clarke and Co., 1872; repr., Cincinnati: Cincinnati Historical Society, 1988), 1, 4, 23, 30, 78, 110.

Chapter 4

1. *Cincinnati Commercial*, May 15, 1878.

2. Cincinnati native A. O. Elzner, who was sent home by the Richardson firm to supervise construction of the Chamber

of Commerce building, documented the design process. After the fire, the Municipal Arts Society and the Cincinnati Chapter of the American Association of Architects joined in a prolonged search for ways to salvage the great stone arches and decorative carvings.

3. The reference to cities of size and culture as "great cities" is ubiquitous. For Cincinnati examples, see Henry A. Ford and Kate B. Ford, *History of Cincinnati, Ohio with Illustrations and Biographical Sketches* (Cleveland: Williams, 1881), and Daniel J. Kenny, *Illustrated Cincinnati: A Pictorial Hand-Book of the Queen City* (Cincinnati: George E. Stevens and Co., 1875),.

4. The women who subsequently attended the Art Academy tended to come from the genteel class, but a number did need steady employment. Some found positions at Rookwood Pottery, which Maria Longworth Nichols (Storer) founded in 1880. Ironically, the women artists at Rookwood received lower pay than male artists for comparable work. Nichols was more interested in art than in reform.

5. *American Architect and Building News,* October 13, 1877, 330; Lawrence F. Mitchell, "The Evolution of the Cincinnati Central Business District and Riverfront: An Historical and Architectural Approach, 1900–1989" (PhD diss., University of Cincinnati, 1998); and Walter E. Langsam, *Architecture Cincinnati* brochure (Cincinnati: Architectural Foundation of Cincinnati, n.d.), citing Gerald Larson, paper delivered at the meeting of the Society of Architectural Historians, Pittsburgh, April 1985.

6. Joe Green, *Cincinnati Enquirer,* September 17, 1961.

7. Barry Horstman, *Cincinnati Post,* October 29, 1999.

8. Ibid.

9. Quoted by George F. Roth, *Cincinnati's Music Hall* (Virginia Beach, VA: Jordan and Co., 1978), 62.

10. Ibid.

11. George Ward Nichols, *The Cincinnati Organ with a Brief Description of the Cincinnati Music Hall* (Cincinnati: Robert Clarke and Co., 1878), 13.

12. Geoffrey J. Giglierano and Deborah A. Overmyer, *The Bicentennial Guide to Greater Cincinnati: A Portrait of 200 Years* (Cincinnati: Cincinnati Historical Society, 1998), 92.

13. *Ohio State Journal,* Columbus, OH, September 24, 1916; and *Cincinnati Times-Star,* November 30, 1934.

14. Elizabeth W. Perry, *A Sketch of the Women's Art Museum Association of Cincinnati* (Cincinnati: Robert Clarke and Co., 1886), 34. See also Sue Ann Brunsman [Painter], "The European Origins of Cincinnati Art Pottery: 1870–1900," MA thesis, University of Cincinnati, 1973.

15. *Cincinnati Gazette,* December 6, 1880.

16. *Cincinnati Times-Star,* December 28, 1888, 20.

17. *Cincinnati Enquirer,* December 2, 1923.

18. Westwood Historical Society Newsletter, January 2005.

19. Sue Ann Painter, *History of Delhi Township* (Cincinnati: Delhi Historical Society, 2002); Peg Schmidt, "Rise of the Urban Township: Mount St. Joseph" (Cincinnati: Delhi Historical Society, 2002).

Chapter 5

1. Cincinnati became a town in 1802 and a city in 1819. Annexing of contiguous territory began in 1849, and large tracts, such as Camp Washington, Price Hill, Mount Auburn, Walnut Hills, and Mount Lookout were annexed to the city in 1870. Resistance to the movement grew in the 1890s, especially among successful villages. Despite opposition, Westwood, Clifton, Avondale, and Linwood were annexed in 1896, and Bond Hill, Hyde Park, and Evanston in 1903. California was annexed in 1908, and the modern waterworks built there encouraged many of the remaining suburbs to join the city between then and 1914. For a map and details, see Zane L. Miller, *Boss Cox's Cincinnati: Urban Politics in the Progressive Era* (New York: Oxford University Press, 1968), 109.

2. Cuvier Press Club, *Cincinnati: The Queen City* (Cincinnati: Cuvier Press Club, 1914), 12.

3. In 1911, Dr. Christian Holmes, the brother-in-law of Cincinnati mayor Charles Fleischmann, succeeded in removing Cincinnati Hospital from the A. C. Nash-designed building at Twelfth and Plum streets to Corryville in the hilltops. Holmes insisted on an expensive, campus-style facilities plan. The GOP machine and some physicians objected to the location far from the poor.

4. As Zane Miller demonstrated in *Boss Cox's Cincinnati,* it was the methods, not the strategies, of the machine that ultimately led to its demise. In some respects, Cox was a "good boss" who brought order and efficiency to the government bureaucracy, but a few Democrat mayors were more effective reformers. See Geoffrey Giglierano, "The City and the System: Developing a Municipal Service 1800–1915," *Cincinnati Historical Society Bulletin* 35, no. 4 (1977): 238.

5. Paul Kraus, Cincinnati Water Works, kindly supplied information about the historic system.

6. Chlorination was introduced in the United States in 1908. With its new treatment plants, the city used the "water club" to annex outlying villages and unincorporated areas where people feared water-borne disease. The typhoid rate dropped dramatically.

7. Cuvier, *Cincinnati,* 11–12.

8. Most major U.S. cities were growing by more than 20 percent. Only St. Louis, Pittsburgh, Philadelphia, and Cincinnati fell below, and all four were controlled by "bosses." Ralph R. Caldwell, "Cincinnati and the Census," in Charles Goss, *Cincinnati: The Queen City* (Cincinnati: S. J. Clarke, 1912), 345–48.

9. Goss, *Cincinnati,* bk. 1, ch. 15, is devoted to a discussion of "bossism."

10. Robert C. Vitz, *The Queen and the Arts: Cultural Life in Nineteenth-Century Cincinnati* (Kent, OH: Kent State University Press, 1989), 242.

11. Burnham was always more of the business agent than the design architect in his partnership or firms.

12. McKinley's "splendid little" Spanish-American War of 1898 was the beginning of an expansion period that took Taft and then Burnham to the Philippines.

13. Burnham had won Taft's admiration and gratitude for his pro bono work in the Philippines.

14. Leland M. Roth, in *A Concise History of American Architecture* (New York: Harper and Row, 1979), 172ff., draws parallels with situation described by Chicago urban historian Robert Wiebe in his classic book *The Search for Order, 1877–1920* (New York: Hill and Wang, 1967).

15. Mark P. Painter, *William Howard Taft: President and Chief Justice* (Cincinnati: Jarndyce and Jarndyce Press, 2004), 89.

16. George McLaughlin, *Art Work of Cincinnati* (Chicago: W. H. Parish, 1893).

17. McLaughlin's unpublished manuscript was preserved by family members and is now in the collection of the author.

18. Miller, *Boss Cox's Cincinnati,* 219–21.

19. Ibid., 191.

20. Kessler had visited Cincinnati in the early 1880s, at the suggestion of Frederick Law Olmsted (1822–1903), to meet Strauch, so he knew that the city had a strong tradition of park design. Kurt Culbertson, "The Origins of Landscape Architecture in Ohio: The Life and Work of George Edward Kessler," *Queen City Heritage* 51, no. 1 (Spring 1993): 15–16.

21. Theodore Wesley Koch, *A Portfolio of Carnegie Libraries, Being a Separate Issue of the Illustrations from "A Book of Carnegie Libraries"* (Ann Arbor, MI: G. Wahr, 1907). A rare reference in the Cincinnati *Western Architect and Builder,* plates 73–74 of the 1907 portfolio, includes exterior and interior photographs and two floor plans of the Walnut Hills Branch Library.

22. See *Inland Architect* 50 (December 1907): 72–73.

23. http://www.pixelp.com.

24. *The New Home of the Procter & Collier Co.* (Cincinnati: Procter & Collier Co., 1922).

25. *Annual Report of the Beau Brummell Co.,* July 1947, n.p.

26. Lee J. Bennish, *Continuity and Change: Xavier University, 1831–1981* (Chicago: Loyola University Press, 1981), 112–13.

27. Ibid., 117, 125–26.

28. Earnshaw worked with Strauch at Spring Grove Cemetery (chapter 2), and Punshon was engineer for the most advanced of the waterworks projects discussed above.

29. *Commercial Tribune,* December 11, 1912.

30. Sharon Irish, *Cass Gilbert, Architect: Modern Traditionalist* (New York: Monacelli Press, 1999), 136.

31. Story related to Painter by Francie Garber Pepper, March 15, 2006.

32. Years later, University of Cincinnati DAAP students used some of the carved stones for a free-form sculpture that they erected in Burnet Woods.

33. *Cincinnati Times-Star,* August 2, 1939.

34. *Downtowner,* August 26, 2003.

35. In 1880, Ingalls consolidated several railroad lines to form the Cincinnati, Indianapolis, St. Louis and Chicago Railway, of which he was the president. It was merged in 1889 with the Vanderbilt-controlled Cleveland, Columbus, Cincinnati and Indianapolis Railway, becoming the Cleveland, Cincinnati, Chicago and St. Louis Railway, commonly known as the Big Four. Ingalls was the new company's president until 1905.

36. John Paul Jones, "The Big Man of the Big Four," *Cincinnati Historical Society Bulletin* 32, no. 3 (1974): 96.

37. Robert Patterson, the owner and CEO of National Cash Register Co. in nearby Dayton, Ohio, is an example of the extraordinary (perhaps compulsive—his company was convicted of antitrust violations in 1912) Progressive reform leader. Almost single-handedly, Patterson shaped his company and his city according to the theories of planners such as Olmsted and Taylor. The Patterson papers are in the Montgomery County Historical Society.

38. Montgomery Schuyler, "The Architecture of Cincinnati" *Architectural Record* 23 (1908): 337–66.

39. Miller, *Boss Cox's Cincinnati,* 210.

Chapter 6

1. Cincinnati suffered less from the depression than many other major cities. The great construction projects underway when the market crashed—the Carew Tower, Union Terminal, and the *Times-Star* Building—bolstered the local economy. See Daniel Hurley, *Cincinnati: The Queen City* (Cincinnati: Cincinnati Historical Society, 1982), 121.

2. Barry M. Horstman, "Seasongood," in *100 Who Made a Difference: Greater Cincinnatians Who Made a Mark on the 20th Century* (Cincinnati: Cincinnati Post, 1999).

3. Lincoln Steffens, "Shame of the Cities," *McClure's Magazine,* 1906.

4. Robert B. Fairbanks, *Making Better Citizens: Housing Reform and the Community Development Strategy in Cincinnati, 1890–1960* (Urbana: University of Illinois Press, 1998), passim.

5. The system has evolved over the years, and since 2000 direct election of the mayor and increased appointment-making authority have enhanced the power of that office.

6. City Planning Commission, *Cincinnati, The Official City Plan of Cincinnati, Ohio* (Cincinnati: The Commission, 1925). For Segoe and his work in Greater Cincinnati, see David J. Edelman, David J. Allor, and April Smith, *Ladislas Segoe and American Planning Practice* (Cincinnati: School of Planning, University of Cincinnati, 2000).

7. Sue Ann Painter, "City Folk Move to the Country: The 1920s," in *Rise of the Urban Township* (Cincinnati: Delhi Historical Society, 2002).

8. Geoffrey J. Giglierano and Deborah A. Overmyer, *The Bicentennial Guide to Greater Cincinnati: A Portrait of 200 Years* (Cincinnati: Cincinnati Historical Society, 1998), 69.

9. Terri Premo and Cindy Bailey, *Visions and Revisions: History of DAAP* (Cincinnati: University of Cincinnati DAAP, 2000), 11, 34–37, 62. Apparently, the Cincinnati program was not immediately popular—the most prominent local architects of the 1920s and 1930s seem to have attended MIT.

10. See Ernest Pickering, *Architectural Design* (New York: John Wiley and Sons, 1933).

11. German architect and theorist Heinrich Hübsch raised the issue in his 1828 book *In What Style Should We Build? The German Debate on Architectural Style* (Santa Monica, CA: Getty Center for the History of Art and the Humanities, 1992).

12. The term "Art Deco" originated with the 1925 Paris Exposition internationale des arts décoratifs et industriels modernes, which showcased current European styles, primarily in the decorative arts and high-fashion retailing. Architecture was represented in a minor way, and Le Corbusier's pavilion was an eloquent statement of the modernism that came to be known as the International Style. Art historian Bevis Hiller published a book about the aesthetic of Art Deco in 1968, but the term did not come into common use until around 1971, following a 4,000-object exhibition at the Minneapolis Institute of Arts. American art historians and curators, and then the popular press, began to call the style Art Deco. Earlier, design with Art Deco characteristics was described by such terms as "Moderne," "Jazz Moderne," "Streamline Moderne," or, in America, simply "Modernism." Although the penchant for taxonomies by critics and historians sometimes distorts the original intent of the designers, use of the terms "Art Deco" and "Art Moderne" to describe the distinctive design programs of the Carew Tower and Cincinnati Union Terminal is helpful in distinguishing them from the "modernism" of what came to be called "International Modernism" (another term coined by curator-critics). In this book, the authors have tried to apply terms to buildings that were used by the architect or by writers of the time.

13. Cincinnati Chamber of Commerce, *Cincinnati Union Terminal: A Pictorial History* (Cincinnati: Cincinnati Chamber of Commerce, 1933; repr., Cincinnati: Cincinnati Historical Society, 1987).

14. City Planning Commission, Cincinnati, *The Cincinnati Metropolitan Master Plan and the Official City Plan of the City of Cincinnati, adopted November 22, 1948* (Cincinnati: City Planning Commission, 1948).

15. Robert Manley, "Recollections of Segoe and Cincinnati," in Edelman et al., *Ladislas Segoe,* 59.

16. Laurence Conway Gerckens, "The Comprehensive Plan in the 20th Century," address for American Planning Association, 2001 National Conference. http://www.asu. edu/caed/proceedings01/GERCKENS/gerckens.htm

17. Sue Ann Brunsman [Painter], *Netherland Plaza Hotel: An Architectural Tour* (Cincinnati: Netherland Plaza Hotel, 1986, 2003). The essay in this booklet was based upon the hotel's collection of documents and publications from the design and construction period. The Netherland Plaza bath has been preserved and the room named the Churchill Suite.

The Churchill quote is from his article "Land of Corn and Lobsters," *Colliers,* August 5, 1933, republished in *Churchill at Large,* vol. 4 of *The Collected Essays of Sir Winston Churchill* (London: Library of Imperial History, 1975), 266. According to Richard M. Langworth, editor for the Churchill Center, Churchill was renovating a flat in 1932 at 11 Morpeth Mansions, near Parliament. He lived there with his wife, Clementine, until 1939.

18. Hurley, *Cincinnati,* 116.

19. David Gebhard, *The National Trust Guide to Art Deco in America* (New York: Preservation Press, 1996), 44.

20. Millard F. Rogers Jr., *John Nolen and Mariemont: Building a New Town in Ohio* (Baltimore: Johns Hopkins University Press, 2001), 8–10.

21. Architects of individual places included national architects Grosvenor Atterbury, Lois Howe, and Eleanor Manning and such local architects as Louis Fechheimer, Elzner and Anderson, George Drach, Charles W. Short, and the Hannaford firm. Paul P. Cret (1876–1945) reviewed some of the designs for public buildings. Charles F. Cellarius (1891–1973) built one section of apartments and served as "resident architect," apparently reviewing construction documents. Ibid. Passim.

22. Rogers, *John Nolen,* 203. Rogers uses Nolen's phrases to summarize the planner's theories for Mariemont.

23. Robert B. Fairbanks, *Making Better Citizens: Housing Reform and the Community Development Strategy in Cincinnati, 1890–1960* (Urbana: University of Illinois Press, 1998), 50.

24. John Zettel (1881–1950) and Walter L. Rapp (1878–1974). The latter was the son of George Rapp (1852–1918), late partner of Zettel.

25. William Fulton, "The Garden Suburb and the New Urbanism," in Kermit C. Parsons and David Schuyler, eds., *The Legacy of Ebenezer Howard: From Garden City to Green City* (Baltimore: John Hopkins University Press, 2002), 166.

26. Ernest Pickering, *Architectural Design (*New York: John Wiley and Sons, 1933), 64, 67. In the 1930s, the building was acclaimed as an example of "Modernism." By the 1970s, the building was used to illustrate the newly coined style of "Art Deco." More recently, because of its round, streamlined forms, it is referred to as an example of Art Moderne, which some critics see as a subset of Art Deco. In this discussion, we use the historical term that was used at the time even though the term "Modernism" subsequently has become associated most often with International Modernism.

27. For discussions on the role of the design team, see Linda Oliphant Stanford, "Railroad Designs by Fellheimer and Wagner," *Queen City Heritage* 43 (Cincinnati: Cincinnati Historical Society, 1985), 3–24; and Denny Carter [Young], "Paul Philippe Cret and the Cincinnati Union Terminal," in *Art Deco and the Cincinnati Union Terminal* (Cincinnati: Art History Department, University of Cincinnati College of Design, Architecture, Art and Planning, 1971), 10–15.

28. Barbaralee Diamonstein, *American Architecture Now II* (Rizzoli: New York 1985), 128. Hejduk, dean of Cooper Union School of Architecture, 1975–2000, had worked for Fellheimer and Wagner.

29. Cincinnati Chamber of Commerce, *Cincinnati Union Terminal,* n.p.

30. Presentation to trustees and staff of the Cincinnati Historical Society.

31. Art Deco's tendencies toward elongation and elegance are akin to those refined traits found in late-medieval International Gothic or in the Mannerist art and architecture that concluded the High Renaissance in Italy, France, and Spain. Some of these characteristics resurfaced in European Art Nouveau of the 1890s, one of the sources of Art Deco.

32. Hugh Ferriss, *The Metropolis of Tomorrow* (New York: I. Washburn, 1929). Scott Gampfer, director of history collections and preservation, Cincinnati Museum Center and an authority on its collection of architectural drawings, kindly shared information about Schulte's library and the drawings reproduced in this book.

33. "Sfumato" is an Italian word frequently used to describe the shadowy, smoky effects achieved by Leonardo da Vinci by blurring the edges of forms and figures so that they seem to dissolve in the environment.

34. Interview with Emery's daughter Lela Emery Steele, December 2005. Emery inherited the extensive Emery family real estate and manufacturing enterprises at the death of his aunt, Mary M. Emery, in 1927.

35. Peter Pennoyer and Anne Walker, *The Architecture of Delano & Aldrich* (New York: Norton, 2003), 51

36. Brunsman, *Architectural Tour.*

37. Robert Taft's private legal work involved him with many important local development projects, including Cincinnati Union Terminal, Indian Hill, and the Emery estate.

38. *Cincinnati Enquirer,* May 25, 1947.

39. This phenomenon was symptomatic of a new way of thinking in the post–World War II period.

Chapter 7

1. David Stradling, *Cincinnati: From River City to Highway Metropolis,* The Making of America Series (Charleston, SC: Arcadia, 2003), 109.

2. Daniel W. Young, *Laurel Homes Historic District Designation Report,* City of Cincinnati City Planning Department, March 1989, 10.

3. George E. Kessler, *A Park System for the City of Cincinnati* (Cincinnati: Park Commission of Cincinnati, 1907).

4. Frederick W. Garber, in "Ohio National Men Rally at New Home," The National Underwriter, The Ohio National Home Office Dedication, September 7, 1934, 6.

5. Christopher A. Cain, *Determination of Eligibility for the Twentieth Century Theater, Cincinnati, Ohio,* City of Cincinnati, Historic Conservation Office, February 1990, 2.

Chapter 8

1. One of CCDC's members was Walter Schmidt, a local real estate developer. Schmidt and six other leading developers instigated the founding of the Urban Land Institute (ULI) in 1936 as an arm of the National Association of Real Estate Boards (now the National Association of Realtors). At the time, there was little public sector planning at the local level and no guidance available to the private sector. According to ULI's Web site, www.uli.org, its charge was "to research, analyze, or encourage responsible patterns for long-term urban growth, or to conduct inquiries into what constitutes sound real estate development projects and practices." ULI became an independent organization in 1940 and now has 20,000 members in fifty states and sixty-five nations.

2. Walter Draper, "Personally Conducted," unpublished paper read at the Cincinnati Literary Club, March 7, 1949.

3. This Bond's interior was designed by Morris Lapidus (1902–2001), an architect who spent two decades as a retail designer before designing his first building. He favored playful elements such as curving walls, columns ending in halos of light, stairs seeming to float in space, even amoeba-shaped cutouts suspended from ceilings. Lapidus built his first hotel in Miami Beach in 1954, the Fontainebleau, which appeared in the 1964 James Bond film *Goldfinger.* Known for his flamboyant style, he designed 1,200 buildings worldwide, including 250 hotels. His showy aesthetic was considered commercial and vulgar by critics, but the public embraced it.

4. Benjamin Baldwin was described by architect Louis Kahn as "the dean of American interior designers." Trained as an architect, Baldwin worked at Skidmore, Owings & Merrill before launching an independent practice that spanned the period 1940–91. *Former Pepsi-Cola Building Designation Report,* New York City Landmarks Preservation Commission, June 20, 1995.

5. "Quaint Is Word for It as One Views 'Old City' from New Hotel's Tower," *Cincinnati Enquirer,* July 17, 1948.

6. According to de Blois, she began work on the Terrace Plaza Hotel project in spring 1946. Gordon Bunshaft transferred to the New York office from Chicago in late 1947. Betty J. Blum, "Oral History of Natalie De Blois," compiled under the auspices of the Chicago Architects Oral History Project, The Ernest R. Graham Study Center for Architectural Drawings, Department of Architecture, The Art Institute of Chicago, 2004, 25, 27; *Former Pepsi-Cola Building Designation Report.*

7. Nathaniel Owings acknowledged this in his 1973 autobiography, in which he praised de Blois: "Her mind and hands worked marvels in design—and only she and God would ever know just how many great solutions, with the imprimatur of one of the male heroes of SOM, owed much more to her than was attributed by either SOM or the client." *The Spaces in Between: An Architect's Journey* (Boston: Houghton Mifflin, 1973), 264–75.

8. "Library," *Progressive Architecture* 36 (December 1955): 78.

9. "Voorhees Walker Smith & Smith," *Architectural Forum* 101 (November 9, 1954): 140–47.

10. "John M. Garber," obituary, *Cincinnati Enquirer,* October 19, 1988, D5:4.

11. "Building Plans Cited by Rector of Christ Church as Significant to City," *Cincinnati Enquirer,* March 12, 1949, 6:1

12. "Artist in Glass," *Cincinnati Enquirer,* July 1, 1956, 10–11.

Chapter 9

1. See chapter 6 in this book for information on the 1925 plan and chapter 7 for information on the 1948 plan.

2. Daniel Hurley, *Cincinnati: The Queen City* (Cincinnati: Cincinnati Historical Society, 1982), 138.

3. Geoffrey J. Giglierano and Deborah A. Overmyer, *The Bicentennial Guide to Greater Cincinnati: A Portrait of 200 Years* (Cincinnati: Cincinnati Historical Society, 1998), 80.

4. Jayne Merkel, "Cincinnati," *Landscape Architecture* (September/October 1985): 122.

Chapter 10

1. Herbert Muschamp, "Zaha Hadid's Urban Mother-ship," *New York Times,* June 8, 2003, 1.

2. Cincinnati, Department of City Planning and Over-the-Rhine Community Council, *The Over-the-Rhine Comprehensive Plan: A Consensus-Based Plan by People Who Care* (Cincinnati: City of Cincinnati, 2002).

3. Sidney K. Robinson, in *The Continuous Present of Organic Architecture,* ed. Elizabeth A. Scheurer (catalogue produced in conjunction with the exhibition, organized by the Contemporary Arts Center, Cincinnati, Ohio, March 22–May 11, 1991), 27.

4. Alice Weston, telephone interview, September 16, 2005.

5. Zaha Hadid, in "Architect in Tune with the Times," by Marilyn Bauer, *Cincinnati Enquirer,* June 1, 2003, S-2.

6. Donald Cornett, personal interview, August 24, 2005.

7. Herbert Muschamp, "A Visionary Has Become a Builder," *New York Times,* June 23, 2002.

8. Hadid, in Bauer, "Architect."

9. Steven Litt, "Touchdown," *Architecture,* April 2002.

10. Ibid.

11. Ibid.

12. Carlos Rojas, Environ Group, in "Ballpark's Too Gaudy, Architects Say," by Marilyn Bauer, *Cincinnati Enquirer,* March 28, 2003.

13. David Niland, in Bauer, "Ballpark's Too Gaudy."

14. Stevan Lipson, personal interview, August 18, 2005.

15. Herbert Muschamp, "A Jigsaw Puzzle Interlocking Layers of Space," *New York Times,* August 9, 1998, 34.

16. Charles Jencks, *The New Paradigm in Architecture* (New Haven: Yale University Press, 2002), 211.

17. Peter Eisenman, in "New College Building True to Form," by Barry M. Horstman, *Cincinnati Post,* September 8, 1996.

18. Suzanne Stephens, "The American Campus," *Architectural Record* (February 2000): 77–79.

Selected Bibliography

Architectural History and Theory

Gelernter, Mark. *A History of American Architecture: Buildings in Their Cultural and Technological Context.* Hanover, NH: University Press of New England, 1999.

Hammett, Ralph. *Architecture in the US: A Survey of Architectural Styles since 1776.* New York: John Wiley and Sons, 1976.

Pickering, Ernest. *Architectural Design.* New York: John Wiley and Sons, 1933.

Roth, Leland. *American Architecture: A History.* Boulder, CO: Westview Press, 2001.

Wiseman, Carter. *Shaping a Nation: Twentieth-Century American Architecture and Its Makers.* New York: W. W. Norton, 1998.

Art, Architecture, and Local History of Cincinnati

Aaron, Daniel. *Cincinnati, Queen City of the West, 1819–1838.* Columbus: Ohio State University Press, 1992.

Clubbe, John. *Cincinnati Observed: Architecture and History.* Columbus: Ohio State University Press, 1992.

Dorsey, Robert W., and George F. Roth Jr., eds. *Architecture and Construction in Cincinnati: A Guide to Buildings, Designers and Buildings.* Cincinnati: Architectural Foundation of Cincinnati, 1987.

Ford, Henry A., and Kate B. Ford. *History of Cincinnati, Ohio with Illustrations and Biographical Sketches.* Cleveland: Williams and Co., 1881.

Giglierano, Geoffrey J., and Deborah A. Overmyer. *The Bicentennial Guide to Greater Cincinnati: A Portrait of Two Hundred Years.* Cincinnati: Cincinnati Historical Society, 1988.

Hurley, Daniel. *Cincinnati: The Queen City.* Cincinnati: Cincinnati Historical Society, 1982.

Kenny, Daniel J. *Illustrated Cincinnati: A Pictorial Hand-Book of the Queen City.* Cincinnati: George E. Stevens, 1875.

Miller, Zane L. *Boss Cox's Cincinnati: Urban Politics in the Progressive Era.* New York: Oxford University Press, 1968.

Stradling, David. *Cincinnati: From River City to Highway Metropolis.* The Making of America Series. Charleston, SC: Arcadia, 2003.

Vitz, Robert C. *The Queen and the Arts: Cultural Life in Nineteenth-Century Cincinnati.* Kent, OH: Kent State University Press, 1989.

Weston, Alice, and Walter E. Langsam. *Great Houses of the Queen City: Two Hundred Years of Historic and Contemporary Architecture and Interiors in Cincinnati and Northern Kentucky.* Cincinnati: Cincinnati Historical Society, 1997.

Writer's Program (Ohio). *Cincinnati: A Guide to the Queen City and Its Neighbors.* Cincinnati: Wiesen-Hart Press, 1943.

Manuscripts

Cincinnati Historical Society Library collections.

Langsam, Walter E. "A Biographical Dictionary of Cincinnati Region Architects." 2004 ed. Architectural Foundation of Cincinnati collections.

Special Subjects

Bennett, Paul. *University of Cincinnati: An Architectural Tour.* New York: Princeton Architectural Press, 2001.

Bruns, James H. *Great American Post Offices.* New York: John Wiley and Sons, 1998.

Craig, Lois, and the staff of the Federal Architecture Project. *The Federal Presence: Architecture, Politics, and Symbols in United States Government Building.* Cambridge: MIT Press, 1977.

Edelman, David J., David J. Allor, and April Smith. *Ladislas Segoe and American Planning Practice.* Cincinnati: School of Planning, University of Cincinnati, 2000.

Fairbanks, Robert B. *Making Better Citizens: Housing Reform and the Community Development Strategy in Cincinnati, 1890–1960.* Urbana: University of Illinois Press, 1998.

Harper, Brett. *Ladislas and Vilma Segoe.* Cincinnati: Segoe Foundation, 2001.

Lee, Antoinette J. *Architects to the Nation: The Rise and Decline of the Supervising Architect's Office.* Oxford: Oxford University Press, 2000.

Rogers, Millard J., Jr. *John Nolen and Mariemont: Building a New Town in Ohio.* Baltimore: Johns Hopkins University Press, 2001.

Shapiro, Henry D., and Zane L. Miller, eds. *Physician to the West: Selected Writings of Daniel Drake on Science and Society.* Lexington: University Press of Kentucky, 1970.

Index

Page references in italics denote illustrations.

About the Authors

Sue Ann Painter is executive director of the Architectural Foundation of Cincinnati, which serves to increase appreciation of the built environment of Greater Cincinnati. She is a principal in PSA Consulting, Inc., which produces history-related books, brochures, and exhibitions.

Painter holds an MA in art history from the University of Cincinnati, where her research was in local art history. She subsequently taught a course there on the Art and Architecture of Cincinnati. For more than a decade, she was a public historian and community development director for the Cincinnati Historical Society. In doctoral studies in American history at UC, her work was in American intellectual and political history. Painter's most recent publications are a biography, *William Henry Harrison: Father of the West,* and a community history, *Rise of the Urban Township.* Her biography of President Rutherford Hayes of Ohio will be published in 2007.

Throughout Alice Weston's career as an environmental artist, her photography has revealed hidden aspects of the natural and man-made worlds. In a previous book, *Great Houses of the Queen City,* her photographs captured the longevity, variety, and beauty in the residential architecture of Cincinnati, the city in which she lives.

In the 1980s, Weston photographed the prehistoric Native American earthworks in the Ohio Valley, especially in relation to the cycles of the sun and moon. Some of these works are on permanent display at the Cincinnati Museum Center; others travel throughout the region.

Weston's series of microphotographs formed the basis of several multimedia productions by the Cincinnati Ballet Company, the Cincinnati Symphony Orchestra, the Contemporary Arts Center, and the Cincinnati Art Museum.

Weston is a recipient of an Apple Award from the Architectural Foundation of Cincinnati, an Architectural Advancement Award from the Cincinnati American Institute of Architects, an Ohioana Book Award, and a Visionary Award from the Contemporary Arts Center.

Weston holds degrees from Vassar College and the College of Design, Architecture, Art and Planning at the University of Cincinnati. A generous and visionary patron of the arts, she serves on several arts boards and is the founder with her husband of the Alice F. and Harris K. Weston Art Gallery at the Aronoff Center.

Beth Sullebarger is principal of Sullebarger Associates, a historic preservation consulting firm based in Glendale, Ohio. A New Jersey native and Ohio resident since 1989, she holds a master's degree in historic preservation from Columbia University and has thirty years of experience in the field, including seven years as Executive Director of the Cincinnati Preservation Association and ten years as a member of the Cincinnati Historic Conservation Board. Sullebarger has assisted local governments, historical societies, and property owners with nominations to the National Register of Historic Places, historic inventories, design guidelines, and historic rehabilitation tax credits. Award-winning projects include exhibits such as Lost Cincinnati for the Betts House Research Center in Cincinnati's West End and A Guide to Art and Architecture in Cincinnati's Parks.

Jayne Merkel, an architectural historian and critic, was the architecture critic of the *Cincinnati Enquirer* from 1977 to 1988, the years covered in chapter 9. She is now the New York–based contributing editor of *Architectural Design/AD* magazine in London, a member of its editorial board, and a frequent contributor to *Art in America* and *Architectural Record* magazines in New York.

From 1994 to 2002 she edited *Oculus,* the monthly magazine of the American Institute of Architects New York Chapter. Her work has appeared in numerous magazines and on public radio. She has also curated numerous exhibitions, lectured widely, and written books about Michael Graves, Richard Dattner, and the firm of Pasanella+Klein Stolzman+Berg. She has recently completed a monograph on Eero Saarinen for Phaidon Press.

Merkel directed the Graduate Program in Architecture and Design Criticism at Parsons School of Design/The New School for Social Research in New York, taught writing in the Department of English and Comparative Literature at the University of Cincinnati, and taught art history at Miami University of Ohio and the Art Academy of Cincinnati. An English literature graduate of Simmons College, Merkel earned an MA in art history from Smith College.

John E. Hancock is Professor of Architecture at the University of Cincinnati, where he has taught architectural design, theory, and history since 1978. His essays on architectural interpretation have been published internationally; his multimedia productions on ancient architecture have been honored widely; and his former students have assumed leadership positions in architectural education throughout the world.